In Need of a Master

In Need of a Master

Politics, Theology, and Radical Democracy

Edited by
Dominik Finkelde and Rebekka Klein

DE GRUYTER

ISBN 978-3-11-110461-4
e-ISBN (PDF) 978-3-11-069924-1
e-ISBN (EPUB) 978-3-11-069946-3

Library of Congress Control Number: 2021931479

Bibliographic information published by the Deutsche Nationalbibliothek
The Deutsche Nationalbibliothek lists this publication in the Deutsche Nationalbibliografie;
detailed bibliographic data are available on the Internet at http://dnb.dnb.de.

© 2022 Walter de Gruyter GmbH, Berlin/Boston
This volume is text- and page-identical with the hardback published in 2021.
Cover image: © Niels Ackermann / Sébastian Gobert: Ukranian House (former Lenin Museum), Kyiv. 12 January 2016, in: Ackermann und Gobert, *Looking for Lenin*, London: Fuel Design & Publishing, London 2017, p. 39.
Printing and binding: CPI books GmbH, Leck

www.degruyter.com

Table of Contents

Dominik Finkelde and Rebekka A. Klein
Introduction: Political Theologies in the Era of Immanence —— 1

I Figurations of the Master

Clemens Pornschlegel
Sklaven ohne Herrn
Goethes Faust als moderner Führer —— 21

Joseph Vogl
Sovereignty Figures in the History of the 'Finance Regime' —— 35

Ino Augsberg
Im Namen des Vaters —— 49

Dimitris Vardoulakis
Spinoza on the Death of the Master
The Hebrew Theocracy after Moses —— 71

Günter Thomas
Enmity as Cast Shadow of Love
Conjectures on Moral-Political Self-Radicalizations in the Protestant Theo-Political Imaginary —— 93

Burkhard Liebsch
Meister, Väter und Surrogate
Mit Blick auf Autorität und Vertikalität, Autoritarismus und identitären Populismus —— 111

II Identity – Diversity – Singularity

Luca Di Blasi
Cis: The Rightist Appropriation of Identity Politics and its Boundaries —— 145

Dominik Finkelde
In Need of A Master
  On the Failure of Radical Democracy in the Era of Liberal-Democratic Authoritarianism —— **165**

Rebekka A. Klein
The Sovereignty of Subversion
  Or: The Masterfulness of the Democratic Revolution —— **187**

Rasmus Nagel
Total Fidelity?
  About the Exclusivity of the Excluded —— **205**

III Post-Political Theology

Philipp Stoellger
Das Relative als das Absolute?
  Das Politische zwischen Kontingenz und Verkörperung —— **221**

John Milbank
Theopolitics Today
  The Crisis of the Symbolic Order —— **253**

Daniel Weidner
Smashing Words
  Prophetic Words and Alternative Political Theologies —— **271**

Florian Grosser
On the Abuses and Uses of Political Theology
  Schmitt, Arendt, and the 'Trump Moment' —— **285**

List of contributors —— 307

Index —— 311

Dominik Finkelde and Rebekka A. Klein
Introduction: Political Theologies in the Era of Immanence

In our so-called 'postmodern' age of widespread ideological critique[1] as presented especially in theories of radical democracy,[2] the correlation between transcendence and immanence proves increasingly problematic.[3] Historically mediated phantasmagoria of state, nation, 'the people' and religious belief can no longer pretend to be part of the basic structures of reality.[4] Their dogmatic form is revealed as contingent and self-made and this insight – trickling down into modern common sense – paved the way for a culture of diversification. The consequences are numerous in our present age. What was once perceived as scandalous and antisocial – e. g. performances like the one presented by Conchita Wurst at the Euro-Contest 2014 – is today regarded as a defining element of contemporary culture.[5] New identities are welcomed and celebrated, new freedoms and individual rights are granted, and, where necessary, fought for in court.[6] Now, potentially, every cultural form and every identity is apparently inherently good.[7]

However, this postmodern process of identity diversification is not necessarily liberating.[8] It may stand both for the victory of a new form of relativism and

---

[1] See Althusser, *Reproduction of Capitalism*, 171–207.
[2] See Comtesse, Flügel-Martinsen, Martinsen and Nonhoff, *Radikale Demokratietheorie*, 11–21; Marchart, *Die politische Differenz* a revised and heavily expanded version of Marchart, *Post-foundational Political Thought*; Abensour, *Democracy Against the State*; Mouffe, *The Democratic Paradox*; Mouffe, *Agonistics*; Laclau, *New Reflections on the Evolution of Our Time*; Laclau and Mouffe, *Hegemony*; Lefort, *Democracy and Political Theory*.
[3] See Claude Lefort's striking analysis of the chiastic interweavement of the theological and the political in the democratic revolution of modernity in Lefort, "The Permanence of the Theologico-Political?", 148–187.
[4] See Balke, *Staat nach seinem Ende*; Santner, *Royal Remains*; Trautmann, *Das politische Imaginäre*.
[5] The term "postmodernism" is treated here in the sense of its widespread popularity as the attitude in philosophy and literary theory that opposes great narratives and ideologies in favour of modes of scepticism, irony, and the persistent questioning of existing premises of meaning and truth.
[6] See on this topic Fukuyama, *Identity*.
[7] See Lefort, "La dissolution", 551–568.
[8] See Žižek, *Ticklish Subject*, 203–205.

the predominance of "singularities" within the polity.[9] Hence, what this process of diversification does apparently not see is that it itself starts from silently accepted ontological and cultural presuppositions which the process of diversification (paradoxically?) questions. The ideological heritage of the 'white heterosexual man',[10] of 'western culture', and the Jewish-Christian legacy[11] is called upon to step willingly aside. In this way, however, the reference to the abstract, ideological and phantasmatic idea of a totality disappears, which – through its ideological power of violence – was also capable of classifying identities in the first place. The open society of decentralization may then discourse-ethically call for the search for 'our' place in the symbolic order (and everybody is invited), but nevertheless this search cannot be mediated democratically as one wishes.[12] Why? Because the search embodies an impossible effort. The place to be found is, on the one hand, constitutively empty,[13] yet it necessarily must be filled with dogmatic phantasmagoria, decisions as scissions and with violent claims nonetheless in the name of the/an absolute.[14] The category of transcendence has not vanished at all since any kind of violence in the name of the law refers to an absolute[15] – even in so called 'post-metaphysical' and discourse-ethical times.[16] Because of this structural necessity, late-modern societies, in their self-emptying and divesting social practices, are increasingly 'haunted' by reactionary-conservative political movements.[17] From the point of view of these movements, the post-metaphysical perspective of the genesis of norms in and through contingency, creates a new form of tragedy as a constant self-questioning of community and order.[18]

Against this background and on the basis of this account of our present age – presented here admittedly with a broad brush – this volume puts up for dis-

---

9 See Reckwitz, *Society of Singularities*, 1–18.
10 See Di Blasi, *Der weiße Mann*.
11 See Agamben, *Potentialities*; Kotsko, *Žižek and Theology*.
12 See for this diagnosis of an insufficiency or crisis of democracy Diamond and Plattner, *Democracy in Decline?*; Levitsky and Ziblatt, *How Democracies Die*; Mounk, *People vs. Democracy*.
13 See Lefort, "Démocratie et avènement d'un 'lieu vide,'", 461–469.
14 See Badiou, *Being and Event*; Finkelde, *Excessive Subjectivity*.
15 See Derrida, *Force de loi*, 47–104.
16 See Habermas, *Postmetaphysical Thinking*, 28–56.
17 See Gordon, "The Authoritarian Personality Revisited", 45–84. See also Rensmann, Hagemann and Funke, *Autoritarismus und Demokratie*, who argue that authoritarianism and democracy persist in a complex interrelation in modernity.
18 See Heitmeyer, *Autoritäre Versuchungen* and his thesis that globalized capitalism has evoked a feeling of the loss of control to which liberal democracy could not act as a counterbalance and which has, therefore, given rise to authoritarian movements.

cussion the non-value laden and descriptive hypothesis that the return of authoritarian ideologies, but also of fundamentalist political religions and the emergence of a new style of post-fatal politics, are both reactionary phenomena as well as symptoms of a political awakening. This thesis, taken up and commented critically as well as approvingly by the authors in this volume, questions deliberately premises of discourse-ethical political philosophies and of theories of radical democracy and fills in lacunae of previous and contemporary debates at multiple intersections, where political philosophy and political theology meet and merge.

1 Political theologies in modernity and late modernity

The question of how authority is born, how social and political orders are instituted and acquire significance, is one that has occupied philosophy since its beginnings. Plato's *Republic* already dealt with this question and saw the state as the image of a 'natural order' of justice. Here, social institutions and social structures, in which order is manifested, are normatively enforced as representations and equivalents of an imaginary order of being. They are legitimized as expressions of a transcendent truth. Since then, questions of political metaphysics and ontology have accompanied all philosophical investigations of the social and political nature of human existence. Even in the context of a critical, post-metaphysical turn in philosophy, they are being further processed in modern thought. Under the banner of Political Theology, the twentieth century in the fields of political science, law, cultural studies and political philosophy attempts to rethink the connection between immanence and transcendence against a logic of separation of both spheres in public space.[19] However, as the influential thesis of the state theorist Carl Schmitt suggests, politics, state, and society can by no means justify themselves on their own.[20] This means that they too seek a foundation in an Other (of themselves) and thus in a phantasmatic transgression of the socially constructed reality that is both rationally and intersubjectively founded.[21]

That the administration of transcendence in the field of politics has not come to an end in the various stages of secularization in the twenty-first century,

---

19 See Schmitt, *Political Theology*.
20 See Böckenförde, *Staat, Gesellschaft, Freiheit*, 60.
21 See Lefort, "The Permanence of the Theologico-Political?"

is shown with precision by the latest publications of Eric Santner.[22] The cultural theorist takes up several theses from Ernst Kantorowicz' famous study on *The King's Two Bodies*,[23] according to which the traditional sovereign combined the sublime, symbolic body of his political-theological mandate with the natural-mortal body of his ordinary humanity. Kantorowicz is for Santner a gateway to modern political theology since this dichotomy of power (metaphysical/sublime vs. physical/naturalistic) lives on, according to him, and it does so even after the fall of the sovereign and his replacement by the *volonté générale* (Rousseau) and the maturity (Kant) and discourse-capacity (Habermas) of the citizen. So, while in pre-modern times the monarchical sovereign was still the representative of the not always easily resisted combination of transcendence and immanence, now and through his abdication the people themselves suffer the pressure of the sublime. Santner calls this theological-political sublimity 'flesh' to denote the medium in which power – i.e. the symbolic order/investment and its never completely self-explanatory demands – tasks, but also privileges its so-called entitlements, which are represented, conveyed and carried. This 'flesh,' which was once historically unified by the sovereign, lives on, according to him, and with it the question of what establishes and maintains communities, be it in the Enlightenment, in Modernity or Postmodernity.[24]

Again and again, the question of reconciliation of immanence and transcendence is at the center of determining the claims to political power, directly or indirectly. It has survived to our present day. The philosophy of the twentieth century has tried to answer this question for its part, because it saw itself less as a medium that simply dissociates itself from theology and religion, but as a new kind of civil religion, as the 'religion of philosophy'.[25] And it is here, where difference, non-identity, discourse and anti-essentialism become basic ethical convictions, which are now – up to the present day – preparing to deconstruct essentialist and fundamentalist traditions. Norms are to be established transparently in the context of their historical-contingent conditions (as far as possible), free of ideology, and free of leading cultural tendencies. The late modern societies of the present are, therefore, characterized by the undertaking to transcend perspectives of political theology towards post-metaphysical thinking, as it was already called for by Habermas, among others, at the end of the twentieth century. In following a transcendental-pragmatic or a discourse- and lan-

---

22 See Santner, *Royal Remains*; Santner, *Weight of All Flesh*; Mazzarella, Santner and Schuster, *Sovereignty, Inc.*
23 See Kantorowicz, *The King's Two Bodies*.
24 See on this topic also Vogl, ed., *Gemeinschaften*.
25 See Di Blasi, *Dezentrierungen*, 15–33.

guage-analytical reduction of political ontology, the attempt is made to deconstruct premises of the various political theologies of modernity: from the ideology of sovereignty to the sacralization of revolutionary movements and the critique of a partly biopolitical production and enslavement of what Giorgio Agamben, following Aristotle, calls "bare life".[26]

Late modern or (if one wants to call it pointedly) *post-post*modern philosophers of our present time, among whom Laclau, Lefort, Badiou can be counted, try for their part to free the political-theological investiture of transcendence (i.e. its invisibility, incorporeality and inviolable truth) from its transcendent power. To do so, a negative universality, a universality 'without' transcendence and an empty signifier is being exposed and proclaimed at the same time.[27] The empty signifier can then, instead of the representative investiture of modern democracy, be recoded as the invasion of the real, the withdrawal of an alterity or as an empty center of political discourse, and subversively and radically democratically be turned against ideologies of representation (which – allegedly – remain pre-modern and contaminated with theological remnants).

In this way, political ontologies of states, communities and societies are 'disenchanted' in their validity and subjected to profanation in a form that goes beyond the logic of what secularization as a process of de-theologization generally stands for. Attributed to their finite, contextually conditioned and thus always relativizable normativity within a social practice, signifiers now appear in their contingency as constantly changing forms of orientation. As such, they pragmatically demand validity and can be changed at any time. But precisely because political forms are no longer ideologically secured by phantasmagoria of a final meaning, a foundation and sufficient reason of social reality, an increased social dynamic of their implementation, annulment, reinterpretation and strategic reversal sets in. (And this *is* the good news, the 'evangelion' of Radical Democracy.[28]) In other words, the post-metaphysical practice of the continuous deconstruction of authorities and their normativity necessarily causes growing unrest, uncertainty and a lack of orientation on the part of large political groups

---

26 See Agamben, *Homo Sacer*, 4–11.
27 See Laclau and Mouffe, *Hegemony*, 186: "[T]he radical difference which democratic society introduces is that the site of power becomes an empty space; the reference to a transcendent guarantor disappears, and with it the representation of the substantial unity of society".
28 See Laclau and Mouffe, *Hegemony*, 187: "It is because there are no more assured foundations arising out of a transcendent order, because there is no longer a centre which binds together power, law and knowledge, that it becomes possible and necessary to unify certain political spaces through hegemonic articulations. But these articulations will always be partial and subject to being contested, as there is no longer a supreme guarantor."

– in the name of political openness. These groups are, as a result, often under normative pressure to disarticulate their collective and individual identity.[29] They can or should no longer essentially create identity, hold on to it, but increasingly only do so under the guidance of a cosmopolitical decentration, shifting and emptying authorities in favor of multiple authorities to come.

But right-wing and left-wing populist parties, identitarian movements, imperial bourgeois ideologies and pseudo-fascist groups, which have emerged with a new self-confidence, especially in the Western world in the last ten years, have revolted against this dynamic. This has caused often an erosion of valid rules of the democratic discourse of the present, but for representatives of political extremism rightly so, since in their point of view, the post-metaphysical perspective of the genesis of norms produces, in and through contingency, a lifestyle that tends towards the tragic and the self-absorption of community and order.

Should this description of the predicaments of our present era be correct, at least approximately, then it may be evident that certain forms of postmodern relativism evoke profound differences between subjects. Reality becomes both the scene of a subjective will to construct one's own self, as well as the impossible realm whose meaning cannot be communicated by me to others. In the face of this development, not only does indifference seem obvious; rather, a new human right to hatred and radical rejection of others or the Other is establishing itself. This right is currently making room for itself and aims at an outspoken discrimination of particular groups against other particular groups – be they identitarian-, gender- or minority-based.[30] The philosopher Alain Badiou speaks in this context of multiple processes of universalization through scission to underline that the surge of universality needs by definition political violence where one group stands against the other.[31]

Against this background, it can be said that certain postmodern processes of decentering, which act against both a metaphysical and ideological heritage, provoke both multiple realities and their respective counter-realities. For this reason, the philosopher Slavoj Žižek sees postmodern multiculturalism, which approves of cultural diversity at the expense of ontological unity, as the expression of a new ethnic fundamentalism in the left political spectrum. It finds necessarily a response in the right political spectrum too:

---

29 See Charim, *Ich und die Anderen*.
30 See the description of dramatic consequences of the struggle for recognition of victimized identities in Fukuyama, *Identity*, 163–183.
31 See Badiou, *Saint Paul*, 98–106; *Being and Event*, chapter II.

"Postmodern relativism is precisely the thought of the irreducible multitude of worlds, each of them sustained by a specific language game, so that each world 'is' the narrative its members tell themselves about themselves, with no shared terrain, no common language; and the problem of truth is how to establish something that – to use the terms popular in modal logic – remains the same in all possible worlds."[32]

Several premises of a post-modern attitude to life are no longer as convincing as they were at the end of the twentieth century and at the end of the Cold War. An effect is a restlessness generated by the post-metaphysical unlocking of life's trajectories which provokes questions of authority and sovereignty, of dwelling and belonging, which cannot be as meaningfully dealt with and solved as promised.[33] What is problematic about radical forms of postmodern thought is its call for the diversification of identities while failing to acknowledge that subjects cannot simply create their own identities either. They must presuppose, among other things, what Lacan, for example, calls the big Other and Habermas the normatively given background knowledge of a common life-world.[34] This background knowledge presupposes certainties that cannot always be renegotiated. Where they are renegotiated, though, there is not 'more' certainty, but 'less'. So, where diversification takes place for the sake of diversification, multiplicities may not phantasmagorically be 'counted as one' anymore (let alone ontologically). They may end up as *less than difference* since only a shared space of reasons can account for differences per se.

2 Perspectives

As we said above, what the process of diversification often fails to see is that it starts out from silently shared ontological and cultural preconditions/commitments, which it calls into question. But the silenced tradition was the precondition to bring, first of all, the critique forward into the debate. So when this tradition with its ideological heritage (of the 'white man,' the 'Western culture,' the Judeo-Christian theologies) is called to step back, then the critique may risk losing its foundation of revolt and give way – necessarily – to both relativism and new forms of political authoritarianism. Hence, paradoxically, when "western"

---

[32] Žižek, *Less Than Nothing*, 367.
[33] For an analysis of the process of attenuating sovereignty in late modernity see Klein, *Depotenzierung der Souveränität*.
[34] See Lacan, *Seminar of Jacques Lacan*, Book II, chapter 19; Habermas, *Theorie des kommunikativen Handelns*, 189.

culture is dwindling, the precondition to classify identities in the face of western values of equality, rights, duties and commitments is dwindling too. Postmodern relativism cannot, in many cases, think and address this paradox. This explains why large sections of the cultural elite often point to phenomena such as LePen, AfD, Trump, Orban, etc. only with incomprehension and radical rejection.[35] This volume attempts, among other things, to clarify why this happens and possibly has to happen.

However, a first working hypothesis concerning this problem could be that the mentioned elites, for their part, lack a convincing narrative that is able to give substantial content to the search for 'our place' in the symbolic form – since a narrative would be phantasmagoric and ideological per se. On the other hand, the search for our place in the symbolic order cannot be mediated by (representative) democratic procedures alone. For the search embodies, as mentioned above, an impossible effort. The place to be found can by its own conditions of existence only be a substantially given or an imposed place. In this sense, the philosophical helplessness of the present is also a symptom of Western civilization. It is increasingly beginning to doubt itself in the name of unspecific concepts like "difference" and "diversification". They embody the rejection of forms of lived models of transcendence of past epochs and often endorse exclusively one ethical injunction: the demand for collective decentration.

Against the background of this panorama, the new dogmatic forms of community building mentioned above can be interpreted as desiderata in the age of an exhausted social and economic liberalism. But they are also the symptom of a world order that is decentering itself, which for its part – despite all differences – unites within the framework of global capitalism. In it, a global leap of faith may indeed be needed for a new narrative that relativizes the world in such a way that an 'Other-of-itself' moderates the hysteria of its inhabitants.

Based on this description of the situation, the papers combined in this volume discuss the deliberately provocative sounding hypothesis that the return of authoritarian ideologies, but also of fundamentalist 'political' religions and the emergence of a new style of post-factual politics should be interpreted less as a reactionary phenomenon of retreat than as a symptom of a political awakening. The volume therefore asks for a new political theology in the age of immanence. This must neither stop at the classical neo-metaphysical approach of the political theology of modernity (Carl Schmitt and the consequences) nor succumb to

---

35 See Frum, *Trumpocracy*; Heitmeyer, *Autoritäre Versuchungen*; Milbradt, *Über autoritäre Haltungen in 'postfaktischen' Zeiten*; Traverso, *New Faces of Fascism*; Zielonka, *Konterrevolution*. A different view is taken by Dieter Thomä who tries to reconcile democratic culture with heroism, see his *Warum Demokratien Helden brauchen*.

the temptations of a deconstructivist, radical profanation of every politics of the community (Derrida, Nancy and its consequences). A political theology that moves into the openness of the present situation has rather to assume that in the supposedly 'reactionary' populist movements, which circle around the signifiers of community, nation, and people, as well as around the ideology of 'America First', no backward-looking thinking announces itself, but a thinking that shifts into a new future and new political implementations.

3 The volume

Part I – Figurations of the Master: The articles in the first section present various interpretations of figurations of the master that are intrinsically linked to the respective fields of research of the authors assembled here. Political theology in the traditions of Schmitt, Taubes, Voegelin et al. is generally, but not exclusively, a point of reference within these investigations, as several authors also consider the issue of the need of a master with reference to the political structure of finances. The authors develop and expose the importance of figurations of the master with reference to Goethe's 'Faust' (Pornschlegel), within the finance regime of the early modern period (Vogl), with a focus on questions of the 'law' (Augsberg), the Hebrew theocracy in Spinoza (Vardoulakis) and contemporary authoritarianism (Liebsch).

Clemens Pornschlegel examines in his text "Sklaven ohne Herrn. Goethes Faust als moderner Führer" how Goethe, in *Faust II*, depicts the historical process of the formation of an industrial and capitalist world-order of production which shaped especially the nineteenth and twentieth centuries through new master-signifiers enrooted in economy and capital. Heidegger, for his part, portrays this process decades later as the emergence of the age of technology. The latter goes hand in hand with what is called secularization: the unreserved absorption of God, his omnipotence and his omniscience into finiteness and a man-made universe of techno-science. For Pornschlegel, Goethe depicts Faust as the leader and pioneer of this new age. He embodies multiple demands which are revealed in the self-conception of modernity as we know it. His life incorporates the project of complete control over nature, including control over human nature itself, which is susceptible to failure. Religion is gradually becoming superfluous for Faust as a new master for a new world. Its vertically oriented piety towards the Divine is transferred into the earthly-horizontal. Now, as Max Weber has shown, a no less pious activity of man sets in, who – as a generic being – becomes the sole author of all riches and gods, of all visible and invisible things.

Joseph Vogl evaluates in his article "Sovereignty Figures in the History of the 'Finance Regime'" how governmental power has been accompanied by the development of financial markets from the modern era onwards. Since then, a new master discourse has permeated social conditions. For where once, according to Giorgio Agamben's theses on Christianity's 'economy of salvation', theological figures of order prevailed in political registers, now financial structures determine the transformation of secularization. Treasury and fiscal authorities become decisive power vehicles in the development of new forms of government. The administration of the population is no longer exclusively based on 'surveillance and punishment' (Foucault), but on the economization of the state. It is one of the last forms in which theologoumena spread into a world of pure immanence. The establishment of the tax-state and regulation through legal guarantees for creditors of public debt are increasingly being put on a permanent basis. The emergence of central banks brings this perpetuation of immanence into the form of an apparently eternal master's discourse without which every modern society cannot exist, especially today.

Ino Augsberg shows in his article "Im Namen des Vaters? Gesetz – Geschlecht – Religion" the extent to which the reference to a 'third' and therefore transcendent dimension of authority is effective not only in authoritarian movements, i.e. in the desire for a leader, for a father figure, but also in modern-secular political discourse as well. The latter, though, refers in turn within its construction of a subject of individual rights to a different 'third' dimension of authority which no longer stands in relation to transcendence. For to the extent that modern law sees itself as constituted by subjects, the subject in return is increasingly understood only as constituted by law. The short-circuit between 'human being' and 'legal subject' is shown, among other things, to incite a structural dilemma in the so-called 'anti-discrimination law'. Its regulations operationalize, on the one hand, legally binding distinctions between persons that, on the other hand, the law formally prohibits since 'all are equal before the law'. The fact that the subject in its assertion of individual rights is at the same time an object of the law or subject to it generates an irreconcilable ambivalence of 'nomos' and 'anomy'. This leads to the fact that even the reference to general normative standards in itself no longer make sense and a logic of radically arbitrary decisions dominates the field of politics.

Dimitris Vardoulakis shows in his article "Spinoza on the Death of the Master: The Hebrew Theocracy After Moses" that the Hebrew state is a consistent point of reference among several political philosophers of the seventeenth century, including Hobbes and Locke. Spinoza's *Theological Political Treaties* participates in this tradition. It refers to the archaic past of Judaism's state-building as a paradigmatic example of a state that relies not only on obedience but also on a concept of theological authority. Problematic becomes the theocratic Hebrew state in itself after the death of Moses. Spinoza insists that the state remains a theocracy, though with the difference that, now, the symbioses of politics and theology embodied by Moses, is fractured and split into co-dependent domains. Theological authority resides with the Levites, whereas political authority is distributed among the Hebrew tribes.

Günter Thomas examines in his article "Enmity as Cast Shadow of Love: Conjectures on Moral-Political Self-Radicalizations in the Protestant Theo-Political Imaginary" the discourse on new masters from the perspective of Christian theology. He emphasizes that this discourse – unlike philosophy – develops new imaginary forms that guide directly the thinking and acting of people in practices in our era. In (post-)secular society, God even transforms into a compassionate therapist and coach and the Protestant Church, within it's 'public theology' agenda, is taking advantage of these modern forms of God's relationship with the world. It is this empowerment of the Church's political role with regard to the church's master discourse on 'Love' that Thomas criticizes. He analyses this master discourse as morally inflated and, more specifically, lacking the multiplicity of antagonisms hidden in a theological concept of divine love itself. According to Thomas, a correct understanding of love that wants to do justice to the theological tradition has to admit that love is intertwined with the concepts of 'enmity' and of 'sin' – both words often lacking in public theology. In short: Divine love cannot be understood without its antagonistic core as it is by no means equivalent with political innocence.

Burkhard Liebsch approaches in "Meister, Väter und Surrogate – mit Blick auf Autorität und Vertikalität, Autoritarismus und identitären Populismus," the call for new masters in contemporary politics on the basis of a diagnosis of decay. In the background of the emergence of authoritarian political movements, he sees the social decline of the father's *imago*, i.e. the vertical structures of authority and truth through which social orders formerly knew how to organize themselves. In this sense, the so-called 'end of verticality' is the great problem of contemporary democratic societies. The decay of "genuine authority" (Taylor) favors not only the emergence of false authoritarian movements, but also, for example, the reattachment to religion. Abandoned social classes are now energized by identitarian policies of radical immanence and see the remedy in the one voice of the people, in the leader; with resentment playing an essential role of motivation. The negation of everything that is different now serves as a total affirmation of the self and as a defense against its losses and traumas. An expression of anti-political self-righteousness takes the lead. On the basis of this diagnosis, Liebsch discusses how authoritarian temptations and seductions, in short 'political infantilism', can best be resisted. Following Paul Ricœur, who equated growing up with renouncing one's father, he calls for the spiritual renunciation of one's father and the abandonment of oneself to others to lay the grounds of political existence again.

Part II – Identity, Diversity, Singularity: The second field of research in this volume is dedicated both to the inevitability of unbound identity formations in modern societies (Di Blasi) as well as to anti-pluralist authoritarian movements which pluralism brings to the fore as its unexpected and often unacknowledged downside (Finkelde). Theology has potentials of liberation within this conflict where heteronomy and hegemony collide. It counters different forms of the fetishization of philosophy and politics (Klein) and presents within its Christian heritage an anti-ideological form of singularity without identity (Nagel).

Luca Di Blasi questions in his article, "Cis. The Rightist Appropriation of Identity Politics and its Boundaries," the extent to which a hegemonic or 'right-wing identity policy' has been able to establish itself in recent years, especially in western societies where it is being marginalized or devalued by liberal elites. To counter this rationale Di Blasi refers to the category 'cisgender', i.e. the apparently 'natural' sexual ascription of a newborn after birth. Can a 'natural' gender take its place in identity politics among other identity demands, asks Di Blasi, or does this give rise to numerous problems in our era of questioned hegemonic structures of identity politics? While 'transgender' (meaning: 'beyond' gender attribution) is regarded as a supernumerary category compared to traditional gender designations (male, female), it provokes a retrospective effect also to its counter-category 'cisgender'. How should 'cisgender' be able to articulate itself identity-politically without the other (transgender) of its own? Di Blasi pursues the division of identity(s) through their counter-identitie(s) with reference to other political group-building processes. They concern both the relationship between Christianity and Judaism as well as the relationship between masters and slaves in contemporary debates within social and political philosophy.

Dominik Finkelde asks in his article "In Need of A Master: On the Failure of Radical Democracy in the Era of Liberal-Democratic Authoritarianism" what happens if subsets of a set are authorized to call into question, time and again, the limits of the set of which they are part. In this case, uncertainties of every set's limit or frontier are potential sites of ever new subsets. This can cause problems as the realm of politics shows. Here the relation of sets and power-sets are a constant struggle for hegemony. This is discussed within radical-democratic theories (presented by authors such as Mouffe, Laclau, Abensour, among others) who postulate plural rights of difference against hegemonic cultures of order. However, the claim of an ontological superiority of difference compared to non-difference produces aporia between hegemony and heteronomy bringing certain radical-democratic theories to the brink of a theoretical breakdown.

Rebekka A. Klein identifies in her article "The Sovereignty of Subversion, or: The Masterfulness of Democratic Revolution" the role of political theology in exploring the metaphysical and imaginary ideas of contemporary politics. Following Jean-Luc Nancy, she shows that the operation of politics and democracy in the present era can best be described as a process of fetishization. Politics within liberal societies is regarded as the last guarantee of a humane and liberal existence. Even various radical democracy theories conform to this understanding, as Klein's reference to Claude Lefort's analysis of the '68 revolt shows. Lefort pointed out that the mastery of a revolutionary act appears here. This act establishes a style of action without precursors, which is characteristic of radical democratic practices. A similar figure of argument can be found in Slavoj Žižek's philosophy. According to Žižek, however, only a leader, a true master can bring about a genuine overthrow, since he is also capable of leaving behind the possibilities and rules of radical democratic theories. Klein finally finds in Carl Schmitt's work the antagonism between radical-democratic politics of unrest and a sovereign reorganization of politics preformed. She shows how revolutionary and authoritarian moments of the political intertwine and mutually reinforce each other.

Rasmus Nagel investigates in "Total Fidelity? About the Exclusivity of the Excluded" the motif of the human being's absolute loyalty to God in the history of religion. He takes up Jan Assmann's well-known thesis, which says that ancient Israel embodies the birth of a 'total religion,' which is accompanied by the violent exclusion of others. Against Assmann, Nagel points out that it is not the quest for truth but the question of faithfulness or disloyalty in the relationship with God which has been the decisive factor in Israel's self-understanding. Israel's religious history is therefore not about the comparison with other religions and their polytheism, but about the inner distinction between friends and enemies of God. The liberation of the Israelites from bondage and the covenant of God based on it is, thus, to be understood as a 'state of emergency' in the sense of Carl Schmitt's political theory. It is a force for enmity and has a highly politicizing effect. Nagel pursues this motive further into Christian theology. He analyzes the concept of *pistis* (faith) as a relationship of loyalty that can be expressed in the New Testament both by God and by the human being. Here, the politically effective distinction between friends and enemies of God continues. But it does so not exclusively in the sense of a fatal distinction between groups of people since the unbelief of the believers themselves proves, from now on, to be an inner exclusion, a rupture of Christian identity itself. The latter's inner split undermines permanently its constitution.

Part III – Post-Political Theology: The third field of research of the volume is dedicated to political theology and its aftermath within postmodern times. Here the figure of the master is reflected upon within the classical theological claim of his absoluteness (Stoellger) as well as within the tradition of Judaism's early prophets (Weidner). And since especially modern capitalism empties the symbolic universe of religion, a return of theological symbolism may be an antidote of the predicaments against secular ideologies (Milbank). Politics proves to be saturated with its faith-based tradition as modern and authoritarian forms of messianic speech-acts demonstrate (Grosser).

Philipp Stoellger explores in "Das Relative als das Absolute? Das Politische zwischen Kontingenz und Verkörperung" the figure of the master within the theological and secular claims to absoluteness. This includes not only the explicit reference to God Almighty in religious discourses in which, for example, Christians express themselves, but also the political call for leaders and experts, universities of excellence and Nobel Prize winners. Stoellger shows that the figure of the master in the theological register is ambivalent. Within the biblical traditions it stands for claims of empowerment which delegitimize the interpretive power of other masters (disqualified as idols) and respectively legitimize the interpretive power of one's own claim to leadership (in the name of God as Lord and Master). The power of interpretation proves to be an antagonistic effort. Stoellger pleads for a theoretical space in-between relativism and the call for absoluteness where especially medium-theoretical questions prove to have an impact on the search for the master.

John Milbank interprets in his paper "Theopolitics Today: The Crisis of the Symbolic Order" the contemporary global political crisis as an impasse of the symbolic order. Human beings are ultimately bound together by objects of their love which are at once concrete and significant. But capitalism rips the symbol apart into empty matter and meaningless sign or number. The extremity of this process has resulted in a division between an elite of the signs and numbers on the one hand and a mass of people reduced to marginalized dependence on leached material resources. The former group tends ideologically to favor liberal universalism, the latter a particularistic nationalism. In order to mediate the particular and the universal we must, according to Milbank, recover the symbolic, which is rooted in a religious mediation of transcendence. Thus, there can only be religious solutions to our current dilemma and Christianity most of all is the religion of the paradoxical coincidence of the most general and the most concrete.

Daniel Weidner investigates in "Smashing Words: Prophetic Words and Alternative Political Theologies" the broad impact of political theology in contemporary theory. He critically examines how political theology time and again refers back to Carl Schmitt's Political Theology of sovereignty, with a special interest in authority and counter-authority which lie at center stage of these debates. But why should this be continued, Weidner asks and presents three different readings of less dogmatic traditions of political theology. He refers to the early prophets in Jewish theology, to the later prophets and their relation to speech, and, finally, to James Baldwin. The latter is a modern prophet who stirs up the liberal public sphere. In all three forms, the prophet has no means of power to execute his words in order to castigate and smash the existing order – a procedure that is always risky since smashing words tend to turn against oneself.

In his article "On the Abuses and Uses of Political Theology: Schmitt, Arendt, and the 'Trump Moment'" Florian Grosser discusses the thesis that it is not postmodernism and its abandonment of a 'realistic' correlation of thinking and being that is responsible for the return of political authoritarianism, but rather the excess of political theology in contemporary politics. It can be uncovered within the seductive power of messianic forms of politics, as it was already propagated by Barack Obama and his administration. Both Obama's politics and Trump's politics were and are time and again based on utopian promises and unverifiable truth-claims. As Theodor W. Adorno has already shown in his analysis of the authoritarian character from 1967, it is not enough to morally reject these gestures of a messianically charged authority. Rather, it is important to make the disastrous consequences of this rhetorically effective political style clear to the public. To counter this development of the present, Grosser refers to the philosophy of Hannah Arendt. According to Arendt, 'real democracy' is only manifest where habitual forms of political community are broken up and the *demós* is conceptualized neither in fundamentalist concepts of community nor in 'anti-foundationalist' concepts of difference and dispute.

Bibliography

Abensour, Miguel. *Democracy Against the State: Marx and the Machiavellian Movement*, trans. Max Blechman and Martin Breaugh. Cambridge, UK: Polity, 2011.
Agamben, Giorgio. *Homo Sacer: Sovereign Power and Bare Life*, trans. Daniel Heller-Roazen. Stanford: Stanford University Press, 1998.
Agamben, Giorgio. *Potentialities: Collected Essays in Philosophy*, ed. and trans. Daniel Heller-Roazen. Stanford: Stanford University Press, 1999.
Althusser, Louis. *On the Reproduction of Capitalism: Ideology and Ideological State Apparatusses*, trans. Geoffrey M. Goshgarian. London: Verso, 2014.
Badiou, Alain. *Saint Paul: The Foundation of Universalism*, trans. Ray Brassier. Stanford: Stanford University Press, 2003.
Badiou, Alain. *Being and Event*, trans. Oliver Feltham. London: Continuum, 2006.

Balke, Friedrich. *Der Staat nach seinem Ende. Die Versuchung Carl Schmitts.* Munich: Fink, 1996.

Böckenförde, Ernst-Wolfgang. *Staat, Gesellschaft, Freiheit: Studien zu Staatstheorie und zum Verfassungsrecht.* Frankfurt a. M.: Suhrkamp, 1976.

Charim, Isolde. *Ich und die Anderen. Wie die neue Pluralisierung uns alle verändert.* Wien: Paul Zsolnay Verlag, 2018.

Comtesse, Dagmar; Flügel-Martinsen, Oliver; Martinsen, Franziska, and Nonhoff, Martin, eds., *Radikale Demokratietheorie: Ein Handbuch.* Berlin: Suhrkamp, 2019.

Derrida, Jacques. *Force de loi. Le fondement mystique de l'autorité.* Paris: Édition Galilée, 1994.

Diamond, Larry Jay, and Plattner, Marc F., eds. *Democracy in Decline?* Baltimore: Johns Hopkins University Press, 2015.

Di Blasi, Luca. *Der weiße Mann: Ein Anti-Manifest.* Bielefeld: Transcript, 2013.

Di Blasi, Luca. *Dezentrierungen: Beiträge zur Religion der Philosophie im 20. Jahrhundert.* Wien: Turia & Kant, 2018.

Finkelde, Dominik. *Excessive Subjectivity: Kant, Hegel, Lacan, and the Foundations of Ethics*, trans. Deva Kemmis and Astrid Weigert. New York: Columbia University Press, 2017.

Frum, David. *Trumpocracy: The Corruption of the American Republic.* New York: Harper Collins, 2018.

Fukuyama, Francis. *Identity. Contemporary Identity Politics and the Struggle for Recognition.* London: Profile Books, 2018.

Gordon, Peter. "The Authoritarian Personality Revisited: Reading Adorno in the Age of Trump," In *Authoritarianism: Three Inquiries in Critical Theory*, ed. by Wendy Brown, Peter E. Gordon and Max Pensky, 31–56. Chicago: University of Chicago Press, 2008.

Habermas, Jürgen. *Theorie des kommunikativen Handelns*, Bd. 2. Frankfurt a. M.: Suhrkamp, 1987.

Habermas, Jürgen. *Postmetaphysical Thinking*, vol. 2, trans. Ciaran Cronin. Cambridge, UK: Polity, 2017.

Heitmeyer, Alexander. *Autoritäre Versuchungen.* Berlin: Suhrkamp, 2018.

Kantorowicz, Ernst H. *The King's Two Bodies: A Study in Mediaeval Political Theology.* Princeton, NJ: Princeton University Press, 1957.

Klein, Rebekka A. *Depotenzierung der Souveränität. Religion und politische Ideologie bei Claude Lefort, Slavoj Žižek und Karl Barth.* Tübingen: Mohr Siebeck, 2016.

Kotsko, Adam. *Žižek and Theology.* London: Continuum, 2008.

Lacan, Jacques. *The Seminar of Jacques Lacan, Book II, The Ego in Freud's Theory and in the Technique of Psychoanalysis, 1954–1955*, ed. by Jacques-Alain Miller, trans. Sylvana Tomaselli. New York: W.W. Norton & Company, 1988.

Laclau, Ernesto. *New Reflections on the Evolution of Our Time.* London: Verso, 1990.

Laclau, Ernesto, and Mouffe, Chantal. *Hegemony and Socialist Strategy: Towards A Radical Democratic Politics.* London: Verso, 1985.

Lefort, Claude. *Democracy and Political Theory*, trans. David Macey. Cambridge, UK: Polity, 1988.

Lefort, Claude. "The Permanence of the Theologico-Political?" In *Political Theologies: Public Religions in A Modern World*, ed. by Hent de Vries and Lawrence Sullican, 148–187. New York: Fordham Press, 2006.

Lefort, Claude. "La dissolution des repères et l'enjeu démocratique," In *Le temps present: Écrits 1945–2005*, ed. by Claude Lefort, 551–568. Paris: Belin, 2007.
Lefort, Claude. "Démocratie et avènement d'un 'lieu vide,'" In *Le temps present: Écrits 1945–2005*, ed. by Claude Lefort, 551–568. Paris: Belin, 2007.
Levitsky, Steven, and Ziblatt, Daniel. *How Democracies Die*. New York: Crown, 2008.
Marchart, Oliver. *Die politische Differenz: Zum Denken des Politischen bei Nancy, Lefort, Badiou, Laclau und Agamben*. Berlin: Suhrkamp, 2010.
Marchart, Oliver. *Post-foundational Political Thought: Political Difference in Nancy, Lefort, Badiou, and Laclau*. Edinburgh: Edinburgh University Press, 2007.
Mazzarella, William; Santner, Eric L., and Schuster, Aaron. *Sovereignty, Inc. Three Inquiries in Politics and Enjoyment*. Chicago: The University of Chicago Press, 2020.
Milbradt, Björn. *Über autoritäre Haltungen in 'postfaktischen' Zeiten*. Opladen: Budrich, 2018.
Mouffe, Chantal. *The Democratic Paradox*. London: Verso, 2009.
Mouffe, Chantal. *Agonistics: Thinking the World Politically*. London: Verso, 2013.
Mounk, Yasha. *The People vs. Democracy. Why Our Freedom is in Danger and How to Save it*. Cambridge, MA: Harvard University Press, 2018.
Reckwitz, Andreas. *Society of Singularities*, trans. Valentine A. Pakis. Cambridge, UK: Polity, forthcoming.
Rensmann, Lars; Hagemann, Steffen, and Funke, Hajo. *Autoritarismus und Demokratie. Politische Theorie und Kultur in der globalen Moderne*. Schwalbach: Wochenschau-Verlag, 2011.
Santner, Eric L. *The Royal Remains: The People's Two Bodies and the Endgames of Sovereignty*. Chicago: The University of Chicago Press, 2011.
Santner, Eric L. *The Weight of All Flesh: On the Subject-Matter of Political Economy*. New York: Oxford University Press, 2015.
Schmitt, Carl. *Political Theology: Four Chapters on the Concept of Sovereignty*, ed. and trans. George Schwab. Chicago: University of Chicago Press, 2005.
Thomä, Dieter. *Warum Demokratien Helden brauchen. Plädoyer für einen zeitgemäßen Heroismus*. Berlin: Ullstein, 2019.
Trautmann, Felix, ed. *Das politische Imaginäre*. Köln: August Verlag, 2017.
Traverso, Enzo. *The New Faces of Fascism. Populism and the Far Right*, trans. David Broder. London: Verso, 2019.
Vogl, Joseph, ed., *Gemeinschaften: Positionen zu einer Philosophie des Politischen*. Frankfurt a. M.: Suhrkamp, 1994.
Zielonka, Jan. *Konterrevolution. Der Rückzug des liberalen Europa*. Frankfurt a. M.: Campus, 2019.
Žižek, Slavoj. *The Ticklish Subject: The Absent Centre of Political Ontology*. London: Verso, 1999.
Žižek, Slavoj. *Less Than Nothing: Hegel and the Shadow of Dialectical Materialism*. London: Verso, 2012.

I | **Figurations of the Master**

Clemens Pornschlegel
Sklaven ohne Herrn

Goethes Faust als moderner Führer

Abstract: The article "Slaves Without Masters" presents Goethe's Faust (in part two of the drama) as a pioneer of modern economic thinking. Religion no longer plays a role in his world of technical-scientific perfection, as every form of transcendence collapses into immanence of production processes. Especially the end of the drama illustrates this, because here, through a huge colonization enterprise with Faust as the leader of modern technological knowledge, land is to be gained on a large scale for the purpose of economic expansion. Max Weber's secularization thesis is anticipated here. This world, which Faust calls his own, is solely organized by economic standards as the singular yardstick of the difference between truth and knowledge.

> "Ceux qui n'ont pas connu l'ancien régime ne pourront
> jamais savoir ce qu'était la douceur de vivre."
> Talleyrand

1

Goethes *Faust* entsteht zwischen 1770 und 1830. Die Tragödie begleitet historisch den epistemischen Umbruch, den Foucault in der *Ordnung der Dinge* beschrieben hat als Übergang vom klassischen Regime der Repräsentation zur Ordnung des produktiven Wissens, in dem der Mensch zum Ursprung und Ziel allen Wissens, das heißt zu einer transzendental-empirischen Dublette wird.[1]

Thematisch wird in Goethes *Faust*[2] – insbesondere im zweiten Teil der Tragödie, der mit der Einführung des Papiergeldes einsetzt, das auf die künftige Hebung von Bodenschätzen spekuliert – der historische Prozess der Ausbildung der industrie-kapitalistischen und techno-wissenschaftlichen Produktionsordnung des 19. und 20. Jahrhunderts, den Heidegger dann als Emergenz des Zeit-

---

[1] Vgl. Foucault, *Les mots et les choses*, 262ff.
[2] Vgl. von Goethe, *Faust: Texte*. – Zitatnachweise im laufenden Text mit einfacher Versangabe nach dieser Ausgabe.

alters der Technik beschrieben wird,[3] der zugleich auch einhergeht mit dem, was ‚Säkularisierung' bedeutet, das heißt, die rückhaltlose Einfaltung Gottes, seiner Omnipotenz und seines Allwissens in die Endlichkeit beziehungsweise in die vom Menschen betriebene Techno-Wissenschaft. Es geht um das Projekt nach Möglichkeit restloser Naturbeherrschung, einschließlich der Beherrschung der störanfälligen Menschennatur selbst. Die alte Religion wird nach und nach überflüssig. Ihre vertikal orientierte Frömmigkeit gegenüber dem Herrn wird umgelegt auf die irdisch-horizontale, dabei freilich – wie Max Weber gezeigt hat – nicht weniger fromme Tätigkeit des Menschen, der als Gattungswesen zum alleinigen Urheber aller Reichtümer und Götter, aller sichtbaren und unsichtbaren Dinge wird. Nietzsche hat den Säkularisierungs- und Verwissenschaftlichungsprozess dann ironisch unter dem Titel *Verheißungen der Wissenschaft* beschrieben, und zwar im Aphorismus 128 der Sammlung *Menschliches, Allzumenschliches*, in dem es heißt: „Verheißungen der Wissenschaft. – Die moderne Wissenschaft hat als Ziel: so wenig Schmerz wie möglich, so lange leben wie möglich, – also eine Art von ewiger Seligkeit, freilich eine sehr bescheidene im Vergleich mit den Verheißungen der Religionen."[4]

Im speziellen Feld der Künste läuft dieser historische Transformationsprozess mitsamt seinen unbescheidenen Fortschrittsversprechen auf den Sachverhalt hinaus, den Hegel mit dem Diktum vom ‚Ende der Kunst' umschrieben hat.[5] Die Wahrheit der Dinge wird den Bewohnern der Wissenschaftswelt nicht mehr im Gewand poetischer Gebilde erscheinen. Gesagt und administriert wird sie stattdessen von *der* Wissenschaft (als Singularetantum), während die ehemaligen Künste ins Reich der Unterhaltung geschoben werden: als zerstreuendes Freizeitvergnügen, das so beliebig wie austauschbar ist und der Regeneration förderlich sein soll. Oder aber die alte Kunst wird im Dienst der Wissenschaft nützlich gemacht, etwa wenn Skulpturen in den Dienst anatomischer Studien gestellt werden. Im Dritten Buch von *Wilhelm Meisters Wanderjahren* beschreibt Goethe diesen Vorgang wie folgt: „‚Ich habe', versetzte der Lehrer [der Bildhauer ist], ‚einen geschickten Mann, dessen Kunst nach Brote ging, indem er Heilige und Märtyrer, die er zu schnitzen gewohnt war, keinen Abgang mehr fanden, ihn hab ich darauf geleitet, sich der Skelettbildung zu bemächtigen und solche im großen wie im kleinen naturgemäß zu befördern.'"[6]

---

3 Vgl. Heidegger, „Einblick in das was ist", 3–45.
4 Nietzsche, *Menschliches*, Nr. 128.
5 Vgl. Hegel, *Ästhetik*, 24 ff.; vgl. dazu auch: Pornschlegel, *Allegorien des Unendlichen*, 14–21.
6 Goethe, *Wilhelm Meisters Wanderjahre*, 356 (Buch 3, Kap. 3) – vgl. dazu auch die Aphorismen 140–143 „Aus Makariens Archiv" (zur Wissenschaft als Theorem und Kunst als Problem), in ebd., 519–520.

Goethes *Faust*, wie gesagt, begleitet in der Textgenese über drei Jahrzehnte hinweg diesen Prozess, der von der Ordnung der Repräsentation in die Ordnung der Produktion führt, und er tut dies affirmativ. Das heißt, die Tragödie ist unter anderem auch die Tragödie der untergehenden Kunst und ihrer Weltdarstellung – weswegen Goethes *Faust* dann auch noch einmal die ganze bisherige Poesie und ihre Formen ‚museal' in sich zusammenzufassen sucht, und zwar in dem Sinn, den Goethe für Calderón geltend gemacht hatte: „Ja, ich möchte sagen, wenn die Poesie ganz von der Welt verlorenginge, so könnte man sie aus diesem Stück widerherstellen."[7]

Albrecht Schöne hat in seinem großen Kommentar zur Faust-Dichtung[8] die unterschiedlichen Metren, Strophenformen und Genres, die in Goethes Text Eingang gefunden haben, minutiös aufgelistet. Verständlich wird die exhaustiv angelegte poetische Formenvielfalt der Tragödie, wenn man sie im Angesicht des Diktums vom Ende der Kunst liest: nämlich als *summa* der Ausdrucksformen der bisherigen Menschheit, die jetzt vom neuen produktiven Menschen abgelöst werden wird: vom Menschen, der um seine Vermögen und Möglichkeiten weiß, einschließlich des ihm bislang verborgenen Vermögens, Götter zu schaffen und die gegebene Natur nach Belieben umzuformen, ja neu zu schaffen.

Das Paradoxon der Selbstermächtigung des Menschen (in seiner Eigenschaft als transzendental-empirischer Dublette, das heißt des Menschen als Gattungswesen im Feuerbachschen Sinn) besteht nun darin, dass die Befreiung aus den Zwängen der alten Natur, aber auch des feudalen Ständewesens sowie der dogmatischen Religion mitsamt ihrem Gott, ihren *regulae* und *praecepta vitae* nicht in die Freiheit führt – jedenfalls nicht in die Freiheit des Müßiggangs, der Kontemplation oder gar des Gebets, der untätigen Bewunderung und des anti-produktiven Genusses –, sondern in die andere Unerbittlichkeit und Zwanghaftigkeit – genau das artikuliert Fausts Teufelspakt –, nämlich die eines ständigen, rast- und ruhelosen Streben-Müssens, in den Zwang der Tätigkeit und der fortlaufenden Produktion, kurzum, in permanente Arbeit – damit aber auch in eine neue Form der Sklaverei.

„Werd' ich beruhigt je mich auf ein Faulbett legen:
So sei es gleich um mich getan
[...]
Kannst du mich mit Genuss betriegen:

---

[7] Johann Wolfgang von Goethe, Brief an Schiller, 28. Januar 1804; zit. nach: Goethe, *Faust: Kommentare*, 11.
[8] Vgl. Goethe, *Faust: Kommentare*, 13–14; vgl. ebenfalls: Ciupke, ‚*Des Geklimpers vielverworrener Töne Rausch'*.

> Das sei für mich der letzte Tag!
> Die Wette biet' ich!
> [...]
> Werd' ich zum Augenblicke sagen:
> Verweile doch! Du bist so schön!
> Dann magst du mich in Fesseln schlagen,
> Dann will ich gern zu Grunde gehen!" (V. 1692–1702).

Die Neuigkeit dieses unentwegten Strebens liegt darin, dass sie keinen Herrn im Sinn der Anti-Produktion mehr kennt, dem sie zu Diensten wäre und der ihre Mühen genießend an sich reißen oder ‚abschöpfen' würde.[9] Die neue Freiheit ist vielmehr ein ständig verbesserndes Tätigsein ohne anti-produktiven Herrn. Denn der neue Mensch ist nur und genau insofern frei, als er rastlos gegen seine Not arbeitet – und zwar um seine alte, fremden Natur-Gewalten unterworfene *conditio humana* (Krankheiten, Tod, Sexualität, Hunger, Durst usw.) zu überwinden. Die Freiheit des Menschen ist nicht mehr die Freiheit eines Herrn – als Freiheit von Arbeit, Zeit zum Müßiggang und zum Genuss –, es ist nicht mehr die Freiheit des Herrn *im (einfachen antithetischen) Gegensatz* zu arbeitenden Knechten, stattdessen die Freiheit *vom* Herrn – und zwar als allgemeine, kollektive Sklaverei auf Dauer gestellter produktiver Arbeits- und Fortschrittsprojekte. Sie werden – so die neue Verheißung – demnächst aus der *conditio humana* erlösen und den alten Menschen mitsamt Sündenfall, Vertreibung aus dem Paradies, Sterblichkeit, Mangel, Krankheit, Not, Leiden usw. überwinden. Damit aber tritt an die Stelle des genießenden Herrn ein moderner, wissenschaftlich prozedierender, das Projekt der Verbesserung und Überwindung des alten Menschen koordinierender ‚Führer' – Chief Executive Officer, Projektleiter, Teamchef, Manager.

> „Wie das Geklirr der Spaten mich ergötzt
> Es ist die Menge, die mir frönet,
> Die Erde mit sich selbst *versöhnet*." (V. 11539–11541; Herv.; C.P.).

Nicht zufällig artikuliert Goethes *Faust* – in der Figur des ordentlichen Universitäts-Professors Wagner (der im ersten Teil noch Famulus und „trockner Schleicher" [V. 521] war) – die techno-wissenschaftliche Verbesserung und Neuschöpfung des Menschen im Laboratorium (V. 6835 ff); nicht zufällig lehnt Faust die ihm von Mephisto angebotene Rolle eines absolutistischen Herrschers und Genussmenschen nach dem Vorbild deutscher Duodezfürsten des 18. Jahrhunderts entschieden ab (V. 10135 ff), um sich stattdessen vom Kaiser ‚des Reiches Strand' geben zu lassen, den er in großem Maßstab kolonisieren wird (V. 11036); nicht

---

9 Vgl. Foucault, *Histoire de la sexualité*, 178 ff.

zufällig liquidiert Faust die traditionale, gastfreundschaftliche Ordnung von Philemon und Baucis, die er gewalttätig enteignen und „beiseite schaffen", das heißt ermorden lässt (V. 11334f); nicht zufällig ist Fausts Palast – von dem aus der Krieg gegen die beschauliche Hütte der mythischen Alten geführt wird – kein repräsentatives Schloss, sondern eine „Zusammenführung von Palast, Kanal, Stapelplatz",[10] Büro und Kontor (V. 1143ff), von wo aus Faust sein Kolonisationswerk diktatorisch lenkt beziehungsweise von wo aus er, wie Gerhard Kaiser formulierte, seine „politische, gesellschaftliche, ökonomische und technische Gewalt"[11] ausübt, bevor er dann am Ort verbrannter, idyllischer Linden seinen Kontrollturm namens „Luginsland" (V. 11344) errichten wird:

> „Dem Blick eröffnen weite Bahn,
> Zu sehn was alles ich getan,
> Zu überschaun mit einem Blick
> Des Menschengeistes Meisterstück" (V. 11245 – 11248).

Dabei ist Fausts imperiales Kolonisationsprojekt, das „vielen Millionen" neue „Räume" eröffnen soll (V. 11563), *planetarisch* konzipiert.[12] Es zielt auf nichts Geringeres als auf die Umgestaltung des bisherigen Menschenwesens und der alten Erde schlechthin. Und zwar im Sinn des biblischen Wortes, das die Schlange an Eva richtet und das in der Tragödie auch explizit zitiert wird: *eritis sicut Deus, scientes bonum et malum* („Ihr werdet sein wie Gott und wissen, was gut und böse ist", Gen 3,5). Mephisto kommentiert das Bibel-Wort im ersten Teil der Tragödie (V. 2048) mit den (besserwisserischen) ironischen Versen: „Folg' nur dem alten Spruch und meiner Muhme, der Schlange, / Die wird gewiss einmal bei deiner Gottähnlichkeit bange!" (V. 2049–2050). Gerhard Kaiser hat das Faust-Projekt zu Recht als post-christliches Heils- und Erlösungsprojekt beschrieben:

> „Faust gebärdet sich als Schöpfer einer neuen Welt und Heilsträger der Völker. [...] Durch sein gewaltiges Kolonisationsunternehmen soll im größten Maßstab Land gewonnen werden. [...] Dass Faust [...] menschlichen Lebensraum durch Trockenlegung des Meeres zu schaffen unternimmt, ist ein Versuch, den Boden der [bisherigen Menschheits-]Geschichte zu verlassen, aus der Geschichte als einer ewigen Kette von Ereignissen auszubrechen. [...] Historische Wirklichkeit soll in absolute Möglichkeit überführt werden. [...] [Faust] überbietet

---

10 Kaiser, *Ist der Mensch zu retten?*, 43.
11 Kaiser, *Ist der Mensch zu retten?*, 43.
12 Goethes *Faust* knüpft damit an die Vorstellung des *theatrum mundi* an. „In Form eines Struktur-Zitats weist die *Faust*-Dichtung auf Calderóns Modell zurück. Aber man wird sie selber kaum noch als ein solches Mysterienspiel verstehen können. [...] Die in das Erdetreiben eintretenden und eingreifenden Himmelsboten der alten Welttheater-Spiele bleiben aus." Goethe, *Faust: Kommentare*, 62–163.

[damit auch] noch [den amerikanischen Traum vom Land der Freiheit und unbegrenzten Möglichkeiten] durch den Traum von einer *tatsächlich* neuen Welt. Der absolute Anfang einer anderen Menschengeschichte soll gesetzt werden, und Faust will es sein, der das tut."[13]

Der entscheidende Punkt des menschheitlichen Freiheits- und Emanzipationsprojekts, das Faust verfolgt, liegt darin, dass die Befreiung des Menschen als Gattungswesen aus der Herrschaft der bisherigen politischen und religiösen Mächte – also der Emanzipationsprozess, wie er historisch Ende des 18. Jahrhunderts sozial, politisch und ökonomisch akut beziehungsweise revolutionär wird – gerade nicht ins Reich individuellen Müßiggangs oder ins Schlaraffenland genüsslichen Nichtstuns oder – gattungsspezifisch formuliert – in irgendeine ‚Idylle' führt, sondern dass er als stetig fortlaufender Emanzipations*prozess* umgehend eine neue, unerhört gewalttätige Form der kollektiven Sklaverei und rastlosen Arbeitsfron auf den Plan ruft. Das kommende Neue Reich fällt niemandem in den Schoß. Faust sagt es völlig offen: „Nur der verdient sich Freiheit wie das Leben, der täglich sie erobern muss." (V. 11575). Die Arbeiter geraten dabei zu halbtoten Lemuren, denen Mephisto neues Eigentum verspricht, von dem sie sich gerüchteweise erzählen: „Es gilt wohl gar ein weites Land / Das sollen wir bekommen." (V. 11517–11518). Faust wiederum befiehlt seinem Arbeitsheer, das heißt: der ganzen Menschheit, deren weltgeschichtliches Schicksal das Himmel und Erde durchmessende *Weltgedicht* des *Faust* darzustellen sucht:

> „Vom Lager auf ihr Knechte! Mann für Mann!
> Lasst glücklich schauen was ich kühn ersann.
> Ergreift das Werkzeug, Schaufel rührt und Spaten,
> Das Abgesteckte muss sogleich geraten.
> Auf strenges Ordnen, raschen Fleiß,
> Erfolgt der allerschönste Preis;
> Dass sich das größte Werk vollende
> Genügt Ein Geist für tausend Hände." (V. 11503–11510).

Und an den diabolischen Aufseher, Mephisto also, ergeht der Befehl:

> „Wie es auch möglich sei
> Arbeiter schaffe Meng' auf Menge,
> Ermuntere durch Genuss und Strenge,
> Bezahle, locke, presse bei!
> Mit jedem Tag will ich Nachricht haben
> Wie sich verlängt der unternommene Graben" (V. 11551–11556).

---

13 Kaiser, *Ist der Mensch zu retten?*, 36–37.

Faust ist in der Tat kein bequem genießender, dekadenter Herrscher, kein antiproduktiver Despot, er ist betriebsamer „Fürst, Ökonom, Kriegsherr, Pirat und Umweltingenieur in einem",[14] und daneben auch: Welt-Besitzer (V. 11242), Groß-Unternehmer (weswegen er ganz ausdrücklich „Patron" [V. 11170] genannt wird), absoluter Wissenschaftler sowie Führer und Schöpfer des Neuen Menschen. Im Verbund mit dem stets verneinenden Dialektiker Mephisto schickt er sich an, die alte Schöpfung im Ganzen aufzuheben.

2

Es ist nicht schwer, Goethes beunruhigend dynamische, alle bisherigen Herrschaftsordnungen hinter sich lassende Faust-Figur mitsamt ihren Fortschritts-, Handels- und Kolonisationsprojekten sozial-historisch und ökonomiegeschichtlich zu entziffern. In seinem tätig-prometheischen, zugleich religionskritischen und techno-wissenschaftlichen Ehrgeiz ist Faust unschwer lesbar als allegorische Figur der triumphierenden *Bourgeoisie* – und zwar in exakt dem Sinn, wie Marx und Engels sie keine zwei Jahrzehnte nach Goethes *Faust* im *Kommunistischen Manifest* charakterisiert haben, nämlich als revolutionäre, sämtliche überkommenen Welt-Ordnungen – in denen die Bücher Moses, Philemon und Baucis, Kaiser, Ritter und Heilige noch ihren Platz hatten – eiskalt destruierende Klasse.

> „Die Bourgeoisie, wo sie zur Herrschaft gekommen, hat alle feudalen, patriarchalischen, idyllischen Verhältnisse zerstört. [...] Sie hat die heiligen Schauer der frommen Schwärmerei, der ritterlichen Begeisterung, der spießbürgerlichen Wehmut in dem eiskalten Wasser egoistischer Berechnung ertränkt. [...] Sie hat, mit einem Wort, an die Stelle der mit religiösen und politischen Illusionen verhüllten Ausbeutung die offene, unverschämte, direkte, dürre Ausbeutung gesetzt. Die Bourgeoisie hat alle bisher ehrwürdigen und mit frommer Scheu betrachteten Tätigkeiten ihres Heiligenscheins entkleidet. Sie hat den Arzt, den Juristen, den Pfaffen, den Poeten, den Mann der Wissenschaft in ihre bezahlten Lohnarbeiter verwandelt. [...] Sie hat ganz andere Wunderwerke vollbracht als ägyptische Pyramiden, römische Wasserleitungen und gotische Kathedralen, sie hat ganz andere Züge ausgeführt als Völkerwanderungen und Kreuzzüge."[15]

Ganz im Sinn dieser umfassenden Decodierung aller bestehenden Verhältnisse durch die neue Welthandelsordnung, die Faust voranbringt – nicht anders übrigens als die weltumspannende Kolonisationsgesellschaft der Wanderjahre[16] –

---

14 Kaiser, *Ist der Mensch zu retten?*, 36–37.
15 Marx und Engels, „Manifest der kommunistischen Partei", 463–464.
16 Vgl. Goethe, *Wilhelm Meisters Wanderjahre*, 415 ff. (Buch 3, Kap. 9).

sagt Mephisto zu den „drei gewaltigen Gesellen", die auf einem prächtigen Kahn, „reich und bunt beladen mit Erzeugnissen fremder Weltgegenden" (V. 11165) in der Unternehmenszentrale anlanden:

> „Krieg, Handel und Piraterie,
> Dreieinig sind sie, nicht zu trennen" (V. 11187–11188).

Die Logik des Zusammenhangs zwischen der Ende des 18. Jahrhunderts revolutionären Bourgeoisie mitsamt ihren gegen die alten Mächte errungenen bürgerlichen Freiheiten und der gleichzeitig anbrechenden neuen, unerhörten Sklaverei haben Gilles Deleuze und Félix Guattari im *Anti-Ödipus* eindringlich beschrieben:

> „Klassen sind *das* Negativ aller alten Kasten und Stände und ihrer Codes, es sind *decodierte* Kasten und Stände. Die Geschichte als Klassenkampf lesen heißt, sie im Hinblick auf die Bourgeoisie als decodierender und decodierter Klasse lesen. Die Bourgeoisie ist insofern die einzige und alleinige Klasse, als sie den Kampf gegen die Codes führt und mit der allgemeinen Decodierung der Ströme verschmilzt. Deswegen reicht sie auch vollkommen hin, das kapitalistische Immanenzfeld auszufüllen. Und in der Tat ereignet sich mit dem Auftauchen der Bourgeoisie etwas vollkommen Neues: der Genuss als Ziel und Zweck der Produktion verschwindet, eine neue Konzeption der Konjunktion bildet sich heraus, wonach der einzige Zweck der abstrakte Reichtum und dessen Realisierung in anderen Formen als denen der Konsumtion ist. Die allgemeine Sklaverei des despotischen Staates implizierte wenigstens noch einen Herrn und einen von der Produktionssphäre geschiedenen Anti-Produktionsapparat. Der bürgerliche Immanenzzusammenhang hingegen, der durch die Konjunktion decodierter Ströme, die Negation jeglicher Transzendenz oder äußerer Grenze sowie das Eingehen der Anti-Produktion in die Produktion bestimmt ist, errichtet eine unerhörte Knechtschaft und eine beispiellose Unterwerfung: es gibt nicht einmal mehr einen Herrn, sondern nur noch Knechte, die anderen Knechten Befehle erteilen. Das Tier muss nicht mehr von außen beladen werden, es belädt sich selbst. Nicht dass der Mensch Sklave der technischen Maschine wäre: der Bourgeois gibt das Musterbild für den Sklaven der Gesellschaftsmaschine ab. Er absorbiert den Mehrwert zu Zwecken, die nichts mit seinem Genuss zu tun haben: Er ist knechtischer als der letzte der Knechte, erster Diener der hungrigen Maschine, Reproduktionsvieh des Kapitals, Verinnerlichung der unendlichen Schuld. ‚Auch ich bin Knecht', werden die neuen Worte des Herrn sein. ‚Nur als Personifikation des Kapitals ist der Kapitalist respektabel. Als solcher teilt er mit dem Schatzbildner den absoluten Bereicherungstrieb. Was aber bei diesem als individuelle Manie erscheint, ist beim Kapitalisten Wirkung des gesellschaftlichen Mechanismus, worin er nur Triebrad ist.'"[17]

Die wesentlich harmloser klingenden Begriffe (oder *mots d'ordre*) Goethes für haargenau dieselben Sachverhalte – nämlich des Eingangs der Anti-Produktion in die Produktion, der Negation jeglicher Transzendenz, der Verinnerlichung der

---

[17] Deleuze und Guattari, *Anti-Ödipus*, 327–328 (Übersetzungsungenauigkeiten sind stillschweigend korrigiert), inhärentes Zitat aus: Marx, „Das Kapital", 618.

unendlichen Schuld, der permanenten Schöpfung abstrakten Reichtums sowie der Ausbildung universaler Knechtschaft – lauten: ‚Entsagung', Erfüllung der ‚Forderung des Tages' und – last but not least – ‚Bildung'. Erich Trunz hat diese *mots d'ordre* Goethes zutreffend charakterisiert: „Kernwörter des Goetheschen Lebensglaubens sind: *'tüchtig, frei, tätig'*."[18] Es sind die normativen Maximen einer bürgerlich kapitalistischen Moderne, welche die Welt des *Ancien Régime*, also der Grafen und Ritter, Mönche und Poeten, Gelehrten und Bischöfe liquidieren. Sie alle werden im eiskalten Wasser egoistischer Berechnung ertränkt.

Die Schlusspassage der Ferdinand-Novelle aus Goethes *Unterhaltungen deutscher Ausgewanderten* von 1795 – in der moralische Schuld rigoros auf zirkulierende Geldschulden und Eigentumsrechte bezogen wird, und sonst auf gar nichts – macht die neue Form der Knechtschaft anschaulich. Was auf den ersten Blick familiär, heiter und respektabel scheint, ist *de facto* unaufhörlicher Dienst am geldheckenden Geld. Und was als ‚individuelle Manie' des Helden der Novelle, Ferdinand, dargestellt wird, ist ‚Wirkung des gesellschaftlichen Mechanismus'. In Goethes Novelle lesen sich die Zusammenhänge wie folgt:

> „Selbst als Mann und Hausvater pflegte er [Ferdinand] sich manchmal etwas, das ihm Freude würde gemacht haben, zu versagen, um nur nicht aus der Übung einer so schönen Tugend zu kommen, und seine ganze Erziehung bestand gewissermaßen darin, dass seine Kinder sich gleichsam aus dem Stegreife etwas mussten versagen können. [...] [Er] untersagte zum Beispiel einem Knaben bei Tische, von einer beliebten Speise zu essen. Zu meiner Verwunderung blieb der Knabe heiter, und es war, als wenn weiter nichts geschehen wäre. Und so ließen die ältesten aus eigener Bewegung manchmal ein edles Obst oder sonst einen Leckerbissen vor sich vorbeigehen; dagegen erlaubte er ihnen, ich möchte wohl sagen, alles, und es fehlte nicht an Arten und Unarten in seinem Hause. Er schien über alles gleichgültig zu sein und ließ ihnen eine fast unbändige Freiheit; nur fiel es ihm die Woche einmal ein, dass alles auf die Minute geschehen musste. Alsdann wurden des Morgens gleich die Uhren reguliert, ein jeder erhielt seine Ordre für den Tag, Geschäfte und Vergnügungen wurden gehäuft, und niemand durfte eine Sekunde fehlen. [...] Er scherzte mit mir als einem katholischen Geistlichen über meine Gelübde und behauptete, dass eigentlich jeder Mensch sowohl sich selbst Enthaltsamkeit als andern Gehorsam geloben sollte, nicht um sie immer, sondern um sie zur rechten Zeit auszuüben."[19]

Konfessionsgeschichtlich prägnanter, genauer und pointierter könnte man Max Webers *protestantische Ethik* und den sie durchwehenden ‚Geist des Kapitalismus' kaum formulieren.

---

18 Trunz, „Anmerkungen", 620.
19 Goethe, „Unterhaltungen deutscher Ausgewanderten", 207.

3

So einleuchtend die Lektüre der Goetheschen Faust-Figur und ihrer kolonisatorischen Unternehmungen als ‚Allegorie der Bourgeoisie' auch sein mag, so plausibel die revolutionäre Dynamik Fausts, die Abschaffung der alten Feudalordnung erscheint, so ungeklärt ist die politische Frage nach dem Zusammenhang zwischen humanistischem Emanzipationsstreben und kapitalistischer ‚Diktatur', die Goethes *Faust* aufwirft.[20]

Man kann Gerhard Kaisers Beschreibung des Faustschen Unternehmens als eines totalitären Diktatoren-Projekts zunächst problemlos folgen:

> „Der Mann, der auf freiem Grund mit freiem Volk zu stehen wünscht, will [...] diesen freien Grund als Diktator durch Druck und Tricks, Zuckerbrot und Peitsche, Entmündigung und Frondienste der Massen erzeugen. Um einer imaginierten freien Menschheit willen erniedrigt er die Menschen hier und jetzt zu Menschenmaterial. Er war nie so unsozial wie im Augenblick seiner sozialen Utopie. Der Reim vom ‚Versöhnen' der Erde auf das ‚Frönen' der Menge pointiert diesen Zynismus. Die industriellen Reservearmeen des 19. Jahrhunderts gehen über in die Heere der Fremdarbeiter und KZ-Sklaven. Die Menschen sind für Faust gerade gut genug zum Sockelfries am zeitresistenten Denkmal seiner Selbstvergötterung als *homo faber*. Untergründig weisen die ‚vielen Millionen', denen Faust Raum schaffen will (V. 11563) auf den Kern seines Traums vor: die ‚Äonen' seines Nachruhms (V. 11584). Das ist wie hellsichtig vorgreifender Hohn auf die sozialen und technischen Welt- und Menschheitsbeglückungskonzepte des 19. und 20. Jahrhunderts, die so unerhörte Menschenopfer gefordert haben. Zwangsarbeit, Trockenlegungen, Kanalbau sind eine berüchtigte Trias."[21]

Man kann der Beschreibung, wie gesagt, problemlos folgen. Fragwürdig ist indes die Wendung vom ‚*wie* hellsichtig vorgreifenden Hohn', welche die totalitären Regime des 19. und 20. Jahrhundert im Blick hat. Das hypothetische ‚Wie' ist kein Zufall. Goethes Hohn nämlich ist keiner. Dieser Eindruck entsteht erst im erschreckten, historischen Rückblick, der um KZ-Sklaven, Kolonialverbrechen, Massenarmut, Massenauswanderung, Tagelöhnerei, Pauperisierung, das heißt, um die Geschichte des 19. und 20. Jahrhunderts und um den horrenden Preis des sogenannten ‚Fortschritts' weiß. Goethes Tragödie – die am Ende, mit dem ‚genießenden' Tod Fausts[22] und seiner himmlischen Erlösung keine mehr ist, je-

---

20 Die Frage nach Fausts Diktatur ist nach 1945 weitgehend aus der Diskussion verschwunden. Vor 1945 ist sie massiv präsent, und zwar als Behauptung einer ‚deutschen' Option der Moderne. Vgl. Pongs, „Faust und die Ehre", 78–105.
21 Kaiser, *Ist der Mensch zu retten?*, 61–62.
22 „Es kann die Spur von meinen Erdetagen / Nicht in Äonen untergehen. – / Im Vorgefühl von solchem hohen Glück / Genieß ich jetzt den Augenblick." (V. 11583–11586).

denfalls nicht für Faust – stellt Fausts kapitalistisch-diktatorisches Kolonisationsunternehmen demgegenüber *ohne* jeden Hohn, ohne jede Kritik und ohne jedes Erschrecken dar. Erich Trunz kommentiert Fausts Projekt zu Recht affirmativ: „[Faust] ist auch jetzt [als brutaler Diktator] ein *Strebender*, seine Vision ist [...] Zukunftsplan."[23] Fausts imperiales Weltschöpfungs-Unternehmen ist und bleibt das grandios visionäre, in der ‚Tragödie' durchgängig *bejahte* und *erstrebte* Welt-Modernisierungs-, Erlösungs- und Menschheitsverbesserungs-Projekt eines rastlos tätigen Helden, der trotz oder besser: *in* seiner Hybris (die über Leichen geht) zuletzt *erlöst* und eben gerade *nicht*, und zwar im Wortsinn nicht, verteufelt wird – wie trügerisch oder zynisch Himmelfahrt, Marienfiguren und Engelsgesänge sich am Schluss des Dramas auch ausnehmen mögen angesichts der Kirchenferne ihres nach Apotheose strebenden Helden. Das heißt aber, dass Goethes *Faust* die bürgerlich-kapitalistische Moderne tatsächlich als brutale diktatorische Moderne entwirft und dass die humanistisch-emanzipatorische Verabschiedung der alten Mächte, also der Feudalherrn, Kirchen, Duodezfürsten des *Ancien Régime*, die neue Sklaverei und die ihr entsprechende Diktatur dezidiert nicht aus-, sondern sie – ‚tüchtig, frei und tätig' – mit einschließt.

Was sich in Goethes Drama nicht findet, sind historische Verweise auf die bürgerlich demokratischen Revolutionen in Frankreich und in den Vereinigten Staaten von Amerika, deren Akteure bekanntlich nicht weniger bourgeois und handelsfreudig waren als Faust und Mephisto. Politisch werden sie keine Diktaturen unter der Führung von nach absolutem Wissen strebenden deutschen Gelehrten oder Professoren (wie Faust) ausbilden,[24] stattdessen Republiken oder konstitutionelle Monarchien mitsamt Parlamenten und liberalen Freiheiten. Erklären lässt sich die fehlende bürgerlich-demokratische Emphase des *Faust* durch die spezifisch deutschen Voraussetzungen, von denen aus Goethe die kapitalistische Moderne denkt. Dass Goethe das Drama als ‚deutsches Drama' entworfen hat, wird anschaulich an den spätmittelalterlichen Studierzimmern, Mummenschanz-Szenen, an den Leipziger Studenten-Kellern, Hexenküchen, Marktplatz-Brunnen und den reinlichen Jungfer-Kammern. Seit dem Sturm und Drang bilden sie das Inventar einer nationalen Ikonographie.[25]

In seiner Studie über *Soziale Ursprünge von Diktatur und Demokratie* hat Barrington Moore darauf aufmerksam gemacht, erstens dass es „verschiedene Wege in die moderne Welt"[26] des Kapitals gibt, nämlich demokratische, faschis-

---

23 Trunz, „Anmerkungen", 620.
24 In Goethes Wanderjahren zielt das kolonisatorische Projekt der neuen ‚Wanderer' auf die Einrichtung eines disziplinären Polizeistaats.
25 Zu diesen ikonographischen Stereotypen vgl. Florack, *Tiefsinnige, frivole Franzosen*, 369–402.
26 Moore, *Soziale Ursprünge von Diktatur und Demokratie*, 475.

tisch-reaktionäre und kommunistische, und zweitens dass sie ganz wesentlich von unterschiedlichen sozio-politischen, aber auch landwirtschaftlich geographischen *Voraussetzungen* abhängen – nämlich von den „Beziehungen der grundbesitzenden Oberklassen zu Monarchie", von deren „Reaktion auf die Erfordernisse der Produktion für den Markt" sowie von den „Beziehungen der grundbesitzenden Oberklassen zu den Stadtbewohnern".[27]

Mit anderen Worten, die kapitalistische Moderne hat mit bürgerlich demokratischen Regimen nur auf historisch kontingente Weise zu tun; es besteht also keinerlei Determinismus – auch wenn Marcel Gauchet oder Francis Fukuyama es sich anders wünschen –, der die kapitalistische Welt an demokratische Regime westlichen, nämlich französischen, englischen oder amerikanischen Zuschnitts binden würde. Was Emanzipation heißt, zielt nicht von sich aus auf Grundrechte, Parlamente, Gleichheit und dergleichen. Der Begriff ist wesentlich negativ. Er bezieht sich auf den Untergang der vor-kapitalistischen Ordnung, aus deren bevormundenden Händen die Menschen freigesetzt werden. Wie Marx sagte: „Die Leibeignen selbst, woneben auch freie kleine Landeigner, befanden sich in sehr verschiednen Besitzverhältnissen und wurden [...] unter sehr verschiednen ökonomischen Bedingungen emanzipiert."[28] Und in der Regel wurden sie derart emanzipiert, dass ihre Emanzipation sie umgehend in vogelfreie Proletarier verwandelte. Die Emanzipation beseitigt deswegen nicht, sondern sie geht einher mit der anderen, neuen, herrenlosen Sklaverei einer Welt, deren einziger Zweck das ständige Wachstum abstrakten Reichtums und dessen Realisierung ist. Deren Motor ist die permanente Decodierung aller sozialen Gebundenheiten oder, mit Karl Polanyi formuliert, aller sozialen „Einbettungen",[29] aller Glaubenssysteme und symbolischer Referenzen, sofern sie der Realisierung von Mehr-Wert im Weg stehen. Dieser Dynamik kann auch das warnende Wort Mephistos nichts anhaben:

> „In jeder Art seid ihr verloren
> Die Elemente sind mir uns verschworen
> Und auf Vernichtung läuft's hinaus" (V. 11548–11550).

Die Warnung vor der Vernichtung läuft deswegen ins Leere, weil dieselbe Vernichtung je schon in die neue, luziferische Ordnung eingelassen ist. Fausts Himmelfahrt – „wer immer strebend sich bemüht, / Den können wir erlösen"

---

27 Moore, *Soziale Ursprünge von Diktatur und Demokratie*, 486.
28 Marx, „Das Kapital", 618.
29 Zu Polanyis Konzept der ‚embeddedness' vgl. Block, „Introduction,", XXIII–XXV.

(V. 11936 – 11937) – ist keine frohe Botschaft. Walter Benjamin hat sie anders entziffert:

„Es liegt im Wesen dieser religiösen Bewegung, welche der Kapitalismus ist, das Aushalten bis ans Ende, bis an die endliche völlige Verschuldung Gottes, den erreichten Weltzustand der Verzweiflung, auf die gerade noch gehofft wird. Darin liegt das historisch Unerhörte des Kapitalismus, dass Religion nicht mehr Reform des Seins sondern dessen Zertrümmerung ist."[30]

Bibliographie

Benjamin, Walter. „Kapitalismus als Religion [Fragment]", In *Gesammelte Schriften*, Bd. 6, Walter Benjamin, hg. v. Rolf Tiedemann und Hermann Schweppenhäuser. Frankfurt a. M.: Suhrkamp, 1991.
Block, Fred. „Introduction," In *The Great Transformation: The Political and Economic Origins of Our Time*, hg. v. Karl Polanyi, 2. Aufl., XVIII – XXXVIII. Boston: Beacon Press, 2001.
Ciupke, Martin. ‚*Des Geklimpers vielverworrener Töne Rausch': Metrische Gestaltung in Goethes ‚Faust'*. Göttingen: Wallstein Verlag, 1994.
Deleuze, Gilles, und Guattari, Félix. *Anti-Ödipus. Kapitalismus und Schizophrenie I*, Bd. 1. Frankfurt a. M.: Suhrkamp, 1977.
Florack, Ruth. *Tiefsinnige, frivole Franzosen: Nationale Stereotype in deutscher und französischer Literatur*. Stuttgart: Metzler, 2001.
Foucault, Michel. *Les mots et les choses: Une archéologie des sciences humaines*. Paris: Éditions Gallimard, 1966.
Foucault, Michel. *Histoire de la sexualité*, Bd. 1, *La volonté de savoir*. Paris: Éditions Gallimard, 1976.
von Goethe, Johann Wolfgang. *Wilhelm Meisters Wanderjahre oder Die Entsagenden*, hg. v. Ehrhard Bahr. Stuttgart: Reclam, 1982.
von Goethe, Johann Wolfgang. „Unterhaltungen deutscher Ausgewanderten," In *Romane und Novellen*, Bd. 1, Johann Wolfgang von Goethe, hg. v. Erich Trunz. München: C.H. Beck, 1988.
von Goethe, Johann Wolfgang. *Faust: Kommentare*, hg. v. Albrecht Schöne. Frankfurt a. M.: Insel Verlag, 1994.
von Goethe, Johann Wolfgang. *Faust: Texte*, hg. v. Albrecht Schöne. Frankfurt a. M.: Insel Verlag, 1994.
Hegel, Georg W.F. *Vorlesungen über die Ästhetik*, Bd. 1, hg. v. Eva Moldenhauer und Karl M. Michel. Frankfurt a. M.: Suhrkamp, 1986.
Heidegger, Martin. „Einblick in das was ist. Bremer Vorträge 1949," In *Bremer und Freiburger Vorträge*, Martin Heidegger, hg. v. Petra Jäger, 2. Aufl., 3 – 45. Frankfurt a. M.: Klostermann, 2005.

---

30 Benjamin, „Kapitalismus als Religion [Fragment],", 100 – 102.

Kaiser, Gerhard. *Ist der Mensch zu retten? Vision und Kritik der Moderne in Goethes ‚Faust'*. Freiburg i. Br.: Romberg, 1994.
Marx, Karl. „Das Kapital," In *Werke*, Bd. 23, *Das Kapital: Kritik der politischen Ökonomie*, Karl Marx und Friedrich Engels, hg. v. Institut für Marxismus-Leninismus beim ZK der SED. Berlin: Dietz, 1962.
Marx, Karl, und Engels, Friedrich. „Manifest der kommunistischen Partei," In *Werke*, Bd. 4, *Mai 1846 bis März 1848*, Karl Marx und Friedrich Engels, hg. v. Institut für Marxismus-Leninismus beim ZK der SED, 463–464. Berlin: Dietz, 1959.
Moore, Barrington. *Soziale Ursprünge von Diktatur und Demokratie: Die Rolle der Grundbesitzer und Bauern bei der Entstehung der modernen Welt*. Frankfurt a. M.: Suhrkamp, 1969.
Nietzsche, Friedrich. *Menschliches, Allzumenschliches. Ein Buch für freie Geister*, Bd. 1. Chemnitz: Schmeitzner, 1878.
Pongs, Hermann. „Faust und die Ehre." *Dichtung und Volkstum: Neue Folge des Euphorion* 44 (1944): 78–105.
Pornschlegel, Clemens. *Allegorien des Unendlichen: Hyperchristen*, Bd. 2, *Zum religiösen Engagement in der literarischen Moderne. Kleist, Schlegel, Eichendorff, Hugo Ball*. Wien: Turia & Kant, 2017.
Trunz, Erich. „Anmerkungen," in *Goethe: Faust*, hg. und kommentiert v. Erich Trunz. München: C.H. Beck, 1977.

Joseph Vogl
Sovereignty Figures in the History of the 'Finance Regime'

Abstract: The paper explores three characteristics of sovereignty in the prehistory of the present-day finance regime: the early-modern *fiscus* (treasury), the status of coinage policy, and the role of public credit. It reveals the impact these characteristics have on the economisation of governmental power with the concept of sovereignty becoming more and more intertwined with private interests, public debt, and tax collection as essential pillars of the emerging modern fiscal state.

1

When, in 1977, two years after the publication of "Discipline and Punish", Michel Foucault turned his attention to the emergence of the modern art of government, he himself raised a number of open questions, or not yet fully exhausted topics, left behind by his previous studies. These concerned the limits of a genealogical analysis of political power based on the model of war, the question of the connection between micro and macro levels of government, and the emergence of new subject-matters, which Foucault recognised, for instance, in populations. With the question of governmentality, a perspective has emerged that makes the state itself appear as an accumulation of heterogeneous governmental practices, which, above all, pursues the "introduction of the economy into political office"[1].

However, when it comes to those procedures that realize the administration of the population through an economization of government, it may be surprising that Foucault almost systematically omitted or ignored some facts that present themselves as essential driving forces for the development of an "economized" governmental power. For the pressing questions of *fiscus* (in the following used to designate the treasury or tax authorities) and finance, dealt with below, have – in contrast to what Foucault once claimed[2] – by no means obstructed the development of the arts of government. On the one hand, they proved to be prominent agencies on the road that leads to the modern adminis-

---

1 Foucault, *Power*, 207.
2 See Foucault, *Power*, 213.

trative state, i.e. to the governmentalisation of state apparatuses in general. On the other hand, it was precisely the associated fields of intervention, such as monetary, coinage and tax policy that directly linked administration of territories with the the administration of populations.

One of the reasons for this omission could be a particular reservation on Foucault's part that is theoretically significant. For if Foucault follows the emergence of political economy – as an assembly of modern governmental knowledge – in strict demarcation from older concepts of sovereignty, he at the same time fades out those conceptual burdens that were connected with the transfer of the 'economy' into the political domain. With the theological economy, which dictated the politicisation of the concept up to the eighteenth century, the precarious relationship between the (transcendent) being and the (worldly) action of God, between ruling and governing was predetermined, as Giorgio Agamben has shown; and precisely the political adaptation of divine business administration can therefore not simply be conceived of as a secularisation of theological figures of order. Rather, with the 'secularisation' of economics, the relation between transcendence and immanence itself became a politico-economical immanence problem. This gave rise to a new governmental sphere of action that entails a redistribution of sovereign rule and the arts of governing.[3] Put in simpler and more direct terms: the matter of tax and finance is not only an essential aspect of the economisation of modern governance, but also an object for the historical analysis of governmentality. It will also become apparent that, in line with Foucault, the state cannot be presupposed as a uniform entity and gauging standard, but, above all – with a slight shift in the question – brings into focus specific distortions, osmoses, and indifference in the relationship between political rule, sovereignty and economic government. It is thus about a form of power of its own kind that accompanies the development of modern forms of government.

Thus, it can first of all be noted that already early modern political theology – Jean Bodin's for instance – was disoriented in a special way by the relation of fiscal and financial questions. For the more these sovereignty theories endeavour to transform the diversity of sovereign powers into a transcendent political unitary framework, the more problematic the discussion of fiscal questions becomes. On the one hand, coinage, tax collection, and the public budget are invoked as essential characteristics of sovereign power; on the other hand, they differ from other sovereign rights (such as legislation, supreme jurisdiction, etc.) in that they are characterized by unclear responsibilities, peculiar consider-

---

[3] See Agamben, *Kingdom and the Glory*.

ations, complicated distinctions, and uncomfortable obligations. In fiscal matters, texts on doctrines of sovereignty are immediately submerged in confusing and unclear casuistry. Questions of coinage, for example, refer to a field of activity in which an erosion of sovereign state power threatens to occur through the trade in offices, through the intervention of tenants and parasites of all kinds; the levying of perpetual taxes brings conflicts with civil property rights, but also raises concerns regarding the autarky of princely households; finally, the negotiation of credit-shaped state financing is accompanied by a horror of its own kind and brings the absolute limit of absolute rule into focus. The cycle of borrowing and debt service through credit – an evil that Bodin first saw raised by Francis I – becomes the epitome of political pathology. In it the "fever" of the state is manifested; in it the sovereign monopoly of power is undermined by economic dependencies.[4]

One could therefore say that the example of state finances reveals a domain that challenges the formation of modern sovereignty theory and encounters incompatibilities with the standard, uniform format of sovereign power. A resistance of objects becomes apparent, which makes the theoretical text hesitant and bears witness to a difficult grasping of the concept of the sovereign state person.

One can see in this the early concern about a sensitive abandonment of sovereign powers. These difficulties bear witness to the fact that the fiscal complex constitutes an essential motive for the stabilisation of early modern state power while at the same time marking its limits and highlighting its fault lines. Fiscal affairs occupy a critical position that resists being clarified by a homogeneous 'concept of the political'.

Using two or three basic elements as examples, I will lay out in the following sections of this paper how modern finance unfolds in close correspondence with political mandates; how a strategic field of its own quality develops in the process; and how this field presents itself as a politico-economic zone of indifference, as a form of economic governance that cannot be grasped in common terms of political power. The basic elements are the concept of the fiscal authorities, the status of coinage policy, and the role of public credit. And I would like to ask the reader to understand the following considerations also as a prehistory of the current financial regime.

---

4 See Bodin, *Les six livres de la république*, 44, 88–92.

2

Already in Roman law, the *fiscus* (literally: the 'money basket' or 'cashbox') was the subject of intricate distinctions reflecting the relationship between private imperial property and state property. These distinctions concerned questions about the legitimate ownership of the *fiscus*, about limitation periods and inalienable possessions, about the relations between the *fiscus* and the immortal entity of the empire. The *fiscus* took on the character of a strange object, whose assignment remained unclear or riddled with exceptions. Thus, as Otto von Gierke noted, the *fiscus Caesaris*, the imperial private treasury, merged in the era of Roman imperialism with the *aerarium* of the *res publica*, the state property; it was, to a certain extent, transformed into state ownership, yet remained subject to the procedural rules of private law. It was precisely through its nationalization that the tax authorities developed a concept of the person under private law and introduced a peculiar form doubling into the format of imperial power. While the state "raised itself ever more decisively above all law, the state, as the tax authorities, subordinated itself to law, and [...] as a private person, placed itself among the private persons." At the same time, the private position of the *fiscus*, of the tax authorities, was fractured by a number of exemptions, which in turn marked a tension between public and private dimensions in the *fiscus* itself. It thus remained unclear who or what – *res publica*, emperor or private person – was acting on behalf of the treasury.[5]

A direct link between the *fiscus* and the state can be proven for the modern era; though, fluctuating regulations of this kind had remained in place. Fiscal law was thus understood as a product or outflow of the *summum imperium* and as a component of the *superioritas*. The treasury is an attribute of sovereignty and can be ascribed to all sovereign authorities – princes, states, imperial cities. The holder of state property rights also exercises state powers of sovereignty; the *fiscus* coincides with the person of the sovereign. But precisely as a sovereignty factor, the *fiscus* now takes on the character of an independent "fund" or asset.

It becomes, as Giercke writes, an immortal and abstract "conceptual entity", its own "fictitious legal personality", which survives the change of its owners. As a sign of sovereignty, it faces the sovereign and binds him to certain obligations – e. g. the prohibition to sell state assets.[6] The *fiscus* occupies an eccentric position and, as a definition of sovereignty, remains beyond the sovereign's control.

---

[5] von Giercke, *Genossenschaftsrecht*, vol. 3, 59–61.
[6] See von Giercke, *Genossenschaftsrecht*, vol. 4, 249f.

The *fiscus* stands therefore in contrast to the ruler as a private individual, but also to the sovereign as the holder of sovereign rights. And the matter becomes even more complicated, because a distinction is again introduced into the fiscal domain itself, clearly attributing some areas (such as the right of coinage) to sovereign prerogatives, and subordinating other elements (such as mines or toll charges) to mere property law – a curious confusion between sovereign rights and private law provisions.

The separation of operations in the name of constitutional law and mere transactions is challenged and problematic at the same time in the example of the treasury. Thus, the objects concerning the *fiscus* somehow belong to the sovereign's jurisdictional powers (Bodin: "sacred, inviolable, inalienable"), but they cannot be separated once and for all from private business activity.[7] If in the seventeenth century the maxim prevailed that "only the sovereign prince has the right to a treasury [...]", this very prerogative is directly connected with restrictive obligations and liabilities.[8]

The effort to achieve a monolithic version of the sovereignty problem is thus pervaded by resistance stemming from fiscal issues and the question of related financial matters.

On the one hand, with the *fiscus* a sovereign district is designated which asserts itself through essential sovereignty features. On the other hand, this district immediately breaks down into different public and private tasks. It cannot be associated with the political figure of sovereignty, or at least not without the expense of great conceptual difficulties.

Similarly, in the *fiscus*, a timeless and non-transferrable entity is formed, a quasi-transcendental thing, that, like the sovereign, stands above the law and denotes a sphere of transpersonal continuity. Yet, by contrast, an independent legal entity is set up in the *fiscus*, with which a tension develops between the ruling authority and the 'sacred' district of finance: The quasi-eternal duration of the sovereign is made dependent on the quasi-eternal duration of the *fiscus*. A process thereby evolved in which, as Ernst Kantorowicz remarked, a decidedly secular phenomenon such as the *fiscus* assumed a numinous character, gaining the capacity to represent the inviolable aspects of prince and state.[9] At the same time, these magical-theological sides to finance highlight a fragility in the concept of sovereign authority. *Fiscus* and finance appear as a scene in which sovereign rule, governmental power, business operations, and civil private traffic

---

7 See von Gierke, *Genossenschaftsrecht*, vol. 4, 251f.
8 Le Bret, *Traité de la Souveraineté du Roy*, 425, 621–626.
9 See Kantorowicz, *The King's Two Bodies*, 164–192.

are intertwined in a peculiar way. Against this background, the special position held by the *fiscus* in the early modern period is thus characterized by the fact that it coincides with the arcane sphere of sovereignty and yet is situated as an area of power of their own quality.

3

Similar problems can be identified in the unquestionable right of fiscal sovereignty: the right to coinage which is also the right to define the value of the coins (German: "*Münzregal*"). I have no intention here of discussing in detail the complex development of the system of coinage in the early modern period, or the problem of the manipulation of coins, or the mints, most of which were run as private companies. Two things should be noted here, however, both of which go hand-in-hand with the formation of sovereign statehood. On the one hand, the minting of coins, i.e. the transformation of goods (precious metal) into means of payment, was associated with the imposition of the so-called monetary "seigniorage" (German: "*Schlagschatz*"), i.e. the amount which resulted from the difference between the nominal value and the metal value of the coins and which for a long time ensured a considerable share of royal income.

On the other hand, the levying of fiscal charges on money meant that the arbitrary act of sovereign power – as expressed in the value of the coins minted – became a sign of recognition of this very power. The coin is a representation of the sovereign; his name or portrait indicates that the coin is "entirely under the authority of the sovereign prince, who prescribes its material, form, course, weight and price at his discretion."[10] The financing of the *fiscus* established the mechanisms of early modern money circulation and the establishment of territorially bound means of payment. This then produced a constellation in which an impressive intermingling of political rule and private enrichment took place.

A situation arose in which sovereign acts in particular led to the development of early financial markets. And this dynamic consists, in short, of two parts. One part is set by the sovereign right of coinage. While cash of all kinds circulated unhindered across borders, the means of payment fixed by the right of coinage were only valid within the respective sovereignty zones. This meant that the market value of foreign coins was not determined by their face value in the country of origin (metal value plus *seigniorage*), but by the price of their respective purity/fineness; the exchange rate resulted from an operation

---

[10] Loyseau, *Traité des seigneuries*, 59.

in which the foreign coin was set in relation to the legal tender, as it were, as a commodity. This situation can be understood as a consequence of the emergence of statehood in the Renaissance and was brought about by acts of sovereignty, by the territorial unification of coinage.

The other part involves business practices with which private merchant bankers had operated since the thirteenth century. This involved bills of exchange, i.e. a means of cash-free payment transactions with which it was possible to transfer money from one place to another, or which allowed a credit to be raised in one place for the purpose of repayment in another. Naturally, these transfers mostly entailed currency exchange, and this set mechanisms in motion in which sovereign implementation and private business contracts were systematically intertwined.

If, for example, a banker bought a bill of exchange for a certain amount of money with which the issuer of the bill of exchange wanted to finance a transaction elsewhere, the price was fixed at a rate calculated at the place of issue on the basis of the ratio between the nominal value of the domestic currency and the metal value of the foreign coin (i.e., minus the *seigniorage*). The amount was calculated on the basis of the legal market value of the coins at the place of issue. It was due, however, at the destination of the transaction, and there it was again calculated according to the local exchange rate, i.e., in the legal currency (including the *seigniorage* associated with it). Through the transfer, the banker thus gained the margin that corresponded to the share of *seigniorage* of foreign coins. However, this profit was only realised when the bill of transaction was taken yet another step further and the amount transferred back again to the place of origin via bills of exchange, whereby the *seigniorage* of the initial currency that was customary there was now added on top. Economic historians speak of a "seigniorage effect": The correlation between the exchange rate when dealing in bills of exchange and the legal market price when converting hard cash resulted in the banker profiting from the corresponding differential of all transactions with a place where *seigniorage* was levied.[11] And so, under the banner of sovereignty rights, an elementary form of capitalist enrichment became established.

Two aspects are remarkable. First, a mutual intertwining of private and political forces can be observed. The princely *seignoriage* enables private enrichment, while conversely the exchange of bills indirectly secures the autonomy of princely prerogatives in matters of money. While the coinage system guarantees sovereign territories and fiscal income, the exchange transactions constitute

---

[11] See Boyer-Xambeu, Deleplace and Gillard, *Monnaie privée*, 179–189, 240–269.

an international monetary system and promote the formation of private financial capital. Second, the circulation of money in the early modern period is therefore characterized by the opposing movements of nationalization and privatization of monetary transactions. The transformation of private goods into legal means of payment in the mints is countered by private, cashless 'coinage' through the exchange of money. With the exchange trade, public money was privatized along with *seigniorage*. The monetarisation of European business transactions in the early modern period cannot therefore be explained by a juxtaposition of state structures and economic dynamics. The political pole of the right of coinage is characterized by an interweaving of public and private actors. Conversely, private business practices do not result in an atomized market, but in a monopoly-like network of exchange processes that develop in direct dependence on princely powers. Against this horizon, like-minded processes of capitalization unfolded that affected private wealth, public finances, and princely power in equal measure. The form of money represents a private-public relationship. All these aspects can probably be situated within the framework of general developments, in which the expansion of sovereign rule over several centuries took place precisely with the selling-off of public tasks.

4

This leads to the third and final aspect. Since the Hundred Years' War, there has been a vehement increase in fiscal debt, and the beginnings of public credit were associated with the double concern of how royal houses could prove to be reliable debtors to their financiers and how the finances of the treasury could once again be secured on a permanent basis. In the dynastic succession, the transfer of previous debts was by no means guaranteed; conversely, the procurement of funds in times of emergency and war remained uncertain. Thus, financing through levies had the character of confiscations of assets born of necessity, which could often only be enforced against resistance.

In the sixteenth century at the latest, a process took place that even contemporaries wanted to see most clearly in the financial policy of Francis I, the French king who had lost a ruinous race (through bribery) for the imperial crown against Charles V. Three elements were repeatedly mentioned. Firstly, interest-bearing bonds were used not only to cover extraordinary monetary needs in times of war, but also to finance current expenses – which led to the formation of financial consortia. Secondly, the interest due in these cases was financed with indirect taxes on consumer goods such as meat, fish, or wine (proving the administrative penetration into the social field). Thirdly, the financial administration was centralised, tax revenues and the revenues from royal domains were combined into a single treasury. The tendency was to identify this as the emergence of a fiscal state, though, this time with a special twist, since what had once been the exception – confiscation in emergencies – had now become an "internal administrative need".[12] This combination of public debt and tax collection placed the imperative of *necessitas* at the centre of the administrative architecture.

This had, broadly speaking, two consequences: On the one hand, the perpetuation of extraordinary capital requirements must be regarded as the motor for the emergence of modern administrative apparatuses. Or, to put it bluntly: before a sovereign and "eternal state power" was recognized in principle, it was preceded by the concept of an "eternal debt" in finance; state debt is the primal scene of the modern state machinery.[13] On the other hand, this state financing has mobilized private monetary power. A process took place in which the antagonisms between political structures and monetary capital collapsed. From this process emerged the most aggressive figures of early modern financial power, and it was probably documented most extensively at first through the example of the city states of northern Italy.

As early as 1148, for instance, the Republic of Genoa was forced to issue bonds, and its creditors joined together to form corporations to which, for purposes of interest repayment, the administration of various tax revenues was assigned. In 1407, a majority of them were grouped together in the *Casa di San Giorgio*, which supplied the Genoese government with credit until the eighteenth century. At the same time a consortium of private creditors was incorporated directly into the administration of the Genoese Republic. Merchants occupied positions in political administration; they controlled government revenues, state loans and public finances; the *Casa* obtained fiscal monopolies, bonded state assets, operated armies and fleets, waged warfare, entered into contracts, and was given jurisdiction and sovereign rights. Genoa was therefore referred to as "the capitalist city par excellence", and the *Casa* as a "true state within the state"[14]. By the middle of the fifteenth century, the *Casa* had already become the most powerful financial institution in the Western world. Genoese bankers transferred profits from mercantile trading into state bonds; they entered into

---

[12] The wording is that of Kantorowicz, who draws on discussions of relations between *necessitas in actu* and *necessitas in habitus* for the levying of perpetual taxes as featured in the commentaries of high- and/or late-medieval jurists; see Kantorowicz, *The King's Two Bodies*, 291–293.
[13] See Ehrenberg, *Capital & Finance*, 40.
[14] Braudel, *Civilization and Capitalism*, 157.

an alliance with Spain in the sixteenth century, pushed German trading houses (Fugger) out of lending to Spain, organized the transport of Spanish silver to northern Italy, financed Spanish troops in the Netherlands, and dominated the money markets at fairs such as Lyon, Besançon, and Antwerp. This interweaving of socialised debt and privatised state income was the prerequisite for non-territorial networks with which Genoa dominated European monetary transactions and could be regarded as a prototype of a cosmopolitically organised accumulation of capital.[15]

This was reflected in a particularly prominent type of enterprise. The protagonists were the Spanish monarchy, the need for money for the armies stationed in the Netherlands, Spanish silver imports from America, and finally the Genoese commercial bankers who organised the aforementioned fairs. This meant in detail the following. The starting point were contracts, so-called "asientos", by which the Spanish crown transferred large sums of money to the troops in the Netherlands, taking advantage of Genoese trade connections and offering American silver imports in return. This resulted in a complex financing system. So, if, for instance, the Spanish finance authorities entered into a contract with Genoese bankers for ten million scudi to cover costs in the Netherlands, they pledged to disburse the sum via Antwerp and to provide advance payments. At the same time, they had to ensure that they received the corresponding compensation from Spain. At the trade fairs held regularly – four times a year – bills of exchange issued in Antwerp were then purchased, as well as bills of exchange made out to Spain, in order to terminate repayments expected from there. These transactions were performed via various detours and intermediate purchases, whereby the bills of exchange themselves were paid with bills of exchange of various origins. In principle, these operations could therefore be carried out without cash, even without any expenditure of capital resources. In the end, the payment obligations were met in the Netherlands (in gold) and compensated for by the Spanish crown (with the shipment of silver to Genoa).[16]

Spanish imperialist politics had thus created a private bond trade that was dominated by the Genoese bankers, and which gave rise to a pan-European financial market. If Genoa presents itself as an exemplary case for the formation of a capitalist 'world system' in the fifteenth and sixteenth centuries, this is due not least to a policy of state credit and a consistent "selling-off of the state".[17] Both the Genoese financial power in the form of the *Casa di San Giorgio* and

---

15 See Arrighi, *Long Twentieth Century*, 151–153.
16 On the Genoese fairs and the associated business practices see Boyer-Xambeau, Deleplace and Gillard, *Monnaie privée*, 283–309.
17 Marx, *Capital*, 779.

the first international capital markets owe their existence to the dynamics of public debt, the entanglement of political action with private business activities.

5

I have tried to demonstrate with reference to three sites of investigation – fiscal policy, monetary policy, public debt – how essential elements of modern politics and economy evolve precisely in their respective zone of indifference. The modern era has not only generated sovereign state apparatuses, internationally operational trading companies, influential financiers, and decentral markets. A specific type of power was also formed that cannot be adequately described either by political structures or by economic strategies as it is constituted solely through the interplay of both forces. In view of the monetarisation of the European economy since the Renaissance and the enrichment effects of fiscal monetary policy, one could speak here of 'seigniorial power' (derived from *seigniorage:* the difference between the face value of coins and their production costs). It differs from the varieties of state power inasmuch as it coincides neither with the political-juridical institution of sovereign power nor with bureaucratic apparatuses and is grounded on the integration of private agents and entrepreneurial practice. It is closely linked to the showgrounds of political-economical zones of indifference which arise in equal degree with the formation of modern political regimes and economic systems.

This area is difficult to access theoretically since, even for reasons of consistency alone, both political and economic theories of modernity are organised around the definition of concepts of system, form, and structure. Political theory is, to this very day, geared towards an examination of the form of political sovereignty, while economic theory formation is oriented towards the form of coherent functional systems of the market. In contrast, the patterns of seigniorial power cannot be characterized by the solidity of forms, the coherence of systems or the stability of structures. Their structure is rather informal, unstable and cannot be translated into a concise systemic framework. One could speak here of a situational interaction of forces of different origins, whose effectiveness results from 'diagrammatic'[18] arrangements (the fluid interplay of disparate elements).

"Seigniorial power" can perhaps be characterised by four features. First, it is characterized by a heterogeneous structure in which the formation of capital power cannot be separated from the activation of power capital. The antagonism

---

[18] On the diagrammatic presentation of power relations see Deleuze, *Foucault*, 34–37.

of 'state' and 'capital' is weakened, suspended or simply not effective. The dominant position of Genoese bankers in the Renaissance, for example, was not based on the accumulation of private wealth, but on the ability to transform political action potentials into business assets and vice versa. This *conversion of state power into capital*, i.e., the capitalization of power in general, is secondly linked to fiscal operations; it takes place through a sell-off of the state in scenarios of its emergence. The process manifests itself exemplarily in the management of public debt, which began in the city states of northern Italy. Administrative means of coercion are linked to the development of new fields of business. The liabilities of public credit are balanced by a constant taxation, in which a state appropriation of the population unfolds. Thus, by securing future fiscal incomes, seigniorial power has coordinated with the *organization of the social sphere*.

Thirdly, this triggered debt cycles that justify talk of primal scenes of capital. If one understands 'capital' as a usable sum of value that carries with it the hope of future earnings, then speculative 'capitalist' financing is perpetuated in the private management of public credit. Along with public debt, the "modern fiscality", which – as Marx maintained – is founded on the taxation of the "most necessary means of subsistence", has made a decisive contribution to the "capitalisation of wealth." Both forces combined manifest the "most powerful lever of original accumulation."[19] With this *accumulation regime*, what once was the extraordinary has assumed the status of the rule and the exception to the norm. (Besides, one should also remember the etymological origin of 'credit', which, with its Indo-European root **kred-* encompasses the religious-economic aspects of trust and demand, faith and creditorship and denotes a position in which the one-sidedness of an irremovable debt claim is manifested).

Fourthly, this has led to a movement that is as effective as it is ambiguous. For to the extent that the modern state has set itself the task of perpetuating the national debt and the tax system in the long term, it has acquired a quasi-sovereign power in fiscal matters, which it loses at the same time due to the system's permanent exceptional character. This marks the precarious position of seigniorial power. In it, the sale, i.e., privatisation of state resources is countered by a political occupation of private finance. It is precisely this reciprocal, private-public incorporation that gives seigniorial power an eccentric position. With its fiscal side, it lays claim to sovereign dignity; as the embodiment of private capital, it

---

19 Marx, *Capital*, 779–781; see Gottlieb, "Political Economy of the Public Debt", 265–279; for a discussion of the term "primitive accumulation" in Marx see Frank, *The World Accumulation 1492–1789*, 238 ff.

claims resistance to the acts of political arbitrariness. The formation of sovereign state apparatuses in concert with business enterprises has released a dynamic that manifests itself in an eccentric sovereignty of seigniorial power. In the matter of finance, a sovereignty reserve of its own order has been established – alongside and away from state authority. A power pattern with a great future can be seen in it, which is constituted in continuous transitions between transcendence and immanence, between sovereignty, the arts of government and financial capital.

The article has been translated into English by James Brown.

Bibliography

Agamben, Giorgio. *The Kingdom and the Glory: For a Theological Genealogy of Economy and Government (Homo Sacer II.2).* Stanford: Stanford University Press, 2011.
Arrighi, Giovanni. *The Long Twentieth Century: Money, Power and the Origins of Our Times*, 2nd ed. London: Verso, 2010.
Bodin, Jean. *Les six livres de la république*, vol. 2. 1593; repr., Paris: Fayard 1986.
Boyer-Xambeu, Marie-Thérèse, and Deleplace, Ghislain, and Gillard, Lucien. *Monnaie privée et pouvoir des Princes.* Paris: Editions du CNRS, 1986.
Braudel, Fernand. *Civilization and Capitalism 15th-18th Century*, vol. 3, *The Perspective of the World.* London: Collins, 1979.
Deleuze, Gilles. *Foucault*, trans. Seán Hand. Minneapolis: University of Minnesota Press, 1986.
Ehrenberg, Richard. *Capital & Finance in the Age of the Renaissance: A Study of the Fuggers and their Connections*, trans. H. M. Lucas. London: Jonathan Cape, 1928.
Foucault, Michel. *Power: The Essential Works of Foucault 1954–1984*, vol. 3. London: Penguin Books, 2002.
Frank, André G. *The World Accumulation 1492–1789.* New York: Monthly Review Press, 1978.
von Gierke, Otto. *Das deutsche Genossenschaftsrecht*, vol. 3, *Die Staats- und Korporationslehre des Alterthums und des Mittelalters und ihre Aufnahme in Deutschland.* 1881; repr., Graz: Akademische Druck- u. Verlagsanstalt, 1934.
von Gierke, Otto. *Das deutsche Genossenschaftsrecht*, vol. 4, *Die Staats- und Korporationslehre der Neuzeit.* Berlin: Weidmannsche Buchhandlung, 1913.
Gottlieb, Manuel. "Political Economy of the Public Debt," *Public Finance* 11/3 (1956): 265–279.
Kantorowicz, Ernst H. *The King's Two Bodies: A Study in Mediaeval Political Theology*, ed. by William C. Jordan and Conrad Leyser. Princeton: Princeton University Press, 1981.
Le Bret, Cardin. *Traité de la Souveraineté du Roy.* Paris: 1632.
Loyseau, Charles. *Traité des seigneuries.* Paris: Abel l'Angelier 1608.
Marx, Karl. *Capital: A critical Analysis of Capitalist Production.* London: Glaisher, 1909.

Ino Augsberg
Im Namen des Vaters

Abstract: The paper focuses on the challenging need for a master as it suggests a proximity of "patronomy" and "patronymics", the meaning of which will be spelled out on the basis of Carl Schmitt's theory of names. The author reads especially Schmitt's conflictive difference between "Name" (name) and "Nahme" (taking) to illustrate how, through linguistic constitutions, legal events have, time and again, the property of being notoriously ambiguous with regard to their dependence on external influences. Finally, a new perspective on the relation of "Name" and "Nahme" will be debated and conclusions for the understanding of law will be drawn.

1

Zu Beginn seines späten, aus dem Jahr 1959 stammenden Aufsatzes über die möglichen Verknüpfungen zwischen Nomos, Nahme und Name erläutert Carl Schmitt eine aus seiner Sicht symptomatische Differenz, die Wortzusammensetzungen mit den Endungen ‚-kratie' oder ‚-archie' von Verbindungen mit ‚-nomie' absetzen soll. Während jene Zusammensetzungen typischerweise das vorangestellte Wort zum eigentlichen Subjekt der Gesamtkonstruktion erklären, also etwa die Demokratie als Herrschaft des Volkes bestimmen, ist Schmitt zufolge in den Verknüpfungen mit ‚-nomie' das vorangestellte Wort „eher Objekt und sogar Materie"[1] des mit dem Nomos bezeichneten Geschehens. „Das mit dem Nomos verbundene Wort wird am Nomos gemessen und ihm unterworfen"[2]. Als Hauptbeleg für diese Behauptung fungiert das Exempel der Ökonomie; weitere Beispiele betreffen die Astronomie, Geonomie und, etwas überraschend in dieser exemplarischen Auflistung, die Gastronomie. Schmitt verweist allerdings auch auf eine Ausnahme von der so statuierten Regel. Die Ausnahme soll an dieser Stelle aber offenkundig, entgegen der bekannten Lehre seiner *Politischen Theologie*, nicht etwa alles – die allgemeine Regel ebenso wie deren Durchbrechung – erklären.[3] Sie fungiert lediglich als mit einer sprachwissenschaftlichen Untersuchung unterfütterter Beleg für die Üblichkeit der anders konstruierten Wortverbindung.

---

[1] Schmitt, „Nomos – Nahme – Name", 92–105. Hier und im Folgenden zitiert nach dem Wiederabdruck in: Schmitt, *Staat, Großraum, Nomos*, 573–591, hier 574.
[2] Schmitt, *Staat, Großraum, Nomos*, 575.
[3] Vgl. Schmitt, *Politische Theologie*, 21.

Entsprechend hat der Verweis auf eine bestimmte Konkretisierung dieses Regelbruchs ersichtlich lediglich den Zweck, dessen Status als „Singularität" zu belegen. Der Versuch dieses Belegs unterläuft allerdings zugleich sich selbst; sowohl der verwendete Plural wie der ausdrücklich als exemplarisch bestimmte Charakter der Inbezugnahme widersprechen implizit der behaupteten Einzigartigkeit der Konstruktion. Bemerkenswert ist an der Konkretisierung aber nicht primär ihre gewisse Selbstwidersprüchlichkeit, auch wenn diese auf eine möglicherweise doch größere Bedeutung der Ausnahme hindeuten könnte. Markant ist vor allem das hierfür angegebene konkrete Beispiel: „Einzelne Besonderheiten, wie Patronomie, dürfen wir hier beiseite lassen, weil ihre Singularität anerkannt ist"[4].

Wie prekär die hier behauptete Anerkennung ist, zeigt eine Fußnote zum 1950 erschienenen, vermutlich aber noch während des Krieges geschriebenen Werk *Der Nomos der Erde*, in der Schmitt im Zuge seiner Erläuterung des Nomos-Begriffs „einen einfachen und sicheren Prüfstein dafür" benennt, „daß der ursprüngliche Sinn des Wortes Nomos verunstaltet worden ist."[5] Bei der Bestimmung dieses Prüfverfahrens bleibt allerdings die später als Differenz zu den Wortverbindungen mit ‚-kratie' hervorgehobene Besonderheit noch unerwähnt; lediglich in der Genitivkonstruktion des Buchtitels klingt sie an. Zwar argumentiert bereits der frühere Text mit einem am üblichen Sprachgebrauch ablesbaren Regel-Ausnahme-Verhältnis, das nun als jener genannte „Prüfstein" normativ scharfgestellt werden soll. Auch das später genannte markante Beispiel taucht schon an dieser Stelle auf. Aber die Einordnung in das Regel-Ausnahme-Schema verläuft noch genau entgegengesetzt. Die in dem jüngeren Aufsatz als Singularität statuierte Wendung ist jetzt auf der Seite des Gewöhnlichen verortet und einer anderen Variante der Ausnahme – die hier zugespitzt wird zu einem allenfalls denkbaren, aber nicht tatsächlich existierenden Fall – gegenübergestellt:

> „Die griechische Sprache kennt viele Zusammensetzungen des Substantivums Nomos zu einem Verbum, wie patronomein, basileuonomein, persinomein und ähnliche Bildungen […]. Das wird richtig übersetzt mit Vater- oder väterliche Herrschaft, Königsherrschaft, Perserherrschaft usw. Wenn es nun aber wirklich eine Nomos-Herrschaft im Sinne des Herrschens abstrakter Gesetze gäbe, dann müßte auch das Wort Nomonomia vorkommen, was natürlich nicht der Fall ist. Eine solche Wortkombination enthüllt nur den Widersinn der ihr zugrunde liegenden Vorstellungen."[6]

---

4 Schmitt, „Nomos – Nahme – Name", 575.
5 Schmitt, *Nomos der Erde*, 40n.
6 Schmitt, *Nomos der Erde*, 40n.

Was in *Nomos – Nahme – Name* als außer Acht zu lassende Singularität bezeichnet wird, bildet demnach im *Nomos der Erde* lediglich ein Beispiel unter vielen. Es ist in dieser scheinbar konträren Zuordnung aber ebenso sehr als irrelevant markiert. Gemeinsam ist beiden Zitaten die Beiläufigkeit, mit der die einschlägige Wendung zugleich genannt und übergangen wird.

Das auf diese doppelte Weise demonstrierte Desinteresse ist umso bemerkenswerter, als der entsprechende Vorgang rechtshistorisch betrachtet mehr Aufmerksamkeit erwarten könnte. Statt die angesprochene Herrschaft des Vaters mit der klassischen Figur der väterlichen Autorität qua *patria potestas* zu verknüpfen und in den Vordergrund einer Erläuterung der Entstehung oder Begründung juristischer Normativität zu rücken,[7] die stärker vom Subjekt als vom Objekt der Herrschaft ausgeht, lässt Schmitts Darstellung diese Form von Autorität und Normativität als bloßes Nebenphänomen erscheinen. Das demgegenüber als dominierend behauptete objektbezogene Verständnis von ‚-nomie' belegt Schmitt mit einem weiteren Exempel, das zugleich die bis dahin nur latente Dimension der Geschlechterdifferenz auf eine charakteristische Weise ins Spiel bringt: „Gynaiko-Nomie zum Beispiel heißt nicht Verwaltung durch Frauen, wie Gynaikokratie Frauenherrschaft bedeutet, sondern: Verwaltung und Bewirtschaftung des Frauenhauses und des Teiles des Haushalts, der die Frauen betrifft."[8]

Das dergestalt nahezu demonstrative Desinteresse gegenüber der Patronomie und damit der offenbar außen vor gelassenen besonderen Rolle des Hausvaters lässt sich auf den ersten Blick durch einen spezifischen antirömischen Affekt erklären, dem gemäß Schmitt in der lateinischen Überformung und Übersetzung des griechischen Rechtsdenkens das *proton pseudos* des gesamten weiteren daran anschließenden abendländischen Rechtsdiskurses erkennen will. Sehr zu Recht, so Schmitt, habe der spanische Romanist Alvaro d'Ors erklärt, dass „die Übersetzung von Nomos durch Lex [...] zu den schwersten Belastungen unserer occidentalen Begriffs- und Sprachkultur"[9] gehört. Aus dem Blick gerät dabei offenbar die zentrale Bedeutung der römischen Konzeption von *domus* und *familia*, die jeweils um die zentrale Figur des *pater familias* kreisen.

Auf den zweiten Blick wird allerdings ersichtlich, dass der Rolle des Hausvaters in Schmitts Analyse doch eine zentrale Bedeutung zukommt. In ihr akkumulieren sich noch einmal alle jene Herrschaftsbefugnisse, die wenig später in

---

7 Vgl. zum Modell der *patria potestas* näher etwa Thomas, *La Mort du père*, 47–49, 165–167; Thomas, „Rom", 277–326.
8 Schmitt, „Nomos – Nahme – Name", 574–575.
9 Schmitt, „Nomos – Nahme – Name", 579.

funktional spezifisch differenzierte Sphären auseinandergerissen werden. „Die Herrschaft des patriarchalischen Hausvaters über Haus und Familie ist eine Totalität, in der sich religiöse und moralische Autorität, juristische potestas und wirtschaftliche Dispositionsbefugnisse vereinigen."[10] Die Erläuterungen zu dem Gegenmodell zu dieser Situation weisen dann darauf hin, dass es aus Schmitts Sicht bei einem primär ökonomischen Verständnis des Nomos nicht sein Bewenden haben kann. Offenkundig fordert das patronomische Element nun doch verstärkt Beachtung. Es soll der zur „Daseinsvorsorge" (Schmitt verwendet diesen von seinem Schüler Ernst Forsthoff in die Diskussion eingeführten und ursprünglich positiv konnotierten Begriff ausdrücklich, ohne jedoch auf seinen Urheber zu verweisen[11]) domestizierten und zugleich anonymisierten Sorge des Hausvaters entgegengehalten werden:

> „Die Verwandlung des Gemeinwesens in einen auf totale Daseinsvorsorge angelegten Verwaltungsstaat führt zu einer hausväterlichen Totalität ohne Hausvater, wenn es nicht gelingt, Archien und vielleicht auch Kratien zu finden, die mehr sind als bloßer Nomos des Teilens und Weidens."[12]

2

Die merkwürdige Dopplung, die den Nomos bzw. das ihm zugrundeliegende Verb *nemein* mit den beiden auf den ersten Blick kaum zusammenhängenden Bedeutungen „teilen" und „weiden" verkoppelt, muss danach um eine weitere Bedeutung ergänzt werden. Die Schmitts Argumentation tragende Grundannahme liegt dabei in einer angeblichen sprachlichen Besonderheit, mit der dann eine sachliche Beziehung kurzgeschlossen wird. Das Wort Nomos, dem Schmitt in seinem *Nomos der Erde* die Grundbedeutung des „Teilens und Verteilens" zugeschrieben hatte,[13] bezieht diese Grundbewegung nun auch auf sich selbst und lässt dadurch die Idee einer einzigen entscheidenden Semantik splittern. Als sich gegen sich selbst kehrende Teilung grenzt es weitere, scheinbar völlig fremde, durch keine sachliche Nähe zusammengehaltene Bedeutungen ab. Zusammengefügt, das heißt aller sachlichen Differenz zum Trotz als Einheit konstituiert, werden sie nur vom Wort selbst, genauer, von der Selbigkeit jenes einen Wortes. Der in seiner

---

10 Schmitt, „Nomos – Nahme – Name", 576.
11 Vgl. Forsthoff, *Verwaltung als Leistungsträger*. Dazu näher Kersten, „Die Entwicklung des Konzepts der Daseinsvorsorge", 543–569.
12 Schmitt, „Nomos – Nahme – Name", 577.
13 Vgl. Schmitt, *Nomos der Erde*, 36–38.

Einzigkeit hervorgehobene Logos des Nomos versammelt und hält zusammen, was die Dynamik des mit diesem Wort bezeichneten Geschehens so sehr auseinandertreibt, dass noch die Bezeichnung als Auseinandertreiben davon erfasst wird. Deutlich wird diese im spezifischen Sinn logisch zu nennende Betrachtungsweise zunächst am Zusammenhang der ersten beiden Bedeutungen:

> „Daß das Weiden und Teilen und Verteilen durch einunddasselbe Wort (nemein) ausgedrückt wird, beweist einen Zusammenhang der beiden in sich selbst und semantisch völlig verschiedenen Vorgänge, eine tiefere Einheit, die durch die Sprache bewahrt und aufrechterhalten wird, auch wenn die Erinnerung dem alltäglichen Bewußtsein längst verloren ging."[14]

Ebenso buchstäblich analog, das heißt an der Sprache entlang, ihr gemäß, argumentiert Schmitt auch mit Bezug auf die dritte, im Wortsinn entscheidende Erweiterung des Nomos-Verständnisses. Sie soll durch den Rückgang vom *nemein* qua pastoral-friedlichen Teilen und Weiden zu einem beinahe homophonen und damit seine ‚Urverwandtschaft' mit dem griechischen Wort demonstrierenden deutschen Verb gewährleistet werden: ‚nehmen', dem als *nomen actionis*, parallel zum Nomos, dann die Nahme entspricht.[15] Schon der *Nomos der Erde* hatte jene Trias von Nehmen, Teilen und Weiden eingeführt, sie damals aber noch in einem Satz so zusammengerückt, dass sie damit zugleich auch inhaltlich in einem Zug, auf einer gemeinsamen Ebene, verortet erscheinen.[16] Diese Positionierung wird nun im Sinne einer sowohl chronologischen wie hierarchischen Einteilung modifiziert, also noch einmal die Bewegung des *nemein* gegen das Wort selbst und seine auf diese Weise herausgearbeiteten Bedeutungen geführt. Ausdrücklich erklärt Schmitt, dass das Nehmen den beiden anderen Aktivitäten als „selbstverständliche Voraussetzung und Grundlage" vorangehen soll.[17] Eigens begründet wird diese Staffelung in aufeinanderfolgende „Stadien"[18] zunächst nicht. Schmitt verweist lediglich auf einen unumgehbaren Zwang in der Sache, der als solcher zunächst schlicht konstatiert wird: „[E]benso unvermeidlich, wie dem Weiden das Teilen vorangeht, geht dem Teilen das Nehmen voran, die Aneignung

---

14 Schmitt, „Nomos – Nahme – Name", 581.
15 Vgl. Schmitt, „Nomos – Nahme – Name", 581. Zur Frage der etymologischen Tragfähigkeit dieser Parallelisierung Schmitt, „Nomos – Nahme – Name", 581–582. Zum ganzen Problem auch bereits Schmitt, „Nehmen / Teilen / Weiden", 489–504.
16 Vgl. Schmitt, *Nomos der Erde*, 40n, wo „die erste Messung und Teilung der Weide, d. h. die Landnahme", genannt wird.
17 Vgl. so bereits Schmitt, „Nehmen / Teilen / Weiden", 492–493.
18 Schmitt, „Nomos – Nahme – Name", 582.

des zu Teilenden. Nicht die Teilung, nicht die *divisio primaeva*, sondern die Nahme ist das Erste."[19]

Die Begründung für diese Behauptung wird zwei Sätze später nachgeliefert. Sie greift auf das theologische Register zurück, indem sie die menschlich-endlichen mit den unbegrenzten göttlichen Handlungsmöglichkeiten kontrastiert. „Kein Mensch kann geben und zuteilen, ohne zu nehmen. Nur ein Gott, der die Welt aus dem Nichts erschafft, kann geben und zuteilen, ohne zu nehmen."[20]

In mehrerlei Hinsicht ist das eine bemerkenswerte Aussage. Unter der Hand revoziert Schmitt damit offenbar seine frühere Position aus der *Politischen Theologie*, der zufolge keine juristische Entscheidung das bloß automatische Resultat einer Reihe feststehender Vorbedingungen sein kann. Im Gegenteil:

> „Jede konkrete juristische Entscheidung enthält ein Moment inhaltlicher Indifferenz, weil der juristische Schluß nicht bis zum letzten Rest aus seinen Prämissen ableitbar ist, und der Umstand, daß eine Entscheidung notwendig ist, ein selbständiges determinierendes Moment bleibt. [...] Die Entscheidung ist, normativ betrachtet, aus einem Nichts geboren."[21]

Jene damals konstatierte Transposition der göttlichen *creatio ex nihilo* in das juristische Entscheidungsgeschehen scheint jetzt aufgegeben. Durch die Hervorhebung des Nehmens modifiziert sich die ehedem fundamentale *Aus*nahme, die in jeder einzelnen Entscheidung am Werk sein sollte, in die nunmehr zentrale, aber nicht näher ausbuchstabierte Figur einer bestimmten *An*nahme. Das Problem der modernen durchindustrialisierten Welt liegt Schmitt zufolge dann in der Verkennung der Angewiesenheit auf jene ursprüngliche Nahme, die der Endlichkeit des Menschen Rechnung trägt. „Heute wird angeblich nicht mehr genommen, sondern nur noch geteilt und industriell entwickelt."[22] Schmitts Annahme einer ursprünglichen Nahme richtet sich demnach, ohne dass dies näher ausgeführt würde, auf eine zugleich transzendentale, da fundamentale, und a-transzendentale, da als Bedingung der Möglichkeit erforderliche und dennoch unverfügbare Bewegung. Wo ihre Notwendigkeit nicht gesehen wird, ist für Schmitt ein echtes normatives Denken nicht mehr möglich. Was dann noch bleibt, ist ein ökonomisch-administratives Kalkül, das glaubt, sämtliche eigene Bedürfnisse selbst befriedigen zu können. In einer rein narzisstischen Weltkonzeption, der jede Form von Fremdheitserfahrung verloren gegangen ist, besteht

---

19 Schmitt, „Nomos – Nahme – Name", 581.
20 Schmitt, „Nomos – Nahme – Name", 581. Vgl. nahezu wortgleich bereits Schmitt, „Nehmen / Teilen / Weiden", 504.
21 Schmitt, *Politische Theologie*, 36, 37–38.
22 Schmitt, „Nomos – Nahme – Name", 582.

keinerlei Sinn mehr für die Unabdingbarkeit der Nahme. Die Konzeption einer politischen Theologie erscheint damit weitgehend abgelöst durch eine neue Form politischer Ökonomie, in der das nomische Element nur noch in einer reduzierten, um seinen entscheidenden nahm-haften Charakter verkürzten Variante Beachtung findet.[23]

Näher besehen ist jedoch selbst in dieser politischen Ökonomie eine vollständige Loslösung von den alten ‚theologischen Mucken' noch nicht vollzogen. An die Stelle der aus der Konfrontation mit dem Gotteskonzept widerfahrenden Einsicht in die eigene Endlichkeit tritt ein neues Verhältnis, das seinerseits aber trotz oder gerade aufgrund der Verdrängung der notwendigen Nahme zumindest krypto-religiöse Züge aufweist, weil es weiterhin auf einer kreditären Struktur beruht:

> „Alles, was sich heute auf unserer Erde, im Osten wie im Westen, auf Fortschritt und Entwicklung beruft, enthält in seinem Kern ein konkretes und präzises Credo, dessen Glaubenssätze lauten: Die industrielle Revolution führt zu einer unermeßlichen Steigerung der Produktion; infolge der Steigerung der Produktion wird das Nehmen altmodisch und sogar kriminell; auch das Teilen ist angesichts des Überflusses kein Problem mehr; es gibt also nur noch Weiden, nur noch das problemlose Glück des reinen Konsums. [...] Die Dinge verwalten sich selbst; die Menschheit begegnet sich selbst; die Wüstenwanderung der Entfremdung ist zu Ende. In einer von Menschen für Menschen – und manchmal leider auch gegen Menschen – geschaffenen Welt kann der Mensch geben, ohne zu nehmen."[24]

Der so skizzierte Gegen-Glaube, der die Endlichkeit der menschlichen Existenz durch die schlechte Unendlichkeit einer Logik des „immer weiter, immer mehr" zu überwinden können meint, verweist darauf, dass Schmitt gegenüber seiner früheren Position nun nicht nur auf ein dem Nomos als „Ur-Teilung und Ur-Verteilung"[25] noch vorausliegendes Geschehen anspielt, das als „Nahme" bezeichnet wird. Durch den Widerspruch gegenüber der suisuffizienten Konzeption, den Schmitt charakteristischerweise nicht ausschließlich als Kapitalismuskritik formuliert, sondern über die – an einer früheren Stelle als ausdrückliches Engels-Zitat eingeführte[26] – Referenz auf die Selbstverwaltung der Dinge ebenso auf die marxistische Tradition bezieht, lässt sich die Argumentation auf eine weitere Ebene verlängern. Sie wird als solche zwar nicht offen benannt, sondern kommt

---

23 Vgl. zu der Idee, dass „the afterlife of political theology in secular modernity [...] essentially its mutation into political economy" bedeute, auch Santner, *Weight of All Flesh*, 81.
24 Schmitt, „Nomos – Nahme – Name", 583.
25 Schmitt, *Nomos der Erde*, 36.
26 Vgl. Schmitt, „Nomos – Nahme – Name", 577, mit Bezug auf Engels, „Die Entwicklung des Sozialismus von der Utopie zur Wissenschaft", 195–196.

allenfalls implizit zur Sprache, entspricht aber offenbar der Logik der vorgeschlagenen Positiv- und Negativvarianten des Nomos-Verständnisses. Die Wendung gegen das Suisuffizienzideal legt es danach nahe, dass die Nahme nicht als eine aktive ursprünglichste Voraussetzung alles weiteren Geschehens verstanden werden kann. Sie bleibt als ausdrücklich so benannte „Grund-Nahme"[27] zugleich eine Grundannahme. Als solche impliziert sie eine dem gesamten in sich gestuften Prozess des Nehmens, Teilens und Weidens notwendig noch vorangehende Gabe, oder genauer gesagt, eine im strengen Sinn aller ökonomischen Logik vorausliegende Vor-Gabe dessen, was nur als Annahme dieser Gabe Recht qua Nomos heißen darf.

3

Insbesondere in der Perspektive auf die Verleugnung und Verdrängung des Nahme-Charakters zugunsten des ökonomisch-administrativen Kalküls ähnelt Schmitts Konzeption damit einer anderen Kritik des modernen Rechtsverständnisses, die diesem ebenfalls seine scheinbar selbstgenügsame, dadurch die Notwendigkeit der Dimension eines Dritten verkennende Grundhaltung vorwirft. Als „Ideologie der normativen Selbstbedienung"[28] bezeichnet Pierre Legendre ein Rechtskonzept, dessen ideologische Dimension gerade in der Verstellung einer aus seiner Sicht für die normative Konstruktion eigentlich unvermeidbaren Struktur besteht. Legendre zufolge wird diese Unvermeidlichkeit gerade im und durch den Prozess der sogenannten Säkularisierung deutlich; sie zeigt an, dass auch in diesem Prozess jene Struktur nicht aufgehoben, sondern lediglich verschoben wurde. Die Verwiesenheit auf den Dritten – *The Need of A Master* – ist demzufolge ein Charakteristikum nicht allein theologischer Konzeptionen und an deren Allmachtsvorstellungen anschließender politischer Totalitarismen. Auch eine vorgeblich säkulare, liberale Politikvorstellung bleibt auf diese Struktur angewiesen. Sie kann sie nicht überwinden, sondern allenfalls verdrängen.

> „Nachdem der das Abendland kennzeichnende schöpferische und kriegerische Gott entlassen wurde, ermöglicht die institutionelle Laizisierung die Erkenntnis, dass es sich bei dem leer gewordenen Platz in Wahrheit um *einen strukturellen Platz* handelt, in den sich ihrerseits zwangsläufig die liberale bzw. gar libertäre Hermeneutik einschreiben wird, die ohnmächtig ist, die Logik zu widerrufen, die die Entstehung der Kulturen wie auch die Entstehung des Subjekts lenkt. So bezeugen es im Übrigen die totalitären Erfahrungen: Die größte Heraus-

---

27 Schmitt, „Nomos – Nahme – Name", 581.
28 Legendre, *Das politische Begehren Gottes*, 28.

forderung der Macht besteht darin, sich des dritten Orts zu bemächtigen und sich diesen als Ort für das Einschreiben der legitimierenden Fiktionen, der Gründungszenarien, zu sichern."[29]

Auf die einzelnen Subjekte bezogen, führt die diese Struktur verdrängende Ideologie zu einer Selbstrekonstruktion in Gestalt von „zu Kleinstaaten beförderten Majestäts-Subjekten"[30], die dem eigenen Selbstverständnis nach keinem ihnen in irgendeiner Form fremd gegenüberstehenden Nomos unterworfen sind, sondern sich ausschließlich selbst regieren.[31] Man mag fragen, ob als das gegenwärtig eindrücklichste Beispiel für den Fluchtpunkt einer derartigen Subjektkonzeption nicht die Figur ‚Donald Trump' angesehen werden kann, dessen Bewunderung durch seine Anhänger möglicherweise entscheidend darauf beruht, dass sich hier ein Subjekt präsentiert, das sich keinerlei Regeln zu unterwerfen scheint – nicht einmal, wie im klassischen Dilemma des kantischen Entwurfs,[32] den selbst gesetzten. In dieser Perspektive wäre Trump weniger ein Exempel für die Fortsetzung einer bestimmten politischen Theologie, die weiterhin klassische soteriologische oder messianische Topoi in das politische Register überträgt, namentlich in Gestalt eindeutig konnotierter Botschaften wie „Mission accomplished" oder, inhaltlich auf der politischen Gegenseite verortet, aber strukturell weitgehend identisch, „Hope".[33] Statt derartiger immer noch den Transzendenzbezug wahrender, ihn lediglich auf die innerweltlich-politische Ebene spiegelnder Verweise läge die Radikalität der Figur Trump darin, dass sie als Übergang zu einer Vorstellung von Welt als reiner Immanenz und damit zugleich letztlich zu einer von Politik qua willkürlichen Entscheidungen nicht mehr abgrenzbaren Anomie erscheint, der gegenüber die Insistenz auf ehedem noch bestehenden allgemeinen normativen Standards keinen Sinn mehr ergibt – ein Übergang, der sich danach weniger als radikale Opposition gegenüber einem

---

29 Legendre, *Das politische Begehren Gottes*, 28.
30 Legendre, *Das Verbrechen des Gefreiten Lortie*, 184.
31 Vgl. zu einer Kritik eines entsprechenden „neuen Rechtsindividualismus" auch Vesting, *Staatstheorie*, 167: „Der neue Rechtsindividualismus kennt nur noch eines: Eine Selbstbestimmung ohne Nomos, eine Autonomie, von der nur das autos, das Selbst, bleibt, während die Notwendigkeit der Erhaltung einer objektiven Kultur und unpersönlichen Ordnung als mit der persönlichen Freiheit unvereinbar angesehen wird." Allg. zu der „Gefahr, dass die Idee der Autonomie zu einer bloßen Tautologie von Selbst und Gesetz wird, die uns weder die Wirklichkeit der Freiheit noch die Verbindlichkeit der Normen verständlich zu machen vermag", Khurana, „Paradoxien der Autonomie", 23.
32 Vgl. Pinkard, „Das Paradox der Autonomie", 45–47.
33 Vgl. zu diesen eher traditionellen Formen politischer Theologie mit Bezug auf die aktuelle Situation in den USA den Beitrag von Florian Grosser in diesem Band.

bestimmten westlich-liberalen Rechts- und Politikverständnis präsentierte, als vielmehr als dessen auf die Spitze getriebene, extremste, eben deswegen eher ordinäre als einfach obszöne Konsequenz.

Dass jedenfalls Legendres Charakterisierung der ‚Majestäts-Subjekte' nicht als scharfe Übertreibung angesehen werden kann, sondern in der Tat das für das westliche Rechtsverständnis dominierende Grundmodell anspricht, zeigt sich daran, dass in einem der Gründungsdiskurse dieses Verständnisses ganz ausdrücklich eine entsprechende Figur herangezogen wird, um das eigene Modell zu erläutern und gegen Kritik zu immunisieren. Auf den denkbaren und sogar als geläufig bezeichneten Einwand, seiner Konzeption eines Naturzustandes, in dem jeder einzelne die ihm von Natur aus zustehenden Rechte – in Form des Dreiklangs von „life, liberty, and estate" – wahrnehmen könne, habe niemals eine Wirklichkeit entsprochen, antwortet John Locke in seiner *Zweiten Abhandlung über die Regierung* mit einem markanten Hinweis, der Legendres Formel stützt, indem er sie einerseits vorwegnimmt, andererseits umwertet, das heißt nicht als Verfalls-, sondern im Gegenteil als Normalform juridischer Normativität begreift. Am Ausgang jenes westlichen Rechtsmodells, das sich entscheidend über individuelle Berechtigungen, *rights*, bestimmt,[34] steht danach in der Tat das Paradigma eines buchstäblich majestätischen Subjekts.

> „It is often asked as a mighty objection, where are, or ever were, there any men in such a state of Nature? To which it may suffice as an answer at present, that since all princes and rulers of ‚independent' governments all through the world are in a state of Nature, it is plain the world never was, nor never will be, without numbers of men in that state."[35]

In dieser Perspektive ist Normativität primär ein Geschehen von Selbst-, nicht Fremdbezüglichkeit. Anstelle eines Ausgeliefertseins gegenüber dem Subjekt von außen auferlegten, ihm fremd bleibenden Geboten und Forderungen bildet das Innehaben eigener Rechtspositionen die prägende Vorstellung. Kaum zufällig fasst Locke bekanntlich die einschlägige Rechte-Trias von Leben, Freiheit und Besitz unter dem einheitlichen Obertitel ‚property' zusammen.[36] Nicht Alterität, als Inanspruchnahme oder Anklage durch andere, steht als Erfahrung im Vordergrund, sondern Identität, im Sinne der Grundvoraussetzung eines über sich selbst, den eigenen Leib, die eigene Freiheit, den eigenen (Land-)Besitz verfügenden Rechtssubjekts, das damit als Ausgangspunkt aller weiteren Rechtsoperationen erscheint. Nicht etwa das Tötungsverbot, sondern das Recht auf Leben

---

34 Vgl. dazu Cover, „Obligation", 240.
35 Locke, *Two Treatises*, 124 (Buch 2, Kap. 2, Paragraph 14).
36 Vgl. Locke, *Two Treatises*, 159 (Buch 2, Kap. 7, Paragraph 87).

bildet demnach das primäre rechtliche Phänomen; jenes ist von diesem abgeleitet, nicht umgekehrt.

Eine dieser grundsätzlichen Differenz entsprechende Verschiebung der Perspektive auf die Rolle der Fürsten für das Verständnis dessen, was als ‚Naturzustand' den Ausgang der kontraktualistischen Konstruktionen bilden soll, findet sich in prägnanter Form bei Moses Mendelssohn. Auch er verwendet ausdrücklich die Analogie zwischen den souveränen Fürsten einer- und den Menschen im Naturzustand andererseits, wendet sie allerdings nun als Kritik gegen Hobbes, indem er gerade nicht die ausgeübten eigenen Rechte, sondern eine aus seiner Sicht darin und damit notwendig implizierte ursprüngliche Verpflichtung hervorhebt:

> „Ferner, der höchsten Gewalt im Staate schreibt *Hobbes* strenge Gesetze vor, nichts zu befehlen, das der Wohlfahrt ihrer Untertanen zuwider sei. Wenn sie auch keinem Menschen Rechenschaft zu geben schuldig seien; so haben sie diese doch vor dem allerhöchsten Richter abzulegen; wenn sie auch nach seinen Grundsätzen keine Furcht vor irgend einer menschlichen *Macht* binde; so binde sie doch die Furcht vor der *Allmacht*, die ihren Willen hierüber hinlänglich zu erkennen gegeben. [...] Allein eben diese Furcht vor der Allmacht, welche die Könige und Fürsten an gewisse Pflichten gegen ihre Untertanen binden soll, kann doch auch im Stande der Natur für jeden einzelnen Menschen eine Quelle der Obliegenheiten werden, und so hätten wir abermals ein *solennes* Recht der Natur, das *Hobbes* doch nicht zugeben will"[37].

Die dergestalt in Bezug genommene „Furcht vor der Allmacht" verweist allerdings offenbar lediglich zurück auf ein sehr traditionelles, im Zuge der Selbstsäkularisierung der Gesellschaft seit der Neuzeit sukzessive aufgegebenes theologisches Paradigma. Lockes Konzeption erscheint demgegenüber moderner. Zu ihr passt zum einen ein gegenwärtig geläufiges, als proprietär-possessiv zu bezeichnendes Grundrechtsverständnis, dem zufolge es sich bei den Grundrechten vorwiegend um Rechtspositionen handelt, die das Individuum haben, besitzen und besetzen kann. Umstandslos presst die herrschende Dogmatik auch jüngere technische Entwicklungen in dieses Schema und konstruiert entsprechend etwa Datenschutz als Schutz des Eigentums an bestimmten personenbezogenen Daten.[38] Auf einer

---

37 Mendelssohn, *Jerusalem*, 37. Eine in eine ähnliche Richtung deutende Argumentation findet sich allerdings auch noch bei Locke zu Beginn des zweiten Buches seiner *Abhandlungen*, in dem Kapitel über den Naturzustand. Danach ist den Menschen die Selbst- und Fremdschädigung untersagt, weil sie „the workmanship of one omnipotent and wise maker" sind und damit „His property" (Locke, *Two Treatises*, 119–120 [Buch II, Paragraph 6]).

38 Vgl. zu dem entsprechenden Vorgehen namentlich des Bundesverfassungsgerichts und seiner Kritik näher Ladeur, „Das Recht auf informationelle Selbstbestimmung", 45–55.

abstrakteren Ebene passt zu diesem Modell zum anderen aber ebenso ein allgemeines Verständnis von Normativität, das in dieser nicht vorwiegend den Aspekt der Begrenzung, das heißt des Aufweises der Endlichkeit von Handlungsoptionen akzentuiert, sondern umgekehrt Normativität vor allem als Eröffnung und positive Markierung bestimmter Möglichkeiten bestimmt.[39]

Dass in der Normativität primär die Begegnung mit einer Referenz liegt, die für das Subjekt als unverfügbare Grenze des eigenen Vermögens erscheint,[40] bleibt auf diese Weise weitgehend ausgeblendet. Kaum noch thematisch wird damit zumal die Frage nach einem möglicherweise irreduzibel traumatischen Kern der Normativität.[41] Wer mit Schmitt an „eine tiefere Einheit, die durch die Sprache bewahrt und aufrechterhalten wird",[42] glaubt, müsste sich dagegen für die entsprechende Mehrdeutigkeit eines einzelnen Wortes interessieren, auf die Legendre ausgerechnet in einem Werk verweist, das diesen Begriff schon im Titel trägt: Das griechische Wort *krima* und entsprechend das lateinische *crimen* meint demnach nicht nur die grundlegende Entscheidung, auch und gerade im juristischen Bereich, also das Verfahren des Urteils, das in dieser Hinsicht zugleich auf die von Schmitt avisierte Ur-Teilung verweist. *Krima/crimen* bezeichnet zugleich das Verbrechen.[43]

Das skizzierte gegenwärtig geläufige Normativitätsverständnis scheint sich von derartigen Zweideutigkeiten fernhalten zu können. In Schmitts Taxonomie der unterschiedlichen Formen von auf ‚-nomie' endenden Wortbildungen wäre vor dem Hintergrund des skizzierten (Grund-)Rechtsverständnisses eine weitere Figur einzufügen, die er selbst erstaunlicherweise nicht aufführt. Wenn man das skizzierte Verständnis, rechtliche Normativität grundlegend im Ausgang von individuellen Berechtigungen statt von objektiven Verpflichtungen zu begreifen, auf den traditionellen Oberbegriff ‚Autonomie' bringt,[44] dann liegt mit diesem Begriff zunächst ein weiteres Beispiel vor für eine Ausnahme von der behaupteten Regel, weil sich hier offenbar vorrangig das Selbst die Normativität zu eigen macht. Zugleich lässt sich allerdings auch eine stärker objektbezogene Lesart der Zusammensetzung rechtfertigen. Denn es geht in der dargestellten Autonomie auch um eine Ordnung des Selbst in dem Sinne, dass das, was als Subjekt seinen sozialen Status geltend machen kann, seinerseits entscheidend durch Rechtsposi-

---

39 Vgl. Möllers, *Möglichkeit der Normen*.
40 Vgl. dazu Legendre, *Verbrechen des Gefreiten Lortie*, 121, 136–137.
41 Vgl. dazu etwa – in seiner Besprechung von Möllers, *Möglichkeit der Normen* – Forst, „Wie utopisch sind Tischsitten?", 43: „Die dunkle Seite normativer Macht kann Möllers nicht erhellen."
42 Schmitt, „Nomos – Nahme – Name", 581.
43 Vgl. Legendre, *Verbrechen des Gefreiten Lortie*, 67–68 (Fn. 25), 131.
44 Vgl. Cover, „Obligation", 240.

tionen bestimmt wird. Beide Bewegungen ergänzen sich: In dem Maße, in dem das Recht als subjektkonstituiert konzipiert ist, wird das Subjekt zunehmend als rechtskonstituiert verstanden. Schärfer noch: Es versteht sich selbst zunehmend nur noch auf diese Weise.[45] Im Kurzschluss von Menschsein mit Rechtssubjektsein, qua Inhaberschaft bestimmter Rechte, erscheinen alternative Betrachtungsmöglichkeiten kaum noch vorstellbar.[46] Darin liegt das strukturelle Dilemma insbesondere des Anti-Diskriminierungsrechts begründet, dessen Vorschriften die Unterscheidungen, die sie untersagen sollen, zugleich rechtlich operationalisieren und damit fortschreiben.

4

Schmitts Kritik an einem vorwiegend ökonomisch-administrativen Nomos-Verständnis erscheint demnach durchaus nachvollziehbar; sie lässt sich auch mit Blick auf gegenwärtige Entwicklungen des Rechts plausibilisieren und mit Beobachtungen verknüpfen, die aus einer zumindest politisch scheinbar vollkommen entgegengesetzten Richtung stammen. „Das herrschende, für alle offenbare Gesetz", heißt es entsprechend etwa bei Alain Badiou, in einer Passage, die sich aus dieser Sicht wie ein zustimmender Kommentar zu sowohl Schmitt wie Legendre lesen lässt, „wird nicht mehr vom Vater bestimmt. Statt seiner gilt das Gesetz des Marktes, ein anonymes, alles und jeden gleichmachendes, von der Figur des symbolischen Vaters gänzlich entkoppeltes Gesetz."[47]

Umso enttäuschender erscheint Schmitts weitere Bestimmung der Nahme. Dabei handelt es sich weniger darum, seiner ersichtlichen Freude an der Provokation durch eine entsprechende moralisch-politische Empörung gewissermaßen auf den Leim zu gehen. Ein solches Bemühen ist kaum zu verkennen, wenn Schmitt über das „Odium des Kolonialismus" spottet,[48] um im Kontrast dazu seine Konzeption einer ursprünglichen Nahme als Landnahme zu bestimmen und diesen Vorgang anhand der Landnahme in der sogenannten ‚Neuen Welt' zu exemplifizieren, unter ausdrücklichem Verweis auf den heroischen Geist, der die „Helden der Conquista" ausgezeichnet habe.[49] Irritierender als diese eher sche-

---

45 Vgl. zum Problem – speziell mit Blick auf die Religion – Reuter, „Religion im Prozess der Ver(grund)rechtlichung der Gesellschaft", 17–19; ausführlich Reuter, *Religion in der verrechtlichten Gesellschaft*.
46 Vgl. Hamacher, „Vom Recht, Rechte nicht zu gebrauchen", 98–99.
47 Badiou, *Versuch, die Jugend zu verderben*, 59–60.
48 Vgl. Schmitt, „Nomos – Nahme – Name", 582.
49 Vgl. Schmitt, „Nomos – Nahme – Name", 585.

matische Entgegensetzung zu einem als herrschend angesehenen Zeitgeist ist die theoretische Dürftigkeit des Vorgehens. Sie fällt, was bereits die frühere Bestimmung der Nahme als „Aneignung des zu Teilenden" nahegelegt hatte, wieder in eben jenes ökonomische Paradigma zurück, das zunächst doch den Anstoß gegeben hatte, über das Teilen und Weiden hinauszudenken. Nicht allein die Ignoranz gegenüber dem Umstand, dass der Appropriation durch die „Helden der Conquista" eine Expropriation der Ureinwohner notwendig vorausgehen musste, also die Aneignung eine gewaltsame Enteignung voraussetzt – wovon der Begriff der ‚Conquista' immerhin hinreichend Zeugnis ablegt –, ist danach das Problem, sondern dass auf diese Weise die Ebene eines um das Paradigma ‚Eigentum' zentrierten Rechtsdenkens gerade noch nicht verlassen, sondern im Gegenteil eher gestärkt wird. Statt einer Ex-appropriation das Wort zu reden,[50] bleibt es dabei, dass das (auch in aktuellen Auseinandersetzungen noch vielberufene) ‚Proprium' des Rechts (und sukzessive, ‚streng akzessorisch', dann ebenso: der Rechtswissenschaft) im Proprietären gesucht wird.[51]

Diese Problematik verschärft sich noch einmal durch den Übergang der Fragestellung von der Nahme zum Namen. Wiederum erfolgt die erste Annäherung unter Verweis auf die sprachliche Nähe beider Wörter, nunmehr allerdings unter ausdrücklicher Hinzufügung der Kautele, sprachwissenschaftliche Diskussionen hierzu nicht führen zu wollen.[52] Ebenso knapp und apodiktisch wie jener Einstieg fallen dann die weiteren Ausführungen aus. Statt zu erörtern, wie man über einen Namen, auch und gerade über den sogenannten eigenen Namen, verfügen kann, ohne zugleich mit dem üblichen Verständnis zu brechen, das die bewusst angenommenen Namen als künstlich versteht und demgegenüber die gegebenen Namen als echt einordnet (immerhin hatte Schmitt mit dem Phänomen eine gewisse eigene Erfahrung, hatte er doch für einige Zeit den, wie sich allerdings erst im Lauf des Scheidungsverfahrens herausstellte: falschen, nämlich keineswegs adeligen Namen seiner Gattin dem seinen hinzugefügt und mit diesem angenommenen falschen Namen auch seine Texte aus jener Zeit signiert[53]), konzentriert sich Schmitt auf die nachgelagerte Frage, inwieweit ein Name zur Bezeichnung und damit zur Begründung von Eigentumsverhältnissen eingesetzt werden kann.

---

50 Vgl. zu diesem Begriff etwa Derrida, „‚Man muß wohl essen'", 280.
51 Vgl. zu diesem juristischen Selbstverständnis charakteristisch etwa Engel und Schön, *Das Proprium der Rechtswissenschaft*.
52 Vgl. Schmitt, „Nomos – Nahme – Name", 584: „Die sprachgeschichtliche Frage, ob die beiden Worte Nahme und Name eine etymologische Verbindung haben, lasse ich ausdrücklich beiseite."
53 Vgl. dazu näher Mehring, *Carl Schmitt*, 57.

Eigentümlicherweise bezieht sich allerdings der erste im Text angeführte Beleg für den in diese Richtung entwickelten Zusammenhang nicht unmittelbar auf klassische Appropriationsprozesse, sondern zunächst einmal auf das Geschlechterverhältnis. Das erste „zur Veranschaulichung jener vergangenen Zeiten, in denen es noch eine Nahme gab",[54] angeführte Beispiel „betrifft die Institution Ehe und der auf die Ehe gegründeten Familie. In jenen Zeiten also *nahm* der Mann die Frau. Die Frau *erkannte* den Mann und unterwarf sich demnach der Nahme."[55] Den Unterschied dieses Vorgangs von einer bloßen Vergewaltigung sieht Schmitt allein in der „eindeutige[n] Publizität"[56] jener Nahme: „Der Mann, der in besonderer Weise die Frau nahm, gab ihr seinen Namen, die Frau nahm den Namen des Mannes, und die ehelichen Kinder wurden mit dem Namen des Mannes geboren."[57] Diese Zeiten seien unter der Herrschaft des Grundgesetzes und der von ihm postulierten Gleichberechtigung beider Geschlechter allerdings vorbei. Dass dennoch „bei uns immer noch" – das heißt zum Zeitpunkt des Erscheinens des Artikels, in der Bundesrepublik Deutschland Ende der 1950er Jahre – „die gesetzlich verheiratete Frau [...] den Namen des Mannes führt, ist ein Überbleibsel aus den vergangenen Zeiten, in denen der Mann die Frau nahm, ein Residuum, das gewohnheitsmäßig vorläufig noch weitergeführt wird."[58] Bei dieser Bestimmung als juristischer Anachronismus lässt Schmitt seine Betrachtung zum Zusammenhang von Nahme, Name, Ehe und Familie aber nicht enden. Er ergänzt seinen „sozusagen zum Abschied"[59] auf jene vergangenen Zeiten geworfenen Blick vielmehr um eine Bemerkung, die die Notwendigkeit einer Erinnerung jener Verhältnisse hervorhebt, also erläutert, warum dasjenige, von dem Abschied zu nehmen ist, zugleich im Gedächtnis festzuhalten ist:

> „Wir tun jedoch gut daran, den tieferen Zusammenhang zwischen Nahme und Namen zu bedenken, damit wir wissen, was die Ehe unserer Väter war, aus der wir stammen und unseren Namen tragen. Wir würden ja nicht einmal mehr unseren eigenen Namen begreifen, wenn die Einheit von Namen und Nahmen aus unserem Gedächtnis gestrichen würde."[60]

Nahme und Name rücken danach in der Erinnerung an die Vaterfigur zusammen. Von ihr her erst sollen wir unseren eigenen Namen und damit uns selbst verstehen

---

54 Schmitt, „Nomos – Nahme – Name", 583.
55 Schmitt, „Nomos – Nahme – Name", 583.
56 Schmitt, „Nomos – Nahme – Name", 583.
57 Schmitt, „Nomos – Nahme – Name", 583.
58 Schmitt, „Nomos – Nahme – Name", 583.
59 Schmitt, „Nomos – Nahme – Name", 583.
60 Schmitt, „Nomos – Nahme – Name", 583.

(und das heißt in der klassischen Hermeneutik: aneignen[61]) können. Was die so begriffene Nahme bedeutet, worin genau ihre spezifische Bewegung liegt, machen dann die weiteren Überlegungen noch deutlicher, die den Akt des Nehmens nicht mehr auf eine Frau, sondern auf neues, auf diese Weise zu gewinnendes Land beziehen. Eine derartige Landnahme soll erst dann vollzogen sein, wenn der Nehmende dem Genommenen etwas gegeben hat: nämlich einen Namen. „Eine Landnahme wirkt nur dann konstituierend, wenn es dem Landnehmer gelingt, einen Namen zu geben."[62]

Die Nahme verweist demnach doch nicht auf eine ihr selbst vorgängige, unverfügbare Gabe. Im Gegenteil: In Gestalt der Namensgebung ist ihr auch diese Aufgabe selbst zugewiesen. Nur im Rahmen einer solchen konkreten Namensgebung – Schmitt verweist auf die „neue[n] Namen Leningrad, Stalingrad und Kaliningrad"[63] –, nicht dagegen in der abstrakten Rede eines Handelns ‚im Namen des Gesetzes', oder entsprechend ‚im Namen der Menschheit' oder der ‚Vernunft', besteht für Schmitt der eigentliche Zusammenhang von Nahme und Name.[64] ‚Name' ist damit nicht nur ein anderer Name für die Nahme als Signum menschlicher Endlichkeit. Er verweist auf ein herrisches Moment im Akt der Selbstgebung, einen kratischen oder arche-haften Charakter, der dem Nomos, Schmitts Ausgangsüberlegungen zu den üblichen Wortverbindungen mit ‚-nomie' zum Trotz, notwendig innewohnen soll und ihn auf diese Weise von der falschen Vorstellung eines allzu idyllischen, pastoral-friedlichen Geschehnisses fernhält. Jener Akt, der die Verstellung und Verdeckung des eigentlichen Charakters des Nomos in der bewusst und offen vollzogenen Namensgebung aufhebt, markiert in dieser Perspektive nicht nur die entscheidende Differenz sowohl gegenüber der *invisible hand* des Marktgeschehens wie gegenüber nackter Gewaltsamkeit. Ihm wird ausdrücklich eine spezifisch theologische Bedeutung zugewiesen:

> „Im Namen und in der Namensgebung wirkt sich die dritte Richtung der Macht aus, die Tendenz zur Sichtbarkeit, Öffentlichkeit und Krönung. Sie überwindet die satanische Versuchung zu einer unsichtbaren, anonymen und im Geheimen bleibenden Macht. Sobald ein echter Name erscheint, hört der nur oikonomische Nomos auf, der sich in Wirtschaft und Verwaltung erschöpft. Der Bienenkorb hat keinen Namen. Sowenig wie Archie und Kratie ohne Nomos bestehen, so wenig lebt der menschliche Nomos ohne Archie und Kratie."[65]

---

61 Vgl. zum Verständnis des Verstehens als Verwandlung des Fremden in Eigenes Schleiermacher, „Über den Begriff der Hermeneutik", 315.
62 Schmitt, „Nomos – Nahme – Name", 584.
63 Schmitt, „Nomos – Nahme – Name", 585.
64 Vgl. Schmitt, „Nomos – Nahme – Name", 585: „Gesetz ist noch kein Name. Auch Menschheit und Vernunft sind keine Namen."
65 Schmitt, „Nomos – Nahme – Name", 584.

5

Wie könnte demgegenüber ein anders konzipiertes Verständnis des Zusammenhangs von Name und Nahme aussehen?[66] In wessen Namen kann eine Nahme erfolgen, die nicht selbst den Prozess der Namensgebung okkupiert? Sicherlich nicht im Namen einer konkreten Instanz, die zugleich als Transzendenz bestimmt ist. Diese Möglichkeit ist durch die Säkularisierung, ganz gleich wie eng oder weit diese selbst verstanden wird, tatsächlich verloren gegangen. Sicherlich aber ebenso wenig im Namen einer konkreten, ein bestimmtes Maß bereits voraussetzenden oder selbst hervorbringenden Teilung, etwa in Gestalt einer Verfassung, sondern allenfalls im Namen dessen, was einer derartigen Teilung je schon vorausliegen muss. Was der Teilung in diesem Sinne vorausliegt, sind jedoch nicht primär eine teilend-zuteilende und eine zu teilende Einheit, also das, was in aller Unbestimmbarkeit der Begriffe bei Schmitt als „Volk" und „Land" auftritt und darin seinerseits nur die konkrete, aber zugleich letztlich kontingente Gestalt einer allgemeinen Sehnsucht nach Substanz, Ursprünglichkeit und Unmittelbarkeit bildet. Ihnen voraus liegt bereits das, was alle Teilung, also auch die Teilung der teilend-zuteilenden und der zu teilenden Einheiten ermöglicht: die abgründige Annahme einer regellosen Teilbarkeit. Sie modifiziert die Idee der Annahme zur An-Nahme im Sinne eines *alpha privativum*, weil sie nicht mehr oder vielmehr noch nicht etwas Konkretes, Einzelnes, namentlich in Gestalt eines bestimmten Stücks Land, als gegeben in Empfang nehmen kann. In diesem Kontext verweist der Nomos als Nahme auf eine ihm je schon vorangehende, ihn heimsuchende Anomie, die nicht deswegen in einem Gegensatz zum Nomos steht, weil sie kein Recht ist, sondern weil sie es zu sehr ist. Wenn Schmitt in seiner *Politischen Theologie* schreibt, es müsste doch „auch den Rationalisten [...] interessieren, daß die Rechtsordnung selbst den Ausnahmefall vorsehen und ‚sich selber suspendieren' kann",[67] dann wäre dem im Sinn einer vernehmenderen Vernunft nur hinzuzufügen, dass die Logik des Exzeptionellen als Fähigkeit zur Selbst-Aussetzung ihrerseits etwas impliziert, was diesseits des aktiven Setzens liegt. Die privativ verstandene An-Nahme lässt sich in dieser Sicht entsprechend als Aus-Nahme lesen. Von ihrem eigenen Namen wie benommen, kann die Nahme nur im Namen des Negativen als solchen geschehen, im Namen des Nichts, oder genauer: im Namen dessen, das (oder der) nichts als Name ist. Im Namen des Namens. Als Sprache.[68]

---

66 Vgl. zum Problem näher bereits Schestag, „Namen nehmen", 544–562.
67 Schmitt, *Politische Theologie*, 20.
68 Vgl. zur „regellosen Teilbarkeit der Wortsprache" näher Schestag, *Parerga*, 156, 178.

Eine solche Perspektive auf ein Ereignis, in dem Selbstbezüglichkeit und Unverfügbarkeit zusammenfallen, auf eine Referenzialität als Angewiesenheit auf Referenz, ohne das referenzierte Objekt selbst garantieren zu können, also auf ein Sprechen ‚im Namen von' im Sinne des Bezugs auf eine Gründungsreferenz, die dabei zugleich als etwas verstanden wird, „das in seiner Substanz, wenn ich so sagen darf, seine eigene Negation enthält"[69], ließe sich dann auch mit einem neuen Blick auf die Konzeption der Rolle des quasi-allmächtigen Hausvaters verknüpfen. Ein derartiger, Patronomie und Patronymie engführender Blick dürfte die *patria potestas* nicht einfach als domestizierte Nachfolgegestalt jener Gewalt verstehen, mit der im Freud'schen Modell die Mitglieder der Urhorde brutal missbraucht und unterdrückt werden. Er müsste vielmehr im Sinne des römischen Rechts die Rolle des Vaters nicht primär biologistisch, sondern funktional begreifen, das heißt mit Bezug auf eine spezifische normative Struktur. Vor allem die Eigenständigkeit der Rolle des *pater familias* macht das deutlich, weil sie keineswegs mit dem bloßen Umstand gleichzusetzen ist, selbst Kinder zu haben. *Domus* und *familia* sind nicht von den bürgerlichen Familienvorstellungen des 19. Jahrhunderts her zu verstehen. Erst recht nicht ist die römische Familie auf die Gemeinschaft von ‚leiblichen' Eltern und Kindern begrenzt. Wie wenig ein derartiges biologistisches Verständnis dem römischen Modell entspricht, zeigt sich an der Üblichkeit der Adoption, das heißt der Annahme als eigenes Kind und Aufnahme in die eigene, dadurch zugleich neu konfigurierte Familie. In Rom galten „Blutsbande [...] nicht als notwendige Bedingung für die Konstituierung dieses Familienkerns. Die Adoption war zur Aufnahme in die Familie durchaus üblich und ebenso ‚natürlich' wie die Geburt."[70] Hieran anknüpfend und zugleich noch etwas weiter ausgreifend könnte man spekulieren, ob Schmitts Desinteresse an dem Konzept der Herrschaft des Vaters möglicherweise durch eine ihm nicht ebenso offenkundig wie der (als ‚natürlich' nicht existierend bezeichneten) Nomonomia eingeschriebene, aber möglicherweise dennoch konstitutive Selbstbezüglichkeit der Patronomie hervorgerufen ist. Statt der gesuchten „volle[n] Unmittelbarkeit"[71], die den Nomos auszeichnen soll, würde danach hier auf eine Konstruktion verwiesen, die sich zwar wiederum in Begriffen von Regel und Ausnahme formulieren lässt, dabei aber nunmehr mit der Ausnahme zugleich den entscheidenden Aspekt der Künstlichkeit des ganzen Geschehens hervorhebt, also mit der vorgeblichen Ausnahme eigentlich, *de facto* wie *de iure*, die Regel benennt. Streng genommen bildet aus juristischer Perspektive die Vaterschaft

---

69 Legendre, *Verbrechen des Gefreiten Lortie*, 137, vgl. auch 132.
70 Thomas, *La Mort du père*, 279–280.
71 Schmitt, *Nomos der Erde*, 42.

auch dort eine *legal fiction*, wo sie mit den biologisch-physiologischen Annahmen übereinstimmt. Ein Vertreter des aus Schmitts Sicht buchstäblich unheimlichen, nämlich durch seine ‚Bodenlosigkeit' charakterisierten ‚Normativismus'[72] bringt diesen Zusammenhang auf den Punkt, wenn er auf die entsprechende Besonderheit der spezifisch juristischen Semiotik verweist:

> „Vater ist im Rechtssinne nur das Zeichen für einen Rechts- und Pflichtenkomplex, der zwar regelmäßig durch die natürliche Vatereigenschaft bedingt ist, ausnahmsweise aber auch völlig losgelöst von diesem natürlichen Tatbestand bestehen kann."[73]

In diesem Verständnishorizont wird die Rede von der Patronomie als eine Wendung lesbar, in der Genitivus obiectivus und Genitivus subiectivus zusammenfallen.

Bibliographie

Badiou, Alain. *Versuch, die Jugend zu verderben*, übers. v. Tobias Haberkorn. Berlin: Suhrkamp, 2016.
Cover, Robert. „Obligation: A Jewish Jurisprudence of the Social Order", In *Narrative, Violence, and the Law: The Essays of Robert Cover*, hg. v. Martha Minow, Michael Ryan und Austin Sarat, 239–248. Ann Arbor: University of Michigan Press, 1993.
Derrida, Jacques. „,Man muß wohl essen' oder die Berechnung des Subjekts", In *Auslassungspunkte: Gespräche*, von Jacques Derrida, hg. v. Peter Engelmann, übers. v. Karin Schreiner und Dirk Weissmann, 267–298. Wien: Passagen Verlag, 1998.
Engel, Christoph, und Schön, Wolfgang, Hg., *Das Proprium der Rechtswissenschaft*. Tübingen: Mohr Siebeck, 2007.
Engels, Friedrich. „Die Entwicklung des Sozialismus von der Utopie zur Wissenschaft", In *Werke*, Bd. 9, *März 1875 bis Mai 1883*, von Karl Marx und Friedrich Engels, hg. v. Institut für Marxismus-Leninismus beim ZK der SED. Berlin: Dietz, 1962.
Forst, Rainer. „Wie utopisch sind Tischsitten?," *Die Zeit*, 14 Jan. 2016, 43.
Forsthoff, Ernst. *Die Verwaltung als Leistungsträger*. Stuttgart: Kohlhammer, 1938.
Hamacher, Werner. „Vom Recht, Rechte nicht zu gebrauchen. Menschenrechte und Urteilsstruktur", In *Sprachgerechtigkeit*, von Werner Hamacher, 93–126. Frankfurt a. M.: Fischer, 2018.
Kersten, Jens. „Die Entwicklung des Konzepts der Daseinsvorsorge im Werk von Ernst Forsthoff", *Der Staat* 44 (2005): 543–569.
Khurana, Thomas. „Paradoxien der Autonomie: Zur Einführung", In *Paradoxien der Autonomie*, hg. v. Thomas Khurana und Christoph Menke, 7–23. Berlin: August Verlag, 2011.

---

72 Vgl. dazu näher Schmitt, *Arten des rechtswissenschaftlichen Denkens*, 9.
73 Merkl, „Justizirrtum und Rechtswahrheit", 207.

Ladeur, Karl-Heinz. „Das Recht auf informationelle Selbstbestimmung: Eine juristische Fehlkonstruktion?", *Die öffentliche Verwaltung* Nr. 2 (2009): 45–55.

Legendre, Pierre. *Das Verbrechen des Gefreiten Lortie: Versuch über den Vater*, übers. Clemens Pornschlegel. Wien: Turia & Kant, 2011.

Legendre, Pierre. *Das politische Begehren Gottes: Studien über die Montagen des Staates und des Rechts*, übers. Katrin Becker. Wien: Turia & Kant, 2012.

Locke, John. *Two Treatises of Civil Government*. London: J.M. Dent, 1962.

Mehring, Reinhard. *Carl Schmitt: Aufstieg und Fall: Eine Biographie*. München: C.H. Beck, 2009.

Mendelssohn, Moses. *Jerusalem oder über religiöse Macht und Judentum*, hg. v. Michael Albrecht. Hamburg: Felix Meiner Verlag, 2005.

Merkl, Adolf. „Justizirrtum und Rechtswahrheit", In *Die Wiener rechtstheoretische Schule. Schriften von Hans Kelsen, Adolf Merkl, Alfred Verdross*, hg. v. Hans Klecatsky, René Marcic und Herbert Schambeck. Wien: Europa-Verlag, 1968.

Möllers, Christoph. *Die Möglichkeit der Normen: Über eine Praxis jenseits von Moralität und Kausalität*. Berlin: Suhrkamp, 2015.

Pinkard, Terry. „Das Paradox der Autonomie: Kants Problem und Hegels Lösung," In *Paradoxien der Autonomie*, hg. v. Thomas Khurana und Christoph Menke, 25–60. Berlin: August Verlag, 2011.

Reuter, Astrid. „Religion im Prozess der Ver(grund)rechtlichung der Gesellschaft", In *Interdependenzen von Recht und Religion*, hg. v. Anne Kühler, Felix Hafner und Jürgen Mohn, 9–29. Würzburg: Ergon-Verlag, 2014.

Reuter, Astrid. *Religion in der verrechtlichten Gesellschaft: Rechtskonflikte und öffentliche Kontroversen um Religion als Grenzarbeiten am religiösen Feld*. Göttingen: Vandenhoeck & Ruprecht, 2014.

Santner, Eric L. *The Weight of All Flesh: On the Subject Matter of Political Economy*. Oxford: Oxford University Press, 2016.

Schestag, Thomas. *Parerga: Friedrich Hölderlin/Carl Schmitt/Franz Kafka/Platon/Friedrich Schleiermacher/Walter Benjamin/Jacques Derrida: Zur literarischen Hermeneutik*. München: Boer, 1991.

Schestag, Thomas. „Namen nehmen. Zur Theorie des Namens bei Carl Schmitt", *Modern Language Notes* 122 (2007): 544–562.

Schleiermacher, Friedrich. „Über den Begriff der Hermeneutik mit Bezug auf F. A. Wolfs Andeutungen und Asts Lehrbuch", In *Hermeneutik und Kritik*, von Friedrich Schleiermacher, hg. v. Manfred Frank. Frankfurt a. M.: Suhrkamp, 1977.

Schmitt, Carl. „Nomos – Nahme – Name", In *Der beständige Aufbruch*, Festschrift E. Przywara, hg. v. Siegfried Behn, 92–105. Nürnberg: Glock und Lutz, 1959.

Schmitt, Carl. „Nehmen / Teilen / Weiden (1953): Ein Versuch, die Grundfragen jeder Sozial- und Wirtschaftsordnung vom Nomos her richtig zu stellen", In *Verfassungsrechtliche Aufsätze aus den Jahren 1924–1954*, von Carl Schmitt, 3. Aufl., 489–504. Berlin: Duncker & Humblot, 1985.

Schmitt, Carl. *Der Nomos der Erde im Völkerrecht des Jus Publicum Europaeum*, 3. Aufl. Berlin: Duncker & Humblot, 1988.

Schmitt, Carl. *Über die drei Arten des rechtswissenschaftlichen Denkens*, 2. Aufl. Berlin: Duncker & Humblot, 1993.

Schmitt, Carl. *Staat, Großraum, Nomos: Arbeiten aus den Jahren 1916–1969*, hg. v. Günter Maschke. Berlin: Duncker & Humblot, 1995.

Schmitt, Carl. *Politische Theologie: Vier Kapitel zur Lehre von der Souveränität*, 7. Aufl. Berlin: Duncker & Humblot, 1996.

Thomas, Yan. „Rom. Väter als Bürger in einer Stadt der Väter (2. Jh. v. Chr. – 2. Jh. n. Chr.)", In *Geschichte der Familie*, Bd. 1, *Altertum*, hg. v. André Burguière, Christiane Klapisch-Zuber, Martine Segalen und Françoise Zonabend, 277–326. Frankfurt a. M.: Campus Verlag, 1996.

Thomas, Yan. *La Mort du père: Sur le crime de parricide à Rome*. Paris: Albin Michel, 2017.

Vesting, Thomas. *Staatstheorie: Ein Studienbuch*. München: C.H. Beck, 2018.

Dimitris Vardoulakis
Spinoza on the Death of the Master

The Hebrew Theocracy after Moses

Abstract: The paper interprets Spinoza's presentation of Moses in the *Theological Political Treatise* in light of antiquity's and early modernity's concept of authority. Moses is the kind of figure who cannot be argued with and whose authority is both theological and political. But what happens when the master of the Hebrew State dies? What happens at the end of authority? And what does this mean for a polity premised on the presence of the master as a figure of authority? These questions are tackled through a close reading of the chapters 17 and 18 of Spinoza's *Treatise*.

The treatise that Spinoza publishes in 1670 is about authority. The concept of authority has a very specific meaning in the tradition – a meaning that remains largely consistent throughout the tradition from the Roman republic onward. A figure has authority when they are impervious to argumentation. As Hannah Arendt puts it, authority "is incompatible with persuasion. ... Where arguments are used, authority is left in abeyance."[1] Or, in Alexandre Kojève's formulation, authority resides with someone whose "action does not provoke a reaction."[2] In this sense, the figure of authority is a "master" because others obey him – the figure of authority in the Judeo-Christian tradition is masculine.

At the same time, the obedience that accompanies a figure of authority has a double source, both theological and political. It is theological when authority is the cause of obedience in the sense that authority is sui generis. It is political when obedience causes authority, that is, when it is constructed through social and legal relations.[3] The double origin of authority distinguishes it from a modern conception of authority, one that arises in the aftermath of the Reformation, intensifies around the time of the French Revolution but is not solidified until the

---

[1] Arendt, "What is Authority?", 93.
[2] Kojève, *Notion of Authority*, 13.
[3] The best description of the double origin of authority is provided by Ricœur, "The Paradox of Authority", 91–105. This traditional conception of authority informs ancient mythology as explained, for instance, in Dumézil, *Mitra-Varuna*.

late nineteenth and the early twentieth century, for instance, in the work of Max Weber.[4]

Spinoza has direct recourse to the traditional determination of authority when he asserts, for instance, that "the authority of the prophet does not permit of argumentation [*prophetae auctoritas ratiocinari non patitur*]" (139/152)[5]. Further, following a tradition that stretches back at least to Machiavelli, Spinoza insists in the opening chapters of the *Theological Political Treatise* that Moses is the greatest of all prophets as he embodies in a unique way both theological and political authority: he derives the law of the Decalogue through revelation but this also becomes the foundation of the Hebrew state.[6] It is because of this authority, both theological and political, that we can understand Moses as the "master" of the Jews. And it is because of the centrality of this theme that Spinoza calls his treatise "theologico-political."

The answer to the question of the title is, however, complicated by the last five chapters of the *Theological Political Treatise*, where the discussion shifts from the prophets and Moses to broader political concerns. Here, Spinoza pursues questions about the political that cannot be circumscribed within the figure of authority. What happens to a state whose main feature is obedience when there is no definitive master? Or, more specifically, what happens when *the* master, Moses, dies? How does mastery and obedience persist in the Hebrew state?

There are three interrelated problematics that we must turn to in order to address the above questions. First, what is the nature of the Hebrew state? To tackle this problematic, Spinoza relies heavily on Josephus who describes the Hebrew state as a theocracy. Second, what are the limits of power or "mastery" in the Hebrew state? This is the question that organizes chapters 17 and 18 of the *Theological Political Treatise* and it is explicitly stated as the question "how far extends the state's right and power [*imperii jus et potestas se extendat*]?" (185/201). Third, in the same chapters Spinoza also explores the reasons for the dissolution of the

---

[4] For an account of the transformation of authority in the aftermath of the Reformation, see Marcuse, "A Study on Authority", 49–155. The importance of Weber in the narrowing of the meaning of authority to refer only to the political has been noted by various commentators. For instance, as Sennett puts it, Weber "identifies authority with legitimacy." Sennett, *Authority*, 22.

[5] All references to Spinoza's *Theological Political Treatise* are to the translation by Samuel Shirley, cited parenthetically by page number. I have often altered the translation. For the Latin, I have used the Gebhardt, *Opera*. The *Tractatus Theologico-Politicus* is contained in Volume 3. All page references to this edition follow after the English edition.

[6] For a detailed discussion of Moses's theologico-political authority in Spinoza, see Vardoulakis, "The Figure of Moses", 771–785.

Hebrew state. The answer he provides makes his discussion of the mastery operative in the Hebrew state resonate with theories of biopolitics.

1 Josephus: The Theocracy of the Hebrew State

Spinoza describes the Hebrew state as a "theocracy [*theocratia*]" on the grounds that "civil law and religion … were one and the same thing" since the tenets of religion were "laws and commands." Spinoza repeats this point a few lines later: "there was considered to be no difference whatsoever between civil law and religion" – to indicate that this form of government is called a theocracy (189/206). The coincidence of civil and religious law is Spinoza's peculiar way of defining a theocracy. The reasons for this idiosyncratic definition will become clear in the next two sections. First, we need to explore how this definition of theocracy is situated within the theological and political discussions of the time.

The compounds of "theocracy" are theos (God) and kratos (power), signifying the rule or sovereignty of God. The word "kratos" does not signify a transcendent kind of sovereignty, such as the rule of God in "heaven." Rather, kratos signifies an immanent rule, such as the rule of a sovereign on earth. The word "theocracy" was coined by Josephus, a first century A.D. Jew who defected to Rome, and who under the protection of the emperor Flavius composed a number of works on Jewish history and culture.[7] These works were written in Greek and the first time that the original was made available widely was in 1544, edited by the Dutch humanist Arnoldus Arlenius. Spinoza held copies of these Latin translations of Josephus's books in his library. Even though Josephus is named only once in chapters 17 and 18, he is one of the authors most often mentioned in other chapters of the *Treatise*, and Spinoza's account of the Jewish state is heavily influenced by him.[8]

---

[7] Josephus's most important are *The Jewish War* that provides an account of the Jewish revolt against the Romans in 66 to 70 A.D., an event that Josephus witnessed; *Jewish Antiquities* expounds on Jewish history and customs all the way from creation to the time of the book's composition; and, *Against Apion* that adumbrates a defense of Judaism.

[8] Omero Proietti has done a remarkable job in creating a matrix of classical references in Spinoza's work in Priorretti, "'Adulescens luxu perditus'", 210 – 257. It is a pity that Josephus is not included in this list, as he does not strictly qualify as a "classical" author. It seems to me that the influence of Josephus is just as, if not more, important than the classical authors in the *Theological Political Treatise*. It would be a worthwhile exercise, for instance, to trace the influences of *Jewish Antiquities* on Spinoza's account of the Hebrew state.

The impact of Josephus and the rise of so-called "Josephism" in the sixteenth and seventeenth centuries has a number of parameters.[9] These provide a significant background to chapters 17 and 18, especially about how the state is governed after the death of Moses. I offer here a schematic typology of these issues.

1.1 The Hebrew republic as a special case of a political regime

First, Josephus's impact can be discerned in the context of the rise of Biblical hermeneutics in the aftermath of the Reformation. To support the principle of *sola Scriptura*, or the authority of the text of the Bible itself as opposed to the personal authority of the Pontiff to interpret the Bible, Protestant theologians start to develop interpretative methodologies. In this context, the discovery of Josephus's text is hugely important. These books are the only detailed source of the culture, history and customs of the Jews written from a Jewish eye-witness and from the time in which Christ lived and the New Testament was composed, and thus become in the sixteenth and seventeenth centuries the most important sources of the study of the cultural milieu of the Bible.

Second, Josephus's writings also have a profound influence on political philosophy from the sixteenth century onward. This influence is due to the fact that they overturn a dominant orthodoxy in political philosophy at least since the time of Plato and Aristotle, namely, that there are three constitutional forms: monarchy, aristocracy and democracy. The distinction between them is quantitative. In monarchy there is one ruler, in aristocracy a few, and in democracy many – a distinction that the Greek names of these constitutional forms clearly describe.[10] A large body of literature develops all through antiquity and the Middle Ages departing from this distinction between three pure constitutional forms, and the distinction between the three pure forms remains the basis of any philosophical or political discussion of constitutional forms.[11]

This orthodoxy is further adumbrated in early modernity due to the rediscovery of Polybius's *Histories*. According to Book 6 of Polybius's *Histories*, the three constitutions conform to a natural cycle of mutation. None of them is absolute, but all are liable to decay, ceding their place to one of the others. Polybius ex-

---

9 On Josephism and Spinoza, see Abolafia, "Spinoza, Josephism", 295–316.
10 See for instance Aristotle, *Politics*.
11 See von Fritz, *The Theory of the Mixed Constitution in Antiquity*.

presses this under the concept of *anakyklosis*, the revolution or rotation of constitutions.¹² This provides a dynamic account of the movement between constitutions that also gives political philosophy concerned with constitutional forms the opportunity to develop a historical account explaining the transmutation of political regimes.¹³

Josephus acknowledges this tradition when he writes that "some peoples have entrusted the supreme political power to monarchies, others to oligarchies, yet others to the masses." But he immediately adds: "Our lawgiver, however, was attracted by none of these forms of polity, but gave to his constitution the form of what – if a forced expression be permitted – may be termed a 'theocracy,' placing all sovereignty and authority in the hands of God."¹⁴ It is this sentence that for the first time introduces the word theocracy. Josephus constructs his neologism by echoing other similar compounds like democracy and aristocracy. But there is a significant difference from the other constitutions identified by classical Greek political thought, namely, that in the Hebrew state God himself is the sovereign. This idea breaks the shackles of the orthodoxy about the three pure constitutional forms and has a liberating effect on political philosophy.

Third, Josephus's designation of theocracy makes the Hebrew republic into a special case of a political regime that was unique and unrepeatable, thereby elevating it to a significant example in political philosophy. During the sixteenth and seventeenth centuries, philosophers consistently refer to the Hebrew state as a way of displacing politically sensitive discussions to a relatively neutral territory – to an example situated in a remote past and beyond reproach as it is a polity of divine rule. This is the case, for instance, with the use of the Hebrew state in Grotius' *De republica emendanda*. Grotius uses the Hebrew state in order to compare it to the Dutch republic.¹⁵ In general, the Hebrew republic becomes a consistent point of reference or an important example in all significant political philosophers of the seventeenth century, including Hobbes and Locke.

1.2 Obedience

The key in this tradition is that political points can be made about the theocracy of the Hebrew state that have a direct relevance for contemporary politics, but

---

12 See Polybius, *The Histories*.
13 It is interesting to consider here the similarities between the biological metaphors of *anakyklosis* in Polybius and auto-immunity in Derrida. See Vardoulakis, "Autoimmunities", 29–56.
14 Josephus, *Against Apion*.
15 See Grotius, "De republica emendanda", 66–121.

which cannot be raised explicitly without fear of offending the theological or political authorities. The *Theological Political Treatise* participates in this tradition of using the Hebrew state as an example. The Hebrew state is – in the schema I outlined above – Spinoza's paradigmatic state that relies on obedience and the path of the emotions leading to virtue. At the same time, it is noteworthy that the last thing Spinoza mentions before he concludes his discussion of the Hebrew sate at the end of chapter 18 is a comparison with the Dutch republic. The estates of Holland, just like the Hebrew theocracy, never had mortal kings, notes Spinoza (210–211), which provided a legitimation for their opposition to Spanish rule. There is an anti-monarchical and anti-authoritarian thrust here.

Fourth, this anti-authoritarian use of the Hebrew state develops in the sixteenth and seventeenth centuries. As Eric Nelson has recently shown, republican authors who were concerned to argue for freedom from coercion, and hence were anti-monarchists, used the idea of theocracy to argue against monarchy.[16] Of particular importance for their argument was the interpretation of *I Samuel 8* by Josephus as well as in Biblical commentaries in Hebrew, according to which God was the sovereign of the Hebrew republic until the people asked Samuel for a mortal sovereign, just as any other nation (*I Sam.* 8.5). In other words, they did not wish to have God as their sovereign any longer. Samuel, as the high priest, consulted with God, who responded by enumerating the evils that a mortal king will bring upon the Hebrews: a king will exploit their sons and daughters, and he will take ownership of the land, the slaves and stock. The inference drawn by the republicans was that this response indicates monarchy as equivalent to the sin of idolatry – since ultimately God will abandon the state with a mortal sovereign (*I Samuel* 8.11–18). This strong anti-authoritarian thrust derived from the tradition is critical to Spinoza's determination of theocracy and the Hebrew state.[17]

To recapitulate, we can discern four distinct uses of theocracy as it enters the vocabulary of thought in the sixteenth century and further develops in the following century. First, the discovery of Josephus's works contributes to the development of Biblical hermeneutics. Second, the Hebrew state becomes a favored example in political philosophy to challenge and complicate the doctrine of the three constitutions. Third, political philosophers use the Hebrew state as a foil to talk about their present political predicament. And, fourth, the growing

---

[16] See Nelson, *Hebrew Republic*, chapter 1.
[17] See Vardoulakis, *Spinoza, the Epicurean*. The argument I put forward there is that Spinoza always contrasts authority with a kind of practical judgment that is responsible for his democratic politics. I refrain from presenting this part of the argument in the present paper.

anti-monarchical movement utilizes the Hebrew republic to argue against authoritarianism. Within this context of theocracy, we can read Spinoza's description of the Hebrew state as paradigmatic of obedience, that is, as a state where mastery persists even after the death of *the* master.

2 Between Tyranny and Revolution: The Limits of the Hebrew State

Spinoza first mentions that the Hebrew state is a theocracy in the sense that it combines civil and religious law (189), and then he returns to the theocratic nature of the Hebrew state when he considers whether it remains a theocracy after the death of Moses (194–95). Spinoza insists that it does remain a theocracy but with a difference. Whereas Moses encompasses both theological and political authority, his succession planning consists in fracturing the theological and the political. Theological authority resides only with the priests taken from a single tribe, the Levites – a crucial point that I will return to in the next section – whereas political authority is divided between the captains of each tribe who are allocated a specific land.

Within the context of the discussion of these arrangements about the distribution of authority after Moses's death, Spinoza determines the limits of the Hebrew state according to "how far a constitution framed on these lines [i.e. the theocracy of the Hebrew state after Moses's death] was able to exercise control over the minds of subjects and *to so restrain both rulers and ruled* that neither would the latter rebel nor the former become tyrants" (195, emphasis added). This provides the new frame for the question of obedience. It consists in the mutual delimitation of rulers and ruled. The limits of the state are established to avoid these two perils – two perils ingrained in the possibility of a state based on obedience.

2.1 Spinoza on ideological state apparatuses

This mutual delimitation between rulers and ruled is not a novel idea in Spinoza. As Stathis Gourgouris argues, the mutual delimitation of ruler and ruled, or *archon* and *archomenos*, is critical for Aristotle and it is clearly stated in his *Politics*.[18] But from this we do not need to conclude, following Gourgouris, that such a mu-

---

[18] Bernstein, Ophir and Stoler, eds., *Political Concepts*, s.v. "Arche" (Stathis Gourgouris).

tual delimitation leads to an anarchic politics. To the contrary, as I have explained above, the thrust of Spinoza's complex relation between rulers and ruled is to frame the question of obedience in such a way so that its origins are untethered from personal authority. This does not obviate the need for obedience, it does not lead to an anarchic position. Rather, it establishes a framework within which it becomes possible to subject authority to the scrutiny of practical judgment – which is to say, it becomes possible to be critical of authority. This is the reason why Spinoza suggests, as I will explain, a distinction within mastery, between what I call the state of authority and authoritarianism.

The mutual delimitation of rulers and ruled within the Hebrew state as the exemplary state of authority that relies on obedience articulates into a series of complex and interconnected concerns in chapter 17. These are often particularly resonant with concerns in contemporary political philosophy. I identify here four such concerns:

First, the Hebrew state presents obedience as an inchoate materialist theory of ideology as the primary means of the exercise of its mastery. Spinoza notes that the power of a state such as the Hebrew one is "not strictly confined to its power of coercion by fear, but rests on all the possible means by which it can induce men to obey its commands. It is not the rationale for obeying, but obedience that makes the subject [*non enim ratio obtemperandi, sed obtemperantia subditum facit*]" (185/201–02). Obedience is not concerned with why people obey. The key to a well-functioning authority is to avoid demanding obedience through threats that instill fear. In a passage that recalls Machiavelli, Spinoza further specifies that the reasons for obedience are secondary if not irrelevant – they can be, says Spinoza almost flippantly, "fear of punishment, hope of reward, love of country or any other emotion [*affectu*]" (186/202). All that matters are the effects that follow from obedience.[19]

It is not hard to discern here a theory of ideology *in nuce:* "From the fact, then, that a man acts from his own decision, we should not forthwith conclude that his action proceeds from his own right, and not from the right of the government [*ex suo, et non imperii jure*]." The reason is that "obedience is not so much a matter of outward action as of the internal acts of the mind [*obedientia non tam externam, quam animi internam actionem*]." And this means that "whoever reigns over the subjects' minds holds the most powerful dominion [*maximum tenere imperium*]" (186/202). We see here the appeal that Spinoza exercised on theorists of ideology in the twentieth century, starting with Althusser and

---

[19] On the importance of Machiavelli for the *Theological Political Treatise*, see Morfino, "Memory, Chance and Conflict", 7–26.

many thinkers subsequently.[20] Ideology is the reproduction of the existing network of power without the need for physical coercion, simply through the control of the minds of the subject.

We see at this point the radical materialism that characterizes Spinoza's philosophy. The subject cannot rise above the given circumstances to assert a "free will" that liberates it from materiality. Nor can the rulers assert their power arbitrarily through their own sovereign decisions. Both ruled and rulers are dependent on the fact of obedience. Differently put, what matters are not the intentions of political actors but the effects of their actions. These effects enable the maximum obedience when people are not coerced through violent means but when their minds are controlled, which is to say, when they believe that they are exercising their free will whereas in fact their actions conform to what those in authority want them to do. That is why, Foucault insists, the free will is a key pillar of neoliberalism.[21] There is no more effective tool for the implementation of obedience than the illusion of free will.[22]

2.2 Obedience via authority not authoritarianism

This suggests that for identifying the limits of the political – the imperative to avoid both rebellion and tyranny – it is crucial to avoid a voluntaristic account of action. Let me underscore this point, as it suggests also a difference from theories of ideology such as Althusser's or theories of power such as Foucault's. Spinoza does not reject authority as such. Rather, he draws a distinction between authority and authoritarianism. If authority can instill obedience that can contribute to the well-being of subjects, authoritarianism seeks to use the subjects' free will to turn them into voluntary slaves so as to "pursue their servitude as if they are striving for their salvation," according to the famous phrase from the Preface (7). At the same time, it is precisely this distinction between authority and authoritarianism that is missing in Althusser and Foucault. Concepts such as the "system" supported by ideology or power incorporate both senses of authority. The effect of this is that neither Althusser nor Foucault have recourse to a discourse about democratic politics.

This materialist presentation of ideology does not lapse into a functionalism according to which we are simply trapped within the apparatuses of power. Spi-

---

20 See Estop, "Beyond Legitimacy", 87–111.
21 See Foucault, *Birth of Biopolitics*.
22 It is well-known that Spinoza is critical of the free will, a point that he tackles directly in Part II of the *Ethics*.

noza does not entrain such an idea in chapter 17. Instead the framework persists on the relation of rulers and ruled that leads to the following problematic: it is unclear what the means for effecting obedience are if "both rulers and ruled, are but human, and as such certainly prone to forsake labor for pleasure [*omnes namque tam qui regunt, quam qui reguntur, homines sunt ex labore scilicet proclives ad libidinem*]" (187/203). It is important that the question of obedience is not confined to the people but extends to the rulers too. Humans – both rulers and ruled – fall victim to bad judgments because of the fact that they can be swayed by their emotions. Thus, the "fact of obedience" is always a negotiation between rulers and ruled, to the point that the control of the people's minds is only possible if their desires also dictate the desires and decisions of the rulers. Obedience indicates a reciprocal influence between authority and its subjects.

At the same time, the significance – even necessity – of obedience and mastery is indicated by the fact that the "fickle disposition of the multitude [*tantum varium multitudinis ingenium*]" drives those who consider politics to "despair" (187/203). The people are swayed by this or that emotion and they forget to calmly calculate their utility. It is this fact that makes the state of authority necessary. But recognizing the problem is not the same as fixing it. A solution to the conundrum of how to make the fickle multitude obey, "this is the task, this the toil [*hoc opus, hic labor*]" (187/203), says Spinoza.[23]

2.3 Authority requires the support of the theological

It is noteworthy what Spinoza suggests that historically has been taken as the solution to this problem: "kings who in ancient times seized power, tried to persuade men that they were descended from the immortal Gods [*se genus suum a Diis immortalibus*], thinking that if only their subjects and all men should regard them not as their equals but should believe them to be Gods, they would willingly suffer their rule and would readily obey" (188/204). Political authority is insufficient on its own. Authority also requires the support of the theological – be that through ancestry or through revelation. This is the ploy, for instance, that Alexander the Great employs, claiming that he was the son of Jupiter. Considering an episode from Curtius, Spinoza notes Alexander's response when his blood ties to Jupiter were challenged by Hermolaus. Alexander responded that "public opinion [*fama*] is an important factor, and a false belief has often done duty for truth [*quod falso creditum est, veri vicem obtinuit*]" (188/204). Alexander is aware

---

[23] This expression is a quotation from Vergil's *Aeneid* (6:129).

here that it is not the motives of obedience that matter but rather the fact of obedience itself. Further, he is aware that for obedience to be effective, authority requires both a political and a theological origin. A functional mastery is theologico-political irrespective of whether the effects arises from true causes. All that matters is the public perception (*fama*) of its theological provenance. To put it in the vocabulary from Machiavelli, what matters for authority is not its veracity but its "effective truth."

Second, clearly, this ideological dimension is insufficient to guarantee that there is no rebellion of the ruled. What is needed in addition is an account of how such a theocracy achieves social and political cohesion. This steers Spinoza's argument about the theocratic coincidence of religious and civil law into a direction that resonates with contemporary accounts of biopolitics.

2.4 The coincidence of religious and civil law

After insisting that the Hebrew state served the utility of the people, Spinoza offers the following remark: "Thus the Hebrew citizens could enjoy a good life [*bene esse poterat*] only in their own country; abroad they could expect only hurt and humiliation" (199/216). There are various elements to this attachment to the Hebrew state enjoyed by its citizens, but they all point to its usefulness "in avoiding civil war" (199). The most significant reason that this is the case is that in such a theocracy civil and religious laws overlap. As such, the law spreads into every aspect of living. The positive side of this is that people feel that their utility is fulfilled by the state. The other side is that they can only achieve this utility within the Hebrew state and by adherence to the state religion. Thus "one who forsook his religion ceased to be a citizen [*civis*] and by that alone became an enemy [*hostis*]" (189/206). This attachment to land and its religious way of life that is identical with civil life is the reason that the Hebrews enjoy "an ardent patriotism" that was "fostered by their daily rituals" determined by law (197). The well-being they enjoyed as a result of following all these laws meant that "their life was one long habituation obedience [*vita continuus obedientiae cultus*]" but because of the benefits they derived, "obedience must have appeared no longer as bondage, but freedom [*non amplius servitus, sed libertas*]" (199/216). Thus, theocracy creates the conditions of a happy life by an expanded system of laws and regulations that dictate every aspect of living in the Hebrew state.

The coincidence of civil and religious law that every citizen ought to adhere prevents movement outside the state: "it was regarded as utterly disgraceful [*flagitio*] even to live outside the state [*extra patriam tantum habitatum*], for the religious rites which it was their constant duty to practice could be performed only on their native soil [*non nisi in patrio solo exerceri*]" (197/214). Simultaneously this imposes a limit to the punishment that the state can deliver: "no citizen was condemned to exile [*nullus civis ... exilii damnabatur*]; for the wrongdoer does indeed deserve to be punished, but not to be disgraced [*flagitio*]" (197/215). Leaving the state, either voluntarily or as a form of punishment, is disgraceful and an outrage because it forces those migrating or being exiled to break the link between civil law and religion that defines them as Hebrews.

The coincidence of religious and civil law of the Hebrew theocracy such as to encompass every aspect of the life of the citizens resonates with what has come to be called in the twentieth century "biopolitical power." In the famous lecture in which Foucault introduces the term biopolitics, he contrasts it with classical sovereign power. Whereas sovereignty is characterized by the prerogative of life and death, that is, by the exercise of power so as to punish anyone who opposes constituted power, biopolitics is characterized by the control and normalization of life. The effect of this move is that power is now distributed across the entire population and it appears as if it has no outside since it regulates every facet of life.[24] Foucault could have used Spinoza's account of the coincidence of civil and religious law to illustrate his point, namely, that the Hebrew religion regulated actions such as when the Hebrews could plough or sow the land, or which days they will rest (199). The effect of this in both Foucault's and Spinoza's analyses is that the state encroaches upon every facet of life, whereby nothing outside the state is conceivable – which is another way of saying that the possibility of rebellion is eradicated.

2.5 From master to mastery

This confluence of what Spinoza calls theocracy and what Foucault calls biopolitics is significant on many levels. From an historical perspective, it suggests that biopolitics is not simply the latest expression of power, but rather a form – for Spinoza, the exemplary form – of power relying on obedience that can be contemporaneous and exists in parallel, even supporting in certain circumstances, other forms of power.[25] From the perspective of the discourse on political theology that has flourished in the past few decades, this suggests that there is no contradiction or incompatibility between the decisionism character-

---

[24] See the last lecture of Foucault's *Society Must be Defended*.
[25] I discuss this point at length in chapter 5 of my *Sovereignty and its Other*.

istic of the sovereign in those political theologies that depart from Carl Schmitt, and the biopolitical theories following in Foucault's footsteps. Rather, Spinoza's analysis of obedience entails that what underlies them both is the operative presence of authority, albeit articulated in different ways. The personal authority of the sovereign requires a genetic account of sovereignty – that is, the question of how the decisions of the figure of authority lead to obedience – whereas the biopolitical account relies on the confluence of theological and political norms so as to expand the field of regulation to the entire field of living – this is the transition from the master to mastery. The insight of the seventeenth century political philosophers that theocracy can be just as relevant to their day holds equally true for us today. I return to this idea at the end.

The Hebrew theocracy has an additional effect, namely, it promotes one particular affect over every other. That affect is hatred – in fact, a double hatred. The Hebrews come to hate others because "their daily worship was not merely quite different, making them altogether unique and completely different from other peoples [*diversus omnino erat*], but also absolutely opposed [*absolute contrarius*] to others. Hence this daily invective, as it were, was bound to engender a lasting hatred [*continuum odium*]" (197–98/215). But the insularity of the Hebrews also provoked the hatred of others toward the Hebrews: "this [i.e. the hatred] was reinforced by the universal cause of the continuous growth of hatred, to wit, the reciprocation [*reciprocatio*] of hatred; for the other nations inevitably held them in bitter hatred in return [*contra odio infensissimo*]" (198/215). Their self-perception of their uniqueness made them hate others and others to hate them back. Thus, the coincidence of religious and civil law may allow for desire to be sublimated in the law and thereby avoid the prospect of rebellion. But the price that the Hebrews pay for their entirely singular society is insularity and the rise of the affect peculiar to it, namely, hatred. The harnessing of hatred in the obedience of the theologico-political law finds an outlet in a single, emotion, hatred, that functions as a *pharmakon*, both protecting the state and infecting it from the inside threatening its very existence.

The coincidence of religious and civil law – the chief characteristic of theocracy – protects the Hebrew state from its own people rebelling against it. This protection from rebellion arises from the unique institution of the Hebrew state – or, at least, unique insofar as one accepts that God was its sovereign, since it is not as unique if the expansion of the law is viewed in biopolitical terms. It provides a cohesive body of citizens who are patriotic and supportive of the state.

Third, the protection from tyranny – that is, the limit on the rulers – is determined by one main characteristic that the Hebrew state shares with other states, namely, the fact that the most powerful entity in a polity is the people. Spinoza repeats this point four times in chapter 17, the first three as a general point not specific to any state, and the last one being explicitly associated with the limitations on the political leaders of the Hebrew state.

The first time the point is raised is at the beginning of the chapter:

> "This is shown I think, quite clearly by actual experience [*ipsam etiam experientiam*]; for men have never transferred their right and surrendered their power to another so completely that they were not feared by those very persons who received their right and power, and that the government has not been in greater danger from its citizens [*propter cives*], though deprived of their right, than from its external enemies [*propter hostes*]" (185/201).

The fact that the most political power rests with the people who are the most fearful entity for the rulers asserts the impossibility of establishing a secure tyranny. This is a point of view that we can find in Machiavelli's *Prince* too, where the sovereign is given license to do anything to perpetuate power except provoke the hatred and resentment of the people.[26]

In the next few pages, Spinoza compulsively returns to the idea that the people are the entity with the most power in a polity. It is used here to assert the limits of the power of the rulers, to show that their power can never be absolute: "there can never be any state so mighty that those in command would have unlimited power to do anything they wish [*potentiam absolute ad omnia, quae velint, habeant*]" (186/203). The reason is that "if the strongest dominion [*maximum tenerent imperium*] were held by those who are most feared [*maxime timentur*], then it would assuredly be held by tyrants' subjects [*tyrannorum subditi*], for they are most feared by their tyrants" (186/202). Thus, it is the threat of rebellion when the rulers do not satisfy the utility of the ruled that prevents tyranny: "the position has never been attained where the state [*imperium*] was not in greater danger from its citizens [*propter cives*] than from the external enemy [*hostes*], and where its rulers were not in greater fear of the citizens than the enemies" (187/204–05). The same point was raised in the course of the discussion of what the limits to the power of the captains of the Hebrew state were (196). Essentially, this solution to the limits of the state's and the sovereign's power due to its delimitation by the superior power of the people is the articulation of the final point about Josephism that I raised at the end of the previous section, namely, that is, its anti-authoritarianism.

It is noteworthy that this idea is not confined to the *Theological Political Treatise*; rather, it is stated as a principle in the *Political Treatise* (e.g. 6.6) and it becomes the motor of the argument. For instance, drawing on the same argument when he talks about monarchy in the *Political Treatise*, Spinoza infers that

---

26 Machiavelli, *Prince*.

"the king's sword or right [*regis gladius,·sive jus*] is in reality the will of the multitude itself or of its stronger part [*ipsius multitudinis, sive validioris ejus partis voluntas*]" (7.25). Spinoza's democratic politics is indebted to this idea – but I am not discussing this topic in the present context.

To recapitulate, the Hebrew theocracy shows how it is necessary to have a reciprocal sense of obedience that delimits the power of both the rulers and the ruled. First, this is possible on condition that obedience is not coercive but rather is exercised over the minds of the people, which is best effected by the combination of the theological and the political sides of authority. Second, the coincidence of religious and civil law protects the community from internal rebellion. In a description that recalls the biopolitical normalization of the population, Spinoza explains how this creates a cohesive citizenry. And, third, the community is protected from the specter of tyranny due to the fact that the most powerful element in any polity are the people. This is the framework of obedience that sustains the theocratic state after the death of Moses.

3 The Fragmentation of the Theologico-Political: On the Reasons for the Destruction of the Hebrew State

If what makes the Hebrew state a model polity relying on obedience, then why – ponders Spinoza – do the Hebrew so often forsake the law (200)? With this question, Spinoza introduces the reasons for the dissolution of the Hebrew state. The dissolution of the Hebrew state ultimately has one main cause that produces a multiplicity of detrimental effects: the cause is the splintering of the theological and the political sides of mastery. To understand this cause, we need to pay attention to how Spinoza describes the formation of the Hebrew state.

Initially, the social contract or *pactum* that established the theocratic state "left everyone completely equal [*hoc pacto aequales prorsus mansisse*]" (190/ 206). But when the Hebrews consult with God for the first time, they are terrified by his voice. In this state of being "overwhelmed with fear" (190), they turn to Moses asking him to represent them to God. This creates Moses's authority. Spinoza identifies a primary cause for the destruction of the Hebrew state that is related to how Moses planned for his succession or for how authority was distributed after his death:

> "In order that we may rightly understand ... the cause of the destruction of the [Hebrew] state [*causa vastationis imperii*], we should observe that it had first been intended to entrust

the entire ministry of religion to the firstborn, not to the Levites (Num. ch. 8 v. 17); but when all except the Levites had worshipped the calf, the firstborn were rejected and defiled [*repudiati et impurati*], and the Levites were chosen in their place [*Levitae eorum loco electi*] (Deut. ch. 1 0 v. 8)" (200/218).

Why does Spinoza place so much import on this fact?

3.1 Fragmenting authority – Israel and the Netherlands

After the establishment of the state, Moses recognizes that if someone is simply to replace him through whatever means – for instance, if the leadership of the Jews were to be inherited – then "the state would have become simply a monarchy" (191). According to Spinoza, Moses tries to maintain the theocratic nature of the state by fragmenting authority between its theological and its political components. The Levites are chosen as the priests. They are entrusted with the administration of the temple and they are charged to communicate with God, but they are deprived of any land ownership (191). The land is divided between the other twelve tribes establishing a confederation – Spinoza adds that it is similar to the confederation of the Estates of the Netherlands – while each tribe retains relative autonomy and has a captain to lead the tribe politically (192–94). The tribes and their captains live autonomously, and do not interfere with each other's affairs. This fragmentation of authority is successful to the extent that when Moses died the Hebrew state – emphasizes Spinoza – "was left neither a monarchy nor an aristocracy nor a democracy, but a ... a theocracy" (194–95).

We should pay attention to one crucial detail of this split of the theologico-political instituted by Moses that makes it incommensurable with the idea of a secular separation between ecclesiastical and temporal powers. The Levites – that is, the priests – are made solely responsible for the interpretation of the law (195). The Hebrew theocracy places the law in the hands of the priests, which is necessary, if the coincidence of religious and civil law – that is, theocracy – is to persist. The fragmented authority that places the law in the hands of the priests is the critical feature that makes the Hebrew state both unique and inimitable, according to Spinoza.

Keeping in mind the critical role of the split between the theological and political, let us return to Spinoza's biblical sources. After the Hebrews ask Moses to be their representative to God because of their fear, Moses climbs Mount Sinai to receive the law. While wandering for forty days, the Hebrews despair at this absence and turn to the veneration of an idol, the Golden Calf. Upon his return, Moses is outraged at the sight of this idolatry. Here is how Moses's reaction to the veneration of the golden calf is described – quoted here in the *King James* translation:

> "Then Moses stood in the gate of the camp, and said, Who is on the Lord's side? [let him come] unto me. And all the sons of Levi gathered themselves together unto him. And he said unto them, Thus saith the Lord God of Israel, Put every man his sword by his side, and go in and out from gate to gate throughout the camp, and slay every man his brother, and every man his companion, and every man his neighbour. And the children of Levi did according to the word of Moses: and there fell of the people that day about three thousand men" (*Exodus* 32:26–28).

We see here the reason why the Levites are chosen as priests – they are the only ones who are not defiled by venerating false idols.

3.2 The Levites as instruments of Moses' political authority

This passage from the *Exodus* describing the descent from Mount Sinai is a famous passage with political philosophers in early modernity but Spinoza himself never explicitly mentions this violence. The closest he comes is his reference to the Levites becoming the priest of the Hebrew state, which can only be understood if the reader knows the biblical passage from the *Exodus* I cited above. This passage is nonetheless critical to understand why authority is fragmented between the Levites and the captains of the rest of the tribes – the key point about mastery in the Hebrew theocracy after Moses. What it is that Spinoza never explicitly cites but to which he heavily alludes is that the Levites achieve their theological authority – their religious purity by refusing to venerate the calf – through the same sequence that puts the sword in their hands to execute the sovereign prerogative of life and death, that is, the punishment against those who defiled God. The first assertion of their authority is a political one – it is the violence of execution that is foundational for the Hebrew state. Thus, their theological (and legal) authority after the death of Moses is tainted with the political from the very beginning, even before the Hebrew state is founded, through this act of violence that they justifiably execute as representatives of political authority. To put it in the visual metaphorics of the frontispiece from the *Leviathan*: they can hold the crosier because they initially held the sword. Their *theological* authority is steeped in blood because initially they were instruments of Moses's *political* authority. The Levites are first representatives of political authority, they become representatives of theological authority only as a result of being representatives of political authority by carrying out Moses's order for the massacre. Thus, the fragmentation of authority pursued by Moses to secure the Hebrew state as a theocracy after his death is doomed to failure because – suggests Spinoza – there is no such thing as an unalloyed theological or a purely political authority.

All the various secondary causes for the destruction of the Hebrew state that Spinoza identifies refer back to this impurity of the theological and the political components in the Hebrew theocracy since Moses's death. The most significant one is that the citizens of the state viewed the priestly tribe as "a constant reminder of their [i.e., the other tribes'] defilement and rejection [*continuo suae impuritatis, et repudiationis arguebant*]" (201/218). The Levites are a constant reminder of the defilement and rejection that the rest of the tribes suffer by venerating the Golden Calf – as well as of the *political* fate of those who were executed by the Levites as a result. This is compounded by other factors, such as the resentment arising from having to provide for the priests, or from the fact that the priests did not hesitate in rebuking the other tribes when they thought that their actions did not conform with the law as they interpreted it.

3.3 A state within the state

This is further compounded by the animosity between the captains and the priests. The animosity between the political and the theological authorities of the Hebrew state was due to the fact that the political authorities, notes Spinoza, felt that it was intolerable for the Levites to be the interpreters of the law, as this created a "state within a state" (202, 203). All these factors gradually erode the notion of authority underlying the Hebrew state from the inside. And with the diminished belief in the value of the separation between the theological authority of the Levites and the political authority of the captains comes the questioning of the value of the theocratic constitution that is based on this fragmentation.

The result is the request of the Jewish people to have a mortal king. This is the reference to *1 Samuel* 8 where the Jews ask the high priest to request that they obtain a mortal king, as opposed to having God as their sovereign. As I mention in the first section of the present chapter, this is a prominent reference to support anti-authoritarian sentiments. Spinoza never cites explicitly this request, made in *1 Samuel* 8:4–5. But Spinoza mentions this request repeatedly, once in chapter 17 (202) and four more times in chapter 18 (twice on 207, 208, and 209). Neither does Spinoza cite explicitly God's response enumerating the evils that follow from monarchy and which was, as I mentioned, so important for the anti-monarchical movements of the sixteenth and seventeenth centuries that referred to the Hebrew state as a way of talking about their contemporary political situation. But Spinoza's brief references to the transition from theocracy to monarchy

– such as the incredible bloodshed and internecine war that it precipitated (207) – leave the reader in no doubt of the catastrophic consequences that followed. Spinoza describes the re-founded Hebrew state as a mere shadow of its former self and refrains from describing in detail its structure. This is consistent with his sharp distinction between authority and authoritarianism. Spinoza participates in the anti-monarchical tradition that characterizes the use of Josephus.

3.4 The end of theocracy

It is instructive to note the way in which the Hebrew theocracy gradually dissolves because of the mutation of mastery. Originally, authority is deferred to God and everyone is equal. Soon, however, authority is transferred to Moses, who subsequently splits authority into a theological component enjoyed by the Levites and a political component attributed to the captains. This fragmentation is meant to safeguard theocracy from monarchy, but it is impure from the beginning – it is contaminated by the exercise of political authority by the Levites in the process of carrying out Moses's order for punishment against those who venerated the golden calf. That which is meant to protect the theocracy – the fragmentation of power – contaminates the Hebrew state from within, like an autoimmune disease, leading to the eventual dissolution of theocracy into a monarchy.

As if this is not bad enough, Spinoza notes a final and most pernicious turn in this unfortunate sequence that has led from authority to authoritarianism. This consists in the eventual usurpation of *political* power by the priests, which results in tyranny. In language steeped in contempt, Spinoza describes the "pontifical authority [*pontificali authoritate*]" (206/222) that the priest sought to obtain as well as their hubris of pretending to emulate the theologico-political authority of Moses. This corruption of the political field is best encapsulated in what I call elsewhere the "ruse of sovereignty."[27] This is the idea that there is nothing outside such an authoritarian rule, whereby the only possibility of political change consists in the substitution of one authoritarian rule with another. Spinoza repeats this point three times, once in chapter 17 and twice in chapter 18. Thus, he describes how the change of those in control of political authority does not change the nature of their authoritarianism: "they merely succeeded in installing a new tyrant" (203). The second reference draws attention to the state of a people accustomed to obey too much, whereby "on removing one king, it

---

27 Vardoulakis, *Stasis Before the State*.

will find it necessary to appoint another in his place" (209). And the third instance describes the logic of the substitution of one monarch with another: If the causes of tyranny are not addressed, warns Spinoza, "a people has often succeeded in changing tyrants, but never in abolishing tyranny or substituting another form of government for monarchy" (210). This discourse shows the disintegration of theocracy into authoritarianism as a direct result of the splintering of theological and political authority.

Bibliography

Abolafia, Jacob. "Spinoza, Josephism and the Critique of the Hebrew Republic," *History of Political Thought* 35, no. 2 (2014): 295–316.
Arendt, Hannah. "What is Authority?," In *Between Past and Future: Six Exercises in Political Thought*, Hannah Arendt. New York: The Viking Press, 1961.
Aristotle. *Politics*, trans. H. Rackham. Cambridge, MA: Harvard University Press, 1998.
Bernstein, Jay, Ophir, Adi, and Stoler, Ann Laura, eds., *Political Concepts: A Critical Lexicon*. New York: Fordham University Press, 2018.
Dumézil, Georges. *Mitra-Varuna: An Essay on Two Indo-European Representations of Sovereignty*, trans. Derek Coltman. New York: Zone Books, 1988.
Estop, Juan Domingo Sanchez. "Beyond Legitimacy: The State as an Imaginary Entity in Spinoza's Political Ontology," In *Spinoza's Authority*, vol. 1, *Resistance and Power in the Ethics*, ed. by Kiarina Kordela and Dimitris Vardoulakis, 87–112. London: Bloomsbury, 2018.
Foucault, Michel. *Society Must be Defended: Lectures at the Collège de France 1975–76*, ed. Arnold I. Davidson, trans. David Macey. New York: Picador, 2003.
Foucault, Michel. *The Birth of Biopolitics: Lectures at the Collège de France 1978–79*, ed. Michel Senellart, trans. Graham Burchell. New York: Palgrave Macmillan, 2008.
von Fritz, Kurt. *The Theory of the Mixed Constitution in Antiquity: A Critical Analysis of Polybius' Political Ideas*. New York: Columbia University Press, 1954.
Gebhardt, Carl, ed., *Opera*. Heidelberg: Carl Windters Universitätsbuchhandlung, 1924.
Grotius, Hugo. "De republica emendanda: On the Emendation of the Dutch Polity," *Grotiana* 5 (1984): 66–121.
Josephus, Flavius. *Against Apion*, trans. Henry St. J. Thackeray. Cambridge, MA: Harvard University Press, 1926.
Kojève, Alexandre. *The Notion of Authority: A Brief Presentation*, ed. François Terré, trans. Hager Weslati. London: Verso, 2014.
Machiavelli, Niccolò. *The Prince*, ed. Quentin Skinner and Russell Price. Cambridge: Cambridge University Press, 1988.
Marcuse, Herbert. "A Study on Authority," In *Studies in Critical Philosophy*, trans. Joris de Bres. Boston: Beacon Press, 1973.
Morfino, Vittorio. "Memory, Chance and Conflict: Machiavelli in the *Theologico-Political Treatise*," In *Spinoza's Authority*, vol. 2, *The Treatises*, ed. by Kiarina Kordela and Dimitris Vardoulakis, 7–26. London: Bloomsbury, 2018.

Nelson, Eric. *The Hebrew Republic: Jewish Sources and the Transformation of European Political Thought*. Cambridge, MA: Harvard University Press, 2010.
Polybius, *The Histories*, trans. William R. Paton, 6 vols. Cambridge, MA: Harvard University Press, 2010–2012.
Proietti, Omero. "'Adulescens luxu perditus': Classici latini nell'opera di Spinoza," *Rivista di Filosofia Neo-Scolastica* 77, no. 2 (1985): 210–257.
Ricœur, Paul. "The Paradox of Authority," In *Reflections on the Just*, von Paul Ricœur, trans. David Pellauer. Chicago: Chicago University Press, 2007.
Sennett, Richard. *Authority*. New York: W.W. Norton, 1980.
Spinoza, Benedictus de. *Theological Political Treatise*, trans. Samuel Shirley, 2nd ed. Indianapolis: Hackett, 2001.
Vardoulakis, Dimitris. *Sovereignty and its Other: Toward the Dejustification of Violence*. New York: Fordham University Press, 2013.
Vardoulakis, Dimitris. "Autoimmunities: Derrida, Democracy and Political Theology," *Research in Phenomenology* 48 (2018): 29–56.
Vardoulakis, Dimitris. *Stasis Before the State: Nine Theses in Agonistic Democracy*. New York: Fordham University Press, 2018.
Vardoulakis, Dimitris. "The Figure of Moses: The Origins of Authority in Spinoza," *Textual Practice* 33, no. 5 (2019): 771–785.
Vardoulakis, Dimitris. *Spinoza, the Epicurean: Authority and Utility in Materialism*. Edinburgh: Edinburgh University Press, 2020.

Günter Thomas
Enmity as Cast Shadow of Love
Conjectures on Moral-Political Self-Radicalizations in the Protestant Theo-Political Imaginary

Abstract: This article describes seven broad theological shifts in liberal Protestantism and thus serve as a tacit background to the changing political imaginary which characterizes our present times. It argues that this changing imaginary is undergirded by the negotiation and deployment of power or enmity, which oftentimes is veiled or obfuscated by the language of love. To take fuller account of our theo-political imaginary, then, the article suggests that liberal Protestantism engages in at least four temptations of love when it fails to acknowledge the implicit power involved in any practice of love. By casting light on these temptations, one not only comes to a greater understanding of our political imaginary but moreover one is able to act as a constructive theologian to resist this 'absolutist' picture of love and recover a 'truer' sense of Christian love.

1 Introduction

What significant changes happened in what I call the liberal protestant religious field over the last one hundred years, changes which have had an enormous impact on the political imagination, on political theologies – not just of academics, but also of people in the pew? What became the dominant political framings – implicit political theologies – among the broadly speaking liberal protestant churches?

My attempt to answer these questions and describe the corresponding frame will proceed in four steps. First, I try to illuminate my own limited space of reflection and my particular object under observations. Second, I will sketch with broad brushstrokes seven far-reaching shifts in Western liberal Protestantism's theological setup. Against this background, I will pronounce ways in which weak and vulnerable love, at least implicitly, needs to claim power. Under conditions of finitude, there is no love without these claims. In the fourth and final step, I will describe four temptations which – in the light of the seven shifts and vis-à-vis the three claims of power – the theo-politics of love enter dynamics of self-radicalization and hence self-absolution. In the end, enmity becomes the cast shadow of radicalized love.

Again, as a short thesis: Any location of love in the theo-political realm needs to consider the vital changes in the background-imaginations that form theopolitical possibility-spaces. Love, even suffering love, requires power and to some degree, sovereignty. Whoever loves is a master. Whoever wants to love the world wants to be the world's master. The denial of such an unavoidable claim to power is in the theologies of suffering love their self-deceptive blind spot. When the connection between power and love is overlooked, denied, or concealed, love is running the manifest risk of creating its opposite: enmity. This is, in short, the bold thesis of the following essay. In particular, the popular claim of unlimited love provokes its opposite, both as resistance and negation. In this respect, the following considerations are 'reactionary' – reacting against developments in liberal Western Protestantism (widely defined). This apparently strange and seemingly opaque thesis needs some explanation.

2 Self-localizations

First, who are we, as we academically reflect on developments in political theology? In philosophy of religion and political theology, we are not in touch with *the* world. The best we can do is to desperately try not to fall into the temptation to offer what Friedrich Nietzsche called "Gelehrtenreligion," that is to say some almost private religious-philosophical meditations without the power of the myth and the community.[1] Large parts of our philosophical reflections are, however, just that: private meditations turned into public confessions.

Second, where are we? As academic philosophers, social scientists, experts in cultural studies, and religion, we are a thoroughly parochial enterprise done by the elite of the West. What is moving the minds and actions of people in the depths of China or Africa is beyond our reasoning. In terms of religious life, our reflections concern just about 15% of World Christianity at most. Furthermore, we should not suppress the nagging doubt that Western liberal Christianity might turn out to be an exciting yet passing short episode in the history of Christianity.

Third, where am I? In what follows, I will work in my small 'sandbox' of Western Protestant theology – mainly of the twentieth century and in Western

---

[1] Nietzsche, "Geburt der Tragödie", 100.

liberal democratic states.[2] Out of my small sandbox, I will take a look at the more current ecclesial-political postures and imaginations.

What is my database? I am working with highly evident and powerful, yet anecdotal evidence, based on readings, invited lectures, numerous pastoral conferences, workshops with laypeople in the Church and the medical field, students, Protestant professionals, church leaders, and the like. Readings and specific encounters are my means and tools in order not to repeat what other great thinkers have said solemnly or to offer the reader little more than private opinions. I need to emphasize this point: theology – contrary to philosophy or sociology – is serving a distinct profession that is in many ways constructively shaping the emotional and cognitive mindset and the imaginative outlook of thousands of people out there, parishes and Christian institutions. We can clearly see that what has been thought and taught about 25, 30, or 40 years ago is now reaching the pew and Christian initiatives. When we talk in our small sandbox about political theology, we do so with an eye on political theology's performance in many layers of ecclesial practice. In this respect, what you will listen too is a kind of empirical political theology alive in the religious field.

3 Theological Shifts in Western Liberal Protestantism / Christianity

Seven tectonic shifts characterize the change of the political imaginary in the liberal Protestant field. These shifts neither follow the classical theological liberal/nonliberal divide nor reflect some post-Kantianism in theology. Secularization, post-secularism, the break-off of religious traditions, or the crisis of theism are all not sufficiently complex tools to analyze and characterize our current religio-political imaginaries. It needs to be emphasized: what I want to describe are shifts, not losses. The latter would require a feeling of loss. Only an observer with normative interests embedded in historical comparisons would identify these shifts as losses.

---

[2] For sandboxes see https://en.wikipedia.org/wiki/Sandbox_(computer_security) (accessed 01 Mar. 2020). Sandboxes provide highly secluded and protected environments in which the 'muddy' world is kept out in order test programs. I use them as a metaphor for academic sandboxes of highly controlled environments.

3.1 The Suffering Companion

The theological imagination of a mighty God still present in many Church hymns shifted to a God who is a suffering companion. As shown by many interpreters, the experiences of two world wars and, in particular the Shoa, pressed Protestant theology to radically emphasize the presence of the suffering God. Dietrich Bonhoeffer, Juergen Moltmann, Michael Welker, Catherine Keller, Wendy Farley with Charles Hartshorn and Alfred North Whitehead in the background, as well as on the Jewish side Hans Jonas, all worked in their particular ways on this shift.[3] It is well-known under the label of post-theism, and whether it confirms or falsifies Ludwig Feuerbach's critique of religion needs to be determined.

3.2 Neither Warrior nor Judge: The Divine Therapist

Parallel to this search for the divine presence in weakness, the leading model for divine reconciliation at the cross changed. How can we today understand the event of the crucifixion of Jesus of Nazareth? What idea of God is disclosed at this cross? The powerful juridical model of both a consequential and a merciful divine judge is in today's liberal Christianity as dead as it can be. This happened despite Karl Barth's latest attempts to work with this model in his Christology and despite Dietrich Bonhoeffer's deep and robust Lutheran background.[4] The divine warrior who later became a judge eventually morphed into a co-suffering therapist with a thoroughly moralistic bend. This is a significant second shift. In the end, this therapist is so enmeshed into human life that there is no conceivable presence of an independent divine agency left. The corresponding changes in public prayer are notable. Theories of prayer look at coping mechanisms and the performance of public prayer becomes a self-demand note (Selbstaufforderung) for political action.

3.3 A World without Conductor or Stage Director

A third shift concerns the total retreat of the trope of God acting in history, theologically speaking, the doctrine of divine providence. There is no God – not even

---

[3] Among many contributions exemplary see Moltmann, *Trinity*; in particular Farley, *Tragic Vision*.
[4] See Barth, *Church Dogmatics*.

among very high Church leaders – who orchestrates the powers in this world towards God's ends.[5] To put it pointedly: in theology, open theism is an evangelical latecomer to the club of those who see the future of the world solely in their own hands.[6] The world-responsibility moved from God to "society" or the Church. The Greek mythic figure of Atlas becomes the hidden image for the liberal, politically active Church. World-responsibility (Weltverantwortung) became the task of the Church.

3.4 Not Collecting People out of the World for the Church but Sending People to the World

The fourth noticeable shift can also be seen taking place at the turn of the twentieth century up to its end. The primary and most crucial inner movement of the Church is not to call people *out* of the world *into* the Church, the ek-klesia, but to *send* people into the world. Early diaconic initiatives in the nineteenth century, Dietrich Bonhoeffer's famous formula "Church for the others," and Juergen Moltmann's messianic ecclesiology, all testify to this radical shift.[7] We should not forget the current attempt of appropriating a Public Theology that sends a rescueship to the Libyan shore.[8] This movement of "being sent to the world" in many initiatives happens even though the churches of Western liberal Christianity are all shrinking churches.[9] In the Netherlands, Protestant church membership has decreased from 64% in the year 1900 to about 9% at the moment, with no end in sight. Empirical realities are brutal.

3.5 Mission as Conversion – what an Embarrassment!

Closely related to the third and fourth shift is the fifth: The death or the fundamental reinterpretation of mission. Classical mission as a conversion is simply dead among liberal Churches, broadly speaking. It would be embarrassing. It

---

5 For an overview see Bernhardt, *Was heißt 'Handeln Gottes'?*.
6 See Teuchert, *Gottes transformatives Handeln*.
7 See Moltmann, *Church in the Power of the Spirit*.
8 See EKD, "Seenotrettung im Mittelmeer," https://www.ekd.de/seenotrettung-im-mittelmeer-46579.htm (accessed 24 Feb. 2020).
9 One might question the notion of 'even though'. This process might well take place because of the secularization. The inflation of acclaimed relevance would then correspond to shrinking social relevance. Future generations might be better equipped to answer this question.

would be an indication of a lack of respect. It would be a sign of missing interreligious sensitivity. For some, it would even be a kind of religious harassment to think or even speak about the mission as conversion. Such an idea appears to substantiate a profound theological disorientation. Again, I am writing about liberal Protestantism broadly understood. There are phenomena, for instance, in migrant churches, which cause embarrassment for our mainline Churches. What the Church is called for and sent for is exclusively the enhancement of this earthly life and its social, cultural, political, and ecological conditions. The diagnosis of the historian Thomas Großbölting is as simple as it is harsh: heaven disappeared, heaven is lost.[10] It is lost in the search for a just peace, just migration, just trade and a better life here and now. Charles Taylor pointedly called this mindset and way of living an "immanent frame" without any robust transcendence.[11] Responsibility for the world, for *this* world, is the Church's specific task. Augustine would have a hard time even recognizing the Church as Church. Faith is not offering a passport to the heavenly city – simply because there is no heavenly city, no 'pie in the sky'.

3.6 Human Dignity and Human Rights as Manifestation of God's Universal Love

The sixth shift is manifest in an insight whose cumulative evidence in the present distracts from the recognition of its slow and long emergence: God's love to every human being as an *imago dei* is translated into human dignity embodied in human rights.[12] God's love for every person on this planet is mirrored in an individualistic and universal interpretation of human rights.[13] Part and parcel of this shift is that one needs to respect the other person's faith tradition, hence no conversion. Most leaders of liberal western Churches assume that human rights are the common ground on which Church and Politics can meet. Human rights can be conceived/perceived by reason and justified by the faith tradition of the Church.[14] So the moral mission of the Church is genuinely 'reasonable.' With the ancient differentiation of three theologies (theologia tripartita) and three corresponding religious practices in mind, one can formulate the following: The respect for human rights becomes the most powerful civil religion

---

10 See the in-depth analysis with radical consequences Thomas Großbölting, *Losing Heaven*.
11 See Taylor, *Secular Age*, 539 ff.
12 See Moyn, *Last Utopia*.
13 See Huber and Tödt, *Menschenrechte*.
14 See Bedford-Strohm, *Radikal lieben*.

which can (if needed) be blended with both the rational religion as well as the particular faith tradition of mythic religion.[15]

3.7 No Worldly Kingdom – the one Realm of Christ

The seventh shift is straightforwardly impacting political theology. Since it happened rather slowly and almost invisibly, it needs some more description. Due to several factors, the classical Lutheran and Calvinist doctrine of the two kingdoms, are also more or less dead.[16] Dietrich Bonhoeffer's vivid rejection of two realms or spheres of God in the world, Karl Barth's strictly universalist notion of reconciliation and emphasis on the brotherhood of humankind, Jürgen Moltmann's optimistic political theology, Michael Welker's threefold office of Christ – they all pour water on this mill. Today's plea for a Public Theology firmly put forth by Heinrich Bedford-Strohm belongs to the same group of approaches.[17] At their core, they all reject the idea that outside of the Church, there is a divinely tolerated battle of antagonistic forces that makes any rule of love just illusionary and dangerous, if not misleading. Compared to the theologies of the nineteenth, eighteenth or seventeenth century this position implies an enormous expansion of Christ's and the Spirit's presence outside of the Church in the sphere of the world.[18] The only difference between the world and the Church is the Church's epistemic advantage: The Church knows that the world is reconciled with God, the place of Christ's anonymous presence and the place of the Spirit's workings. This shift raises the enormous moral claims addressed towards the world, because what in terms of politics is considered to be possible in the world is dramatically changed. The world is not just a realm of sin which needs to be managed in some way by law. In short: the social-democratic welfare state appears to have hijacked the theo-political agenda. The only way forward is to add some green elements. Many of the key theological agents carry the matching party membership. Is this a solution or a problem? Is this the ultimate triumph of two impressive liberal minds – Richard Rothe and Trutz Rendtorff – because it is the ultimate dissolution of the Church? Too

---

15 See Luhmann, "Grundwerte", 293–308; recently see von Scheliha, "Die 'Zwei-Reiche-Lehre'", 182–206.
16 See von Scheliha, *Protestantische Ethik*; Andersen, *Macht aus Liebe*.
17 See Bedford-Strohm, *Liberation Theology*.
18 See in this respect a classic: Tillich, *Systematic Theology*; not with respect to culture, but with an expansion to creation Moltmann, *Spirit of Life*; Moltmann, *God in Creation*; the spirit of Christ is transcending the Church also in Welker, *God the Spirit*.

early to tell! At the very least, it profoundly changes the expectations concerning the possibility-space of the political: Moral progress is possible; moral enhancement is no illusion, real approximations to the kingdom of God can be achieved. "Yes, we can." Any fight for justice by expanding the welfare state and in the work towards a more sustainable ecosphere – to name just a few fields of action – is a sign of God's presence and God's peace. Nota bene: all of this can keep you away from the necessary secularization of Marxism and socialism in the Protestant field.[19]

What is crucial in this more recent shift: The close alliance of a) love, b) imago Dei and c) human rights, make love *reasonable*.[20] This is why there are no two kingdoms. Not to love is not only morally wrong but stupid. This is, seen from a distance, the shared assumption of left-wing Barthianism, of a progressive reading of Dietrich Bonhoeffer, of the import of Juergen Habermas into the Church and the matching green-left consensual field in politics. Love has to be accepted. Selfishness is unreasonable. To question love can quickly become hate speech.

3.8 Quo Vadis?

So again: What is the situation of liberal Christianity broadly understood? What is the prospect of liberal Churches (if we abstract from Orthodox worlds, from Catholicism outside of Europe, from Pentecostalism in Asia, Africa, and Latin America, etc.)? What is their theo-political imaginary?

Sent to the world by the suffering companion, coach, and therapist, the shrinking Christian churches have to take over divine providential care in the act of responsibility for nothing less than the world: for the world's justice, for

---

[19] See Thomas, "Karl Barth's Political Theology", 181–198; Thomas, "On the Limits of Responsibility", 243–264.

[20] For the very same reason, the common synod of all German Churches issued a programmatic statement in which they argued for radical pacifism on utilitarian grounds: "Experience shows that individuals, communities and states are able to handle problems and conflicts in all areas of societal and political life in a constructive and nonviolent manner. There are tried-and-tested strategies and instruments for finding ways out of violence and guilt, protecting one another from violence and shaping reconciliation processes – in peace times as in crisis and war situations." See for the German version https://www.ekd.de/kundgebung-ekd-synode-frieden-2019-51648.htm (accessed 10 Feb. 2020). An English version is also available: https://www.ekd.de/ekd_de/ds_doc/Kundgebung-Kirche-auf-dem-Weg-der-Gerechtigkeit-und-des-Friedens-EN.pdf (accessed 10 Feb. 2020). Any type of coercive violence is literally unreasonable.

the world's peace, for the "world order" and for the world's ecosystem.²¹ Without bothering so much about faith and mission, Christians care for the poor, search for justice, and are fighting for the human rights of every human being – regardless of where he or she is living and from what place he or she is coming. For good reasons, many adherents of 'no border' are Church-people.

It is evident that these seven shifts are relevant in the presence, assumption, negotiation, and eventually the use of power. These seven shifts provide a formatting framework and a tacit background, a set of assumptions for our current talk about love in the religiopolitical field and the relation between love, power, and sovereignty, in all its subtle manifestations.

Such is the situation we live in Western Europe in all mainline churches – because we are called to love and to follow this suffering love of the suffering companion in our practice of active world-responsibility. This is the *basso continuo* in our churches and faculties, at the "Kirchentag," in Churches and our Synods. At this point, I will not debate whether these shifts represent a solution, a problem, or both. I hypothesize that these shifts represent, in all cases, legitimate solutions, which at the same time create overwhelming new problems. Regardless of any final assessment, they represent the powerful theological context in which we are reasoning today – even though we communicate a broader set of ideas at the university. Even if I do not embrace all of these shifts wholeheartedly, these shifts are not just an 'academic idea' but an empirical reality in the life of the mind of many people in our Christian churches, from Bishops down to the laypeople in the pews. They do not live just in minds and on paper, they form actions. This significantly changed theo-political imaginary is forming the stage for the current political-religious discourse on love. Thus, the overarching question is: What happens to the Church's notion of love when the seven shifts are changing the theological imagination all the way down to the benches, the synods, and Church-conventions?

Consequently, my more specific question is: Given this strong emphasis on love, how are love and power intimately connected? To phrase it differently: Why is the concept of powerless love not a meaningful concept but rather a misleading and even deceptive concept? Why would the total absence of sovereignty also be an absence of love?

---

21 For an impressive document of such general and wide-ranging responsibility – and correspondingly wide-ranging lament about the state of the world – see the same document issued by the Synod 2019.

4 Unveiling Love's Need for Power

Any finite love lays claim on power in at least three ways: first, the power of selection, second, the power of interpretation, and third, the power of intervention. Let me start with the power of selection.

4.1 The Power of Selection

Let us first ponder on the intimate connection between love and action – be it perceived and accompanied by feelings of love or not. Any social *action* is directed to some social entity and not to another. In terms of time, space, social address, and subject matter, it is selective. Any act of love has to draw a distinction, even multiple distinctions. In a media society, any act of love as action forces shifts or establishes a focus of shared attention. At the same time, it is already influenced by the media's focus of attention. An act of love can be observed, and since others are observing it, the acting entity has to try to observe it too. No act of love can escape the intricacy of mutual observations, hence the loss of immediacy, which makes evident love's distinctions.

If the acting agency is not entirely just responding to other actions, if it is not only in the mode of perceiving and experiencing, it has to make a decision: do I love A or B? Do I love now or later? What action is now the proper medium to communicate love? Can I act in such a way? Do I have the means and media to do so? Can this action be understood and interpreted as an act of love? As an action, to be very simple-minded, love has no reciprocity based on a contract![22] Any act of love occurs in a triage situation – even more in late-modernity without stable orders in a society that could provide a kind of preformed corridor for love's selectivity. Any act of love – even suffering love – needs to master this complex selectivity. Again, in media-saturated societies with the media-induced shifting attentions, this fundamental selectivity can be delegated to the news or talk-shows. Accordingly, the churches can absorb the media attention for their orientation and practice of love. The management of these multiple selectivities inevitably presupposes a 'master.' Hence even suffering love seems to be entangled into a tragic moment.

This problem of selectivity is, to a far-reaching extent, expended and interrupted on a large scale in functionally differentiated societies, which never emerge based on I-thou personalized encounters. When love is practised through

---

[22] See Thomas, "The risks of love", 265–274.

organizations, things become even more difficult. Any organization exists of decisions concerning inclusion and exclusions. Its services cannot be communicated to anyone, but only to a limited number of people.

4.2 The Power of Interpretation

Whoever is communicating love is transforming the possibility-space of another agent. Such transformation concerns new possibilities. This transformation can also change unreal and distant possibilities into real ones. Both types of transformation help the practice of freedom in unfolding the other agent's life. Love contributes to human beings flourishing by supporting and enhancing other agencies' possibility-spaces for their life. The other agent's perspective is taken into account – not to cross its path, but to support and enhance his or her possibilities. To interact with others like playing chess is the opposite of love. To outpace, outsmart, and cross out the other's path is not love. Even in creating a nourishing environment for the other agent, love is never powerless. Any practice of love is deeply embedded in a vision of life, and what counts as flourishing can vary to a high degree. What possibility should become an impossibility and what impossibility should become a possibility depends not only on a historic contingent framework for action but on one's vision of life.

Consequently, to love is to practice the power of interpretation and definition of reality. This power can be marked as invisible by merely claiming to be self-evidently what counts as a good life. In doing so, power is shifted to the claim that something is evident against seeing its contingency. Whatever strategy is used against this corrosive contingency, it needs power: The power to interpret, the power to define and frame, the power to negotiate, the power of seeing clearly, and of assisting the revelation.

4.3 Love and the Power of Intervention

Beyond being a detached observer or, alternatively, a fully engaged good Samaritan, the position of any agent of love is very likely a much more complex one. Dualistic one-to-one relationships are scarce. More likely is the constellation in which agent A is relating to B, but at the same time C has a relation to B too. As a consequence, A's relation to B has a direct or indirect impact on C's relation to B. Quite often the loving relationship of A to B has to intersect the destructive relationship of C to B. While A's relationship to B might emphasize passivity and receptivity, A needs the power of intervention to interfere with C's destructive relationship to B. It is the complexity of life in which any loving agent is embedded, which asks for the power of intervention. When co-suffering companionship continues the suffering and the agony caused by other agents, more than empathy is asked for.[23]

5 Four temptations of love within the space formed by the seven shifts

What happens to love under the framing conditions of the seven shifts described above and when it cannot acknowledge the exercise of power implicit in any practice of love? This paper's general thesis is that both the framing conditions of the seven shifts and the negation of power in love leads to four temptations that form the theo-political imagination powerfully present in current Western societies and Western liberal Churches. The result is a self-empowerment of love, which in the end creates what it is fighting against, namely, enmity.

5.1 The first temptation: generalization, or: there is no alternative to love

To understand this temptation, we must shuttle back to the death of the theological tool of the two-kingdom doctrine. This theological theory worked with three values, not with one and not with two. Love was one option. There had been, however, two alternatives to love. The first alternative to love: A network of sin, violence, stupidity, and works of evil and eventually the devil (God's apparent enemy, the devil, was in itself a complex option, but with an overall negative value). There was a second alternative to love, which could be observed from two sides. It could be observed from the position of sin or the position of love. The third position was the law. The law provided some limitation of violence, was reasonable, somehow working, decent, and helpful in the containment of sin, even though not perfect. The law is open to compromise and presents a form of order that can be transformed and superseded by love. However, it is neither a manifestation of love nor of sin, but a limited manifestation of justice – regardless of how and where the law can be found.[24] In some respect, the law needs to

---

23 See Thomas, "Kampf der Theologie", 470–476.
24 For a recent discussion on the Protestant side of natural law see Dalferth, *Naturrecht in protestantischer Perspektive*; Welker, "Gottes Gerechtigkeit", 409–421.

negotiate interests and searches for pragmatic adjustments – at least seen from a distance. Without any doubt, the law can be misused. It is, however, a quite preliminary form of order pushing back sheer chaos.

If this triangle of a) chaos and sin, b) the rule of law, and c) the rule of love falls apart at the law's cost, the only opposition to and the only alternative to love is chaos, sin, and evil. The opposition to love is the manifestation of the enemy, the whole picture of sin, stupidity, evil, and devilish power, the denial of all good forces of love. In order to battle sin, love was in the triangle not the only alternative. In some respect, to battle chaos and sin, the rule of law could often be sufficient.

When the third value disappears from the triangle, the whole moral landscape changes. Who does not love, who does not fight ultimate justice and for universal individual human rights, is now considered to be unreasonable and seen as a being without any decent identity.[25] Love knows no valid other, no opponent. It knows only what needs to be rejected and overcome. Love eventually sees itself in a position where it justifies the hate of hate and the silencing of otherness. Love without alternatives is the death of a fair negotiation of interests. With the 'other,' seen as enemy, love cannot cut a compromise. Love has to hate evil. However, what happens in politics if this is the only alternative?

5.2 The second temptation: the speed of love, or: no time for patience

Without the framework of providential care and a divine conductor – left alone with total world responsibility, with only the support of a powerless coach and therapist – living in a world of conflict, fate, selflessness, destruction, and manifest self-endangerment becomes a heavy burden. No doubt about that. It is the world of Lamech described in the first pages of the Bible. Lamech said to his wives: "Adah and Zillah, hear my voice; you wives of Lamech, listen to what I say: I have killed a man for wounding me, a young man for striking me. 24 If Cain's revenge is sevenfold, then Lamech's is seventy-sevenfold." (Genesis 4:23–25 (English Standard Version (ESV))

In the actual world, love is sent on a racetrack. Every day without more transformative love will cost too much. No time is to be left. The catastrophes come like a thief in the night. Only the moral flaneur can rumble. When panic is the proper posture, a conversation is a distraction from the action. Even talk-

---

[25] See Bedford-Strohm, *Radikal lieben*.

ing needs to be left behind. Impatience becomes a virtue and imperative. The wrath of a God is replaced by the loving human agent's wrath, the just, the missionary, the saviour. To hesitate by looking back transforms any impatient revolutionary into salt (Gen 19,26). Whoever looks back on the way through the divided sea will be covered by the waves (Ex 14,26 ff). When utopias are replaced by dystopias, when the redeeming Messiah is substituted by the avenger called mother earth, speed becomes so essential that any call for patience turns out to be an act of betrayal. When the world is endangered, true love will take every shackle away and will take away everyone out who is standing in its way. Love will remove all human and nonhuman, all institutional barriers. When democracy is too slow other political means need to overrun it, literally. Love has the right to declare an exceptional state.[26] Human rights can overrun any exclusive rights.

5.3 The third temptation: the force of reason, or: no chance for foolishness

The marriage with universal reason transforms love. Truly vulnerable and particular love is not only risk-taking and extravagant but always shares a long border with foolishness.[27] Universal reason disciplines love, moderates its temper, and universalizes it. However, it also gives love in exchange for a forceful weapon in hand. Whoever questions the acts of love is unreasonable or even wicked and insane. Only the intellectually insufficient develop minds and, metaphorically speaking, the ill and truly sick minds that need a therapist, can resist both love and reason. After the marriage of love and reason, the resistance to acts of love is a resistance against the universal power of reason. It is something truly unthinkable. Whoever searches for alternatives is misled and eventually stupid, maybe just ill-minded. Such a person is an agent in need of help. He cannot be a conversation partner, only the object of therapy. The unreasonable agent becomes a case of medicine broadly conceived. Only mean people cannot favour reasonable love when true love is responsible for nothing less than the whole world.

---

26 On the connections between exceptional states and human rights see Heller, *Mensch und Maßnahme*.
27 See Thomas, "The risks of love".

5.4 The fourth temptation: forceful immediacy, or: there is no place for reflexively observing contingency

The one possible alternative, speed, the claim of coherent reason, is the support of forceful immediacy. What love needs to do needs to be done, now, and here. "Just do it" [Nike]. Do not hesitate! Grasp life. Fight now! Do what is evident! Second thoughts are merely second. Forget self-observation![28] Dare to do it! There was enough talk! To discuss is to distract! To distract is to stop love and give space and time to the enemy! Do not slow down the momentum of the movement! This question is always the question of the snake. It is the devilish temptation. Seize the moment, the Kairos, the revolutionary moment of intensified love, immediate certainty, go for the power of the non-reflexive! Whoever introduces contingency, second thoughts and clear doubt needs to be silenced. So do not listen to the devil as the agent of second-order observations.[29] Love overcomes evil by eliminating it! Do not befriend the devil. Hate the haters. Exclude the excluding ones. Stay away. Mark the enemy! Reflexivity is infectious. Kill the virus! Cut out the cancer ulcer. Love needs to be blind and forceful; it is the powerful light conquering the night. The night has progressed; the day is not far off.

6 Looking forward: The end is near

There is no simple determining causality present between the seven shifts identified earlier. They raise, however, a likelihood. They increase proximity. They establish relations of resonance.[30] They become strange attractors. They lure into a theo-political mindset of a quite particular kind. It is a mindset that might be directly called Christian, yet it also permeates current Western societies' public spaces. Is it dangerous or truly salvific? Is it a problem or rather a solution? Does it need to be developed or changed? "Too early to say!" (Zhou Enlai). At any rate, it comes at a high cost.

To tentatively answer these questions, we need to leave the comfort zone of a philosopher and an academic observer. We need to leave behind the devilish position of second-order observation without taking up responsibility. To answer these questions, we need to become normative philosophers or constructive theologians,

---

28 On speed and reflexivity see Luhmann, *Gesellschaft*, 87 ff.
29 For the specific observation of the devil see Nickel-Schwäbisch, "'Ich bin ein Teil des Teils'", 117–125.
30 For a very broad notion of resonance see Rosa, *Resonance*; Peters and Schulz, eds., *Resonanzen und Dissonanzen*; more specifically see Thomas, *Gottes Lebendigkeit*, 12–24.

be it implicit or explicit. At the end of this paper, I want to sketch an alternative route with very broad brush strokes. Unquestionably, it would need more elaboration.

As a constructive theologian, I want to question the absolutist love described above. Moreover, I will not underwrite all of the shifts which create the background of absolutist love. First and foremost, true love will remain vulnerable and be aware of the risk of death for the power of the resurrection. This vulnerable love is the one that hope in Jesus Christ live's out. It is not the love of a Jacobin or a Zealot. True love will never stop to lament in the practice of patience.[31] True love will draw a distinction that lies at the core of faith. Every human love, finite and factual, needs to be distinguished from the life of divine love and hope. True love will accept the surpassing creativity of divine love. In Christ, God successfully loves his enemies. Love which hates and also desperate hope grow in the twilight of the weak God, in an orchestra without a conductor, in a Church without borders, in an unleashed optimism and celebrated loss of the third value of the law.

Do we need to revive metaphysics and follow Charles Taylor?[32] Are these good reasons to escape immanence? No![33] We need to trust in the Spirit of Christ, who sabotages both the very projects of metaphysics and all inclinations for post-metaphysical solitude and heroism. The Spirit calls into question cold metaphysics *and* hotly running this-worldliness. It is not the Church, but the Spirit who is continuing the incarnation and is the drive towards embodiment in the vulnerable flesh. The Spirit as the power of the resurrection violates this distinction between immanence and transcendence permanently. This is – to anticipate the joyful mystery of Christmas – the secret of the Virgin Mary. This is the profound secret of the Father's response to Christ's god-forsakenness at Good Friday.[34] It is the nocturnal Spirit of new life mentioned in Nicodemus' night-talk, evoking and eroding the border between the old and the new world. Between the Spirit of life and the Spirit of the new creation, there is a subtle quarrel. The Spirit shifts the shifts and evokes a realism of genuine hope and love without the cast shadow of love: enmity. One might call this the Spirit of hopeful realism. In terms of the necessity of politics of the law and the chances of the pol-

---

31 See Thomas, *Weltabenteuer*.
32 See Taylor, *Secular Age*.
33 See Thomas, "Temptation of Religious Nostalgia", 49–70.
34 See Clarke, *A Cry in the Darkness*; for the reception of Psalm 22, a Psalm of lament, see Janowski, "'Mein Gott', 371–401.

itics of love, hopeful realism is seeking a place beyond a politics of strong optimism and a politics of morbid skepticism.[35]

Bibliography

Andersen, Svend. *Macht aus Liebe: Zur Rekonstruktion einer lutherischen politischen Ethik.* Berlin: de Gruyter, 2010.
Barth, Karl. *Church Dogmatics*, vol. 4: *The Doctrine of Reconciliation*, Pt. 1, ed. Geoffrey W. Bromiley and Thomas F. Torrance, trans. Geoffrey W. Bromiley et al. Edinburgh: T&T Clark, 1961.
Bedford-Strohm, Heinrich. *Radikal lieben: Anstöße für die Zukunft einer mutigen Kirche.* Gütersloh: Gütersloher Verlagshaus, 2017.
Bedford-Strohm, Heinrich. *Liberation Theology for A Democratic Society: Essays in Public Theology.* Vienna: Lit, 2018.
Bernhardt, Reinhold. *Was heißt 'Handeln Gottes'? Eine Rekonstruktion der Lehre von der Vorsehung.* Gütersloh: Gütersloher Verlagshaus, 1999.
Clarke, Anthony. *A Cry in the Darkness: The Forsakenness of Jesus in Scripture, Theology, and Experience.* Oxford, UK: Smyth & Helwys, 2002.
Dalferth, Ingolf U. *Naturrecht in protestantischer Perspektive.* Baden-Baden: Nomos, 2008.
Farley, Wendy. *Tragic Vision and Divine Compassion: A Contemporary Theodicy.* Louisville, KY: John Knox Press, 1990.
Großbölting, Thomas. *Losing Heaven: Religion in Germany since 1945*, trans. Alex Skinner. New York: Berghahn, 2016.
Heller, Jonas. *Mensch und Maßnahme: Zur Dialektik von Ausnahmezustand und Menschenrechten.* Weilerswist: Velbrück Wissenschaft, 2018.
Huber, Wolfgang, and Tödt, Heinz Eduard. *Menschenrechte: Perspektiven einer menschlichen Welt*, 3rd ed. Munich: Kaiser, 1988.
Janowski, Bernd. "'Mein Gott, mein Gott, wozu hast du mich verlassen?' Zur Rezeption der Psalmen in der Markuspassion," *Zeitschrift für Theologie und Kirche* 116 (2019): 371–401.
Luhmann, Niklas. "Grundwerte als Zivilreligion," In *Soziales System, Gesellschaft, Organisation*, Niklas Luhmann, 293–308. Opladen: Westdeutscher Verlag, 1981.
Luhmann, Niklas. *Die Gesellschaft der Gesellschaft*, vol. 1. Frankfurt a. M.: Suhrkamp, 1997.
Moltmann, Jürgen. *The Trinity and the Kingdom of God: The Doctrine of God.* San Francisco, CA: Harper & Row, 1981.
Moltmann, Jürgen. *The Spirit of Life: A Universal Affirmation*, trans. Margaret Kohl. Minneapolis, MN: Fortress Press, 1992.
Moltmann, Jürgen. *God in Creation: A new Theology of Creation and the Spirit of God*, trans. Margaret Kohl. Minneapolis, MN: Fortress Press, 1993.
Moltmann, Jürgen. *The Church in the Power of the Spirit: A Contribution to Messianic Ecclesiology.* Minneapolis, MN: Fortress Press, 1993.

---

[35] The Spirit of Christ is not destroying, but transforming the distinction made in Oakeshott, *Politics of Faith.*

Moyn, Samuel. *The Last Utopia: Human Rights in History.* Cambridge, MA: Belknap Press of Harvard University Press, 2010.

Nickel-Schwäbisch, Andrea. "'Ich bin ein Teil des Teils, der anfangs Alles war': Überlegungen zum Begriff des Teufels bei Niklas Luhmann," In *Luhmann und die Theologie*, ed. by Günter Thomas and Andreas Schüle, 117–125. Darmstadt: Wissenschaftliche Buchgesellschaft, 2006.

Nietzsche, Friedrich Wilhelm. "Die Geburt der Tragödie," In *Werke in Sechs Bänden*, vol. 1, Friedrich Wilhelm Nietzsche, ed. Karl Schlechta. Munich: C. Hanser, 1980.

Oakeshott, Michael. *The Politics of Faith and the Politics of Scepticism*, ed. Timothy Fuller. New Haven, CT: Yale University Press, 1996.

Peters, Christian H., and Schulz, Peter, eds. *Resonanzen und Dissonanzen: Hartmut Rosas kritische Theorie in der Diskussion.* Bielefeld: transcript, 2017.

Rosa, Hartmut. *Resonance: A Sociology of the Relationship to the World*, trans. James Wagner. Cambridge, UK: Polity, 2019.

von Scheliha, Arnulf. *Protestantische Ethik des Politischen.* Tübingen: Mohr Siebeck, 2013.

von Scheliha, Arnulf. "Die 'Zwei-Reiche-Lehre' im deutschen Protestantismus des 20. Jahrhunderts," *Zeitschrift für evangelisches Kirchenrecht* 59 (2014): 182–206.

Taylor, Charles. *A Secular Age.* Cambridge, MA: Belknap Press of Harvard University Press, 2007.

Teuchert, Lisanne. *Gottes transformatives Handeln: Eschatologische Perspektivierung der Vorsehungslehre bei Romano Guardini, Christian Link und dem 'Open theism'.* Göttingen: Vandenhoeck & Ruprecht, 2018.

Thomas, Günter. "Karl Barth's Political Theology: Contours, Perspectives, and Lines of Development," In *Dogmatics after Barth: Facing Challenges in Church, Society and the Academy*, ed. by Günter Thomas, Rinse H. Reeling Brouwer and Bruce McCormack, 181–198. Leipzig: Create Space, 2012.

Thomas, Günter. "Der Kampf der Theologie mit der Utopie: Beobachtungen zu 'The War of the Lamb. The Ethics of Nonviolence and Peacemaking' von John Howard Yoder," *Evangelische Theologie* 75 (2015): 470–476.

Thomas, Günter. "The Temptation of Religious Nostalgia: Protestant Readings of a Secular Age," In *Working with a Secular Age: Interdisciplinary Perspectives on Charles Taylor's Master Narrative*, ed. by Florian Zemmin, Colin Jager and Guido Vanheeswijck, 49–70. Berlin: De Gruyter, 2016.

Thomas, Günter. "On the Limits of Responsibility," In *Responsibility and the Enhancement of Life: Essays in Honor of William Schweiker*, ed. by Thomas and Heike Springhart, 243–264. Leipzig: Evangelische Verlagsanstalt, 2017.

Thomas, Günter. *Gottes Lebendigkeit: Beiträge zur Systematischen Theologie.* Leipzig: Evangelische Verlagsanstalt, 2019.

Thomas, Günter. "The risks of love and the ambiguities of hope," *Angelaki: Journal of the Theoretical Humanities* 25 (2020): 265–274.

Thomas, Günter. *Im Weltabenteuer Gottes Leben: Impulse zur Verantwortung für die Kirche.* Leipzig: Evangelische Verlagsanstalt, forthcoming.

Tillich, Paul. *Systematic Theology*, vol. 3: *Life and the Spirit, History and the Kingdom of God.* Chicago, IL: University of Chicago Press, 1963.

Welker, Michael. *God the Spirit*, trans. John F. Hoffmeyer. Minneapolis, MN: Fortress Press, 1994.

Welker, Michael. "Gottes Gerechtigkeit," *Neue Zeitschrift für Systematische Theologie und Religionsphilosophie* 56 (2014): 409–421.

Burkhard Liebsch
Meister, Väter und Surrogate

Mit Blick auf Autorität und Vertikalität, Autoritarismus und identitären Populismus

Abstract: In the light of historical experiences of the twentieth century the paper defends the 'renunciation of the father-figure' (Paul Ricœur following Sigmund Freud) as being indispensable for modern politics. The loss of the father must not be compensated for. Rather, it marks the disclosure of the true dimension of the political, in which one is willing to listen to each other even under the maintenance of vertical and not horizontal power relations. In addition, the paper contradicts any attempt to take advantage for theological and identitarian purposes to push an agenda of reinstating in our 'secular age' (Charles Taylor) a master who, as a surrogate of the 'father-figure', promises to liberate the people from the burden of their freedom.

> „Der Mensch ist ein Tier,
> das, wenn es unter andern seiner Gattung lebt,
> einen Herrn nötig hat [...].
> Wo nimmt er aber diesen Herrn her?
> Nirgend anders als aus der Menschengattung.
> Aber dieser ist ebenso wohl ein Tier, das einen Herrn nötig hat."[1]
> Immanuel Kant

> „Der Autoritärste befiehlt im Namen eines anderen,
> eines geheiligten Parasiten – seines Vaters –,
> er überträgt die abstraktesten Gewalttaten weiter,
> die er erlitten hat."[2]
> Jean-Paul Sartre

---

1 Kant, *Anthropologie*, 40. Weiter heißt es: „[D]enn jeder derselben wird immer seine Freiheit missbrauchen, wenn er keinen über sich hat, der nach den Gesetzen über ihn Gewalt ausübt. Das höchste Oberhaupt soll aber gerecht für sich selbst, und doch ein Mensch sein. Diese Aufgabe ist daher die schwerste unter allen; ja ihre vollkommene Auflösung ist unmöglich: aus so krummem Holze, als woraus der Mensch gemacht ist, kann nichts ganz Gerades gezimmert werden" (Immanuel Kant, „Idee zu einer allgemeinen Geschichte in weltbürgerlicher Absicht", in Kant, *Anthropologie*, 41.
2 Sartre, *Wörter*, 13.

https://doi.org/10.1515/9783110699241-008

1 Vorüberlegungen zwischen Bewunderung und Knechtschaft

‚Meisterlich' – mit diesem Attribut spendet man höchstes Lob für eine gewisse Kunst, deren Ausübung besondere Anerkennung und größte Bewunderung verdient. Das gilt für die faszinierende Cellistin ebenso wie für den subtilen Dichter, für die ausgezeichnete Choreografin ebenso wie für den unbekannten Meister gotischer Baukunst. Aber kann man ‚meisterhaft' Mensch sein? Wird der Meisterdenker innerhalb und außerhalb seines Faches von autoritären Anwandlungen frei sein, wie sie selbst einem unbestrittenen *maestro* von den Mitgliedern seines Ensembles womöglich nicht verziehen werden? Auf den ersten Blick stellt es sich paradox dar: wirkliche Autorität bedarf keines autoritären Auftretens; und letzteres tendiert zu etwas ganz anderem: zum Autoritarismus, der sich mit einschüchternder Macht und Gewalt die Bevormundung Anderer anmaßt, ohne jemals akzeptieren zu können, dass die bzw. der Autorität Ausübende allenfalls ein *primus inter pares* sein kann, wie es für wirkliche Autorität selbstverständlich zu sein scheint, die idealiter in persönlicher und sachlicher Hinsicht Bewunderung verdient – nicht zuletzt, weil sie menschlich ohne jegliche autoritäre Attitüde auskommt. Ganz ähnlich hat Richard Sennett Autorität mit Blick auf das Vorbild eines guten Dirigenten diskutiert.[3] Aber so attraktiv es zunächst erscheinen mag, auch politisches Zusammenwirken nach dem Vorbild eines Orchesters als ein *acting in concert*[4] zu deuten, in dem man wie im palästinensisch-israelischen *West-Eastern Diwan-Orchestra* ungeachtet tiefster Differenzen zusammenspielt, so sehr fallen doch Unterschiede ins Auge: agonale und antagonistische Konflikte, die nicht einfach unter Rückgriff auf Heraklit als (zwieträchtige) Harmonie des Zusammenwirkens auszulegen sind sowie Leitungsfunktionen der Machtausübung und des Regierens, die auf der Ebene staatlicher Politik nicht per Dirigat auszuüben sind.

Und doch wird letzteres suggeriert durch das aktuelle Fragen danach, ob man (‚heute', wieder einmal oder wie seit jeher[5]) einen neuen *Master* (Meister, Herrn oder gar Quasi-Vater als ‚starken Mann') brauche[6] – ob in den USA (wie Donald Trump), in Russland (wie Vladimir Putin), in China (wie Xi Jinping), in Italien (wie Matteo Salvini) oder in Deutschland (wo sich – noch – keiner ganz aus der

---

[3] Vgl. Sennett, *Autorität*, sowie Mouffe, *Für einen linken Populismus*, 83, die sich dagegen wendet, „starke Führung mit Autoritarismus gleichzusetzen".
[4] Vgl. Arendt, *Denktagebuch*, 207.
[5] Vgl. Moscovici, *Zeitalter der Massen*, 220.
[6] Ich verweise auf die Einleitung der Herausgeber dieses Bandes.

Deckung wagt). Offenbar meidet man, aus guten Gründen, an dieser Stelle den Begriff ‚Führer', schien sich doch aus einschlägiger, unvergessener deutscher Geschichte als erstes Gebot politischen Lebens eindeutig ergeben zu haben: ‚Du sollst keinen Führer haben und dich auch nicht gleichgültig dazu verhalten, wenn Andere sich einer Führerfigur unterwerfen.'[7] Wohin letzteres führt, wissen wir vom Extremfall bedingungsloser Unterwerfung her, wie sie mit dem auf die Person Adolf Hitlers abgelegten Fahneneid einherging.

Das mag erklären, warum man ins Englische ausweicht und auf diese Weise den einschlägig belasteten, wenn nicht gar politisch endgültig diskreditierten Begriff ‚Führer' meidet. Möglicherweise möchte man auch nur Formen ‚hündischer' Hörigkeit in der Unterordnung unter eines *Master's Voice* oder der Unterwerfung unter einen Meister, Herrn oder Quasi-Vater in Betracht ziehen, die an widerrufbare Bedingungen geknüpft werden können, so dass man den besagten Extremfall nicht unbedingt in Betracht ziehen müsste. So oder so handelt es sich um ein ernstes, zugleich uraltes und in immer neuen Variationen zum Vorschein kommendes Thema, nämlich um das im Zeichen moderner Freiheiten vielleicht nur verschärfte, tatsächlich aber viel tiefer verwurzelte und so leicht nicht zu eliminierende Bedürfnis nach *soumission*[8] (wie es bei Michel Houellebecq heißt), das man seit Étienne de la Boëtié, Fjodor Dostojewski und Saul Bellow nach dem Muster ‚freiwilliger Knechtschaft' als Angst vor der Freiheit zu deuten neigt.[9] Letzterer hat dieser Angst ein Denkmal gesetzt mit seinem 1944 erschienenen Roman *Dangling Man*, dessen Protagonist sich zunächst nur eingesteht, dass er nicht weiß, „what to do with my freedom", um dann zu realisieren, dass es ihm wie im Grunde jedermann vor allem darum gehen muss, „to stop living so exclusively and vainly for our own sake [...], self-fastened"[10]. Die subjektive „inability to be free" manifestiert sich am Ende in der vermeintlichen Aufgabe der eigenen Freiheit, mit dem zweifelhaften Ergebnis: „I am no longer to be held accountable for myself; I am grateful for that, I am in other hands, relieved of self-

---

7 Dieser politische Imperativ geht m. E. aus der frühen Auseinandersetzung klar hervor, die Karl Jaspers kurz nach dem Ende des Zweiten Weltkriegs mit der berüchtigten ‚Schuldfrage' geführt hat; Jaspers, *Schuldfrage*; vgl. Liebsch, „Verfehlte Ethik und politische Schuld". Bei näherer Betrachtung zeigt sich, dass jenes ‚erste Gebot' des Politischen allerdings nur irreversible Ermächtigungen zu einer Führerschaft ausschließen kann, die jeglicher Kritik und Absetzung entzogen würde.
8 Im Deutschen wiedergegeben mit ‚Unterwerfung'.
9 Vgl. de la Boëtié, *Rede von der freiwilligen Knechtschaft*. Vgl. Löwith, *Rezension* von „H. Kuhn", 429–431.
10 Bellow, *Dangling Man*, 125, 127.

determination, freedom cancelled."[11] In der politisch-zoologischen Sprache Kants bedeutet das in dreifach paradoxer Weise: Der Einzelne erweist sich so als Tier oder macht sich erst dazu, indem er sich einem Herrn (in diesem Fall militärischen Vorgesetzten) aus freien Stücken unterwirft (was ein Tier scheinbar nicht kann) und auf diese Weise vermeintlich die Last seiner Freiheit loswird, obgleich der fragliche Herr seinerseits aus der Menge der Tiere stammen und daher das gleiche Problem haben muss.

Wir haben, ungeachtet der Angst vor der Freiheit und der Unfähigkeit, von ihr den rechten Gebrauch zu machen, rückhaltlos selbst verantwortlich zu sein, besagt dagegen eine ohne derartige zoologische Anleihen auskommende Philosophie, die noch in menschlicher Passivität, im befremdlichen Widerfahrnis und im Erleiden einer Krankheit Spuren eines unaufrichtigen Bewusstseins entdeckt, das sich gewissermaßen über sich selbst hinwegtäuscht, so als sei es in dem, was ihm widerfährt, was es erduldet und erleidet, gar nicht im Spiel. Vor allem Jean-Paul Sartre hat sich als Entlarver der inneren Widersprüchlichkeit einer *mauvaise foi* hervorgetan, die sich selbst belügt und als solche noch im Hass auszumachen ist, der die Hassenden glauben macht, es genüge, die hassenswerten Anderen ein für alle Mal loszuwerden. Liegt nicht darin, dass *sie* hassenswert *sind*, aller Grund zum Hass, den man ihnen entgegenbringt? Und wird der Hass demnach nicht gegenstandslos, wenn man seine hassenswerten Objekte liquidiert hat? Demnach wäre der Hass, den sie sich zugezogen haben, ganz und gar ‚ihre Schuld', die Hassenden selbst aber hätten damit nichts zu tun. Sie würden vielmehr nur auf das von sich aus Hassenswerte reagieren, auf diese Weise aber keineswegs den Hass ihrerseits erst hervorbringen. Wer diese Strategie, den Hass zu genießen und sich zugleich jeglicher Verantwortung für ihn zu entziehen, wie Sartre nicht gelten lassen will, muss den Hassenden umgekehrt nachweisen, dass sie in Wahrheit nur *aus* und *in* Freiheit hassen können, d.h. dass sie ihrer eigenen Freiheit auch dann nicht entkommen, wenn sie bloß noch auf pathologisch und heteronom Widerfahrendes zu reagieren meinen. So lässt die Analyse des Phänomenologen streng genommen überhaupt keine Entschuldigung zu. Schließlich stößt sie uns in die eigene Verantwortung auch dort, wo alles Missliche am ‚Anderen' zu liegen

---

[11] Bellow, *Dangling Man*, 159. Weiter heißt es mit der Aussicht, in der Armee unter autoritärer Führerschaft unterzukommen:
  „Hurray for regular hours!
  And for the supervision of spirit!
  Long live regimentation!"
  Von fälligen Unterscheidungen zwischen bewundernswerter Meisterschaft und tierisch-,hündischer' Hörigkeit angesichts autoritärer Figuren, deren Autorität gar nicht mehr befragbar ist, ist bei Bellow nicht die Rede.

scheint – Missetaten ebenso wie die Missstände, deren Andauern tiefgreifende Ressentiments nährt. Man täuscht sich nur, wenn man glaubt, man habe allein aufgrund ‚Anderer' unter ihnen zu leiden, und *sie* seien, wie Sündenböcke, allein dafür verantwortlich zu machen.

Gemäß der phänomenologischen Theorie der Freiheit muss das auf uns selbst zurückfallen. Ihr zufolge bekommen wir nichts je geschenkt, was nicht in unserer Freiheit läge; auch die Verantwortlichkeit der Anderen nicht. *Wir müssen sie* verantwortlich *machen* und unsere Verantwortlichkeit dafür beruht auf nichts anderem als auf unserer Freiheit. ‚Mangels eines Vaters wurde ich meine eigene Ursache', steht sinngemäß in Sartres autobiografischem Text *Die Wörter* zu lesen.[12] Wer keine zureichende Ursache seines Selbstseins in einem Anderen hat – niemand kann über eine solche Ursache verfügen, insofern wir grund-los ‚zur Freiheit verurteilt' sind, wie der Phänomenologe lehrt –, dem bleibt scheinbar keine andere Wahl, als sich auf seine eigene Freiheit zu besinnen, die jeden für alles *selbst verantwortlich* macht, auch für das, was scheinbar nur widerfährt wie eine Krankheit, ein Überfall oder ein unanfechtbarer Befehl.

2 Erneute Flucht vor der Freiheit?

Erklärt sich die vielfach diagnostizierte Karriere, die das Autoritäre in unserer politischen Gegenwart erfährt, aus der seit de la Boëtié immer wieder bemerkten Flucht vor der Freiheit, d.h. davor, selbst verantwortlich sein zu müssen? Möchte man die eigene Freiheit jemand anderem übertragen, um selbst nicht frei bleiben zu müssen und um sich der Verantwortung dafür entziehen zu können – was der phänomenologischen Lehre von der *mauvaise foi* zufolge nur darauf hinauslaufen kann, sich selbst zu belügen? Erweisen sich das nicht nur im europäischen Osten festzustellende Liebäugeln mit einer ‚illiberalen' Demokratie ebenso wie die chinesische Staatshörigkeit und der nord- und südamerikanische Populismus als Symptome des gleichen Ausweichens vor der eigenen Freiheit, die man einem Anführer, *Master* oder ‚starken Mann' und Quasi-Vater ersatzweise anvertrauen möchte? Handelt es sich – ungeachtet aller regional sehr verschiedenen politischen Problemlagen – um die gleiche Krise der Freiheit zumindest insofern, als erhebliche Teile der jeweiligen Bevölkerungen selbst keinen Anspruch auf eine politische Freiheit mehr zu erheben scheinen, die ihnen nicht auf sehr bequeme Art und Weise von einem *Master*, Herrn oder Ersatzvater abgenommen werden könnte? Hat eine Philosophie, die nach dem Bekunden Noam Chomskys „stakes

---

12 Sartre, *Wörter*, 65.

all on freedom",[13] diesen offenbar verbreiteten Wunsch, entweder ‚unmündig' zu bleiben oder sich uneingeschränkter Mündigkeit wieder weitgehend zu entledigen, noch immer ebenso wenig verstanden wie das seit langem prophezeite Bevorstehen eines „Jahrhunderts des Autoritarismus"[14]?

Diese Frage ist aus Bruno Latours Sicht verfehlt, insofern es stimmt, dass das Volk, das man massenhaft zu polemischen Wortführern überlaufen sieht, *tatsächlich verraten* wurde und dass es eben deshalb nach einer klaren Sprache verlangt, die nach Lage der Dinge nur groben Vereinfachern zu Gebote steht, die sich, sei es von ‚links', sei es von ‚rechts', für keine populistische Propaganda zu schade sind.[15] Immerhin hat die rhetorische politische Vereinfachung noch einen realen Anhalt an einer komplexen Wirklichkeit, die sie vereinfacht, sei es die alle politisch-rechtlichen Grenzen sprengende Globalisierung durch die ungezügelte Freiheit eines desozialisierten Wirtschaftens, das immer mehr Menschen von ökonomischer Teilhabe ausschließt und ihrem ‚prekären' Leben überlässt, sei es der massive Abbau sozialstaatlicher Leistungen, durch den sich selbst wohlhabende Staaten des Westens dem nunmehr global herrschenden Kapitalismus anzupassen versuchten – mit maßgeblichem Nachdruck von Sozialdemokraten, die sich bis heute nicht genug darüber wundern können, dass ihnen die besonders Betroffenen die Gefolgschaft verweigern und Beteuerungen, man habe die entscheidenden Fehler begriffen, keinerlei Glauben mehr schenken mögen.

In dieser unübersichtlichen Lage, wo große Teile der Bevölkerungen offenbar seit langem aufgehört haben, an eine effektive politische Repräsentation ihrer elementarsten Lebensprobleme zu glauben, wimmelt es nun von Diagnostikern vielerlei Couleur, die für sich in Anspruch nehmen zu verstehen, wie es zu dieser

---

13 Chomsky, *Essential Chomsky*, 76.
14 Man beruft sich in diesem Zusammenhang oft auf Dahrendorf, „Anmerkungen zur Globalisierung,", 52 f. Dabei hat schon der Schweizer Historiker Jacob Burckhardt im 19. Jahrhundert in schneidenden Worten das Heraufziehen eines „Pathos der Masse" beschrieben, die am „Besserlebenwollen" interessiert sei, sich aber einer bequemen „Mediokrität" hingebe und dabei ein „heftiges Begehr nach großen Männern" verrate. Dabei wolle keiner mehr „ein einzelner existierender Mensch sein", wie Søren Kierkegaard im gleichen Kontext meinte feststellen zu können. Dass sich in der „Masse" auch viele „unberechtigte Existenzen" und „stummgemachter Jammer" finden, tut dem keinen Abbruch, bietet sich doch auch denjenigen, die nicht gesehen und nicht gehört oder verachtet werden, jederzeit die Möglichkeit, ihre „Wut gegen zum Teil unfassbare innere Feinde" zu richten, was schließlich zu „endlosen Hinrichtungen" führen kann, zumal wenn nur noch „Majoritäten" statt „Autoritäten" entscheiden. Aber wenn die nationalisierte Masse nicht weiß, was sie abgesehen von einem komfortablen ‚sozialen' Leben will, wird sie nur allzu leicht bereit sein, sich einem „allmächtigen Staat" zu unterwerfen, der von *terribles simplificateurs* angeführt werden kann, unter denen das „Maulhalten allgemein consigne sein wird"; vgl. Löwith, „Jacob Burckhardt", 143 ff., 159 f., 247, 249, 257 f.
15 Latour, „Refugium Europa", 143.

Situation hat kommen können. Man spricht von Abgehängten und Marginalisierten, von ‚überflüssig' Gewordenen und dauerhaft prekär Lebenden, die allesamt nur noch im Modus ihres Nichtdazugehörens, d. h. gewissermaßen nur noch formell, Mitglieder ihrer jeweiligen Gesellschaften zu sein scheinen. Indem man ihre Lage ‚verstehen' will, will man auch bei Dritten Verständnis für Andere nicht selten herabwürdigende und verbal zum Abschuss freigebende Protestformen wecken – so als sollte man froh darüber sein, dass die Benachteiligten sich mit ihren viel zitierten ‚Ängsten' und sonstigen ‚Gefühlen' überhaupt noch demonstrativ artikulieren, und als sei es von zweitrangiger Bedeutung, *wie* sie dies tun. Stehen sie nicht in der Tat ‚existenziell' unter Druck, wenn es stimmt, dass insbesondere der Ort, wo sie leben, infolge des monierten Verrats „als wichtigste Quelle ihrer Identität seine Bedeutung verloren"[16] hat, dass dieser Ort keine definitiven territorialen Grenzen mehr hat[17] und dass *deshalb* Fremde scheinbar ungehindert eindringen können, die sich vor Ort angeblich aller Vorteile bedienen, in deren Genuss die Deklassierten nur durch jahrelange Erwerbsarbeit hätten kommen können, die ihnen indessen weder jetzt (wie im Fall sog. ‚Aufstocker') noch gar im Alter tatsächlich ein Auskommen sichert? Der rezente Populismus erkennt hier keine Notwendigkeit zu fragen und nach differenzierten Antworten erst zu suchen. Die Fragen sind für ihn bereits die Antwort. D. h. sie werden, als ‚rhetorische', um ihre Fragwürdigkeit gebracht.

3 Autoritäre und identitäre Rede

Jetzt, wo sich Populisten unterschiedlichster Provenienz diese Lage zunutze machen, um das Wasser, das den Betroffenen vielfach bis zum Hals steht, auf ihre politischen Mühlen zu lenken, treten zahlreiche ‚Versteher' dieser Lage hervor, die wissen wollen, wie es um den ‚ursprünglichen' Zusammenhang von Ort und Identität, von nicht-prekärer Erwerbsarbeit, sozialer Zugehörigkeit und politischer Mitgliedschaft bestellt ist und, mehr noch, was für den Fall droht, dass man diesen inneren Zusammenhang aus den Augen verliert, wie es offenbar einer Politik passiert ist, die nur darauf bedacht war, die Konkurrenzfähigkeit des eigenen Staates zu weitgehend unbestrittenen neo-liberalen Bedingungen sicherzustellen. Dabei gehen die entsprechenden therapeutischen Vorschläge durchaus in verschiedene Richtungen. Kommunitaristen legen uns ans Herz, uns ‚an Ort

---

16 Mason, „Keine Angst vor der Freiheit", 153.
17 Vgl. Bauman, „Symptome", 47. Dort spricht Bauman von einer „unvermeidlich traumatische[n] Trennung von Zugehörigkeit und Territorialität".

und Stelle' verwurzelt zu begreifen und loben die Werte der Nachbarschaft, der Gemeinschaft und des identitären Wissens, wer man im Unterschied zu Fremden ist, die sich als Heimatlose der kalten Globalisierung der Lebensverhältnisse rückhaltlos ausgesetzt sehen oder, wie einstige ‚Luftmenschen', gerade als nicht ‚Verwurzelte' glücklich zu werden scheinen.[18] Umverteiler dagegen insistieren auf dem legitimen Anspruch der ökonomisch Benachteiligten auf einen fairen Anteil am erwirtschafteten Reichtum, der längst die Form unaufhörlicher und endloser Bereicherung Weniger angenommen hat, die sich nationalstaatlicher Kontrolle weitgehend entziehen. Und wieder andere wollen ‚verstehen', warum Millionen den mehr oder weniger unglaubwürdigen Versprechungen von Populisten auf den Leim gehen, eben diese Kontrolle rigoros wiederherzustellen mit Hilfe einer faktisch nirgends mehr verfügbaren politischen Souveränität alten, klassischen Zuschnitts.[19] An deren Stelle tritt vielfach eine rhetorisch angemaßte Autorität, von der sich die jeweiligen Anhänger gerne einreden lassen, man müsse sich nur entschlossen genug zu dem Willen bekennen, das eigene Selbst an Ort und Stelle territorial eindeutig abgegrenzt zu behaupten und zu verteidigen, notfalls auch durch konsequente Abweisung fremden ‚Menschenfleisches' an den Grenzen, wie es der in diesen Dingen kein Blatt vor den Mund nehmende ehemalige italienische Innenminister Matteo Salvini ausdrückte.

Ob solche Rhetorik ‚wirklich' für sich in Anspruch nehmen kann, für das eigene Selbst aller Betroffenen zu sprechen, ob sie es nicht vielmehr ganz und gar entleert, indem sie es als idealiter von allem Fremdem zu reinigendes vorstellt, kümmert die bekannten Wortführer wenig. Es genügt ihnen offenbar, die fragliche Entschlossenheit nur immer wieder in Szene zu setzen, so dass sie sich geradezu selbst beweist. Wer immerfort und (ungefragt) im Namen aller den Willen bekundet, das Eigene zu behaupten und zu verteidigen, personifiziert diesen Willen und *ist* in diesem Sinne am Ende dieser Wille oder erweckt ständig diesen Anschein – so klein der Anteil an der jeweiligen Wählerschaft auch sein mag. Die ‚echten' Ungarn, zahlenmäßig eine Minderheit, *sind* dann *die Ungarn* (oder glauben es zu sein), so wie die ‚wahren Finnen', ebenfalls eine Minderheit, und nur sie wirklich Finnen sind (wie sie glauben). Jeder von ihnen darf dann glauben, in seiner Person ‚das Volk' zu sein, als ob er „die ganze Polis wäre"[20].

Jedes Mal, so scheint es, spielt die mehr oder weniger angemaßte Autorität einiger weniger eine entscheidende Rolle, die als Wortführer anderer auftreten, welche sich ihnen offenbar nur allzu gerne unterwerfen, indem sie ihnen unwi-

---

18 Vgl. Berg, *Luftmenschen*.
19 Vgl. Klein und Finkelde, *Souveränität und Subversion*.
20 Löwith, „Jacob Burckhardt", 194.

dersprochen ein weitgehend unbeschränktes Rederecht im Namen Benachteiligter (oder sich benachteiligt Fühlender), Vernachlässigter, Übersehener, Marginalisierter oder Diskriminierter zubilligen. Je weniger diese glauben, überhaupt noch in den Augen Anderer ‚jemand' zu sein, und je komplexer die Umstände der wirklichen oder vermuteten Vernachlässigung, Benachteiligung, Marginalisierung und Diskriminierung sich darstellen, desto stärker ist offenbar das Bedürfnis, sie rhetorisch zu vereinfachen, um sich wenigstens auf diese Weise dessen vergewissern zu können, *dass* man politisch existiert und *wer* man ist. Wenn das die eigene Situierung im sozialen und politischen Zusammenleben nicht mehr hergibt, verspricht wenigstens Solidarisierung mit Anderen im Zeichen von Zorn, Empörung und Protest klar zu beweisen, wer man ist – nach der Logik: ‚Wir protestieren, *also sind wir ‚da'*; wir bringen durch öffentliche oder virtuelle Zusammenrottung unseren Zorn zum Ausdruck (oder lassen ihn von Wortführern zum Ausdruck bringen), *also sind wir identisch*; wir pflichten demonstrativ den Reden unserer Anführer bei, *also existieren wir politisch als ‚jemand', als identitäre, durch die Rede unserer Wortführer verbürgte Wesen, die nicht zu ignorieren sind.*'

Die Attraktivität identitärer Rede speist sich offenbar wesentlich aus dem öffentlich erzeugten Eindruck, durch sie die eigene politische Existenz unübersehbar manifestieren zu können. Wenn er, der Wortführer, ruft, ‚Wir sind das Volk!', so hat es den Anschein, als habe sich die Existenz derjenigen, die ihm frenetisch beipflichten, als Volk in diesem Moment manifestiert. Zu behaupten, das Volk zu sein, genügt im Sinne eines derart schlichten Existenzbedürfnisses schließlich, um zu beweisen, dass man das Volk *ist* – im Unterschied zu Anderen freilich, die man im gleichen Zug ausgeschlossen hat. Je eindeutiger, desto besser, selbst wenn es sich bei den jeweils Ausgeschlossenen im Grunde um die Mehrheit der jeweiligen Bevölkerung handeln sollte. Wenn die einschlägigen politischen Demonstrationen eines beweisen, dann dies: Die für viele unerhörte Attraktivität eines Verhaltens, durch das man mittels identitärer Rhetorik sichtbar machen kann, dass man existiert. Im Grenzfall einfach dadurch, dass einer, den man dazu wie auch immer ermächtigt hat, schreit: „Wir sind das Volk"; d. h. ‚die Existenz des Volkes spricht sich durch meinen Mund aus; insofern bin ich das Volk, das durch mich zu Wort kommt und sich auf diese Weise identitär manifestiert'.

Wer derartigen Manifestationen beiwohnt, wird scheinbar reich belohnt: Wie aus dem Nichts seiner Marginalität heraus partizipiert er am allein durch Worte hervorzubringenden Sein eines Kollektivs, das gar keiner *voces populi*, sondern nurmehr einer einzigen Stimme bedarf, um als *vox populi* zu affirmieren, dass man existiert – was mangels einer solchen Stimme radikal ungewiss ist. Die Abgehängten, Benachteiligten, Überflüssigen und prekär Lebenden müssen ständig daran zweifeln, ob sie (politisch) überhaupt noch ‚da' oder bereits (politisch) ‚tot' sind. Umso größer ist offenbar die Versuchung, sich mittels rhetorisch-identitärer Gewaltstreiche einer kollektiven Existenz zu versichern, die Theoretiker der Identität von Gilles Deleuze bis hin zu Zygmunt Bauman längst in einer uferlosen Liquidierung von allem und jedem aufgehen sehen. So schlägt nicht nur (wieder einmal) die Stunde des autoritären Denkens, das damit Schluss zu machen verspricht,[21] sondern auch die Stunde derjenigen, die die Renaissance dieses Denkens aus dem Verfall ‚echter' Autorität erklären. Charles Taylor beispielsweise beklagt (in Park Honans Worten) „das Fehlen einer das spirituelle Leben bestimmenden, starken Autorität" in geistiger „Leere, Oberflächlichkeit und Fragmentierung" anheimgegebenen Gesellschaften und preist wie andere vor ihm eine „neue Bindung" an Religion als Ausweg an.[22]

4 Vater-Imago, Vertikalität, Autorität und Autoritarismus

Dergleichen erscheint anderen umso notwendiger, als wir es angeblich seit langem mit einem weitgehenden Zusammenbruch väterlicher Autorität bzw., in Jacques Lacans Worten, mit einem „gesellschaftlichen Verfall der väterlichen Imago" zu tun haben, auf der nicht weniger als die eigentliche „Vertikalität" heutiger Gesellschaften bzw. ihrer autoritativ verbürgten hierarchischen Struktur zu beruhen scheint.[23] Erodiert die väterliche Imago, so lassen sich demzufolge letztlich keine vertikalen, autoritativen gesellschaftlichen Strukturen mehr verlässlich ausbilden, die ihrerseits das ‚Image' des Vaters sollten ratifizieren können, da es niemals aus sich heraus, bloß als psychologisches, Bestand haben kann. Dieses Image hängt demnach mit einer entsprechenden gesellschaftlichen, autoritativ-hierarchisch ausgeprägten Vertikalität heutiger Gesellschaften zusammen, die es stützen und sich ihrerseits auf das generelle Funktionieren von Internalisierungen dieses Images verlassen müssen.

So ergibt sich scheinbar mühelos eine suggestive Verkettung von Problemen, die auseinander folgen und sich in zirkulärer Weise gegenseitig verstärken: Wo das Ansehen des Vaters bzw. des Väterlichen als solchen schwindet, fehlt es an einer ‚wirklichen' Fundierung von Autorität nicht nur innerhalb familialer Zu-

---

[21] Man denke nur an Carl Schmitts Politische Theorie, die nicht zuletzt von seiner Kritik der Romantik als einer angeblich alle klaren Unterscheidungen auflösenden Bewegung inspiriert ist.
[22] Suggestiv diskutiert Taylor so Matthew Arnold in Taylor, *Säkulares Zeitalter*, 632–644, vgl. Chaouat, *Is Theory Good for the Jews?*. 244 ff.
[23] Ehrenberg, *Unbehagen*, 212, 218, 320 ff.

sammenhänge, sondern auch in vertikalen gesellschaftlichen Dimensionen, die sich infolgedessen nicht mehr verlässlich hierarchisch ausbilden können und im Übrigen durch ‚horizontale' Sozialbeziehungen[24] nicht zu ersetzen seien. Genau das soll wiederum eine Schwächung väterlicher Autorität zur Folge haben, letztlich auch derjenigen Gottes selbst, usw. Man spricht in diesem Zusammenhang geradezu vom „Ende der Vertikalität" und sieht darin „das große Problem der demokratischen Gesellschaft",[25] nämlich den Verfall jeglicher Autorität, der antiliberalen, autoritären Tendenzen geradewegs in die Hände spiele (als ob es sich nicht auch genau umgekehrt verhalten könnte). So gesehen ist nicht etwa die familiale Internalisierung väterlicher Autorität, die man lange im Verdacht hatte, sondern gerade deren Erosion für das Aufkommen politischer Autoritarismen verantwortlich.[26] Und letzteres scheint ganz und gar einer moralischen Analyse zugänglich zu sein, die weitgehend ohne sozio-ökonomische Fundierung auskommt.

Wenn es darüber hinaus aber zutrifft, dass auch die psycho-sozio-politische väterliche Autorität als solche nur in einer *über sich selbst hinausweisenden Vertikalität* zu verstehen ist,[27] verweist sie dann nicht ‚letztlich' auf Gott als Inbegriff des Vaters, der allein auch das psychische, soziale und politische Leben selbst noch ‚vertikal' ausrichten kann?[28] Ist also der ‚Tod' oder die ‚Abwesenheit' Got-

---

[24] Vgl. Frankenberg, *Verfassung*, zur Suche nach „säkularisierter Ersatztranszendenz" in der „Sehnsucht nach einer absoluten Quelle von Autorität jenseits aller von Menschen beschlossenen Gesetze" (ebd., 85, 87).

[25] Ehrenberg, *Unbehagen*, 154, 322. Ricœur, *Le Juste 2*, 181 ff. zu Antoine Garapon.

[26] In diese Richtung zielt die Argumentation von Vargas Llosa, *Alles Boulevard*, der beklagt, Antiautoritäre hätten das Autoritative gleich mit abgeschafft (69, 85). Und deshalb könne auch politisch reaktionäres Denken wieder aufkommen (87). Schon die einschlägigen Untersuchungen der sog. Frankfurter Schule bzw. der ehemaligen Kritischen Theorie zielten freilich darauf ab, eine nicht-autoritäre Weise der Ausübung väterlicher Autorität herauszuarbeiten. Sie sollten nicht etwa darauf hinauslaufen, jegliche familial begründete Autorität zu rechtfertigen, obgleich sich gelegentlich genau dieser Eindruck aufdrängt. Vgl. Frankfurter Institut für Sozialforschung, *Soziologische Exkurse*, Kap. 9.

[27] Wie es schon Numa Denis Fustel de Coulanges nahegelegt hatte, indem er behauptete, die Autorität des Vaters (im antiken Rom) sei „religiösen Ursprungs" (De Coulanges, *Der antike Staat*, 62). So öffnet sich das thematische Feld auf einen unermesslichen Horizont verschiedener Konstellationen von Filiationen, Vaterschaft, Autorität, Gesetzlichkeit, Vertikalität und religiöser Suprematie, die wir vom alten Ägypten über das Judentum und das Christentum bis in den modernen Faschismus und Nationalsozialismus hinein höchst unterschiedlich ausgeprägt finden. Vgl. Hegel, „Der Geist des Christentums", 274–418, bes. 302–308; Bataille, *Psychologische Struktur*, 31–37; Assmann, *Herrschaft und Heil*.

[28] Hier haben wir es mit einer komplexen Verschränkung (psycho-)ökonomischer, phänomenologischer und hermeneutischer Problematiken zu tun, die Ricœur im Anschluss an Freud

tes²⁹ der letzte Grund für den Autoritätsverlust, dessen Symptom die rezenten Autoritarismen sind? Und wäre gegen diese demzufolge eine Rückkehr *der* bzw. *zur* Religion im Sinne der Wiedereinsetzung eines absoluten Vaters das einzig angemessene Gegenmittel? Oder sind entsprechende Vorschläge ihrerseits Ausdruck einer im Grunde autoritären Haltung, die der Versuchung nachgibt, offenbar weitgehender Verwirrung in der Frage, wer wir sind, durch eine neue Form der Unterwerfung zu begegnen?

Ein absoluter Vater – sei es nun der *polemós* Heraklits, der Krieg „als Vater aller Dinge",³⁰ oder Gott – bedürfte solcher Unterwerfung angesichts der ihm attestierten ‚Herrlichkeit' ohnehin nicht.³¹ Jede(r) wäre ihm gegenüber als schlechterdings und unüberwindlich inferior einzustufen. Und das müsste auch für jeden gewöhnlichen Vater gelten. Mag das ursprünglich in der Kindheit tief verankerte *sentiment filial*³² von diesem Unterschied zunächst auch nichts wissen, die ‚Enttrohnung' eines jeden Vaters erweist sich in ontogenetischer Perspektive als unvermeidlich. So sehr ein Gott als ‚Vater' verehrt werden mag, so wenig kann die Umkehrung funktionieren. Kein gewöhnlicher Vater ist Gott. Keine ‚väterliche' Macht der Welt kann bzw. darf göttliche Ambitionen verfolgen. Keine väterliche Autorität hat Anspruch auf Glaubwürdigkeit, in deren Sinn es nicht liegt, auf göttliche Prätentionen zu verzichten. Entweder sie dementiert von sich aus, über göttliche Befugnisse zu verfügen, beschränkt sich entsprechend selbst und stellt sich darauf ein, nicht als unumschränkt souveräne gelten zu dürfen, oder aber sie zerstört ihre Glaubwürdigkeit selbst. Väterliche Autorität, die quasi-göttliche Souveränität beansprucht, ist absolute Anmaßung und kann nicht Bestand haben. Sie programmiert gleichsam ihren eigenen Ruin vor.

Weit entfernt, sich gewisse Souveränitätsverzichte allenfalls von Anderen in einem Kampf um Leben und Tod abnötigen zu lassen, sich im Übrigen aber unter allen Umständen souverän behaupten zu wollen, muss im Grunde jede überlegene Macht darauf aus sein, sich von denjenigen, über die sie ausgeübt wird, ‚etwas sagen zu lassen'. Michel Foucault hat das in seinen Vorlesungen am *Collège de France* gut auf den Punkt gebracht: Damit der Stärkste vernünftig regieren

---

und Hegel auf imaginären und symbolischen Ebenen differenziert hat, um deren einfache Vermischung zu vermeiden. Darauf sei hier nur am Rande hingewiesen; vgl. Ricœur, „Die Vatergestalt", 74 ff.

29 Ehrenberg, *Unbehagen*, 154.
30 Taureck, *Wurzeln des Krieges*, 270 f.
31 Agamben, *Herrschaft und Herrlichkeit*.
32 Bovet, „Le sentiment religieux", 157–175; Bovet, „Le sentiment filial", 141–153.

kann, müssen die Schwächsten ‚freimütig' zu ihm sprechen können.³³ Das gilt in politischer wie auch in generativer Hinsicht. Keine Macht der Welt kann auf Dauer Bestand haben, die in diesem Sinne nicht zuzuhören imstande ist. Die Selbstherrlichkeit einer Macht, die darauf keine Rücksicht meint nehmen zu müssen, programmiert, da sie nicht ‚zuzuhören' imstande ist, gleichsam ihren eigenen Machtverlust vor, der nötigenfalls auch durch mehr oder weniger brutale Absetzung, durch Vater- oder Gottesmord erzwungen werden wird. Das gilt bereits innerhalb familialer und quasi-familialer Lebenszusammenhänge, in denen man den Ursprung väterlicher, quasi-göttlicher Souveränität und aller Autorität vermutet hat, die ohne ihre mehr oder weniger *‚vorbildliche'* Selbstbeschränkung nur auf eine *Despotie ohne Ansehen* hinauslaufen kann – auf die noch Hannah Arendt die väterliche Autorität glaubte reduzieren zu können. Erst recht aber gilt *das Angewiesensein jeglicher überlegenen Macht darauf, Schwächeren Gehör zu schenken,* für deren politische Formen.

Wie auch immer es heute um die ontogenetischen Bedingungen der Ausbildung, Anerkennung und ‚Relativierung' väterlicher, vertikaler und hierarchischer Autorität sowie um deren sei es religiöse, sei es gesellschaftlich-ökonomische Rückendeckung bestellt sein mag: mir kommt es hier darauf an, die *Schwelle ihrer Politisierung* eigens zu bedenken, die in der Klage über den angeblichen Zusammenbruch der vertikalen Dimension der Autorität allzu wenig bedacht wird.³⁴ Keineswegs kann letztere einfach im Rekurs auf ‚autoritäre' familiale Voraussetzungen begründet werden. Umgekehrt müssen diese sich ihrerseits auf eine politische Welt hin öffnen, an der sie von Anfang an Anteil haben und in die sie die Heranwachsenden früher oder später entlassen müssen; und zwar nach einschlägiger historischer Erfahrung so, dass diese keinerlei Bereitschaft dazu haben, sich einem ‚Führer' zu unterwerfen. So gesehen trennt familiale und gesellschaftliche bzw. öffentliche Autorität kein absoluter Hiatus, wie es stellenweise bei Arendt den Anschein hat, wo sie die quasi-despotische Herrschaftsstruktur der Familie dem republikanischen und demokratischen Sinn politischer Koexistenz gegenüberstellt. Vielmehr muss die Familie ihrerseits jeglicher späteren politischen Unterwerfung vorbeugen und kann nur so zu diesem Sinn beitragen.

---

33 Vgl. Foucault, *Regierung des Selbst*, 179; Liebsch, *Einander ausgesetzt. Elemente einer Topografie des Zusammenlebens*, Kap. 20.
34 Vgl. Rieff, *Crisis*.

5 Verzicht auf den (politischen) ‚Vater'

Paul Ricœur hat in seinem Freud-Buch *Die Interpretation* dafür die schlichte Formel gefunden, erwachsen zu werden heiße, auf den Vater zu verzichten.[35] Damit war bei näherem Hinsehen vor allem gemeint, weder den Vater noch irgendeine Ersatzfigur noch als unumschränkte, nicht ‚diskutable', also unanfechtbare und souveräne Autorität gelten zu lassen, um sich auf diese Weise von der Last der eigenen Freiheit zu befreien.[36] Dass jener Verzicht auf jeden Fall einen nach Hegel'schem Vorbild gedachten Kampf um Anerkennung erforderlich macht, wie es stellenweise auch bei Ricœur den Anschein hat, erscheint allerdings kaum glaubhaft, wenn es stimmt, dass es gar nicht im recht verstandenen Sinn der Ausübung väterlicher Autorität liegen kann, sich *nicht auch von sich aus* auf ihre eigene Überwindung einzustellen, d. h. freimütige Rede, Kritikfähigkeit und Widersetzlichkeit gegen jegliche Form der Unterwerfung unter Bedingungen der Zugehörigkeit zum Leben Anderer zu fördern. Zugespitzt gesagt: Der politische Sinn der Ausübung väterlicher Autorität liegt (mindestens) gerade darin, die Heranwachsenden so weit wie nur möglich gegen jeglichen *Need of A Master*, sowie gegen jedes entsprechende *Begehren* immun zu machen, *so dass niemals eine psycho-politische, imaginäre oder symbolische direkte Linie vom Vater zum Meister und Führer verlaufen kann, dem scheinbar alles zuzutrauen ist,*[37] der aber jederzeit mit einem ‚Vatermord' rechnen muss.

So gesehen wird man den oft beklagten Weg in die ‚vaterlose', genealogisch konturlose Gesellschaft, die alle Einzelnen angeblich einem haltlosen, nach

---

[35] Vgl. Ricœur, *Interpretation*, 335f., 562.

[36] Im gleichen, zwischen Archäologie und Teleologie des Psychischen gleichsam aufgespannten Werk lesen wir allerdings auch, dass über eine archäologische Dimension Wesen verfügen, die Kind gewesen sind, ohne dass man annehmen dürfte, die darin liegende Verspätung sich selbst gegenüber lasse sich jemals aufholen oder die Kindheit lasse ihre Überwindung derart zu, dass man ein für alle Mal nicht mehr befürchten müsste, regressiv zu ihr ‚zurückgerissen' zu werden (Ricœur, *Interpretation*, 335f., 455, 459, 467). So wird denn auch hier an keiner Stelle angenommen, der erwähnte Verzicht auf den Vater, die Befreiung von ihm (oder auch die Trauer um ihn) lasse sich jemals radikal und endgültig zum Ziel bringen.

[37] Auch aus eigener Machtvollkommenheit ‚das Recht zu schützen', wie Schmitts berüchtigte Formulierung lautete, oder auch das ‚Volk' zum Tode zu verurteilen, wie es im Kontext des sog. Nero-Befehls symbolisch geschehen ist. Vgl. Bazyler, *Holocaust*, 214. Was diesen Befehl Hitlers vom 19. März 1945 im Hinblick auf das Volk angeht, beziehe ich mich auf die dokumentierte Antwort Albert Speers auf ihn, online abrufbar unter: http://germanhistorydocs.ghi-dc.org/docpage.cfm?docpage_id=2382&language=german (letzter Zugriff im November 2019; B.L.).

terribles simplificateurs sich sehnenden Leben in der „Masse"[38] überantworten muss, kaum bedauern, sofern er nur diese Linie durchkreuzt hat.[39] Längst hat dieser Weg andere Formen der Väterlichkeit denkbar werden lassen, andere (nicht-souveräne, nicht bloß repressive[40]) Formen väterlicher Autorität und andere Formen ihres Ansehens, die auch Trauer über den abwesenden, vermissten oder verlorenen Vater zulassen, ohne die nach dem Zeugnis von Albert Camus in ihr liegende „furchtbare Leere" in eine politisch fatale, nämlich autoritäre Richtung zu lenken.[41]

Tatsächlich hat die kritische Diagnose gesellschaftlicher ‚Vaterlosigkeit' zwei komplementäre Seiten. Sie besagt einerseits, dass niemand ohne eine psychodynamisch angemessene Internalisierung ‚väterlicher' Autorität wirklich ‚erwachsen' werden kann, besteht andererseits aber darauf, dass letztere von sich aus auf die egalitäre Entmachtung ihrer asymmetrischen Überlegenheit hinarbeiten muss, um endlich mündige Nachkommen aus jeglicher Vormundschaft zu entlassen und dazu zu befähigen, sich als Bürger jeglicher Unterwerfung unter Ersatzvaterfiguren zu widersetzen, als die ‚Führer' regelmäßig anmaßend auftreten. Nichts ist in Anbetracht einschlägiger historischer Erfahrung politisch gefährlicher als das; nichts an der gesellschaftlichen Funktion der Vaterschaft demzufolge wichtiger, als durch Einwilligung in ihre eigene Entmächtigung den Weg in eine Mündigkeit freizumachen, deren Ziel es sein muss, sich jeglicher Unterwerfung unter ‚Führer' widersetzen zu können.[42]

So gesehen liegt die politische, über ihren familialen Sinn hinausweisende Bedeutung der Vaterschaft in der Etablierung akzeptabler ‚autoritativer' Verhältnisse, die keiner ‚autoritären' Versuchung oder Verführung nachgeben; auch nicht

---

38 Vgl. Löwith, *Rezension von „Nicolai Berdjajews"*, 416 ff. Strauss, *Naturrecht und Geschichte*, 299, zu Rousseau.
39 Zur „Masse", zur „Vaterlosigkeit" sowie zur genealogischen Entsicherung vgl. Arendt, *Vita activa*, 41; Mitscherlich, *Auf dem Weg zur vaterlosen Gesellschaft*; Sloterdijk, *Die schrecklichen Kinder der Neuzeit*.
40 Vgl. Merleau-Ponty, *Keime der Vernunft*, Kap. 2; Sartre, *Moralphilosophie*, 334–343.
41 „Jetzt, wo mir alles abhanden kommt, wo ich das Bedürfnis habe, daß jemand mir den Weg weist, mich tadelt und lobt, nicht aufgrund von Macht, sondern von Autorität, brauche ich meinen Vater", schreibt Camus in seinem posthum veröffentlichten, offenbar autobiografisch grundierten Roman Der erste Mensch, 37; vgl. ebd. 165 ff. Das Possessivpronomen ist hier entscheidend. Es geht nicht um irgendeinen Vater, der ersatzweise den Verlassenen „tadelt und lobt" und dessen entsprechende Infantilisierung erfordern würde.
42 Diese m. E. politisch unumgängliche Einsicht müsste dazu führen, das gängige, von Nietzsche über Heidegger bis hin zu manchen Foucault-Adepten verbreitete Vorurteil zu revidieren, demzufolge jegliche Macht nur auf ihre eigene Steigerung hinauswollen kann. Allerdings stellt sich auch die Frage, ob jene Entmachtung wiederum nur in der Macht derjenigen liegt, die sich zu ihr bereitfinden bzw. herablassen.

im Sinne freiwilliger Unterwerfung.[43] In dieser Perspektive *kommt vermittels autoritativer Verhältnisse eine ‚vertikale' gesellschaftliche Dimension ins Spiel, die gerade den Verzicht auf einen ‚politischen Vater' erfordert und nur unter dieser Bedingung noch (anfechtbare) Autorität legitimieren kann*. Alles andere müsste auf die eine oder andere Art eines politischen Infantilismus hinauslaufen, der den psychodynamisch entscheidenden Schritt des Verzichts auf den Vater und die darin liegende Befreiung niemals wirklich vollzogen hat und politischen Ersatz für – sei es schwache und amorphe, sei es gewaltsame oder überhaupt fehlende – väterliche Autorität sucht, wo er in Wahrheit niemals zu finden sein wird: in ‚Führerfiguren',[44] denen es im Narzissmus ihres politischen Daseins vor allem um sich selbst geht, während ihre Gefolgsleute und Bewunderer eher Verachtung als möglicherweise ersehnte Anerkennung erfahren, es sei denn, einige wenige von ihnen werden gnädig zu Ersatz-Töchtern und Ersatz-Söhnen erhoben, die in ihrer Inferiorität politisch allerdings niemals um ihrer selbst willen geliebt werden; zumal dann nicht, wenn sie sich im Zuge ihrer Unterordnung oder Unterwerfung im Grunde selbst aufgegeben haben.

So gesehen läuft jene Diagnose darauf hinaus, dass wir normalerweise zwar eines Vaters[45] bedürfen, durch den wir in die vertikale und autoritative Dimension des Politischen eingeführt werden; nicht aber eines Vaters, für den politischer Ersatz gesucht werden müsste. Im Gegenteil: *Die Aufgabe des ontogenetisch ersten Vaters wäre es, den Verzicht auf den politischen Vater vorzubereiten*. Nur wer nicht vaterlos aufgewachsen ist, kann demzufolge auf die Vaterlosigkeit angemessen vorbereitet sein, die von allen, die als Gleiche miteinander politisch koexistieren, abzuverlangen ist, ohne indessen autoritative Verhältnisse unmöglich zu machen.

---

43 Die sich in der genealogischen Perspektive des bis hierher Gesagten keineswegs als zweifelhafter Erfolg, sondern gerade als ein Versagen der politischen Funktion der Vaterschaft deuten ließe.

44 Man vergleiche in diesem Sinne nur die Streitschrift von Jaspers, *Die geistige Situation der Zeit*, in der als Gegenmittel gegen anscheinend vaterloses Leben in der „Masse" mehrfach „Führer" empfohlen werden (41, 49).

45 Bzw. des Väterlichen, wie es genauer heißen müsste, wenn es denn stimmt, dass dessen Funktionen im Hinblick auf die Etablierung einer vertikal und autoritativ (aber nicht autoritär) orientierten Gesellschaft ebensowohl von Frauen und Müttern übernommen werden können. Die gleiche Frage stellt sich im Fall einer ‚mütterlichen' Dimension des Sozialen, die nicht auf das entsprechende Geschlecht beschränkt zu denken ist. Es liegt außerhalb der Reichweite dieses Beitrags, diese Fragen zu klären. Dass die Funktion des Väterlichen ggf. von weiblichen Identifikationsfiguren zu übernehmen ist, so wie auch die Funktion des Mütterlichen zumindest teilweise von männlichen Identifikationsfiguren übernommen werden kann, versteht sich jedoch von selbst.

Aus dieser zweifellos normativen Deutung der Psychoontogenese folgt gerade nicht, dass wir politisch wie im Grunde seit jeher *in need of a master* existieren müssten und dass wir insgeheim nicht ohne entsprechende Formen der Bewunderung, der Idealisierung, der Idolisierung und der Unterwerfung auskommen könnten. Normativ fällt diese Deutung nicht zuletzt in der Erinnerung an fatale Zeiten aus, die uns die politische Fragwürdigkeit solcher Formen reichlich genug vor Augen geführt haben dürften; und zwar auf Seiten derer, die zur Unterwerfung bereit waren, wie auch auf Seiten derer, die sich als ‚Führer' aufgespielt haben und auf der Suche nach entsprechender Gefolgschaft waren; sei es als anti-politische Demagogen (wie Adolf Hitler), sei es auch als akademische Lehrer (wie Martin Heidegger).

Seitdem erweist sich das politisch-theoretische Denken als außerordentlich sensibilisiert für die Frage, wie der familiale Raum, in dem zunächst die Vaterschaft ihren sozialen Ort hat, mit dem Raum des Gesellschaftlichen und Politischen in Verbindung gebracht wird, in dem es zu keinerlei Unterwerfung unter ‚führendes' Personal, dessen Reden und ideologische Programme mehr kommen soll. Hannah Arendt war darum derart besorgt, dass sie keine andere Wahl zu haben glaubte, als die genealogischen Verbindungen zwischen Familialem und Privatem einerseits, dem Politischen und Öffentlichen andererseits zu durchtrennen. Folgt man ihrer Theorie, so muss man im Überschreiten der Schwelle zum Politisch-Öffentlichen die nach Arendts Dafürhalten unvermeidliche Despotie des Privatlebens ebenso wie die ‚Weltlosigkeit', die Liebesbeziehungen auszeichnet,[46] definitiv hinter sich lassen und ‚vergessen', um sich in politischen Beziehungen zwischen Gleichen bewegen zu können, die grundsätzlich nur zusammen vertikale (legale und legitime) Beziehungen zu Anderen stiften sollten, denen darauf aufbauend autoritative, im Prinzip jederzeit zu widerrufende Befugnisse zustehen.

6 Was es bedeutet, eine Meinung zu äußern und sich etwas sagen zu lassen

Im Rahmen eines solchen Ansatzes kann man allerdings nicht zeigen, wie denn der familiale Raum auf solche Beziehungen vorbereitet und was er zu ihnen ggf. beitragen kann. Wie aus dem Nichts soll, nachdem man ihn verlassen hat, ein freies Spiel der Meinungen in politischen Auseinandersetzungen um gemeinsame Angelegenheiten möglich werden. Aber muss dieses Spiel nicht unweigerlich

---

46 Arendt, *Denktagebuch*, 279, 428.

die Form eines Kampfes gegeneinander, um Hegemonie und womöglich unumschränkte Vorherrschaft annehmen, wenn es keine anderen Ressourcen voraussetzen kann als derart kümmerliche, wie sie nur aus einer ‚despotischen' und mehr oder weniger repressiven Sozialisation hervorgehen können? Was sollte man aus einer entsprechenden Vorgeschichte anderes lernen, als dass jede politische Meinung und Überzeugung – wie schon die autoritär, despotisch und repressiv sich manifestierende Übermacht des Vaters auch – unter allen Umständen so zu vertreten ist, dass man jeweils möglichst ‚recht behält'? Kann es unter diesen Voraussetzungen überhaupt um Anderes und um mehr gehen, als sich in diesem Sinne ständig ‚durchsetzen' und gegen Andere behaupten zu wollen?

Tatsächlich scheint Arendt den öffentlich-politischen Meinungsaustausch, der nach ihrer Überzeugung auf jeglichen unbedingten Wahrheitsanspruch, auf jegliche Suprematie des Ansehens und auf jegliche unanfechtbare Vormacht zu verzichten hat, aber ganz anders aufgefasst zu haben, nämlich als ein freies In-Erscheinung-treten derjenigen, die sich an Andere auf Erwiderung hin wenden.[47] Um sich mit Anderen überhaupt auseinandersetzen zu können, muss man *vor ihnen* und *mit ihnen* in Erscheinung treten können, *sie* erscheinen lassen, seine Stimme erheben und etwas zu bedenken geben können, von dem man zunächst nur sagt, dass man es so oder so ‚finde'. ‚Ich finde, dass ...', ‚Ich meine, dass ...' und vergleichbare Ausdrücke[48] sind aber weit mehr als nur *etwas feststellende* Äußerungen. Implizit beinhalten sie, wenn sie im Geist wirklichen, freien Meinungsaustausches getätigt werden, eine an Andere gerichtete *Frage* dieser Art: ‚Meinst du nicht auch ...?' ‚Was meinen Sie dazu?' Äußert man eine Meinung (*dóxa*[49]), so ist damit gerade keine ‚unerschütterliche' Überzeugung zu verknüpfen, die Andere nur noch zur Kenntnis zu nehmen und zu übernehmen hätten. Vielmehr bedeutet es, eine gleichsam provisorische Einschätzung an Andere zu adressieren, auf deren Korrektur oder wie auch immer geartete Modifikation man sich dabei zugleich einstellt und zu der man geradezu einlädt.

Nur so können sich auch Meinungen ‚bilden'; und genau das ist auch der Sinn politischen Austauschs, von dem wir nicht umsonst als einem Prozess der ‚Meinungsbildung' (und nicht nur ihres Abgleichs) sprechen. Das aber bedeutet, dass jeder, der eine Meinung politisch äußert, damit zugleich zu erkennen gibt, dass er sie für ergänzungs- und korrekturbedürftig hält und in diesem Sinne den jeweiligen Adressanten einen eigenständigen und unverfügbaren Antwortspielraum

---

[47] Arendt, *Vita activa*, §§ 5–9.
[48] Vgl. Held, *Phänomenologie*.
[49] Von deren konstitutivem Weltbezug, den Arendt betont, sehe ich hier ab; Arendt, *Denktagebuch*, 399.

einräumt. Im Prozess der Meinungsbildung und -äußerung wird den Adressaten ihre Bedeutung als grundsätzlich unvorhersehbar Antwortenden bestätigt, so dass sich die eigene Meinung nur infolge fremder Antworten (weiter) bilden kann. Selbst wenn man an ihr festhält und auf ihr beharrt, geschieht das demzufolge erst, nachdem man die Erwiderung Anderer zur Kenntnis genommen hat. Das ist etwas ganz anderes als nur ein Kampf ohnehin verschiedener Meinungen um ihre Durchsetzung gegen Andere – so als ginge es in politischer Kommunikation nur darum, ‚recht zu behalten' – was Paul Valéry nicht umsonst als das Widerwärtigste überhaupt bezeichnet hat.

Jede politische Meinungsäußerung impliziert also nicht nur den Anspruch, selbst gehört werden zu wollen, sondern auch das Signal an die Adresse der jeweils Angesprochenen, ihrer Erwiderung Gehör schenken zu wollen, und anerkennt sie insofern als Gleiche, ganz gleich, in welcher inferioren oder überlegenen gesellschaftlichen Stellung sie sich gerade befinden. Wer sich mit Anderen in einen Meinungsaustausch begibt, anerkennt sie als freie Adressaten und Subjekte einer grundsätzlich nicht vorwegzunehmenden und nicht durch Anderes zu ersetzenden Erwiderung, die ablehnend, neutral oder auch beipflichtend ausfallen kann, aber nicht muss.

Bereits im familialen Erscheinungsraum sind wir darauf angewiesen, dass sich in diesem Sinne Meinungen überhaupt erst *bilden* können, die man niemals einfach wie aus dem Nichts heraus ‚hat'. Und hier können sie sich nicht originär bilden, wenn überlegene Subjekte alle Möglichkeiten, die ihnen zur Verfügung stehen, dazu nutzen, über die noch kaum artikulierten anfänglichen Meinungen Jüngerer zu triumphieren (was in einem rein despotischen Herrschaftsverhältnis ja vollkommen genügen würde). Alles hängt hier davon ab, dass die Überlegenen ihre Vormacht selbst beschränken und Meinungen überhaupt erst sich bilden, artikulieren und behaupten lassen. Genau das bereitet – in einer zunächst autoritativen familialen oder quasi-familialen Sozialstruktur – dann auch auf den freien politischen Meinungsaustausch im Horizont einer überwiegend anonymen Öffentlichkeit vor, in der man – statt Meinungen als fertige Überzeugungen nur gegeneinander in Stellung zu bringen, um möglichst die eigenen den Sieg über andere davontragen zu lassen –, echtes Interesse an der Artikulation der Meinungen Anderer aufbringt; diesmal aber unter Gleichen, die als Subjekte freien Meinungsaustauschs keine privilegierte Position für sich in Anspruch nehmen. In diesem Sinne muss es sich um eine zutiefst anti-autoritäre Angelegenheit handeln, auf die, recht verstanden, gerade eine autoritative Sozialstruktur vorbereitet, welche darauf angelegt ist, keinerlei ‚Vaterersatz' nötig zu machen.

Im Geist des ‚Verzichts auf den Vater' also überschreiten wir die Schwelle der Öffentlichkeit vom Privaten zum Politischen, vorausgesetzt, wir haben gemäß autoritativem Vorbild, das seine überlegene Macht selbst eingeschränkt hat, gelernt, uns ‚etwas sagen' zu lassen. Statt Andere geradewegs mit rhetorischen Mitteln übertrumpfen oder sogar mundtot machen zu wollen, äußern wir Meinungen *spezifisch politisch* überhaupt erst dann, wenn wir (a) sie stets zugleich mit der offenen (wenigstens impliziten) Frage verknüpfen, was Andere zu ihnen meinen, wenn wir (b) einen entsprechend freien Antwortspielraum aller politischen Zeitgenossen und Mitbürger anerkennen und gleichzeitig (c) das Interesse an ihrer Erwiderung bekunden. Darin liegt, mehr noch, (d) das implizite Versprechen, dass wir unsere Meinung infolge *ihrer* Meinungsäußerungen möglicherweise revidieren werden.

Fehlt es auch nur an einem einzigen dieser für jede genuin politische Meinungsäußerung und -bildung sinnkonstitutiven Momente, so haben wir es überhaupt nicht mit spezifisch politischem Meinungsaustausch, sondern viel eher mit *anti-politischem Verhalten* zu tun.[50] Anti-politisches Verhalten lässt demzufolge jede Frage danach, was Andere zu ihm meinen, vermissen (a'); es anerkennt keinen eigenständigen, freien Antwortspielraum aller politischen Zeitgenossen und Mitbürger (b') und bekundet kein Interesse an deren Erwiderung (c'). Zudem verspricht es in keiner Weise, die eigene Meinung infolge der Meinungsäußerungen Anderer möglicherweise zu revidieren (d'). Alle diese Punkte manifestieren das genaue Gegenteil politischer Offenheit, die für jeden echten Meinungsaustausch vorauszusetzen ist, und geben nur Selbstgerechtigkeit zu erkennen. Wer sich selbstgerecht äußert, genügt sich politisch anscheinend vollkommen selbst, bedarf widerstreitender Ansichten Anderer überhaupt nicht und lässt sie allenfalls noch als Objekte von Äußerungen gelten, über die bereits mehr oder weniger feststehende Meinungen kundgetan werden. Nichts beugt solcher Selbstgerechtigkeit besser vor als eine sich selbst einschränkende, auf Schwächere hörende Autorität, die sich überwinden lassen hat.[51] Nichts trägt dagegen mehr zu ihr bei als das negative Vorbild eines autoritären Verhaltens, das stets über Andere zu triumphieren sucht, ohne Interesse daran zu zeigen, sich

---

[50] Lediglich *en passant* sei darauf hingewiesen, wie weitgehend sogenannte radikal-demokratische Theorien jegliche Besinnung auf jene Momente vermissen lassen. Mit einer Apologie des Agonalen oder Antagonistischen allein, die sich um die ‚zivile' Form politischer Auseinandersetzungen keine besonderen Gedanken macht, ist gewiss keine Gesellschaft und kein Staat zu machen.

[51] Und zwar nicht wiederum ‚aus eigener Machtvollkommenheit'. Wenn jegliches Zuhören nur einer Selbsteinschränkung souveräner und autoritärer Macht zu verdanken wäre, bliebe diese auch dann, wenn sie sich ‚etwas sagen lässt', uneingeschränkt. In Wahrheit erweist sich aber noch die stärkste Macht *nolens volens* vom Anspruch des Schwächsten grundsätzlich affizierbar und kann nur nachträglich zu ihm Stellung nehmen. Nur so lässt sich eine Beschränkung solcher Macht denken, die nicht wiederum auf deren Selbstbeschränkung hinausliefe.

etwas sagen zu lassen[52] – wie es in jeder *listening citizenry* unabdingbar ist, die es den Schwächeren erspart, sich erst mit gewaltsamen Mitteln Gehör verschaffen zu müssen.[53]

Paradoxerweise rekurrieren nun aber gerade autoritäre und populistische politische Bewegungen auf diesen Zusammenhang. Angeblich im Namen derjenigen, ‚die nicht gehört werden', ermächtigen sich identitäre Wortführer dazu, ihnen Geltung zu verschaffen. Dass diese ihrerseits elitären und nicht selten superreichen Kreisen entstammen, tut dem offenbar keinerlei Abbruch, Hauptsache, sie bedienen das Bedürfnis, durch identitäres Reden bestätigt zu bekommen, dass man politisch existiert und als ‚jemand' ernst zu nehmen ist – im Gegensatz zu Anderen, ohne deren möglichst eindeutig bestimmte negative Identität man dabei allerdings nicht auskommt. Wer man ist, weiß man offenbar nicht aus eigener Kraft, sondern primär durch Ablehnung Anderer – von alltäglicher Diskriminierung über polemische Anfeindungen bis hin zur *hate speech*, die sich darin gefällt, sie ganz und gar auf Objekte denunziatorischer, verächtlicher und symbolisch vernichtender Rede, virtueller Kommentare oder *posts* zu reduzieren. All das geschieht offenbar nicht mehr, um mit Anderen in ein Spiel der freien Meinungsäußerung einzutreten – dessen Regeln man zwar in Anspruch nimmt, aber systematisch missachtet, insofern es dieses Verhalten gar nicht mehr darauf anlegt, auf unvorhersehbare Art und Weise erwidert zu werden. Insofern verhält es sich *antipolitisch im Politischen*. Es nimmt für sich in Anspruch, die Identität der Gefolgschaft populistischer Rhetorik zum Ausdruck zu bringen, lässt aber nicht mehr erkennen, ob und inwiefern es ihm überhaupt noch auf Erwiderung ankommt, die ihm möglicherweise nicht zustimmt. Wer sich aber politisch äußert, ohne dabei das Dissenspotenzial möglicher Erwiderung im Sinn zu haben oder es sogar unterdrücken will, verhält sich anti-politisch.

Dabei geht es nur noch um die Manifestation und Behauptung eigener Identität gegen Andere, ohne die Frage, als wer man sich versteht, noch einer offenen Auseinandersetzung auszusetzen.[54] Geäußerte Meinungen und Überzeugungen gehen dann nicht mehr mit der Frage einher, wie Andere sie empfinden und beurteilen. Identitäre Rede will sich nur noch gegen Andere durchsetzen,

---

[52] Bezeichnenderweise unterstellt eine politische Theorie, die in der Familie nur eine despotische Herrschaftsstruktur erkennen kann, genau diese ‚Ignoranz' auf der Seite ‚autoritärer' Elternschaft.
[53] Vgl. Barber, *Strong Democracy*, 207; Grüny, „Der Sensibelste aller Sinne", 253–280.
[54] Bezeichnenderweise wird auch in Apologien eines ‚linken' Populismus, der dem Politischen wieder Leben einhauchen soll, kaum je bedacht, wie ein agonales und antagonistisches Gegeneinander überhaupt die Form einer offenen Auseinandersetzung annehmen kann und ob es dazu ‚ziviler' Umgangsformen bedarf.

denn das scheint der einfachste und vielversprechendste Weg zu sein, sich dessen zu vergewissern, wer man überhaupt ist. Sich durchzusetzen, ohne sich dabei Anderen als solchen auszusetzen, das ist offenbar der anti-politische Traum derjenigen, die sich nicht damit abfinden können und wollen, unter Bedingungen einer öffentlich in Erscheinung tretenden Pluralität unter Gleichen überhaupt erst herauszufinden, wer sie unter der politischen Grundbedingung des ‚Verzichts auf den Vater' sind oder erst werden könnten.

Dieser Verzicht macht es unumgänglich, sich die Frage nach eigener Identität nicht von irgendjemandem einfach *beantworten zu lassen*, auch nicht von Meistern öffentlicher Rhetorik, die wissen wollen, wer das Volk ist, und von vermeintlich weisen Führern in künftiges Geschick. Sich von einem Anderen vorsagen lassen zu wollen, wer man ist – sei es auch nur als Unterdrückter, als Marginalisierte, als ‚Überflüssiger' oder Diskriminierte –, verrät politischen Infantilismus, der in polemischer Wendung gegen Andere, auf die man sich nur zum Zweck negativer Abgrenzung eigener Identität bezieht, ohne ihren Dissens noch im Geringsten ernst zu nehmen, die Gefahr irreversibler Spaltung jedes politischen Gemeinwesens heraufbeschwört, das nur dadurch bestehen kann, dass man sich im Interesse an freier Erwiderung Anderer möglichem Dissens aussetzt.

Tatsächlich sind wir unvermeidlich von Geburt an einander ausgesetzt; zunächst aber im Rahmen familialer oder quasi-familialer Lebensformen, die ebenso unvermeidlich eine Dimension autoritativer Vertikalität zwischen Mächtigen (Müttern und Vätern, Vormündern oder anders ‚Erziehungsberechtigen' usw.), die sie ökonomisch tragen, und Abhängigen ins Spiel bringt, die zur Welt Anderer und zur Sprache überhaupt erst kommen. So weit wie möglich frei kann das nur geschehen, wenn sich die autoritative Vertikalität dieser Lebensformen von sich aus auf eine öffentliche Sphäre der Gleichheit hin jenseits des Privaten öffnet, in der man sich und Andere dem Dissens aussetzt, ohne noch zu erwarten, Wortführer mit durchgreifender Interpretationsmacht sollten bestimmen, wer man ist bzw. als wer man sich zu verstehen hat. Politisch käme der ‚Verzicht auf den Vater' erst dann voll zum Tragen, wenn überhaupt niemand mehr in diesen Fragen vorrangig oder einseitig ‚das Sagen' hätte,[55] wenn vielmehr jede(r) in diesen Angelegenheiten ‚zur Sprache kommen' könnte und es dabei ertragen würde, dass niemand zustimmen muss.

Darin liegt nicht etwa die Auflösung ‚gegebener' Identität in uferloser Kontingenz, sondern gerade die Chance ihrer dissensuellen Artikulation. Nur wo sie im Spiel *anders möglicher* Artikulationen zum Vorschein kommen kann, ist sie *überhaupt* zu bestimmen, vorausgesetzt, man fasst sie nicht anachronistisch nach

---

55 Vgl. Stoellger, *Deutungsmacht*.

dem Vorbild der Selbigkeit (*mêmeté*) als etwas irgendwie Vorhandenes auf. Im Gegensatz zu reidentifizierbarer Selbigkeit ist Identität als Selbstheit (*ipséité*) nur in und aus Verhältnissen zu Anderen zu bestimmen;[56] und das wiederum nur, wenn sie wenigstens zu artikulieren und dem Dissens auszusetzen ist. Dabei entzündet sich Dissens primär an der Negativität dessen, was als nicht erträglich, als nicht zumutbar, am Ende nicht ‚lebbar‘ (*liveable*) erfahren wird, ohne dass irgendjemand ganz allein und aus eigener Kraft zu bestimmen vermöchte, wie, auf welchen Wegen und bis zu welchen Grenzen sich eigenes und fremdes Leben überhaupt als ‚lebbar‘ erweisen kann.[57]

Auch dazu bedarf es des Sichaussetzens in sozialer Auseinandersetzung, die nur im möglichst freien Austausch miteinander erweisen kann, wer man ist. Auch in diesem Fall muss es die Auseinandersetzung auf freie Erwiderung Anderer anlegen, andernfalls schlägt die Negativität des als ‚unlebbar‘ Erfahrenen, in identitäre Empörung, Zorn und Wut um, die sich scheinbar in ihrer schieren Manifestation bereits genügt – nach dem alten, von Albert Camus mehrfach variierten Schema: ‚Ich empöre mich, also sind wir …‘;[58] ‚Indem wir unseren Zorn herausschreien, beweisen wir, dass wir politisch existieren‘; ‚Indem wir unserer Wut freien Lauf lassen, machen wir unmissverständlich klar, dass wir *jemand* sind‘ usw. Doch bei all dem handelt es sich um nichts als Missverständnisse, Fehldeutungen oder gezielte Manipulationen des Politischen, die auf dessen Leugnung hinauslaufen, wenn sie suggerieren, es komme auf die freie Erwiderung Anderer gar nicht mehr an, nur noch darauf, sich (selbstgerecht) ‚thymotisch‘ in Szene zu setzen und dabei selbst die elementarsten ‚zivilen‘ Umgangsformen missachten zu dürfen.

7 Schuld der Philosophen?

Daran, dass es so weit hat kommen können, wird nun in der letzten Zeit immer wieder der Philosophie bzw. speziellen Richtungen der Philosophie wie der Dekonstruktion, Theorien der Postmoderne, der Dezentrierung des Subjekts und der Kontingenz sowie der Reduktion jeglicher Vertikalität auf die ‚Immanenz‘ des Sozialen die Schuld gegeben, das überhaupt kein ‚Außen‘ mehr zu kennen und

---

56 Vgl. Ricœur, *Selbst als ein Anderer*.
57 Vgl. Liebsch, Hetzel und Sepp, *Profile negativistischer Sozialphilosophie*.
58 Vgl. Liebsch, *Europäische Ungastlichkeit*, Kap. 9.

insofern sich selbst zu genügen scheint[59] – als ob all das schierer Beliebigkeit Tür und Tor öffnen würde, die subjektiv nur noch als völlige Haltlosigkeit zu erfahren sei.[60] Das in der Einleitung dokumentierte Exposé[61] zu diesem Band schlägt zumindest dem ersten Anschein nach ebenfalls in diese Kerbe. So heißt es, „historisch vermittelte Phantasmagorien von Staat, Nation, Volk und Religion können" – unter dem Eindruck jener Richtungen – „nicht mehr auf ihre Verankerung in den Grundstrukturen der Wirklichkeit verweisen, sondern sind in ihrer Dogmatik als kontingent offengelegt". Auf diese Weise sei „einer Kultur der Diversifizierung von Identitäten der Weg bereitet" worden, die als radikal „dezentrierte" nunmehr jeglichen festen Anhalts beraubt zu sein scheinen. Genau darauf reagieren angeblich bestimmte Formen der Behauptung eigener Identitäten repressiv, indem sie auf identitäre und populistische Art und Weise dogmatisch festlegen, wer jemand, ,die eigenen Leute' bzw. ,das Volk' im Gegensatz zu abgelehnten Anderen sei, die sich entsprechend herabwürdigende Sprache gefallen lassen müssen.

Die bemerkenswerte Karriere identitären Denkens wurde in der öffentlichen Diskussion nun u. a. damit erklärt, dass allen voran stereotyp als ,postmodern' titulierte Philosophen nicht nur ,die Rechten', sondern im Grunde jedermann jeglichen festen bzw. verlässlichen Anhalts eigener Identität beraubt hätten. Also brauche man sich gar nicht darüber zu wundern, dass diejenigen, die das unerträglich finden, gewissermaßen zum Notbehelf identitärer Selbstvergewisserung greifen, die ihre Identität auf ein exklusiv vorhandenes, territorial abgegrenztes und aversiv gegen Fremde zu behauptendes Sein zu reduzieren tendiert.

Nun ist es aber abwegig zu unterstellen, identitäre Politik bzw. Anti-Politik sei in erster Linie das Ergebnis genauer Lektüre philosophischer Texte – und nicht etwa primär das kognitiv höchst unzulänglich bewältigte Resultat sozio-ökonomischer Verwerfungen, wie sie die Globalisierung, die Exzesse des Finanzkapitalismus, der weitgehende Abbau sozialstaatlicher Absicherungen von Millionen Menschen und die weitgehend erlahmte Gegenwehr politischer Parteien mit sich gebracht haben. In dieser Lage betreiben zumindest einige Philosophen eine radikale Kritik der Begriffe, mit deren Hilfe man sich die menschlichen Verhältnisse der Vergangenheit, der Gegenwart und der Zukunft verständlich zu machen hofft. Wobei Kritik, wie Emmanuel Levinas mit Blick auf Jacques Derrida angemerkt hat, durchaus noch in einem radikalisierten kantischen Sinne verstanden werden

---

[59] Wäre es so, dann würden sich allerdings auch alle Formen der Distanzierung von einer Sozialität erübrigen, die totale Formen angenommen zu haben scheint. Jene Immanenz kann bzw. darf aber in Wahrheit nicht ,alles' ausmachen, wenn sie sich als effektiv kritisierbar erweisen soll.
[60] Vgl. Poppenberg, „Eine einzige Wahrheit gibt es nicht", 40.
[61] Ich verweise auf die Einleitung der Herausgeber dieses Bandes.

kann.⁶² Indem diese Kritik mit ‚dekonstruktiven' Mitteln zeigt, dass beispielsweise Ungerechtigkeit in der Gerechtigkeit selbst zuhause ist, dass Identität zutiefst mit Nicht-Identischem kontaminiert ist und dass jede Frage nach Gründen ‚abgründige' Implikationen hat, macht sie nur deutlich, in welcher Lage wir uns ‚wirklich' befinden, wenn wir den Anspruch erheben, sie begreifen zu wollen. In diesem Sinne *klärt sie auf*, auch wenn sie sich von jeglichem naiven Verständnis von Aufklärung glaubt verabschieden zu müssen. Ohne eine weitgehende Entsicherung, Verunsicherung und Befremdung derjenigen, die sich diesem Prozess aussetzen, kann es dabei nicht abgehen. Aber sollte darin nur ein Verlust oder gar ein Trauma liegen, das man mit allen Mitteln, auch mit Mitteln identitärer Leugnung, abzuwehren versuchen müsste?

Nein. Denn in der Entsicherung gerade der Identitätsfrage als der Frage, wer wir (im Verhältnis zu Anderen) sind, liegt deren eigentliche Öffnung, die sie auf die Antworten Anderer verweist, ohne die überhaupt niemand je ‚zu sich' kommen könnte. Diese Antworten mögen unter gegebenen Umständen ‚kontingent', d. h. anders möglich, ausfallen; das bedeutet aber keineswegs, dass sie beliebig, ‚arbiträr' sein müssten, um prompt wieder nach autoritärer Rückendeckung verlangen zu lassen. Jeder, der als leibhaftiges Wesen zur Welt kommt, wird allein schon aufgrund seiner leiblichen Konstitution ‚nein' sagen müssen zu allem, was ihm als unerträglich, schmerzhaft, verletzend und ein wirklich ‚lebbares' Leben schließlich unmöglich machend bzw. vernichtend vorkommt.⁶³ Aus der Adressierung der entsprechenden Negativität an Andere, mit denen man dissensuell um Verständigung in diesen Fragen ringt, kann solidarisches Potenzial des Politischen hervorgehen, wo eine offene Auseinandersetzung gesucht und in nicht-autoritärer Einstellung der freie Antwortspielraum Anderer bejaht wird. Schließlich kann auch die Frage, als wer man sich angesichts der Negativität des als unerträglich Erlebten versteht, nur infolge von Deutungen beantwortet werden, mit denen man Andere auf Erwiderung hin konfrontiert. Erst wenn man darin scheitert, auf artikulierten Dissens in diesen Fragen keine Hoffnung mehr setzen mag und keinen anderen Ausweg mehr sieht, wird man gegebenenfalls der identitären Versuchung nachgeben und sich auf Führerfiguren berufen, die in einer derart verfahrenen Lage angeblich für ‚Klarheit', bzw. für ‚Eindeutigkeit' als deren Surrogat, sorgen. Auf diese Weise werden tatsächlich komplexe und zu dekonstruierende Lebenslagen, in denen weder eine sicher ‚zentrierte' Identität noch ersatzweise ein identitärer Signifikat politischer Macht verfügbar ist, auf gegebenenfalls auch brutale Art und Weise einer Vereinfachung dessen unter-

---

62 Vgl. Levinas, *Eigennamen*, 67 ff.
63 Vgl. Liebsch, *Verletztes Leben*.

zogen, was von sich aus keineswegs ‚einfach' *ist*.⁶⁴ Die gängige Rhetorik ist bekannt und kabarettistisch bereits vielfach aufs Korn genommen worden: ‚Wir sind wir und waren schon immer hier' (Wilfried Schmickler); ‚Dieser Ort gehört uns und niemandem sonst'; ‚Wir und niemand sonst entscheidet darüber, wer sich hier zu welchen Bedingungen und wie lange aufhalten darf'; ‚So ist es und so wird es immer bleiben'; etc. Der identitären Rede des jeweiligen Wortführers ist all das jedes Mal mit gewissen Variationen zu entnehmen.

Dabei handelt es sich um Symptome der Schwäche, auch des Versagens, der Defensive, in die man geraten ist und die dazu zu zwingen scheint, zum letzten Mittel identitärer Selbstverteidigung um den Preis gewaltsamer Vereinfachungen dessen zu greifen, was sich von sich aus keineswegs derart ‚einfach' verhält. Allerdings kann ein derartiger identitärer Notstand auch eingeredet werden. Keineswegs geht identitäres Denken stets aus Notfalllagen benachteiligter Subjekte hervor; im Gegenteil kann es sich auch um eine Strategie derjenigen handeln, die nur um ihren relativen Reichtum und Status fürchten.

Jedenfalls sind nicht die (von Identitären ohnehin wohl nicht studierten) Philosophen, die im radikal-kritischen Geist unsere Begriffe ‚auseinandernehmen' und revidieren, an deren gewaltträchtiger Verkürzung durch politische Subjekte schuld, denen offenbar nur an einer möglichst eindeutigen und somit verkürzten Definition dessen liegt, wer sie im Unterschied zu abgelehnten Anderen sind – wobei ihnen eine polemogene Ablehnung ohne genaue Kenntnis des jeweils Abgelehnten vielfach schon völlig genügt. Wie schon der antisemitisch eingestellte frühere Wiener Oberbürgermeister Karl Lueger sagte: ‚Wer Jude ist, bestimme ich', so können auch die Identitären sagen: ‚Wer ‚die Anderen' sind, die wir ablehnen und die wir ‚hier' nicht dulden wollen, das bestimmen wir selbst'. Was sie dabei verschweigen, ist, dass sie sich offenbar nur durch die Form der Ablehnung selbst eine kümmerliche Identität zu verschaffen wissen, so dass sie von den ‚Anderen' ungeachtet ihrer eigenen Ignoranz ganz und gar abhängig bleiben. Darüber hinaus droht diese Identität auf ein exklusives Bei-sich-sein hinauszulaufen, das am Ende jegliche ‚Andersheit' zurückweist und auf diese

---

64 Wer den sozialen ‚Umweg' dissensueller Artikulation leibhaftigen Lebens in der Auseinandersetzung mit Anderen gar nicht erst in Erwägung zieht oder scheut, wird zu solchen Vereinfachungen neigen, ob in der sog. Realpolitik oder auf theoretischer Ebene. Dafür sind die offenkundig autoritären Tendenzen in Slavoj Žižeks politischem Denken ein bezeichnendes Beispiel. Er geriert sich als exklusiver Kenner des Lacan'schen Realen und zeichnet ein derart von letzterem subvertiertes Bild des Sozialen, dass am Ende nur noch die Flucht in pseudo-leninistisches, angeblich nur „mit erbarmungsloser Entschlossenheit" zu vertretendes Denken Abhilfe versprechen soll. Vgl. zum theoriegeschichtlichen Kontext Breckman, „Žižek, Laclau und das Ende des Postmarxismus", 199–214.

Weise auch die Koexistenz mit Seinesgleichen ruinieren muss. Denn jeder ist unvermeidlich *anders* ‚anders', ohne je in einer die Ander(s)heit aufhebenden Identität aufgehen zu können.[65] Die identitäre Leugnung jeglicher politisch maßgeblichen ‚Andersheit' im Innern derer, die sich zu einer von außen undurchdringlichen Gemeinschaft zusammenfinden wollen, muss auch letztere zerstören. Es handelt sich um eine letztlich selbst-destruktive Angelegenheit, was nur solange unbemerkt bleiben wird, wie sich noch ‚Fremde' finden, von denen man sich abheben kann.

8 Bilanz

Jede(r) ist zur Welt gekommen, ohne um vorherige Einwilligung gefragt worden zu sein. Insofern sind wir wirklich „condamné à être libre", wie Sartre behauptete.[66] Untersuchungen der Frage aber, *in welchem Sinne* wir frei sein müssen,[67] haben seit de la Boëtié gezeigt, wie beunruhigend es ist, sich als frei zu wissen, und wie attraktiv es sein kann, die eigene Freiheit in freiwilliger Knechtschaft, Hörigkeit oder Unterwerfung aufzugeben oder sie an Andere zu delegieren – was streng genommen ‚ein Ding der Unmöglichkeit' ist. Die in menschlicher Freiheit offenbar liegende, auf diese Weise sichtbar werdende Ambiguität stellt sich im unvermeidlichen Durchgang durch die meist als ‚väterlich' eingestufte imaginäre und symbolische Dimension des Autoritären und des Autoritativen deshalb als politisch außerordentlich gefährlich heraus. Vor dem Hintergrund einschlägiger historischer Erfahrungen zumal erweist sich der ‚Verzicht auf den Vater' in politischer Hinsicht als unabdingbar.

Nach dem hier beschriebenen Verständnis handelt es sich dabei gerade nicht um einen bloßen Verlust, den man unter allen Umständen kompensieren müsste, sondern um die Freigabe einer responsiven Dimension des Politischen, in der man

---

65 Vgl. Ricœur, *Anders*.
66 Sartre, *L'existentialisme*, 39.
67 Gerade das erklärt Sartres Theorie der Freiheit *nicht* überzeugend. Liebsch, „Passionierte Freiheit", Kap. 9. Diese Theorie wirft jeden rückhaltlos auf sich selbst zurück, zeigt aber nicht, wie menschliche Freiheit responsiv *im* und vor allem *als* Verhältnis zu Anderen Gestalt annehmen kann, ohne in die bekannten Fallen des Dezisionismus, purer Arbitrarität und ‚Absurdität' zu gehen. Insofern ist auf der Basis dieser Theorie der Freiheit allein keine wirklich befriedigende Antwort auf die Herausforderung des Autoritarismus zu geben, wenn sie nur darauf hinausläuft, Formen freiwilliger Unterwerfung, Gefolgschaft und Hörigkeit gegenüber ‚Führerfiguren' als ‚verlogene' zu brandmarken. Auf dem Spiel steht ja auch die Frage, warum es nicht gelingt, sozialresponsive Formen der Ausübung von Freiheit attraktiv erscheinen zu lassen, die das Politische nicht dem Bedürfnis oder Begehren nach einem *Master* oder nach Surrogaten unterordnet.

auch in vertikalen Machtverhältnissen aufeinander zu hören bereit ist. Daraus ergibt sich die skizzierte Kritik populistischer und identitärer Bewegungen, die sich *ungenügenden Verzicht* zunutze machen. Zu warnen ist allerdings auch davor, aus der beschriebenen Situation religiöses bzw. politisch-theologisches Kapital schlagen zu wollen – so als bestätige das angebliche Ausgeliefertsein an ein ‚säkulares Zeitalter'[68] ein unstillbares Bedürfnis, Verlangen oder Begehren nach einem Meister, Herrn oder unanfechtbaren Gebieter, der uns von der Last der eigenen Freiheit zu befreien verspricht, sei es auch nur dadurch, dass er uns den Sinn ihrer Ausübung offenbart und auf diese Weise vorgibt. Der Raum des Politischen als einer zur Freiheit bestimmten und gerade deshalb auch Angst machenden Sphäre ihrer praktischen Ausübung eröffnet sich jedoch unvermeidlich nur, wo Dissens auch in dieser Hinsicht zugelassen und zudem schließlich bejaht wird. Dem aber stehen zweifelhafte Angebote autoritärer Provenienz entgegen, die darauf hinauslaufen, das fragliche Bedürfnis, Verlangen oder Begehren durch politisch gefährliche Surrogate zu befriedigen.

Daran kommt auch keine ‚Politische Theologie' vorbei. Das heißt, dass sie sich fragen lassen muss, inwiefern sie diesen Titel für sich in Anspruch nehmen kann, ohne sich theologischer Anleihen zu bedienen, die der Freiheit im Politischen und der Freiheit des Politischen direkt zuwiderlaufen. Doch das bedeutet nicht, dass nunmehr das Politische zum Maß aller Dinge zu erheben wäre. Nicht nur ‚lebt' es von vor-politischen Voraussetzungen, die es selbst nicht verbürgen kann, so dass es niemals sich selbst genügen wird; angesichts der zum Verzweifeln ungenügenden Formen, die es vielfach annimmt,[69] zehrt es auch von trans-politischen Energien, darunter religiöse unterschiedlichster Herkunft, die es heraus- und überfordern, inspirieren und tödlich bedrohen. Nicht zuletzt dadurch, dass sie dahin tendieren, das Politische seinerseits unter Berufung auf unanfechtbare Quellen verabsolutierten Maßgaben zu unterwerfen, so dass wir nicht nur *im Politischen*, sondern auch *angesichts des Politischen selbst* in unaufhebbaren Widerstreit normativer Anforderungen geraten, denen das eigene Leben, das Leben von Nächsten, Mitbürgern und selbst anonymen Zeitgenossen gerecht werden sollte.[70] Wie es scheint, sind Formen der Berufung auf ein vor-

---

68 Vgl. Taylor, *Säkulares Zeitalter*.
69 Vgl. Liebsch, „Religiöse Lebensformen", 139–170.
70 Vgl. Liebsch und Staudigl, *Bedingungslos?*.
Anmerkung: Da bis heute Begriffe wie Meister und Führer eindeutig männlich konnotiert sind (was die Ausübung entsprechender Funktionen angeht), wurde in der Auseinandersetzung mit den politischen Implikationen dieser Begriffe durchgängig auch die männliche Form gewählt. Durch grammatikalische Weichenstellungen allein wäre ohnehin nicht quasi nebenbei die *gender*-theoretische Frage zu erledigen, ob sich die aufgeworfenen Probleme in ›weiblicher‹ Hinsicht

politisches, politisches oder transpolitisches Bedürfnis, Begehren oder Verlangen nach einem *Master*, Herrn oder Führer nicht in Sicht, die nicht Gefahr laufen, mit dieser elementaren Einsicht in fatale Konflikte zu geraten.

Bibliographie

Agamben, Giorgio. *Herrschaft und Herrlichkeit: Zur theologischen Genealogie von Ökonomie und Regierung (Homo sacer II.2)*, übers. v. Andreas Hiepko. Berlin: Suhrkamp, 2010.
Arendt, Hannah. *Vita activa oder Vom tätigen Leben*, 4. Aufl. München: Piper, 1985.
Arendt, Hannah. *Denktagebuch 1950 bis 1973*, hg. v. Ursula Ludz und Ingeborg Nordmann, Bd. 1. München: Piper, 2003.
Assmann, Jan. *Herrschaft und Heil: Politische Theologie in Altägypten, Israel und Europa*. München: Carl Hanser, 2000.
Barber, Benjamin R. *Strong Democracy: Participatory Politics for a New Age*, 2. Aufl. Berkeley, CA: University of California Press, 2004.
Bataille, Georges. *Die psychologische Struktur des Faschismus: Die Souveränität*, hg. v. Elisabeth Lenk, übers. v. Rita Bischof, Elisabeth Lenk und Xenia Rajewsky. Berlin: Matthes & Seitz, 1978.
Bauman, Zygmunt. „Symptome auf der Suche nach ihrem Namen und Ursprung", In *Die große Regression: Eine internationale Debatte über die geistige Situation der Zeit*, hg. v. Heinrich Geiselberger, 2. Aufl., 37–56. Berlin: Suhrkamp, 2017.
Bazyler, Michael. *Holocaust, Genocide, and the Law*. Oxford: University Press, 2016.
Bellow, Saul. *Dangling Man*. Harmondsworth: Penguin, 1974.
Berg, Nicolas. *Luftmenschen: Zur Geschichte einer Metapher*. Göttingen: Vandenhoeck & Ruprecht, 2008.
Boëtié, Étienne de la. *Rede von der freiwilligen Knechtschaft*, hg. u. übers. v. Horst Günther. Frankfurt a. M.: Europäische Verlagsgesellschaft, 1980.
Bovet, Pierre. „Le sentiment religieux", *Revue de Théologie et de Philosophie* 7 (1919): 157–175.
Bovet, Pierre, „Le sentiment filial", *Revue de Théologie et de Philosophie* 8 (1920): 141–153.
Breckman, Warren. „Žižek, Laclau und das Ende des Postmarxismus", In *Unbedingte Demokratie*, hg. v. Reinhard Heil, Andreas Hetzel und Dirk Hommrich, 199–214. Baden-Baden: Nomos, 2011.
Camus, Albert. *Der erste Mensch*, übers. v. Ulli Aumüller. Reinbek: Rowohlt, 1997.

ähnlich stellen würden. Sie bleibt deshalb ausgeklammert. Das Gleiche gilt für die verschiedenen Spielarten eines illiberalen, kompetitiven und renationalisierten Autoritarismus, die in Europa zu beobachten sind; vgl. die aktuelle Situationsbeschreibung von Rupnik, „Wohin treibt Europa". Weitgehend ausgeklammert bleibt weiterhin die wichtige Frage, ob man sich – gewissermaßen ›von unten‹ – nach einem neuen Autoritarismus sehnt oder ob er, etwa auf der Linie einer amerikanischen *imperial presidency*, wie sie sich von Richard Nixon bis Donald Trump gezeigt hat, ›von oben‹ durchgesetzt und gerechtfertigt wird. (Beides könnte zutreffen.)

Chaouat, Bruno. *Is Theory Good for the Jews? French Thought and the Challenge of the New Antisemitism*, Liverpool: Liverpool University Press 2017.
Chomsky, Noam. *The Essential Chomsky*, hg. v. Anthony Arnove. London: The New Press, 2008.
de Coulanges, Numa Denis Fustel. *Der antike Staat* [1864], hg. v. Alexander Kleine, übers. v. Paul Weiß. München: Klett-Cotta, 1988.
Dahrendorf, Rolf. „Anmerkungen zur Globalisierung", In *Perspektiven der Weltgesellschaft*, hg. v. Ulrich Beck. Frankfurt a. M.: Suhrkamp, 1998.
Ehrenberg, Alain. *Das Unbehagen in der Gesellschaft*, übers. v. Jürgen Schröder. Berlin: Suhrkamp, 2012.
Foucault, Michel. *Die Regierung des Selbst und der anderen: Vorlesung am Collège de France 1982/83*, hg. v. Alessandro Fontana und Frédéric Gros, übers. v. Jürgen Schröder. Frankfurt a. M.: Suhrkamp, 2009.
Frankfurter Institut für Sozialforschung, *Soziologische Exkurse*, 2. Aufl. Frankfurt a. M.: Europäische Verlagsanstalt, 1983.
Frankenberg, Günter. *Die Verfassung der Republik: Autorität und Solidarität in der Zivilgesellschaft*. Frankfurt a. M.: Suhrkamp, 1997.
Grüny, Christian. „Der Sensibelste aller Sinne: Das Hören als Hoffnungsträger", In *Sensibilität der Gegenwart: Wahrnehmung, Ethik und politische Sensibilisierung im Kontext westlicher Gewaltgeschichte*, hg. v. Burkhard Liebsch. Hamburg: Felix Meiner Verlag, 2018.
Held, Klaus. *Phänomenologie der politischen Welt*. Frankfurt a. M.: Internationaler Verlag der Wissenschaften, 2010.
Hegel, Georg W.F. „Der Geist des Christentums und sein Schicksal", In *Frühe Schriften*, Georg W.F. Hegel, hg. v. Eva Moldenhauer und Karl M. Michel. Frankfurt a. M.: Suhrkamp, 1986.
Jaspers, Karl. *Die Schuldfrage: Ein Beitrag zur deutschen Frage*, 5. Aufl. Zürich: Lambert Schneider, 1946.
Jaspers, Karl. *Die geistige Situation der Zeit* [1932], 5. Aufl. Berlin: de Gruyter, 1979.
Kant, Immanuel. *Schriften zur Anthropologie, Geschichtsphilosophie, Politik und Pädagogik*, Bd. 1, hg. v. Wilhelm Weischedel. Frankfurt a. M.: Suhrkamp, 1977.
Klein, Rebekka, und Finkelde, Dominik, Hg. *Souveränität und Subversion: Figurationen des Politisch-Imaginären*. Freiburg i. Br./München: Karl Alber, 2015.
Latour, Bruno. „Refugium Europa", In *Die große Regression: Eine internationale Debatte über die geistige Situation der Zeit*, hg. v. Heinrich Geiselberger, 2. Aufl., 135–148. Berlin: Suhrkamp, 2017.
Levinas, Emmanuel. *Eigennamen: Meditationen über Sprache und Literatur*, hg. v. Felix Philipp Ingold, übers. v. Frank Miething, 2. Aufl. München: Carl Hanser, 1988.
Liebsch, Burkhard. *Verletztes Leben: Studien zur Affirmation von Schmerz und Gewalt im gegenwärtigen Denken: Zwischen Hegel, Nietzsche, Bataille, Blanchot, Levinas, Ricœur und Butler*. Zug, Schweiz: Graue Edition, 2014.
Liebsch, Burkhard. *Einander ausgesetzt – Der Andere und das Soziale*, Bd. 2. *Elemente einer Topografie des Zusammenlebens*, Freiburg i. Br.: Karl Alber, 2018.
Liebsch, Burkhard. *Europäische Ungastlichkeit und ‚identitäre' Vorstellungen: Fremdheit, Flucht und Heimatlosigkeit als Herausforderungen des Politischen*. Hamburg: Meiner Verlag, 2019.

Liebsch, Burkhard. „Verfehlte Ethik und politische Schuld: Zur systematischen Aktualität von Karl Jaspers' Abhandlung Die Schuldfrage (1946) – mit Blick auf John K. Roths The Failures of Ethics (2015/8)", *Wiener Jahrbuch für Philosophie* 51 (2019): 125–156.

Liebsch, Burkhard, Hetzel, Andreas, und Sepp, Hans Rainer, Hg., *Profile negativistischer Sozialphilosophie: Ein Kompendium*. Berlin: de Gruyter, 2011.

Liebsch, Burkhard. „Passionierte Freiheit: Jean-Paul Sartres Entwürfe für eine Moralphilosophie nach dem letzten ‚Weltkrieg'", In *Unaufhebbare Gewalt: Umrisse einer Anti-Geschichte des Politischen. Leipziger Vorlesungen zur Politischen Theorie und Sozialphilosophie*. Weilerswist: Velbrück Wissenschaft, 2015.

Liebsch, Burkhard. „Religiöse Lebensformen und deren KritikerInnen in der Kritik", In *Gelingen und Misslingen religiöser Praxis*, hg. v. Katharina Eberlein-Braun und Dietrich Schotte, 139–170. Münster: LIT, 2020.

Liebsch, Burkhard, und Staudigl, Michael, *Bedingungslos? Zum Gewaltpotenzial unbedingter Ansprüche im Kontext politischer Theorie*. Baden-Baden: Nomos, 2014.

Löwith, Karl. „Jacob Burckhardt. Der Mensch inmitten der Geschichte [1936]", In *Jacob Burckhardt*, Stuttgart: J.B. Metzler, 1984.

Löwith, Karl. *Rezension von „Nicolai Berdjajews, Das Schicksal des Menschen in unserer Zeit (1935)"*, In *Wissen, Glaube und Skepsis: Zur Kritik von Religion und Theologie*, 416–420. Stuttgart: Metzlersche Verlagsbuchhandlung, 1985.

Löwith, Karl. Rezension von „H. Kuhn, *Freedom, Forgotten and Remembered* (1943)", In *Wissen, Glaube und Skepsis: Zur Kritik von Religion und Theologie*, 429–431. Stuttgart: Metzlersche Verlagsbuchhandlung, 1985.

Mason, Paul „Keine Angst vor der Freiheit", In *Die große Regression: Eine internationale Debatte über die geistige Situation der Zeit*, hg. v. Heinrich Geiselberger, 2. Aufl., 149–174. Berlin: Suhrkamp, 2017.

Merleau-Ponty, Maurice. *Keime der Vernunft: Vorlesungen an der Sorbonne 1949–1952*, hg. v. Bernhard Waldenfels, übers. v. Antje Kapust. München: Fink, 1994.

Mitscherlich, Alexander. *Auf dem Weg zur vaterlosen Gesellschaft: Ideen zur Sozialpsychologie*, 15. Aufl. München: Piper, 1984.

Moscovici, Serge. *Das Zeitalter der Massen: Eine historische Abhandlung über die Massenpsychologie*, hg. v. Wolf Lepenies, übers. v. Michael Sommer. Frankfurt a. M.: Fischer, 1986.

Mouffe, Chantal. *Für einen linken Populismus*. Berlin: Suhrkamp, 2. Aufl. 2018.

Poppenberg, Gerhard. „Eine einzige Wahrheit gibt es nicht: Das postmoderne Denken soll alte Gewissheiten zerstört haben und sogar schuld sein an Fake-News und Donald Trump: Das ist Unfug", *Die Zeit* 11 (2019): 40.

Ricœur, Paul. „Die Vatergestalt: Vom Phantasiebild zum Symbol", In *Fragen nach dem Vater*, hg. v. Jochen Storck, 315–353. Freiburg i. Br.: Karl Alber, 1974.

Ricœur, Paul. *Die Interpretation: Ein Versuch über Freud*, übers. v. Eva Moldenhauer, 5. Aufl. Frankfurt a. M.: Suhrkamp, 1974.

Ricœur, Paul. *Le Juste 2*, Paris: Editions Esprit 1991.

Ricœur, Paul. *Das Selbst als ein Anderer*, übers. v. Jean Greisch. München: Wilhelm Fink, 1996.

Ricœur, Paul. *Anders: Eine Lektüre von Jenseits des Seins oder anders als Sein geschieht von Emmanuel Levinas*, hg. u. übers. v. Marco Gutjahr. Wien: Turia & Kant, 2015.

Rieff, Philip. *The Crisis of the Officer Class: The Decline of the Tragic Sensibility*, hg. v. Kenneth S. Piver. Charlottesville, VA: University of Virginia Press, 2011.

Rupnik, Jacques. „Wohin treibt Europa" Dreissig Jahre nach 1989 – Die liberale Demokratie und ihre Feinde", In *Lettre International*, Sommer 2019, 7–16.
Sartre, Jean-Paul. *Die Wörter*, übers. v. Hans Mayer. Reinbek: Rowohlt, 1968.
Sartre, Jean-Paul. *L'existentialisme est un humanisme*, hg. v. Arlette Elkaïm-Sartre. Paris: Gallimard, 1996.
Sartre, Jean-Paul. *Entwürfe für eine Moralphilosophie*, übers. v. Hans Schöneberg und Vincent von Wroblewsky. Reinbek: Rowohlt 2005.
Sennett, Richard. *Autorität*, übers. v. Reinhard Kaiser. Frankfurt a. M.: Fischer, 1985.
Sloterdijk, Peter. *Die schrecklichen Kinder der Neuzeit: Über das anti-genealogische Experiment der Moderne*, 3. Aufl. Berlin: Suhrkamp, 2014.
Stoellger, Philipp, Hg. *Deutungsmacht: Religion und* belief systems *in Deutungsmachtkonflikten*. Tübingen: Mohr Siebeck, 2014.
Strauss, Leo. *Naturrecht und Geschichte*. Frankfurt/M.: Suhrkamp 1977.
Taureck, Bernhard H.F. *Drei Wurzeln des Krieges: Und warum nur eine nicht ins Verderben führt*. Zug/Schweiz: Graue Edition, 2019.
Taylor, Charles. *Ein säkulares Zeitalter*, übers. v. Joachim Schulte. Berlin: Suhrkamp, 2012.
Vargas Llosa, Mario. *Alles Boulevard: Wer seine Kultur verliert, verliert sich selbst*, übers. v. Thomas Brovot, 3. Aufl. Frankfurt a. M.: Suhrkamp, 2013.

II **Identity – Diversity – Singularity**

Luca Di Blasi
Cis: The Rightist Appropriation of Identity Politics and its Boundaries

Abstract: Ever since Donald Trump's election in 2016, people have repeatedly spoken of a 'right-wing identity policy'. But how is such a policy conceivable given the fact that the category of identity politics has been, so far at least, applied rather to disadvantaged and marginalized political groups? This paper explores this question and starts with an analysis of the 'Cisgender'-category. Unlike familiar and socially embattled categories, like 'white,' 'male' or 'heterosexual,' it received relatively little attention so far and is insightful precisely because it is still relatively unloaded. This helps to illustrate the structural position of those whom have been considered privileged and their specific characteristics and problems. In a second step, this paper reconstructs a brief epistemo-political genesis of 'identity politics' and tries to demonstrate on that basis, that not only did some positions have no legitimate place that could be assigned to them, but that (third step) the interrelatedness of identity and politics as it occurs here necessarily formed the seedbed for that brand of right-wing populism which appropriates identity politics for itself. However, at the point where instruments of identity politics are used to fight against other identity politics, in other words, where identity politics turns against identity politics, it has reached its own limits.

'Identity politics' in the form it has hitherto taken can be defined as collective self-determination based on a devalued identity with the political objective of overcoming the hierarchy that lies behind it. If one applies this definition, then *right-wing* identity politics would appear to be a *contradictio in adjecto*, since it is manifestly a species of politics in which the *favoured* join forces to fight for the continuance of their prerogatives. But why, then, especially since the election of Donald Trump, is there talk in the debate of 'white' or 'right-wing' or 'hegemonial' identity politics?

As I aim to substantiate in the following, the term 'identity politics' is indeed perfectly apposite, for what is constituted here (and this is an aspect that is often overlooked or denied from the progressive side) is also a group based on a shared sense of devaluation or neglect. At the same time, however, such identity politics is not progressive, for it is precisely *not* interested in overcoming hierarchies, but rather in the preservation or re-establishment of a state of affairs in which one's own group was secure or protected or, especially in the eyes of others (one's own privileges are not always easily recognisable as such), privileged.

In doing so, I do not wish to approach right-wing identity politics by means of the standard categories white, male and heterosexual,[1] but rather by examining the aporias of a category that is still new and seldom reflected, and therefore less fraught or loaded, namely, cisgender. Cisgender (or simply cis) denotes a correspondence of natural and assigned gender. This gender correspondence is not normally called into question and – as opposed to the 'trans' underlying cis – appears to be largely uncomplicated and unproblematic in terms of lifeworld and society. It is all the more remarkable that this lifeworld unquestionability, non-marked-ness and protected-ness involve considerable structural difficulties as soon as any attempt is undertaken to find an acceptable identity-political place for cis.

Taking an analysis of this problem as my starting point I will, in the second section of this paper, reconstruct a brief epistemo-political genesis of 'identity politics' and attempt to demonstrate on that basis, that not only did some positions have no legitimate place that could be assigned to them, but that, as I outline in the third section, the interrelatedness of identity and politics as it occurs here necessarily formed the seedbed for that brand of right-wing populism which appropriates identity politics for itself. However, at the point where instruments of identity politics are used to fight against other identity politics, in other words, where identity politics turns against identity politics, it has reached its own limits.

1 Cisgender Trouble

Viewed formally, the term 'cis' differs from other dyadic terms such as 'left' or 'above'. Cis not only requires a counter term (trans), it even presupposes that term, insofar as it is only in the moment of transition or moving beyond (and be it only imagined or conceived) that it is possible to recognise a boundary, from the perspective of which one side can be identified as cis. But trans itself also presupposes something, though not a cis, but a breach or a rift that makes cis and trans differentiable in the first place. From a breach, what is broken retrospectively becomes recognisable and can thus be transcended.

The breach renders transcendence possible and makes of a horizon a recognisable (and disputed, contested) boundary. Transcending this boundary can,

---

[1] See Di Blasi, *Der weiße Mann*.

namely, be legitimated as an act of emancipation, and affirmed as *moving beyond and progressing* into new spheres of freedom. And it can be abnegated as *transgression*, as the violation of a boundary, as the breaching of a taboo or barrier that *should never have happened*. This dichotomy of interpretative possibilities is a fundamental conflict, since unambiguous and unilateral evaluations (the *'beyond'* of moving beyond, the *'pro'* of progressing are always to be evaluated as liberations from a repressive 'narrowness'; they are always to be rejected as loss and displacement, as curse and escape) prove untenable after even the briefest of reflections, which means, consequently, that they constantly remain contested.

The gender category is founded on a breach between so-called 'biological' and 'social' gender, as was already theoretically implemented by Simone de Beauvoir, and for decades this has stood at the centre of progressive policy. In the meantime, however, it has become a core element of right-wing populist mobilisation along with migration and a supposed climate hysteria. How is this politicising effect of the gender category to be explained?

In formal terms, the category of gender can be understood as a product of the splitting apart of gender-sexual non-difference. Precisely that which was not differentiated, sex and gender, is divided and forms the basis both for *moving beyond* this non-difference (trans) and for various marginalised gender identities (and hence also for identity politics based on them) as well as for the deconstruction of the distinction between natural and social gender, for which the expression *queer* is frequently used.[2]

An ambivalence of each and every trans and of all transiting or moving beyond boundaries (which might better, as in more dialectically, be termed boundary visualisation qua transiting) consists in the residual uncertainty as to whether *trans* means the movement beyond in itself or the other side (the beyond) of moving beyond. This also pertains to the category of transgender. It can mean 'transsexuality' in the sense of otherness over against the relationship of sex and gender (biological and social gender) assigned qua birth (or qua ultrasound), but it can also stand for the transcendability of the boundary itself ('transgender'), out of which many possibilities and possible identities can arise, of which transsexuality is but one. From the very outset, then, trans is thus characterised by the ambivalence that it represents the separation of a non-difference in gender and sex including the possibility of deconstructing the distinction arising out of that separation; and that, *at the same time*, it stands

---

[2] Butler's, *Gender Trouble* is widely regarded as one of the founding texts of queer theory, even though the very term 'queer' is of practically no significance.

for *one* side of the distinction, for the change from an *identity* of sex and gender, that can be retrospectively maintained to be 'natural', to a *multiplicity* of selectable identities arising out of this distinction.

Less attention has been given to the fact that this division also leads to a decentering of that (former) non-difference and that this presents contingencies, which at this point I wish to describe as cis.

The first and simplest option for determining this cis is already inscribed in the name itself, with the naming, the act of baptism, so to speak. Cis would simply be the counterpart (this side, the 'here') of trans, an agreement or coincidence of one's own biological and social gender that is experienced as being unproblematic. Volkmar Sigusch, who introduced the term roughly a quarter of a century ago, wrote: "Given that there are transsexuals, there must logically also be cissexuals."[3] That does indeed *sound* logical, but it is at the same time undialectical, for it is only valid if the trans is misunderstood as the trans of a cis. But it was in fact genetically exactly the other way around: What came first was trans, and this was the fundament on or from which the need arose to create a corresponding counterpart. It was only with and through trans that cis was also able to become a subject for reflexion and, ultimately, for self-reflexion. But, as such, it is also no longer a 'here', on this side, but the return from a beyond (accessible at least qua reflexion), that is, no 'here' at all. Such a cis is unthinkable, inconceivable.

It is possible to distinguish from this inconceivable 'natural' cis a further option, an option that I wish to describe as the reactionary cis. In order to understand this, one can work from the premise of the shared root or ground of cis and trans, what I already described earlier as the *non-difference* of gender and sex, which is posited qua separation as cause or reason. Then and only then does this non-difference appear as the object of a *choice which, however, cannot be chosen as a choice*. Due to the under-lying pre-condition, the choice is not only rendered possible, but is *enforced*. In consequence of the separation, *all* appear fundamentally no longer free *not* to choose their own relation of sex and gender. The non-difference of sex and gender, which appears retrospectively as 'natural' or is ideologically tenable as such, is subjectivized (as with all 'naturalness', all 'substantiality' in the modern era), but, and this is the ambiguity of the Enlightenment as of all transitions since the Fall, there is retrospectively no alternative to this subjectivization. The freedom gained (the additional freedom

---

[3] Sigusch, "Transsexueller Wunsch", 811–837. Sigusch had already introduced the term ‚cissexuell' in 1991 in the variant spelling ‚zissexuell'. An overview of the genealogy of the term cisgender is offered in Enke, "Education of Little Cis", 234–244.

rendered possible by the new options to choose the relation of sex and gender) is accompanied by a new compulsion, an obligation also to choose the former non-difference of sex and gender as a voluntary or self-chosen 'identity', that is, to make of this a cis. Cis thus stands for the conversion of the former non-difference into an identity.

The breach of the gender-sexual non-difference thus not only opens up new spheres of freedom, it also enforces them. The breach and the enforced decentering proceeding from it is thus accompanied by the reactionary temptation to restore what has been overcome in the form of retroactive naturalisation of precisely that which has just been proven to be *not* natural. This is given expression in the reactionary temptation to *deny* the distinction between sex and gender. The trans of transgender is simply adjudged as having no legitimate *epistemic* place, and the category gender itself is consequently also denied; it no longer exists or, more precisely, since the term does exist, it is without content, it is empty, it is delusion, madness, 'gender madness'. Consequently, no legitimate *politics* can have its source in it, but only illegitimate ideology, 'gender ideology', whereby the irony lies in the fact that precisely such an attempt at the re-naturalisation of a particular relation of gender and sex and/or at rendering the distinction itself invisible once more can, in the strictest sense of the word, be described as 'gender ideology', as an ideology that seeks to recentre and defend qua naturalisation a social (power) relationship (that is already decentered). The reactionary temptation accompanies each and every breach and each and every resultant crossing of boundaries, and it is the lastingly impotent inverse of it. Even when it is directed against progressive identity politics, it is not specifically bound to that *identity politics*, but far rather to its *progressive* character. It therefore equally opposes everything that would appear to make a change of lifestyle necessary, e. g. man-made climate change, and even though it has gained in influence with the rise of right-wing populism, the reaction does not point to the limits or boundaries of identity politics but, conversely, it bears testimony to its effectiveness beyond the universities in which it had its origins.

A further cis can be distinguished from the inconceivable natural cis and the reactionary cis with its attempt at retroactive re-naturalisation of the gender-sexual non-difference. This third cis acknowledges the trans as well as the breach between sex and gender, thereby affirming its own decentering. As a means of highlighting the distinction from the reactionary cis, one might also operate, analogously to the distinction transgender and transsexuality, with the distinction cisgender and cissexuality. Cisgender includes in its name the very gender category that, in its turn, only came about through the breach, and is thereby implicitly accepting of it. Accordingly, it represents the awareness of the relative nature of the correspondence between 'biological' and 'social' gender that arises out of a confrontation with the breach. By contrast, 'cissexual' could describe the (reactionary) attempt to re-naturalise this correspondence qua opposition against the gender category.

However, this poses a double problem for the decentered cis: It must preserve and communicate the distinction from naive non-reflexion as well as from a reactionary standpoint; it must resist a double misunderstanding and, accordingly, guard against a double mistrust: If cis, as the word misleadingly suggests, can be understood as the 'site' of a division, as that which lies *this side* of rupture and division, then it is accordingly located this side of the innumerable options that first become visible through trans, including the option of deconstructing gender and sex, the two sides of the former gender-sexual non-difference that, qua trans, have been disconnected into two separate entities; structurally it does not belong to that diversity facilitated qua trans, that chain of possible gender identities, just as "heterosexual" does not belong. However, if cis is understood as the result or consequence of a trans and as 'decentered cis', as the conscious choice of an option that is known to be particular, this can come under suspicion of being reactionary, the conscious choice of a repressive and privileged identity, which seeks to exclude trans. Cis can thus come under suspicion of being a naive *precondition* and evil *consequence* of trans.

By way of illustration, some examples from other fields may prove helpful here. In the West, the Moslem hijab or headscarf is only accepted if and when it has become a matter of individual, 'self-determined' choice, that is, once it has undergone the Enlightenment and is not simply 'naively' adopted and thereby approved when others do not wish to wear a headscarf. But as soon as it becomes a matter of choice, the same symbol promptly comes under suspicion of being a reactionary political sign. In general, everything that is 'natural' is, in the progressive modern world, caught in the crossfire between suspicion of naivety and suspicion of ideology, just as the *light* of the Enlightenment transforms unknowing into a shady *ignorance* that consistently oscillates between naivety and malignly willed ignorance.

An analogy to the relationship between Christianity and Judaism is evident. Judaism can appear as and/or perceive itself as being in unbroken continuity with the Old Testament/Tanakh and can always therefore appear and/or perceive itself both as the legitimate bearer or heir of an unbroken continuity with the Old Testament/Tanakh – in contrast to Christianity, which unambiguously arises out of division. Judaism can, at the same time, be understood/understand itself, like Christianity, as the product of a separation (as 'rabbinic Judaism') arising out of a fundamental rupture (destruction of the Temple, diaspora). In consequence (from a Christian perspective), the Jews either do not belong to the community of nations made possible qua Christ (or Saint Paul) but instead, they constitute a problematic exception (given that Judaism is understood as the site of the Christ event). Or they are also understood as the outcome of a rupture or breach, and this in turn is seen as a consequence of their not making a decision for Christ (destruction of the Temple, diaspora as consequence/punishment of a non-acceptance of Christ). Their being non-Christian is thus de-neutralised as a conscious choice or option against Christ.

The underlying problem of the confusability of enlightened (decentered) and reactionary (totalitarian) cis can be illustrated using the hermeneutic model of a *Kippbild* (multistable or ambiguous image), which I have developed in greater detail elsewhere[4]. The breach, which I have assumed to be the starting point for cis and trans, can be described as akin to the so-called aha moment of the reversible figure, that spontaneous moment when the other aspect suddenly appears (the rabbit or the duck in the famous rabbit-duck *Kippbild*). With its appearance, the image breaks apart into two aspects. The 'trans' can be understood accordingly as the 'new aspect'. Since the separation of the picture as a single entity (= non-difference of gender and sex) only becomes recognisable through the trans, this trans is, on the one hand, a new aspect whilst, on the other, it *represents* the separation. Consequently, it is (ontologically) a particular aspect, but appears (phenomenologically) as representing the *separated whole*. Analogously, cis constitutes the 'first aspect' which, however, as long as the new aspect had not emerged, appeared as a whole picture. The cis therefore remains no more than a particular aspect after separation has occurred, but at the same time it retains the remembrance of the *lost whole* and *appears* therefore also as more than a particular aspect.

A possible and (over against the other) disputable claim – and, with it, a potential conflict – can be recognised on both sides here, namely the claim to represent the whole. If, for instance, the cis is identified with the lost whole, it is not simply one of the options arising out of the split, but is far rather the *site* which, after the emergence of the new aspect, has been rendered impossible or untenable. If, however, cis is understood as the choice of this site, that choice cannot be clearly differentiated from a reactionary choice of a claim to wholeness or naturalness. It is therefore not only true that cis either knows nothing of the split and hence of itself as cis (using the language of a Kippbild-hermeneutics: it is 'aspect blind') and is, as soon as it knows itself, no longer such a cis. Worse than that: Even if it tries to choose to be particular and decentered, this choice can thus always appear as a claim to the former whole.

---

[4] See Di Blasi, *Dezentrierungen*, esp. 39–64. See also Di Blasi, "Splitting Images", 67–87.

This structural ambiguity appears in an early example of a political interpretation of cis by the activist Emi Koyama:

> "I learned the words 'cissexual,' 'cissexist,' and 'cisgender' from trans activists who wanted to turn the table and define the words that describe non-transsexuals and non-transgenders rather than always being defined and described by them. By using the term 'cissexual' and 'cisgender,' they de-centralize the dominant group, exposing it as merely one possible alternative rather than the 'norm' against which trans people are defined."[5]

Prima facie, cis would indeed appear to have been allocated a legitimate place here. On closer examination, however, it stands for both: for the decentering (qua cis designation) of a dominant group which, as such, can constitute a possible alternative to trans *and* for that dominant group itself. Cis is thus manifested *at once* as legitimate alternative *and* as illegitimate dominant group.

This structural problem applies not only to the comparatively young cis category, but also, analogously, to all other "groups" which, in the course of the identity politics of the so called "cultural left", came to be understood as dominant: whites, men, heterosexuals. It would appear that, irrespective of their lifeworld reality, they all reached a structural impasse on account of identity politics, out of which there would seem to be no possible escape, particularly as even non-reflexion or non-consideration of their own situation came to be criticised as objectionable 'self-invisibilisation', de-politicisation or as universalist 'God trick', as an attempt at "seeing everything from nowhere".[6]

2 The epistemo-political roots of identity politics

The gender category and the breach out of which it arose is a fundamentally epistemo-political category;[7] it can, as with identity politics in general, only be grasped as a response to political conflicts. Although the *expression* 'identity politics' first originated in the 1970s and only came to gain acceptance in the course of the 1980s, it is possible to trace the epistemo-political roots of contemporary identity politics back to developments in the period between the end of the First World War and the end of the Second World War. Jean-Paul Sartre's essay "*Anti-Semite and Jew: An Exploration of the Etiology of Hate*" dating from 1944[8] is of

---

5 Koyma, "Cissexual/Cisgender".
6 Haraway, "Situated Knowledges", 581.
7 For the terms political epistemology and epistemo-political see Lapidot, *Jews Out of the Question*.
8 Sartre, *Anti-Semite and Jew*.

particular relevance for this. The text was the product of a specific historical situation – the withdrawal of German troops from France – and it was based on fundamental insights in his first major work *Being and Nothingness* dating from 1943.[9] This in turn arose out of the interplay of the Hegelian master-slave dialectic, its class-struggle *transformation* by Karl Marx and its *re-actualisation* by Alexandre Kojève, as well as Edmund Husserl's phenomenological intersubjectivity and its existentialist and ontological enlargement by Martin Heidegger.

Here, between *Being and Nothingness* and *"Anti-Semite and Jew"*, decisive theoretical figures are developed for later identity politics: the explicitly atheistically founded (that is, qua denial of *religious* transcendence) precedence of existence over essence, which recurs in progressive identity politics in the form of a consistent anti-essentialism; the category 'being for others', which arises out of a fundamentally conflictual understanding of intersubjectivity (master and slave) and the transferral of these insights to collective subjects (in the case of Sartre: anti-Semites and Jews). This transferral creates the necessary conditions for new master-slave dialectics that 1) need not (necessarily) be bourgeoisie and proletariat and which 2) nevertheless refer to non-essentialised collectives.[10] Consequently, at that moment when essentialised or essentialiseable collectives such as peoples, races, nations are repudiated, a new and progressive option is created for conceptualising collective subjects.

The slaves are products of the masters; they are, as it were, created by their masters reifying them, viewing them as objects. Ever since Sartre's *Being and Nothingness* and especially since his *"Anti-Semite and Jew"*, this has become a central figure in post- or anti-essentialist identity politics, meaning accordingly: not to slip, with respect to the reifying perspective of the 'masters' towards specific marginalised 'identities', into evasive irony and other forms of inauthenticity, nor to subject or submit oneself to it, but to accept it and to grasp it as the fundament (thrownness, place) thus rendered possible for group formation, in other words, to make out of the 'identity' defined by the 'master' (it "is the anti-Semite who creates the Jew"[11]) the starting point for solidarisation, group formation and politicisation. As already anticipated at the outset, 'identity politics' can be defined accordingly as collective self-determination on the basis of a

---

9 Sartre, *Being and Nothingness*.
10 A highly readable critique of identity politics using Sartre's approach was published in the late 1990s by Sonia Kruks. See Kruks, "Identity Politics and Dialectical Reason", 229–252. On the difficulties involved in transferring 'anti-Semite' and 'Jew' from *Reflections on the Jewish Question* to other collective subjects see Bell, "Different Oppressions", 123–148.
11 Sartre, *Anti-Semite and Jew*, 143.

devalued identity with the objective of overcoming the hierarchy that lies behind it.

What Sartre attempted using 'anti-Semites' and 'Jews' was able to be transferred to other discriminated identities, especially clearly so in Simone de Beauvoir's application to the category of gender.

> "[B]iological and social sciences no longer believe there are immutably determined entities that define given characteristics like those of the woman, the Jew or the black; science considers characteristics as secondary reactions to a *situation*. [...] Rejecting the notions of the eternal feminine, the black soul or the Jewish character is not to deny that there are today Jews, blacks or women: this denial is not a liberation for those concerned, but an inauthentic flight. Clearly no woman can claim without bad faith to be situated beyond her sex."[12]

Frantz Fanon's pioneering studies in postcolonialism, in which he analyses relations between whites and blacks and/or colonial masters and the colonialised, are also influenced by Sartre's operation (and, as is well-known, Sartre also wrote the foreword to Fanon's *The Wretched of the Earth*[13]), and the comparatively new expression 'cisgender', of which I spoke in the first section, can, in spite of complex transformation and translation processes,[14] be located in this epistemo-political setting.

There is also a second discursive thread that must be considered in order to conceptually grasp the identity politics of recent decades. This discourse appears especially in the (often polemical) term 'cultural left', and its proximity to and overlaps with what is understood as 'identity politics' is already apparent in the fact that both terms became the subject of countless debates at roughly the same time and for the same reason (the successes of right-wing populism). In spite of their differing genealogies, the terms 'cultural left' und 'progressive identity politics' are almost interchangeable in these debates, with the difference that liberals, for whom collective subjects are just as suspect as any facticity which is seen as restricting freedom, tend rather to use the term 'identity politics' critically, whereas the term 'cultural left' is viewed critically by the 'traditional' or 'social' left in order to point to the, in their view, insufficient consideration given to the issue of ownership, and to the social or class category. (I shall return to this in the third section.)

---

12 de Beauvoir, *Second Sex*, 13 f.
13 See Fanon, *The Wretched of the Earth*.
14 These primarily include the structuralist transformation of psychoanalysis in Jacques Lacan, the de-personalisation of the master-slave relation in the form of 'invocation' by 'ideological state apparatuses' in Louis Althusser, the work of Michel Foucault and its poststructuralist and queer reception.

Richard Rorty already associated the cultural left with a partial substitution of Freud for Marx and, explicitly, with a politics of identity.[15] And, as is the case with identity politics, the cultural left is often interpreted, by Rorty too, as a postmodern phenomenon. But this term can also be expanded upon genealogically and ultimately traced back to the neo-Marxism of the interwar years. This is true for the emphasis there on the significance of 'culture' and particularly for the combination of Marxism and psychoanalysis in the earlier *Frankfurt School*. Taking this starting point into account also allows one to free oneself from the misleading yet widespread notion that the recognition emphasised by the 'cultural left' is concerned with 'soft' questions and is even a symptom of a neoliberally oriented left that eschews the 'hard' redistribution questions and busies itself with comparatively irrelevant questions of cultural recognition (gender-sensitive language, unisex toilets, etc.)

For, by the same token whereby such an interpretation is partially correct, it is in other respects false. Just as existentialism, the discovery of facticity, paved the way for an *ontological expansion* or enhancement of phenomenological intersubjectivity theories, so too neo-Marxism was able qua psychoanalysis to expand on recognition questions. Whereas, as Sartre ironically remarked, the Marxists of his day only dealt with adults ("[r]eading them, one would believe that we are born at the age when we earn our first wages"[16]), the 'cultural left' and progressive identity politics based on it reach far back into childhood, especially qua psychoanalysis, and, in the case of gender, even as far as the prenatal classification of foetuses according to a two-gender matrix. Skin colour and sexual orientation also not only affect adults, but they already affect childhood and youth, which is where designations or interpellations, education and other forms of constitution of the subject and the underlying (biopolitical) dispositives are already operational, and where formative experiences of misjudgement or non-recognition already take place and usually anticipate even early forms of dominance and exploitation in working life (child labour).

As with other psychotherapeutic and medical procedures, however, psychoanalytical instruments require the voluntary consent of those undergoing the psychoanalysis. Wherever this does not happen, and wherever it is applied to whole groups, psychoanalysis quickly becomes an instrument for political ends, an instrument for the reversal of perspectives, for the pathologisation of the pathologisers, the objectification of the objectifiers. Expanding on recognition categories is therefore only one dimension of psychoanalysis, the second

---

15 See Rorty, *Achieving Our Country*, 76f.
16 Sartre, *Search for a Method*, 62.

is the potential objectification of the other as a patient and as an object of analysis, like the early *Frankfurt School* applied psychoanalytical instruments to explain anti-Semites and/or the 'authoritarian character'.

Precisely such objectification of the other interlinks the cultural left with Sartre's groundwork on identity politics and its fundamental problem, namely, that it laid the foundations for a concept of intersubjectivity based on the reversal and thus continuation of reification or objectification of the other.[17] And exactly this very problem of identity politics comes now to light in the shape of its rightist appropriation.

3 Right-wing identity politics

In 2013, in my book *Der weiße Mann* ("The White Man"), I described a development in which those who had been spared longest, namely white heterosexual men, begin to see themselves in terms of identity politics as a marked minority.[18] At the latest, this became clearly apparent with the election of Donald Trump in 2016. Only two days after his election, the American historian Nell Irvin Painter wrote:

> "Though white Americans differed sharply on their preferences for president, the election of 2016 marked a turning point in white identity. Thanks to the success of 'Make America Great Again' as a call for a return to the times when white people ruled, and thanks to the widespread analysis of voters' preferences in racial terms, white identity became marked as a racial identity. From being individuals expressing individual preferences in life and politics, the Trump era stamps white Americans with race: white race."[19]

Can this development be better comprehended in the light of what has been said until now? The reconstruction of the epistemo-political fundament of identity politics has shown that people who were subjected as Jews, as women, as

---

[17] Some theoretical problems of this conflictual approach were addressed and presented in detail at an early stage. Michael Theunissen regarded Sartre's problem as the "reversal of my objectification by the other into the objectification of the other" (see Theunissen, *Other*, 238 ff). A consequence of this is the fundamental problem of Sartre's conception of intersubjectivity in *Being and Nothingness:* the "dynamic of reciprocal reification" through which, according to Axel Honneth, "an element of conflict [enters into] all forms of social interaction ... so that the prospect of a state of interpersonal reconciliation is quasi ontologically excluded." See Honneth, *Struggle for Recognition*, 156.
[18] See Di Blasi, *Der weiße Mann*, esp. chapter 7.
[19] Painter, "What Whiteness Means in the Trump Era". See also Coates, "First White President".

blacks, etc. to negative interpellations hardly have any other option than either to skim over their own situation, to ignore it, to respond ironically to it and thereby to become *inauthentic* in Sartre's sense of the word or, indeed, to conform, to accept the negative constructions of others, to assimilate them and to deny themselves. For precisely this reason, Sartre's answer, the recognition of this 'facticity' as the starting point for politicising empowerment and a struggle against power relations, appeared as an enthusing option.

But something else also becomes apparent in the light of this reconstruction: Sartre's proto-identity politics were founded on a figure that, by virtue of the Shoah, has since been and remains unsurpassably negative: the anti-Semite. And all other groups of subsequent identity politics who are understood analogously as creators of discriminated and devalued identities – whites, men, heterosexuals – thereby also land in the slipstream of a politically and morally repudiated position. Even the apparently harmless correspondence of biological and social gender (cis) mutates into a problematic, dominant, discriminating "identity" and falls foul of structural aporias.

Those who, in identity political terms, occupy the side of domination are caught in an impasse. The culturally determinant left and the progressive identity politics they support offer them no satisfactory place in the structure. The non-consideration of their own situation has the appearance of *ignorance*, of an ambivalent mixture of naivety and deception; the self-thematisation that does not restrict itself to an internalisation of the critical gaze of others immediately arouses distrust; group formation on the basis of these categories has the appearance of a reactionary provocation.

What is more, precisely the appeal of the master-and-slave dialectic, that it offers the 'slave' the prospect of overcoming the power relations, means that *eventually* the point at which the power relations become blurred must be reached. And although that is desirable, it does mean that this point, when it is reached, must be unsettling for *all parties*, because not only must the 'masters' learn and accept that they are no longer 'masters', but the 'slaves' must also learn that they are no longer 'slaves'.[20] And the growing polarization in Western societies, emerging debates on "threatened majorities" (Ivan Krastev) and "cultural majority rights" (Ruud Koopmans and Liav Orgad) might indicate that this point has already been reached in some fields.

This raises the unpleasant question: Need the identity political constitution of collective subjects not *of necessity* have brought forth devalued 'dominant',

---

[20] For an exploration of the associated term 'wounded attachment' see Brown, *States of Injury*, 52–76.

'repressive' identities, which were able, for their part, eventually to become the fundament for analogous group building processes? Need not precisely the success of progressive identity politics *sooner or later* of necessity raise the question as to what happens when those who once took an abasing view of others, for their part, are subjected over longer periods, to criticism and degradation? The persistent and international success of right-wing populism can be understood as an indicator that something of this nature is taking place, that people who, from a culturally left or progressive identity political perspective, appear privileged and dominant experience themselves as neglected and degraded and, on that basis, subjectivize themselves.

In order to understand this process better, it is necessary to clarify how the underlying dissensus is to be explained. How can it be that those who, from a progressive-liberal viewpoint, are clearly dominant and privileged consider themselves to be victims? In order to probe this question further, I would like to elaborate on a specific characteristic of the cultural left that I referred to earlier, and that appears to me to be highly relevant for an understanding of both leftist and right-wing identity politics: the tendency to neglect or ignore social or socio-economical questions. This problem has been repeatedly discussed (at least) since the 1990s, just as, since then, important academic debates have been held on the issue.[21] Rather than replicating these debates once more, which would go beyond the scope of this paper, I wish to illustrate this problem by means of a short and relatively topical text. Its author is Carolin Emcke, who can be described as one of the most prominent exponents of the cultural left in Germany. As a pupil of Axel Honneth's[22] and, as such, in a sense an offshoot of the *Frankfurt School,* she can also be seen as belonging in an academic sense to the cultural left as it was outlined earlier.

In a column she wrote for the *Süddeutsche Zeitung* in May 2019, Emcke seeks to defend progressive identity politics against its liberal opponents, developing a simple yet incisive thought experiment: Just imagine there is an (implicit) rule whereby only people with a body height of more than 1.85 metres are allowed to go to the opera. At some point, those excluded in this way would become aware of the commonality of their exclusion and the exclusion criterion (smaller than 1.85) would gradually become a relevant category.

---

21 See esp. Fraser and Honneth, *Redistribution or Recognition*. At an earlier date, Fraser had already engaged in a controversial exchange on this question with Judith Butler. See Butler, "Merely Cultural", 265–277 and in response see Fraser, "Heterosexism", 279–289.
22 Emcke, *Kollektive Identitäten*.

"Whether they like it or not, body height is relevant, because a significance is ascribed to it from outside, because it determines who is allowed to go to the opera and who is not. (...) You must take seriously what, to you personally, seems unimportant, you must have an awareness of yourself as a member of a group that would not exist in this way if all opera lovers were treated alike."[23]

In ultra-short form, this is a popularising summary of the fundamental elements of progressive identity politics and, at the same time, an affinity to Sartre's "*Anti-Semite and Jew*" is recognisable. The powerful and the power structures they sustain create qua discrimination the very *identity* that, for the powerless, can serve as the fundament for *politicising group formation:* identity politics. This category is thus *nolens volens* important.

But whereas Emcke thereby succeeds in effectively defending progressive identity politics against liberal objections ('particularism'), she fails to notice that she involuntarily confirms the main objection raised by the left against progressive identity politics: the neglect of socio-economic problems. Significantly, the central exclusion mechanism in capitalism, the ticket price, plays no role whatsoever in Emcke's thought experiment. The thought experiment simply assumes that people can afford the ticket. "They look at their ticket, the date, themselves – everything is just right."

But this blind spot has problematic epistemic consequences, for it favours the misperception that since, in the language of the thought experiment, only people taller than 1.85 were allowed into the opera, *all people* taller than 1.85 would have been admitted to the opera. But, regardless of which non-socially privileged group is substituted for 'taller than 1.85', even among those who belong to one of these categories it was always *only small minorities* who could afford the expensive admission tickets for the opera. Indeed, it is necessary to go even further than this. Especially in institutions for 'high' culture such as the opera, *social* exclusion always plays the central role. Moreover, not only does diversity in elite institutions (renowned universities, museums, opera houses, etc.) *alone* not solve any social problems, it can even help to obfuscate them. The literary theorist Walter Benn Michaels has found the following pointedly polemical expression for this:

"The neoliberal dream is that the top one percent of the population, in terms of wealth, is just as diverse as the remaining 99 percent, so that no one can any longer blame his/her economic situation on discrimination. The rich can then claim that everyone has the

---

23 Emcke, "Raus bist du".

place in society that he/she deserves or has earned. The pursuit of diversity is not primarily concerned with minimising inequality so much as with justifying it."[24]

A consequence of the emphasis placed on recognition questions paired with insufficient consideration given to social exclusion is that those who fall into the categories white, heterosexual, male, since recently also cis, run the risk of being unilaterally equated with 'privileged', or even 'repressive'. Consequently, there is a general assumption that it is legitimate to speak disparagingly of these categories ('white trash', 'hillbillies', 'toxic masculinity', 'old white men', etc.), even amongst those who are in many ways clearly privileged by comparison with them. In one well-known and spectacularly extreme case, precisely those who regarded themselves as already ignored, were labelled by a presidential candidate who was herself privileged in every conceivable way as a *basket of deplorables*, a phrase that has by now become almost proverbial.

However, it is not the symbolic devaluation alone, but the combination of symbolic devaluation, the impossibility of finding a recognised place for oneself, *and* the absence or the inadequacy of any consideration given to socioeconomical questions that forms the breeding ground for that which has become unmistakably obvious with the election of Donald Trump, namely that identity politics spreads to those who have long represented its other side. The psycho-political fundament for right-wing identity politics arises precisely at the intersection of several categories that are devalued in progressive identity politics (masculinity, whiteness, heterosexuality) and precisely where the social reality contradicts the equation of these categories with domination, privileged status, and oppression.

Contrary to what right-wing populists would have us believe, let it be understood, this does *not* mean that – compared with other groups – white, heterosexual men are in the meantime disadvantaged, quite the opposite. Both with regard to their socio-economic situation as well as to the recognition given to their colour, gender or sexual orientation, they are not more badly off, but better off, than most other groups. What they have experienced in the course of progressive identity politics – being the objects of negative marking – is something that *all* others have already long since had to face in far more painful form before them (and from or through them).

'Plus' plus 'plus', in this case, does not simply amount to yet more plus. Since the majority of whites and men and heterosexuals have to struggle with social decline or are already 'left behind', while unilaterally appearing from a cultural-left, identity-political perspective as being privileged, they were the

---

24 See Michaels, "Diversity".

only group whose specific difficulties experienced little attention[25] and absolutely no recognition and who appeared to deserve no empathy.[26] On the contrary, as David Wong wrote in a widely acclaimed article shortly before Trump's election:

> "It really does feel like the worst of both worlds: all the ravages of poverty, but none of the sympathy. 'Blacks burn police cars, and those liberal elites say it's not their fault because they're poor. My son gets jailed and fired over a baggie of meth, and those same elites make jokes about his missing teeth!' You're everyone's punching bag, one of society's last remaining safe comedy targets."[27]

Even if, in the light of this, it is possible to understand *that* people can here perceive themselves as victims, as well as why they are *not* recognised as such by progressive identity politics, this does not make the rightist appropriation of identity politics somehow more reassuring, quite the opposite. By virtue of the fact that, along with identity politics, the insufficient consideration of social and economic questions also migrates to the other side, it there becomes particularly *acute*. For precisely that reason, people who are *also* able to understand themselves as victims, run the risk of failing to address the inequalities and the exploitation of a particular economic system, but misconstrue themselves as victims of those who set themselves up against all forms of degradation and against insufficient recognition. And this is also the reason why right-wing populists are frequently supported by conservative liberal billionaires.

Due to the neglect of the economic question, its rightist appropriation can delude people into misunderstanding themselves as *victims of the victims*, on the basis of which they empower themselves, an empowerment that can extend as far as violence and terror against minorities, as demonstrated in the murderous attacks by white men on young Social Democrats, on Muslims, on Jews, on foreigners. The new and alarming phenomenon of so-called 'incels' vividly demonstrates this danger. What we are dealing with here is white, heterosexual men who feel they are spurned or despised by women and who see themselves as victims, empowering themselves on that basis qua group formation (to violence).

---

25 Little attention was given by the media with their metropolitan focus or by academia with its left-wing liberal dominance to the fact that roughly half a million people died between ca. 2000 and 2016 in the opioid crisis, in which the northeast of the United States was hardest hit, especially the industrial region between the Great Lakes and the East Coast, and in which those predominantly affected were white Americans and men.
26 An exception worth reading is Hochschild, *Strangers in their Own Land: Anger and Mourning on the American Right*.
27 Wong, "How Half of America Lost Its F**king Mind".

The fact that the apparent masters are now beginning to understand themselves as victims and are politicising themselves on that basis thus understandably arouses fears and general resistance, mobilising a vast and broad political and moral front of culturally left identity politics and liberal trans-tribalism for whom collective identities are, in any case, nothing more than the metier of losers. Yet the problem is not so much that white men identify themselves as victims. That can, at least, be interpreted as an inevitable consequence of current horizontalizing tendencies. As soon as it is affirmed, even experiencing the loss of an unmarked position, although painful, can lead to a symmetrisation of relations, unlike the liberal lack of consideration given to the categories white, male, heterosexual. Even the forms of political expression of right-wing identity politics, however dangerous they are, force the others to take cognizance of new forms of neglect and inadequate recognition. The main problem, I repeat, is therefore not the fact that whites and men are also able to see themselves as victims here, but the fact that and/or when they misunderstand themselves as *the victims of the victims*.

This main danger arises in part from a problem that also shapes progressive identity politics and that I just mentioned: the tendency to disregard socio-economic questions. This disregard allowed the cultural left to ignore the specific problems of white men (and women) – and it allows right-wing identity politics to ignore the socio-economic dimension of their situation including their instrumentalization by neoliberalism. The constantly fuelled identity-political conflicts have caused this to move out of the firing line into which it had come in the wake of the financial crisis of 2007.[28] More fundamentally, however, this main danger of right-wing identity politics – the self-perception as victims of the victims – has to be understood as a consequence of an epistemo-political precondition of identity politics in general: its inherent "dynamic of reciprocal reification".[29]

One consequence of these conflicts, therefore, is the cognizability of identity politics itself. By its appropriation of identity politics, right-wing populism turns against progressive identity politics, that is, identity politics is turned against identity politics, whereby it becomes unavoidably reflexive – and it is

---

28 Shortly after the financial crisis and the profound undermining of confidence in neoliberalism that it caused, the Koch brothers gave their support to the Tea Party, which is understood by some to be the real starting-point of right-wing identity politics. Elsewhere too, right-wing populists serve as a useful *thumos* for neoliberalism. But left-wing liberals also benefit from this 'tribalist' polarisation. With Trump's election, they were immediately able to present themselves as a sensible alternative to a society divided by leftist and right-wing identity politics. See e.g. Lilla, *Once and Future Liberal*; Fukuyama, "Against Identity Politics".
29 See Honneth, *Struggle for Recognition*, 156.

not until then that its boundaries or (de)limitations are to be truly recognised. And where boundaries can be recognised, they can be transcended. We therefore find ourselves at the end of an era shaped by identity politics. For those young people who are currently becoming politicised in their recognition of the dramatic finitude of Planet Earth, the era of identity politics may already be a thing of the past.

The article has been translated into English by James Brown.

Bibliography

de Beauvoir, Simone. *The Second Sex*. London: Vintage, 2011.
Bell, Linda A. "Different Oppressions: A Feminist Exploration of Sartre's Anti-Semite and Jew," In *Feminist Interpretations of Jean-Paul Sartre*, ed. Julien S. Murphy, 123–148. University Park, PA: Pennsylvania State University Press, 1999.
Di Blasi, Luca. *Der weiße Mann: Ein Anti-Manifest*. Bielefeld: transcript, 2013.
Di Blasi, Luca. "Splitting Images: Understanding Irreversible Fractures Through Aspect Change," In *Multistable Figures: On the Critical Potentials of Ir/Reversible Aspect-Seeing*, ed. by Christoph F.E. Holzhey, 67–87. Vienna: Turia & Kant, 2014.
Di Blasi, Luca. *Dezentrierungen: Beiträge zur Philosophie der Religion im 20. Jahrhundert*. Vienna: Turia & Kant, 2018.
Brown, Wendy *States of Injury: Power and Freedom in Late Modernity*. Princeton, NJ: Princeton University Press, 1995.
Butler, Judith. *Gender Trouble: Feminism and the Subversion of Identity*. New York: Routledge, 1990.
Butler, Judith. "Merely Cultural," *Social Text* 52 (1997): 265–277.
Coates, Ta-Nehisi. "The First White President. The Foundation of Donald Trump's Presidency is the Negation of Barack Obama's Legacy," *The Atlantic*, Oct. 2017, https://www.theatlantic.com/magazine/archive/2017/10/the-first-white-president-ta-nehisi-coates/537909/. (accessed 05 Dec. 2019)
Emcke, Carolin. *Kollektive Identitäten: Sozialphilosophische Grundlagen*. Frankfurt a. M.: Fischer, 2000.
Emcke, Carolin. "Raus bist du," *Süddeutsche Zeitung*, 13 May 2019, https://www.sueddeutsche.de/politik/carolin-emcke-kolumne-rassismus-1.4439103. (accessed 05 Dec. 2019)
Enke, Anne F. "The Education of Little Cis: Cisgender and the Discipline of Opposing Bodies," In *The Transgender Studies Reader*, vol. 2, ed. by Susan Stryker and Aren Z. Aizura, 234–244. New York: Routledge, 2013.
Fanon, Frantz. *The Wretched of the Earth*, trans. Richard Philcox. New York: Grove Press, 2004.
Fraser, Nancy. "Heterosexism, Misrecognition, and Capitalism: A Response to Judith Butler," *Social Text* 52 (1997): 279–289.
Fraser, Nancy, and Honneth, Axel. *Redistribution or Recognition: A Political-Philosophical Exchange*, trans. Joel Golb, James Ingram, Christiane Wilke. London: Verso, 2003.

Fukuyama, Francis. "Against Identity Politics: The New Tribalism and the Crisis of Democracy," *Foreign Affairs*, Sept./Oct. 2018, https://www.foreignaffairs.com/articles/americas/2018-08-14/against-identity-politics-tribalism-francis-fukuyama. (accessed 05 Dec. 2019)

Haraway, Donna J. "Situated Knowledges: The Science Question in Feminism and the Privilege of Partial Perspective," *Feminist Studies* 14 (1988): 575–599.

Hochschild, Arlie Russell. *Strangers in their Own Land: Anger and Mourning on the American Right*, New York: The New Press, 2016.

Honneth, Axel. *Struggle for Recognition: The Moral Grammar of Social Conflicts*, trans. Joel Anderson. Cambridge, UK: Polity, 1996.

Koyma, Emi. "Cissexual/Cisgender: Decentralizing the Dominant Group," In *eminism: Putting the Emi Back in Feminism*, http://www.eminism.org/interchange/s2002/20020607-wmstl.html. (accessed 05 Dec. 2019)

Kruks, Sonia. "Identity Politics and Dialectical Reason: Beyond an Epistemology of Provenance," In *Feminist Interpretations of Jean-Paul Sartre*, ed. by Julien S. Murphy, 229–252. University Park, PA: Pennsylvania State University Press, 1999.

Lapidot, Elad. *Jews Out of the Question: A Critique of Anti-Anti-Semitism*. Albany, NY: SUNY Press, 2020.

Lilla, Marc. *The Once and Future Liberal: After Identity Politics*. New York: HarperCollins Publishers, 2017.

Michaels, Walter B. "Diversity kann Ungleichheit rechtfertigen," *DIE ZEIT*, 11 July 2019, https://www.zeit.de/politik/2019-07/us-wahlkampf-demokraten-vielfalt-identitaetspolitik-klassenkampf-oktopus/komplettansicht. (accessed 05 Dec. 2019)

Painter, Nell I. "What Whiteness Means in the Trump Era," *New York Times*, 12 Nov. 2016, https://www.nytimes.com/2016/11/13/opinion/what-whiteness-means-in-the-trump-era.html (accessed 05 Dec. 2019)

Rorty, Richard. *Achieving Our Country: Leftist Thought in Twentieth-Century America*. Cambridge, MA: Harvard University Press, 1998.

Sartre, Jean-Paul. *Being and Nothingness: An Essay on Phenomenological Ontology*, trans. Hazel Barnes. New York: Philosophical Library, 1956.

Sartre, Jean-Paul. *Search for a Method*. New York: Vintage, 1963.

Sartre, Jean-Paul. *Anti-Semite and Jew: An Exploration of the Etiology of Hate*, trans. George J. Becker. New York: Schocken, 1995.

Sigusch, Volkmar. "Transsexueller Wunsch und zissexuelle Abwehr," *Psyche* 49 (1995): 811–837.

Theunissen, Michael. *The Other: Studies in the Social Ontology of Husserls, Heidegger, Sartre, and Buber*, trans. Christopher Macann. Cambridge, MA: MIT Press, 1986.

Wong, David. "How Half of America Lost Its F**king Mind," *Cracked*, 12 Oct. 2016, https://www.cracked.com/blog/6-reasons-trumps-rise-that-no-one-talks-about/. (accessed 05 Dec. 2019)

Dominik Finkelde
In Need of A Master

On the Failure of Radical Democracy in the Era of Liberal-Democratic Authoritarianism

Abstract: If subsets of a set are allowed to question the limits of the set of which they are a part, and this questioning has a priori ontological priority over the stability of the set, then the indeterminacy of limits is constantly in danger of generating new sets time and again. A large number of such new sets may then generate a truly exceptional superset, which restricts subsets to question and limit its borderlines. When this happens within the political activities associated with the governance of a country or a state – as it does today within the rise of authoritarian anti-liberal political movements (from Orban to Trump) – premises of radical democratic theory are in peril since authoritarianism shows to be its flip-side and the unwanted child it nurtured unintentionally.

1 Introduction

In his text *Inhibitions, Symptoms, and Anxiety* from 1926, Freud addresses bodily reactions that, as symptoms, indicate a lack of representation of psychic forces in the mental-value system of the human mind.[1] These forces, coming from the outside of the "ego-organization", have an influence on the latter. Freud interprets them as "signs and a substitute for an instinctual satisfaction which has remained in abeyance."[2] This can be a trembling eyelid for example, a compulsive cough, or a recurring stutter in front of a certain person. These symptoms assert, as indeterminate entities, their existence in the abnormality of a body reaction. The subject simply fails to bring something into words and meanings and transforms the (partly traumatic) congestion into a corporeal reaction which lacks mental causation. In these "extra-territorialit[ies]"[3], as Freud calls them, the subject has no other solution than a "hysterical conversion"[4] of the repressed into the physical sign of disorder. Literally, an *Other* (with capital O) in the ego takes the floor and waits to be either reintegrated by the mind or to be accepted

---

1 See Freud, *Inhibitions*, 87–156.
2 Freud, *Inhibitions*, 91.
3 Freud, *Inhibitions*, 97.
4 Freud, *Inhibitions*, 98.

resignedly as an inner-psychical irritation which is now, unpleasant as it may be, part of the self itself.

Freud's observation of a blocked and conversion provoking force striving for sublation is mentioned here, since it can reveal insights into the emergence of authoritarian political movements in the nations of the so-called "western world" (Europe and the USA). Because, from the point of view of these movements, an inhibited, traumatic core that is characterized by collective identity crises vis-à-vis gender roles, questions of immigration, questions of "Leitkultur", questions of social inequality, "victimhood" or the like, cannot be adequately discussed in public – allegedly.[5] And this may lead to the Freudian symptoms mentioned above, but now – within the body politic of a nation – in the distorted form of extreme political views toward political "elites", "liberals", and/or "the left" in general. And these views, often commented on in public media, may include crude rejections of the value systems of the ruling class, "identitarian" political movements with their criticism of immigration policies, and taboo violations with regard to the respective culture's histories.[6]

It appears as if in 'culture war'-like clashes as these, a repressed substance comes to the surface with a hysterical articulation and leads to forms of various political schisms. In the present year of 2020 we are only too familiar with them through multiple political battles of the last years in the US and Europe and their frequent binary options of "they" vs. "we"; "fake news" vs. "good journalism"; enlightened liberal establishment vs. reactionary nationalists and simple-minded folks.[7] This kind of existential dramatization of political disagreements is not only caused by conflicts of interest, but, as I want to show in the following, by theoretical and philosophical failings as well. They unfold a "hysterical theatre" (Žižek)[8] around what cannot be said out loud. And what we are currently experiencing in right-wing authoritarian movements in the aforementioned countries corresponds to such hysterical theatre exemplarily. They express themselves even like psychotherapeutic interventions in the context of a theoretical break-

---

[5] The title-page of the German weekly *Der Spiegel* mirrors the political atmosphere with its heading: "(Anti-)Freedom of Speech. About real and perceived limits of what can be said" ("Meinungsunfreiheit. Über echte und gefühlte Grenzen des Sagbaren"), Issue 45, November 2019.
[6] This can concern the historic value given to reflecting nationwide upon the age of National Socialism in Germany (as Alexander Gauland's annihilating comparison with "birdshit" illustrates), the history of colonialism in France or that of a Southern-state culture in the eighteenth and nineteenth centuries in the United States, where a dispute about monuments and their influence on the cultural heritage has erupted in recent years.
[7] The topic has provoked multiple publications, such as: Farkas and Schou, *Post-Truth, Fake News and Democracy*; Babones, *New Authoritarianism*.
[8] Žižek, *For They Know Not What They Do*, 143.

down for which various aspects of radical democracy theories are co-responsible. At least this is the thesis that will be defended in the following paragraphs. Because it is precisely by giving ontological priority to the internal differentiation of multiple forms of life over leading cultural forms of life, through which radical democracy theories unintentionally paved the way for the return of their theoretical counterpart: authoritarianism. And indeed, authoritarian figures from Trump in the United States, to Johnson in Great Britain, and the Far Right in Germany surged unexpectedly in liberal-democratic societies of the present era. But how did we get there? Are large parts of the population simply too ignorant and uneducated to participate responsibly in democratic processes? Or have, within the field of philosophy at least, proponents of radical democracy theory set the expectations of liberal elites too high with the promise that only an ever more open and plural society will lead the way into the future of a modernized and globalized world? These are some of the questions discussed in the following sections with reference to aporia between hegemony and heteronomy as provoked by radical democracy theories. The concept of enjoyment, developed by Slavoj Žižek, will play a role from time to time in this analysis as it can be a refuge to protect communities from what they perceive as alienated societies. In that sense, enjoyment will prove to be a political factor.

2 The impasse of "transparticularism"

In his book *The White Man: An Anti-Manifesto*, the philosopher Luca Di Blasi has given a thought-provoking conceptual definition of the theoretical impasse that I just mentioned, since he dedicates himself exclusively to the normative status of the group mentioned in the title of his book. His thesis is that "white, heterosexual men" are representatives of hegemonic power in politics and society and therefore not able "to position themselves as a group of an equal normative identity-status vis-à-vis other groups", as for example minorities of all kinds, in the political field of discourse. They are no "particularity among other particularities".[9] In the antagonistic process of striving for hegemonic power they simply lack a "status of discrimination." As such, the most important political tool, to opt for "victimhood", is for this group obsolete. Only from the perspective of "discrimination" could a group defend normatively its rights to political power and social influence. At least this is the thesis presented according to a rather unspecified scale of victimhood and oppressorship, in which skin color, gender,

---

9 Di Blasi, *Der weiße Mann*, 92.

and sexual orientation are the outstanding criteria of assessment, although not sufficiently justified.

Di Blasi points to a way out of the dilemma for these men. It consists in the deliberately paradoxical simultaneity of paying respect to one's own particularity while at the same time crossing it out. This, he suggests, could result in the specific form of a universalism that – via "crossing all (im)possible particularizations"[10] out – anti-universalizes itself to form a new universal. White heterosexual men are, therefore, called upon to follow the normative imperative of having to want ever new particular identities at their side and it is their responsibility to encourage other social groups to articulate their forms of identity in such a way that they receive their "share" within the framework of the distribution of political power. So, while particular groups are therefore "empowered" to articulate their identities, the "white, heterosexual man" is not supposed to go this way, but with Di Blasi to favor "transparticularism,"[11] i.e. the questioning of every identity in the existing political hegemonic structure for the sake of an ever more plural future to come.

As an example, from Realpolitik this would mean that a male, white, heterosexual candidate for a university position would have to want that position to be given to a woman. In this decision according to gender, an institutional injustice lasting for centuries towards the groups concerned (women) would find a form of inter-generative justice and compensation. Though the female applicant for the aforementioned position herself may no longer have been an individual victim of discrimination (compared to, let's imagine, her grandmother, who was refused university studies); and she may also come from a higher social class than the male applicant, and yet it is only in her appointment as woman that a form of historical reparation and compensation takes place. The reason why in this case the female quota is the decisive criterion for the appointment to the academic position and not skin color, minority-status or social origin (in which the man might have had a better victim status), may still be part of contingent circumstances for the time being. And yet also the women, as applicant, must want to point out this circumstance in order to potentially assign her victim status to another victim, which is even more victimized, if there is one. (And I dare to say, that there is *always one* who is more victimized as oneself). Now what matters within this victimhood schematism is not what the individual is as an individual. What matters is someone's belonging to a group and its group-identity.

---

10 Di Blasi, *Der weiße Mann*, 79.
11 Di Blasi, *Der weiße Mann*, 81–88.

The pressing question as to whether there is not a danger within this narrative that an area of political self-assertion by identitarian groups will emerge, in which no one wants to be a non-victim, cannot be answered here for reasons of space.[12] And yet such a panorama seems possible and to be able to permanently harm the social contract in an unexpected way. Nor can reference be made here to the question of why the victim status of gender or minority discrimination should be rated higher than the victim status of a bookseller, for example, who loses his business due to a corporation like Amazon. In fact, in view of multiple levels of victimization in modern capitalist societies, the question would have to arise again whether it is not precisely in the gender difference itself that a hegemonic position of supremacy is articulated. In this case, though, it would of course not be plausible to attribute the moral prerogative to this kind of victim status in the first place.

Be that as it may, according to Di Blasi, the group of white, heterosexual men is turning into a new avant-garde. Compared to women, homosexuals, blacks et al. who are still struggling for identities, recognition and political power, this group manages to eat the cake of its identity by not touching it. Identity, similar to the state-critical Marxism of the French sociologist Miguel Abensour, is to be thought of as reconciling the universal and the non-identical via the creation of a new anti-universal-universal.[13] New identities and differences are supposed to pave the way for an ever more plural society to come. In it, subsets or sub-elements are no longer counted by a universal and controlling superset, but are free to strive for difference which is only limited by other differences in an eternal agonistic struggle.[14] In this world of transparticularism, "singularities" (Reckwitz)[15] exist on an equal footing in their own "agonistic" (Mouffe)[16] but not antagonistic (Laclau) identity – namely as groups of whites, blacks, women, men, Germans of Turkish origin, Moroccan Frenchmen, homosexuals, heterosexuals, vegans etc. all striving creatively and conflictively for political representation.

Chantal Mouffe has, next to Ernesto Laclau, Etienne Balibar, Claude Lefort and many others, famously laid specific theoretical grounds for this political phi-

---

12 On victimhood see: Campbell and Manning, *Rise of Victimhood Culture*.
13 See Abensour, *Democracy Against the State*, XLII–XLVI.
14 The fact, however, that this very same theory must accept as collateral damage in the name of a better future the constant discrimination of individuals (on the basis of their gender, skin color or sexual orientation) is rarely acknowledged.
15 Reckwitz, *Gesellschaft der Singularitäten*.
16 Mouffe, "Deliberative Democracy or Agonistic Pluralism?", 745–758. See also: Mouffe, *Agonistics*, 8.

losophy as she understands "agonism" as a "democratic outlet".[17] Political polarization is allowed, but only insofar as the breaking off of democratic processes through friend-enemy antagonisms can be prevented. In this way, Mouffe wants to "disavow ... the possibility of an act of radical refoundation that would institute a new social order from scratch."[18] Always new worlds of multiple multiplicities are supposed to open up within radical democracies. Within them, identity narratives, which refer to concepts such as people, race, property, religion, are interpreted only in terms of their future non-identity. Every identity as well as every culture, every way of life appears good per se, at least as long as one reflects on the identity of non-identity of it. This is the meta-theoretical narrative that various representatives of radical democracy theory proclaim, sometimes with reference to the horrors of twentieth century ideologies as something that should never repeat itself. And who would want to dispute this ambition?

However, as Alex Demirović (and many others before him) has shown, Mouffe's rationale necessarily contradicts itself. "For she suggests that the dynamics of discourse can be controlled and fixed in a specific way. It gives the impression that political actors can consciously and strategically decide to constitute and maintain a certain, namely liberal social order" with agonistic properties.[19] In fact, the ontology of political contingency postulated by both, Mouffe and Laclau in *Hegemony and Socialist Strategy*, is suspended here, since a certain liberal understanding of both "politics" *and* "the political" is always already presupposed as normative. But if the founding gesture of politics via the disruptive gesture of the political has always been, is, and will always be unfounded and contingent, then it is not clear from which normative presupposition contingency should only be allowed within radical-democratic societies. Or, to say it differently: There is just no normative ground of argument that can justify the exclusion of an anti-radical democratic contingency that proclaims (exactly in the name of contingency) the rule of authoritarianism. As such Mouffe's theory is similar to "political moralism".[20]

---

17 Mouffe, *On the Political*, 30; Mouffe, *Agonistics*, 30.
18 Mouffe, *On the Political*, 31.
19 Demirović, "Scheitern der Agonistik", 197.
20 Cross, "Normativity", 180. The "absent ground" of society has been repeatedly addressed by philosophers of the Radical Democracy Theory. Claude Lefort, for example, refers to the democratic age as one in which the constant elimination of certainties is one of the central characteristics. Often, however, this does not express the risk of political anarchism, but on the contrary, the joy of the fact that through the absent ground the fundamental plasticity of society is guaranteed. Lefort, "La dissolution", 551–568.

Anti-"identitarian" theoretical approaches cannot protect themselves from their dialectical reversal to create a new political ideology, since – with Willard V. O. Quine – there is just no way for entities to exist without identities. So, the proclaimed transparticular identity of an anti-universal universalism is just that: an identity with political properties, beliefs, desires and it is only outstanding insofar as its ideological background-conditions are often unacknowledged. But even independently of this, the radical democratic viewpoint, which is only touched upon here, is problematic since it can, within the axiomatic limits of its premises, only defend increasingly pluralistic rights against hegemonic cultures without sufficiently pointing out the conditions of the possibility of the functioning of hegemonic structures through mechanisms of suppression tout court.

While, according to Mouffe, pre-modern communities are "organized around a single substantive idea of the common good"[21] modern communities highlight "the lack of a final ground"[22] as well as the lack of an "organic identity". And the "logic of the contingent" as a political factor brings this to the fore.[23] What does the reference to contingency explain? It conveys the fact that there is nothing within an established form of power that can be regarded as "natural". But it refers also to all claims, to natural orders, and to "every essence".[24] In the same line of argumentation and in the tradition of Miguel Abensour, Mouffe emphasizes that radical democracy theory should not question the plurality-pushing premises from which it started, but at most should radicalize them time and again.[25] This, though, reinforces the idea that reality is not only the stage of a subjective will to construct one's own self as singularity, but that it also seems impossible to communicate the meaning of my reality to other subjects (due to divided ideologies). In the face of this development, not only does indifference seem obvious; rather, a new human right to hatred and radical rejection of others or the Other is establishing itself.

---

21 Mouffe, *On the Political*, 17.
22 Mouffe, *Agonistics*, 131.
23 Mouffe and Laclau, *Hegemony*, 7.
24 Mouffe and Laclau, *Hegemony*, 155.
25 "What we need is a hegemony of democratic values, and this requires a multiplication of democratic practices, institutionalizing them into ever more diverse social relations, so that a multiplicity of subject positions can be formed through the democratic matrix." Mouffe, *Return of the Political*, 18.

3 Universality and scission

The concepts "transparticularism" (according to Di Blasi), "agonism" (according to Mouffe) and "contingency" (according to Mouffe/Laclau et al.) are mentioned here since we see in the USA of the present era a political right-wing movement that is taking place in defiance of all three concepts which are central pillars in the theoretical edifice of radical democracy theory. As such it stages what according to the theory of "transparticularism" should not have been staged: a successful self-presentation of victimhood of the group of white and heterosexual men. This group's victim-status outlines its contours in the self-proclaimed opposition to left-liberal hegemonic powers and from this opposition its political universality finds its ground. Do the followers of this movement lack insight and empathy for minorities since many of them possess political hegemonic power? This is difficult to say as this group is dissimilar within itself. But not only that. It might simply be the case that – as mentioned above – the group has different categories of victimhood. Social categories are political battlefields themselves and not simply empirical facts. A word-to-world relation of fit is instantiated in them which explains why social facts have a lesser degree of modal robustness, as, let's say, scientific facts.

What is striking is the fact that people of different social backgrounds appear to be united by an unconcealed longing for a "master", a paternal authority, which becomes particularly evident in the career of Donald Trump. Even after loosing his re-election in 2020 he forces his most bitter opponents into an almost pathological dependency to "work themselves off" at the scandal of his personality. And even a structural analogy to Freud's "Urvater" of the pre-civilizational "brother-hord", as presented in *Totem and Taboo*, cannot be overlooked. Because Trump incorporates this position of being the headman of enjoyment where all the other 'brothers' are deprived from their real desires within the politically correct form of the modern social contract: with regard to beliefs, sexuality, classical gender-roles and the will to bend political power as they want to. As such, Trump creates a bizarre place of universality and exception especially in being an outlaw of its own kind at the summit of political power as president of the United States. He, thus, becomes almost automatically the incarnation of resistance to the social contract which is, allegedly, too neutral, too libertarian, and which develops itself into pluralistic and anti-social differences of ever more sub-groups. For this is the gesture of power that Trump, but also other right-wing conservative movements (led by Marien le Pen in France or Alexander Gauland in Germany) have established in liberal democratic societies in the last two decades. And, as I have said, this obviously contradicts various premises of Di Blasi's theorem of "transparticularism" and the dogma of an anti-identitarian concept of identity within radical democracy theories.

This is mentioned here, not to unilaterally criticize philosophers of pluralism against their nationalistic opponents, but to lay bare that theories of radical democracy are lagging behind in giving accounts of unexpected political movements in liberal, western societies.[26] And it is not clear if radical democracy theory can integrate the phenomenon of Trump or not. (A side-note: This became apparent at the conference "In Need of a Master" at the University of Bochum where proponents of radical democracy theory could not agree if Trump is a political symptom that radical democracy theory can incorporate, or if he represents exactly political beliefs which have to be shunned so that the theory can maintain its normative axioms.)

Confronted with a surge of identity-political activism in the public sphere where movements such as LGBT, "Me-too" and "Black Lives Matter" are supported especially by representatives of the Democratic Party, the Republican Party sees its role primarily concerned with the reestablishment of a hegemonic culture that is felt as having been lost to liberal mainstream. And the question is whether this anti-liberal movement with Trump at center stage can be contained within the normative premises of radical democracy theory (as presented by Mouffe or Di Blasi in the context of this essay) or whether, as mentioned above, it is a theoretically unexpected avant-garde that, in turn, makes radical theories of democracy look apolitical and backward-looking.

Mouffe (but also authors such as Butler, Laclau and Balibar) normatively state repeatedly that radical democracy theory must not fall back on traditional "essentialist" or "substantialist" narratives to promote a community's unity, since narratives like these are contaminated by contingent historical processes and blind-making phantasmagorical illusions. The only alternative is an anti-essentialist communal future where plurality trumps "organic" explanatory pat-

---

26 Trump embodies the paternal authority in a particularly exemplary manner through his uncompromising questioning of traditions of left-liberal elites about what the term "USA" denotes, or of how cultural achievements such as plural and cultural openness towards minorities should be interpreted in the political sphere. His strategy is deliberately based on his much-commented taboo-breaking of traditional political background assumptions, as for example his blatant form of public lying and multiple defamation campaigns against political opponents show. To still adopt in this context Mouffe's term "agonism" seems difficult to justify, since in the struggles between Democrats and Republicans the political legitimacy of the opponents themselves is constantly being questioned and the dispute repeatedly referred to judicial decisions on the correct interpretation of the constitution. Agonism seems to have given way to antagonism in Realpolitik.

tern in guiding cultural ideals.[27] But this is precisely what many US-Republicans, but also other authoritarian-political movements mentioned above, seem to deny. And it is within this denial that a "chain of equivalence" among political signifiers is, according to Laclau/Mouffe, achieved.[28] Different signifiers bring themselves into antagonism towards a particular signifier and become, in confrontation with the latter, a political force.

4 Consensual minimum

According to Carl Schmitt – to whom Mouffe refers in her conception of "agonism" – it is evident that the concept of *anta*gonism (known as friend-enemy schematism) could only be usefully applied if it is supported by a phantasm of national identity. According to him, this keeps pluralism and contingency at a consensual minimum. "Every actual democracy rests on the principle that not only are equals equal, but unequals will not be treated equally. Democracy requires, therefore, first homogeneity and second – if the need arises – elimination or eradication of heterogeneity."[29]

In contrast to Hans Kelsen and his school, Schmitt maintains that a society's consensus cannot be grounded on a purely positivistic legal formality as the ultimate guarantor of political freedom. Law's community-building effect is rooted in a space of shared traditions and unreflected background assumptions. It marks a normative minimum of options for action that can be carried out without being sanctioned. As such, however, the law presupposes a cultural maximum of forms of behavior that is not regulated by law itself. In other words: In order that laws can be invoked as a normative minimum in exceptional cases, a maximum of non-legally defined forms of life is required. For this reason, societies in which cultural pluralisms interact with one another in relation to the legal positivism are in danger of losing a communitarian understanding of solidarity (among "my peers" and against "the others") as the foundation of the political. At least this is Schmitt's famous interpretation of what "*the* political" is about.[30]

---

[27] Mouffe, *Return of the Political*, 18.
[28] See Laclau, "Why do Empty Signifiers Matter to Politics", 36–46.
[29] Schmitt, *Crisis of Parliamentarian Democracy*, 9.
[30] From this line of argumentation, bizarre and dogmatic as it may seem, one may understand the political motivation of Britain's withdrawal from the European Union between the years 2018–2020. Advocates of "Brexit" may have wanted less universalistic notions of equality among Europeans, but rather a less complex autonomy of "us" as political agents through

He speaks repeatedly of essences of national and ethnic identity. But does he mean these terms in an "essentialistic" manner? How else, one might ask? And yet it is not at all clear what the term "essence", often negatively connoted in radical democracy theory, is supposed to denote. Perhaps Schmitt himself already understood terms such as "the people", "the nation" etc. in a "post-foundational" sense of Oliver Marchart's interpretation.[31] Why should Schmitt not have known about the contingency and phantasmagorical basic structure of "essences" (whatever "essence" is supposed to mean here) and yet use words like "the people", "our nation" as phantasmagorically as Di Blasi uses his concept "transparticularism" or as Mouffe uses her concept "agonism"? The terms mentioned are memes with a specific domain of reference. They are imagined postulates in the midst of inferential justifications and all serve as post-foundational foundations and reasons.

According to Schmitt, a community only comes about as a community of solidarity through normatively shared phantasmagorias. Do these phantasmagorias break away if their "essences" are proven to be phantasmagoric? To hold this opinion is rather naive, since "essence" itself has, as concept, both phantasmagoric and epistemic properties from ancient philosophy onwards. What else is the platonic theory of forms if not phantasmagoric in explaining epistemically the relationship between multiple universals and particular entities instantiating them? Therefore, it is not intelligible by Mouffe's own light of reasoning how Schmitt becomes her source in the development of her concept of "agonism". Transforming "antagonism" (as it is present in the friend-enemy schematism) into "agonism" deprives Schmitt's political philosophy of both its phantasmagoric and epistemic-ontological core-idea of what reality is all about: "us" vs. "them".

For Schmitt, the "enemy" as concept is a purely formal figure of difference to the citizen of any body politic. Enmity defines citizenship existentially as the limit to what one, as citizen, is not. "The political enemy need not be morally evil or aesthetically ugly; he need not appear as an economic competitor, and it may even be advantageous to engage with him in business transactions."[32] The criteria of morality (good vs. evil) do not concern Schmitt. For this reason, however, he also rejects those theories that paradoxically do not accept the "we" vs. "they" difference precisely because of a supra-human perspective of hu-

---

the (questionable?) cultivation of an "essential" and "substantial" *Leitkultur*. And they apparently wanted this even if this form of national identity-politics has an impact on the national economy.
31 Marchart, *Post-foundational Political Thought*.
32 Schmitt, *Concept of the Political*, 27.

manity that has an inhuman core exactly via the greatness of its values. As Schmitt reveals in his *Theory of the Partisan*, supra-human values may lead to another form of enmity, one in which "[e]nmity will be so terrifying that one perhaps mustn't even speak any longer of the enemy or of enmity. ... Annihilation thus becomes entirely abstract and entirely absolute. It ... serves only an ... ostensibly objective attainment of highest values, for which no price is too high to pay."[33] This may explain why Schmitt saw in the friend-enemy schematism a political humanism that resisted "an allegedly objective enforcement of highest values" in the name of humanity that undermines the contingent property clusters of communities. And as it seems, radical democracy theory is lagging behind these both existentialist and structural insights.

5 The fabric of fantasies

Independently of the diagnosis of the 'state of theory in the age of Trump' presented here, people in a body politic desire time and again foundational acts of politics – especially in times of crisis – to retrieve the community from the expense of a society divided by differences. (I have published on this elsewhere.)[34] This becomes particularly a pressing subject matter when aporias emerge in the ideological fabric of society that threaten the formal conditions of community. Especially in these situations, fantasies must not only be managed, but also instrumentalized in such a way that divisions and scissions can re-establish a new community of political enjoyment on the basis of Schmitt's friend-enemy schematism and anchor it effectively in human structures of desire. And Trump succeeded in doing exactly that: articulating – via "chains of equivalence" (Laclau) – an exception precisely at the level of that class which should not have been able to relate to a form of exception and victimhood at all. He achieved this both in the phantasmagorical cultivation of being a victim of a politically corrupted society where identitarian groups of victimhood see often all the evil in the class, that Trump is a member of; and in cultivating at the same time the image of the patriarch, who allows himself various excesses and special rights in a world cleansed by, allegedly, microaggressions of "political correctness". But, as I mentioned above, the thesis presented here is that defective premises of radical democracy theory make this success of Trump theoretically comprehensible.

---

33 Schmitt, *Theory of the Partisan*, 67.
34 See Finkelde, *Phantaschismus*; see also, Finkelde, "The 'Secret Code' of Honour", 232–261.

The structural objective of politics, as Trump understands it apparently, consists in invoking an illegal act of founding a community in demarcation to a disillusioned society – especially in times in which contradictions threaten the pleasure structures of the administered hegemonic fantasies within society. A performative act of self-positing creates space for itself, which, as a paradoxical element, thereby reconnects chains of signifiers in the ideological field of the community that have become unstable. And I think that this is where the avant-garde potential of all authoritarian, anti-liberal, national-political movements in the so-called "Western countries" lies, regardless of whether they are considered to have great chances of remaining in power or not. For if, in the realm of theory, premises of the political refer exclusively to their moral value with reference to transparticularism, to contingency, difference and identity in non-identity (which is confirmed by a recent anthology on Radical Democracy Theory published in 2019)[35], then, within the framework of this (theoretical) hegemonic culture of difference, a structural site of an excluded Other is automatically created. And this Other is waiting to bring about via chains of equivalence a new form of freedom against the superiority of singular identity groups through an authoritarian gesture of power.[36]

From the perspective of US-Republicans, then, to put it very simply, a certain form of hegemonic identity is crossed out (from Trump's perspective: the United States of a liberal culture of order) to found a new identity in the creation of a radical scission ("we" vs. "them"). What is articulated here is a phantasmagorically radical-identitarian outburst in the sense of a hysterical conversion mentioned at the beginning of this paper. From now on, facts concerning, for example, immigration at the border with Mexico, split society into enemies and friends, into "them" and "us". Especially in times of crisis, when it cannot be de-

---

35 Comtesse, Flügel-Martinsen, Martinsen and Martin Nonhoff, *Radikale Demokratietheorie*, see especially the introduction: 11–16.

36 Representatives of radical democracy theories may object that, in their own view, this place of a non-articulable (right-wing authoritarian position) does not exist, since there is never the absolutely ascertained position which can be fully articulated nor the opposite: the position of what can absolutely not be politically articulated. Only "strategic essentialisms" (Gayatri Spivak) are therefore allowed politically within certain limits of justifications. See Spivak, "Can the Subaltern Speak?", 66–111. But thinking along these lines does not only underestimate the ideological blindness of radical democracy theories towards their own fantasies. It also underestimates the extent to which they themselves prepare, as I said, the way for a return to antagonism in the midst of agonisms. Because it is precisely by allowing "all-inclusively" all positions of articulation of political interests under agonistic premises, except the fundamentalist, essentialist one, that radical democracy theory opens up a space out of space. And in certain situations, it may be only here that freedom and truth have a chance to come to unconceal themselves.

termined with empirical-scientific precision who is "entitled" to proclaim the fact that a crisis truly exists (at the border to Mexico for example), the task of political representatives can be to reconstitute the community around imaginary forms of universalities (precisely through forms of, for example, dividing the nation). And the US government under Trump is succeeding in this so far. Fantasies about identity-formations, about the wall to Mexico and the superiority of one's own culture (MAGA = Make America Great Again), prove to be effective, especially since transgressions towards dominant hegemonic cultures are expressed in them. So, excessive fantasies that Trump's administration injects into political debates are aimed at reinventing the space of community through a moment of constitutive division, so that it will have retroactively surrendered in its legitimacy as a 'natural place' – similar to a religious conversion. And the converts are precisely those who unite in the obscene enjoyment of the "master" and his ability to divide and in the adoption of a universality in the act of scission. The one who shares the fantasies mentioned (of the wall to Mexico, of a national heritage 'without immigration' etc.) then belongs to us – and watches, for example, Fox News – knowing full well that facts now take on a different value in the everyday language of the political – especially since the political opponent, just as in a political-radical counter-reaction, cannot help but put political facts as well into the limelight of their own political bias. One need only recall how left-center liberal media (Washington Post, New York Times, CNN) have tendentially treated the so-called "Russian Collusion" as if the proof of Trump's guilt was for sure.

6 On behalf of the law against the law

Slavoj Žižek describes violations of the allegedly failing neutral law in the name of patriarchal power as the normative re-appearance of what he calls "nightly law". In his far-reaching analyses of the ideological character of culture, he shows the extent to which the idea of law is inherently divided into a public appearance of the law on a symbolic and supra-individual level and its "id"-like desires swarming undercover in the mental states of rebellious and resentful subjects. According to Žižek, the "id"-like desires can take on even a "super-ego"-like authority in confrontation with the neutral-public law, especially when the neutral law is perceived as too liberal and too human for the well-being of the general public. In cases like these an "obscene" enjoyment of the law follows a super-ego-like injunction: to do everything possible for the sake of the law – even to break the law in the name of the law. And this process is by no means unprecedented to our experiences, since the majority of detective series like "Bosch" or "True Detective" build their plots on the same structure of enjoyment. The protagonists of these series are heroes who, according to their will, cross the law – within the bounds of a neutral, reasonable structure of guidelines, values and norms – for the sake of the law. In cases like these (where a super-ego injunction acts with enjoyment contra the law in the name of the law), a kind of "reenactment" of the foundation of society, described by Freud in *Totem and Taboo*, gains a new political power of action. But it does not get this power by killing the "Urvater" again; on the contrary: that he may rise again as representative of an urgently needed universal principle for the suppression of singularities that have become unruly: the brothers of a brother-horde at the brink of collapse. In Žižek words: "[W]hat now erupts ... is precisely the authoritarian-patriarchal logic that continues to determine our attitudes, although its direct public expression is no longer permitted."[37]

Since every form of a social contract cannot answer the question of its own provenance and therefore has no response to how the law was able to establish itself in the first place – without being simply lawless – a hidden illegality is constitutively inscribed into the law. This illegality, though, can (and must) always re-emerge when fantasies about the ruling neutral principles of law are no longer shared. A singular (lawless) authority that was once abandoned in favor of social democratic consensus among equals returns in these cases. And Donald Trump is truly an outstanding example of this return. Acting in the name of the patriarchal "nightly law" gives his followers an understanding of community that surpasses the purely formal understanding of society and constitutes its plea for the new community, which is to be strengthened or to be re-established by legal-illegal forms of singular-patriarchal exceptions. And it is in political situations of this kind that Carl Schmitt's dictum, taken from Thomas Hobbes, fits adequately: "Auctoritas, non veritas [facit legem]."[38]

The normative value of fantasies of authority, which are included and excluded in the new communitarian reality they create, can often no longer be vindicated by traditional justifications (like fact-checking) since the classical reasons themselves constituted the non-thematic background condition of the new community. (This also applies to the fantasy of a "Russian Collusion".) For what denotes a fantasy like "Make America great again"? The proposition pretends that the greatness conjured here is real as soon as the proposition's counterpart is adopted as well: that America is not yet great. As a condition of affective attachment, fantasies are conditions of the "space of reasons", and that is a condition of political rationality.

---

37 Žižek, *Metastases of Enjoyment*, 56.
38 Schmitt, *Leviathan*, 55.

Right-wing populist parties, identitarian movements, and neo-fascist groupings, which have emerged especially in "western" nation states in the last ten years, deliberately undermine and shift the rules of the democratic discourse of the present. And the polemics that are being raised against them are proof for them of their universality in particularity. From their point of view, the post-metaphysical and radical democratic perspective of the genesis of norms produced in and through contingency, pushes a political form of life that tends towards the tragic and the self-absorption of community and the fantasies of order. This must be resisted by all means, because the discourse of universalism leaves them, allegedly, not enough room for the community as fantasized.

Against this background, the accusation often made by theorists of radical democracy theory that right-wing and nationalist political philosophers like Schmitt or Heidegger rest their political convictions only on *false* fantasies (i.e. ideological ones) is actually a naive argument. It is guileless, since radical democracy theorists can only base their reasons on fantasies as well, fantasies that are supposed to be primitive and foundational. These fantasies may have good reasons. But they have good reasons also because they are grounded in fantasies. And that is fine. How else could it be?

Shouldn't theoreticians of radical democracy theory acknowledge that the power of particularity is also formally nothing but power, if every form of Leitkultur formation is seen as a historical-contingent phantasm, waiting to be set aside similar to the premise of "transparticularism" that will be set aside as well? This is how the struggle for recognition is seen: as power for power's sake and not for the common will. For this common will is supposed to be non-existent, respectively transparent in the horizon of the always "coming" plural society, the coming universalism of non-identity.

7 Victimhood

To detect the true political impact of conflictive relations of sets and their subsets in political communities, one should recall the controversy between the Canadian student Lindsay Shepherd and the *Wilfrid Laurier University* in Ontario, which was much debated in North America. The teaching assistant was accused of hurting students of her study group in November 2017 when she showed the video of a discussion with the conservative cultural theorist Jordan Peterson. In the recording a new law in Canada, known as "Bill C-16", was controversially discussed as it punishes the refusal to use a personal pronoun for trans-gender people with severe penalties. Shepherd was summoned for an interview by employees of the university, but was denied information about who had made the charge against her. She was also not told whether the accusation was made by one or more participants of her study group. Apparently, the only decisive factor that mattered for those responsible at the university was that a victim exercised his/her right to non-discrimination without it becoming clear why showing a video with Jordan Peterson on the aforementioned debate should be perceived as discriminatory at all.[39]

The conflict between Shepherd and the university finally provoked the question, much discussed in Canadian media but also in the United States, how much formal right can be granted to the vulnerability of an individual or an identitarian group in the space of political discourse without that space itself losing its own universality as a framework for discussion due to too many internal counter-norms of what is supposed to be worthy of discussion, or what victimizes a person in the first place. This question concerns precisely the question mentioned above, of how many particular rights may be distributed, so that sub-groups of all kinds (women, Trump supporters, Latinos etc.) are supposed to split off from the hegemonic field of universality, from the community/society putting their status as victims first according to their definition of what a victim is.

The relationship between a cultural texture that shapes a shared background knowledge of a political community (through post-fundamentalist ideologies) and the formal determination of rights by the law, as commented on above with reference to Carl Schmitt (and his nationalistic ideology), returns here in an exemplary fashion. For here, in the conflict between Shepherd vs. Laurier, a cultural maximum was apparently used up in the past to such an extent that particular groups could possibly only meet each other with the accusation of mutually bending the law. But in a society which has to be "open" by definition this can only be a beginning, so that one has to ask oneself whether an antisocial society with a perfect legal conscience must not actually await us in the future. And there may not be an alternative to this development – but not because we people of the twenty-first century explicitly agreed to go this way. It may rather be the case that our contemporary understanding of freedom, which Christoph Menke coined with the term of "subjective rights", can no lon-

---

[39] On the Facebook page of *Wilfrid Laurier University's* "Rainbow Center," the following comment was posted on 21 November, 2017: "These debates, regardless of how 'neutrally' they are presented, constitute a form of epistemic violence that dehumanizes trans people by denying the validity of trans experience. ... We cannot allow for this profound violence to be continued." See: https://m.facebook.com/WLURainbowCentre/posts/1628430573891091 (accessed 02 Feb. 2020).

ger help but split society with ever more subjects as victims of the universal.[40] Why, however, an individual, even in a banal everyday area such as the choice of a health insurance, should then still show solidarity with people who are not of his or her "race", "identitarian-" or "victim-group", can then no longer be conveyed.

The *Wilfrid Laurier University* ultimately found itself in a predicament of no longer being able to distinguish between the rights of singularities and the duties of institutions defending universals – since universals are bundles of contingent phantasmagoria themselves. As such the conflict revealed exemplary aporias in multiple dogmas of radical democracy theory. Proponents, who, like Mouffe or Abensour, defend an unbound pluralism against hegemonic structures without pointing out that the very preconditions of plurality is the hegemonic dominion of ideological suppression of difference, cannot, in my opinion, provide any answers with regard to the conflictive dimension of a formal-structural superiority of victimhood within the space of discourse. For if sub-sets of a set are allowed to question all too quickly the limits of the set of which they are (as victims) subsets of, and this questioning is a priori to be valued ontologically as of a higher value (as certain aspects of radical democracy theory insinuate, in which, according to formal definitions, particular identities are allowed to proclaim themselves as "essential", whereas hegemonic identities are not), then the limit between set and subset is constantly in danger of generating even sets of such radical exception that philosophers like Mouffe or Abensour might qualify them as anti-political. Because such an exception may in the end generate a phenomenon like Trump or even worse a new totalitarian state-function. In a nutshell: if the fear of violated singularities leads to a space of discourse which is in danger of no longer being able to preserve its ideological authority, then the anecdote at *Wilfrid Laurier University* seems to be a kind of *mise en scene* for public conflicts surging possibly in the future.

As I said, stopping this process may be just as impossible as a return to "good old times" which of course never existed. For this reason, the analyses presented here sees its primary goal not in questioning the importance of radical democracy theories, but rather in undermining the moral pathos of their acolytes and in revealing the theory as just as ideologically burdened as representatives of radical democratic theory repeatedly accuse their opponents of.

---

40 See Menke, *Kritik der Rechte*, 17–18.

8 Difference to come

One can compare the theoretical approach of radical democratic theory with Hegel's analysis of "stoicism" as well as with his comments on the "ascetic position," as mentioned with a brief reference to the early Christian scholar and ascetic Origen of Alexandria, in his *Phenomenology of Spirit*.[41] Stoicism tries to hold onto universal categories, like the true and the good, wisdom and virtue, but shies away from giving them a specific meaning. But this lack of concrete content effects radical democracy theory as well. Just as it is impossible for radical democratic approaches to elude their ontic life-world and the Eurocentric facts, norms and values that have always been normatively prescribed therein – let us call them either Eurocentrists of a "first level" (Schmitt, Strauss, Mohler …) or Eurocentrics on a "second, meta level" (Mouffe, Laclau …) – so they have, as well, no other choice than to constantly address the issue of their denial, their renunciation of ideology, and their radicality for the sake of *renunciation per se*. But since Euro*decentrism* cannot in turn renounce its Euro*centrism*, or in other words: because Euro*decentrism* is the fundamental political gesture of Euro*centrism*, it is left – or so it seems – only with the eternally embodied Euro*decentrism*-rejection-thematization. But just like Hegel recognizes stoicism as a stage of political impotence, which is reflected in the formality of its abstract aspirations, so radical democracy theory appears to be just as much a battle of constant retreat, where a small group of like-minded people with universal categories of the true and the good are surrounded by reactionary forces. Decentralization becomes a duty of constant denial of that which historically and contingently defines the actual status.

This might explain why conferences on radical democracy theory seem (at least to my knowledge) to be constantly preoccupied with their radicality in order to find new ways to universalize this radicality without essentializing it. But this, as such, is not what is too problematic about this approach, because, after all, everyone should be free to do what makes him or her happy. What is problematic, however, is the moral rank that advocates of this theory attribute to themselves, as well as the inability to think a concept such as "Leitkultur" without already locating it either on the side of some kind of proto-fascism or – from the a priori framework of the theory – in the genealogy of its permanent decentralization.

Radical democracy theory is, as such, the machine of desire, which wants to maintain itself as being the ultimate theory of universality. What, though, this de-

---

[41] See Hegel, *Phenomenology of Spirit*, 119–139 (stoicism), 348 (Origen).

sire produces is its own opposite: singularity. From the radical decentralization without end, which is experienced as senseless repetition, only the desire for centering can come to the fore. And Trump embodies this. He is the hysterical symptom of conversion which radical democracy theory both nurtured and has been waiting for. In Trump, radical democracy found truly its master. The theory was in need of him.

Bibliography

Abensour, Miguel. *Democracy Against the State: Marx and the Machiavellian Moment.* Cambridge, UK: Polity Press, 2011.
Babones, Salvatore. *The New Authoritarianism: Trump, Populism, and the Tyranny of Experts.* Cambridge, UK: Polity Press, 2018.
Campbell, Bradley, and Manning, Jason. *The Rise of Victimhood Culture: Microaggressions, Safe Spaces, and the New Culture Wars.* Cham, CH: Palgrave Macmillan, 2018.
Comtesse, Dagmar; Flügel-Martinsen, Oliver; Martinsen, Franziska, and Nonhoff, Martin, eds., *Radikale Demokratietheorie: Ein Handbuch.* Berlin: Suhrkamp, 2019.
Cross, Ben. "Normativity in Chantal Mouffe's Political Realism," *Constellations* 24 (2017): 180–191.
Demirović, Alex. "Das Scheitern der Agonistik: Zur kritischen Theorie des Politischen," In *Kritische Theorie der Politik*, ed. by Ulf Bohmann and Paul Sörensen, 179–208. Berlin: Suhrkamp, 2019.
Di Blasi, Luca. *Der weiße Mann – ein Anti-Manifest.* Bielefeld: transcript, 2013.
Farkas, Johan, and Schou, Jannick. *Post-Truth, Fake News and Democracy: Mapping the Politics of Falsehood.* New York: Routledge, 2020.
Finkelde, Dominik. *Phantaschismus: Zur totalitären Versuchung unserer Demokratie.* Berlin: Vorwerk 8 Verlag, 2016.
Finkelde, Dominik. "The 'Secret Code' of Honour: On Political Enjoyment and the Excrescence of Fantasy," *Culture, Theory and Critique* 59 (2018): 232–261.
Freud, Sigmund. *Inhibitions, Symptoms and Anxiety*, ed. by James Strachey. Toronto: The Hogarth Press, 1959.
Hegel, Georg W.F. *Phenomenology of Spirit*, trans. Arnold V. Miller. Oxford: Oxford University Press, 1977.
Laclau, Ernesto. "Why do Empty Signifiers Matter to Politics," In *Emancipation(s)*, Ernesto Laclau, 36–46. London: Verso, 1996.
Lefort, Claude. "La dissolution des repères et l'enjeu démocratique," In *Le temps present: Écrits 1945–2005*, Claude Lefort, 551–568. Paris: Belin, 2007.
Marchart, Oliver. *Post-foundational Political Thought: Political Difference in Nancy, Lefort, Badiou and Laclau.* Edinburgh: Edinburgh University Press, 2007.
Menke, Christoph. *Kritik der Rechte.* Berlin: Suhrkamp, 2018.
Mouffe, Chantal. "Deliberative Democracy or Agonistic Pluralism?," *Social Research* 66 (1999): 745–758.
Mouffe, Chantal. *On the Political.* Abingdon: Routledge, 2005.
Mouffe, Chantal. *The Return of the Political.* London: Verso, 2006.

Mouffe, Chantal. *Agonistics: Thinking the World Politically.* London: Verso, 2013.
Mouffe, Chantel, and Laclau, Ernesto. *Hegemony and Socialist Strategy: Towards a Radical Democratic Politics.* London: Verso, 1985.
Reckwitz, Andreas. *Die Gesellschaft der Singularitäten: Zum Strukturwandel der Moderne.* Berlin: Suhrkamp, 2018.
Schmitt, Carl. *The Crisis of Parlamentarian Democracy*, trans. Ellen Kennedy. MA: MIT, 1988.
Schmitt, Carl. *The Theory of the Partisan: A Commentary on the Concept of the Political*, trans. A.C. Goodson. Michigan: Michigan State University Press, 2004.
Schmitt, Carl. *The Leviathan in the State Theory of Thomas Hobbes*, trans. Georg Schwabe and Erna Hilfstein. Chicago: Chicago University Press, 2005.
Schmitt, Carl. *The Concept of the Political*, trans. Georg Schwab. Chicago: University of Chicago Press, 2007.
Spivak, Gayatri. "Can the Subaltern Speak?," In *Marxism and the Interpretation of culture*, ed. by Larry Grossberg and Cary Nelson, 66–111. Houndmills: Macmillan, 1988.
Žižek, Slavoj. *Metastases of Enjoyment: Six Essays on Woman and Causality.* London: Verso, 1994.
Žižek, Slavoj. *For They Know Not What They Do: Enjoyment as a Political Factor.* London: Verso, 2002.

Rebekka A. Klein
The Sovereignty of Subversion
Or: The Masterfulness of the Democratic Revolution

Abstract: In the context of late-modern society with its loss of metaphysical assurances, the quest for a renewed significance of contemporary politics is being pursued with substantial vigour. On the one hand, politics may reveal itself to be a 'fetish' that pursues the progress of the world in an immanent domain, and on the other hand, it could be understood as the source for a 'masterful revolution' which aims to alter reality through its very subversion of this ideological endeavour. With analyses of key figures from Nancy to Badiou, as well as a return to the early work of Carl Schmitt, this article treats the latter as the principle task of a reformulated political theology, which seeks to lay bare the contingency of ideological attachment, and thereby set a course for genuine political action.

> "The word politics denotes 'the omnipotence
> of a life and/or of a conscience
> that evolves and perfects being.'"[1]
> Jean-Luc Nancy

1 Politics as a fetish of human omnipotence, or: What is political theology today?

In his essay *Que faire? / What is to be done?* published (in French) in 2016, Jean-Luc Nancy characterises politics from its creation in antiquity down to the present as a fetish. In our present-day society, it has undergone a special form of sanctification[2] as a "venue of full justice or of true happiness".[3] Politics is regarded as the ultimate horizon of a humane and liberal Dasein and is a guarantor for the meaningfulness of shaping a collective existence. With recourse to politics and to the political, i.e. to the foundation of symbolical processes for the shap-

---

[1] Nancy, *Que faire?*, 24 (trans. J.B.).
[2] Compare here the thesis of Ágnes Heller that politics and more precisely democratic politics is the singular realm where decisions are still possible in a globalised modernity after the end of philosophy and the end of history. See Heller, *Hegel*.
[3] Nancy, *Que faire?*, 24.

ing of a collective political existence, it is possible to sustain the illusion that human beings are indeed able to make decisions and determine matters in their own affairs.

In the modern age, politics is additionally seen as guaranteeing an arena for the communication of reason that is revealed in sovereign, higher-level decision-making. This higher-level decision-making, as a modern survival of divine forms of the principle of sovereignty, is preferentially assigned to the people (*das Volk*), in whom it is embodied and enshrined. The progressive demise of the state – which at least since the rise of communism and the labour movement is no longer looked upon as an autonomous institution and the embodiment of the political community – is also to be found in the context of its rise to the status of a political subject. Yet, even in the course of the nineteenth century, during which the decline of national states began, 'the people' started becoming increasingly impalpable and unidentifiable. As a reaction to its increasing loss of identity in its embodiment of a unitary entity, the nation, the people in the shape of the populace have become a mere administrative object of politics. The people are reduced to the electoral clientele or the populace to be administered, the masses or the crowd.[4] On the other hand, however, on the basis of its existence in the structure of natality, the people continues to be a life-source of the new, an awakening and an inventiveness in politics. The people stand for that collective existence of humanity that transcends politics and that creates transformation and change.[5] This goes beyond politics, even as far as "the price of remaining politically unlocatable"[6].

According to Nancy, it must now be clear – as can be elucidated with the use of the term 'fetish' – that the social ascription of greater significance to politics and/or, as is currently the case, to democracy, ultimately serves the ends of capitalism, which replaces a world that is able to reveal the infinite within the finite (the world of antiquity) with "a second world that has its final end or cause in itself"[7] (the modern world), presenting that final end or cause as infinite and inexhaustible. Following Nancy's argument, politics in this sense can also be described as the fetish of a world of progress within immanence, and as a commodity that is traded, produced and exploited at high value in that world.

At this point, Nancy emphasises that the efficacy of this fetish has presently reached a point of crisis. He poses the question as to how we can live and act in a world that no longer permits any utopias whatsoever of a *wholly other* world and

---

4 See Nancy, *Que faire?*, 33.
5 See Nancy, *Que faire?*, 34.
6 Nancy, *Que faire?*, 41.
7 Nancy, *Que faire?*, 18.

that has instead become amalgamated into one single world that no longer offers us any scope for actually or effectively doing anything in the sense of real change. It becomes increasingly clear that, in the locus of politics – the arena of rational deliberation and systems of the state – people are no longer able to decide or change anything.[8] The national and constitutional state are therefore destined to be "left behind in the wake of history"[9].

What Nancy invokes in his characterisation of politics as fetish is the insight that it is not only the various practices, forms, or styles of politics that can be investigated, but politics as an ideological endeavour as such, i.e. a desire for the omnipotence of humanity. By no means should this desire after omnipotence be affirmed, in his view, but far rather it calls for critical distantiation. Nancy himself deals with this further, in line with Kant and Lenin, by posing the question, 'What is to be done?' For him, the desire for political action, for conduct that is decisive in its efficacy, that creates justice for our collective existence, can only escape the pretensions of omnipotence if and when it deconstructs itself, i.e. pushes itself to the limits of an "impossibility of completion", and at the same time opens up the "necessity of incompletion".[10] The action that Nancy envisages, that substitutes the fetish of politics, is thus open to question and should remain open to question.[11] It represents politics in a redundant sense.

In the light of Nancy's considerations, the deconstructive 'ends' and 'departures' and 'openings' of which will not be further pursued here, it is possible to reformulate the question as to what political theology is or can be today. Political theology, one might say, means undertaking a special form of attaining detachment – to the ideological transcendence of finitude, mortality, fragility and limitations of all forms of collective existence that are manifested in political practices, systems, the embodiment of communality, and in the institution of the political. The specific aspect of the distance over against politics created by political theology as opposed to other forms of social and ideological critique lies in its 'theological' reading, and in its investigation of the metaphysical and notional world formulae of politics. In revealing precisely these references of politics to imaginary totalisation and metaphysical foundations of collective existence, there arises a latitude of freedom, which refuses all forms of self-absolutisation. In thus attaining detachment from the ideological aspect of all politics, political theology can then act critically as well as formatively, creatively

---

[8] See Nancy, *Que faire?*, 30.
[9] Nancy, *Que faire?*, 36.
[10] Nancy, *Que faire?*, 97.
[11] See Nancy, *Que faire?*, 83.

as well as destructively. Liberation from politics as a fetish of the system is made possible by attaining detachment, and political theology can set a course of reformative restructuring for that liberation, just as it can also set a course for revolutionary discontinuance.

Taking this approach as a starting point, the focus in the following will be on a mode of politics that is central for political modernity and especially for modern democracy, yet which at the same time is itself not normally at the centre of any ideology critique of politics, namely: revolutionary politics. The aim is to further develop the reflections on this concept with reference to a 'revolutionary' act that has come back into fashion in our own day, that is, student occupations of universities.

2 Student occupation – variations from 1968 and 2017

There is a famous photograph by Henry Cartier-Bresson which can be characterised as an ironic persiflage that undermines the supposedly anti-authoritarian character of the May '68 student revolution, by focussing our sights on the prominently displayed heroes of the revolt, Mao and Lenin. At odds with myths and photo narratives of May '68 such as this, however, is an interpretation that places special emphasis on the masterly aspect of revolutionary politics and that was jointly responsible for establishing the myth of the anti-authoritarian May '68 revolution and of democratic politics. This is to be found, for example, in the texts of Claude Lefort, a pioneer of so-called radical democratic theory.[12]

To 'breach' is to assert a "form of action ... for which no precursors are known to us"[13]. These are the words of Claude Lefort in his essay "The New Disorder", written in 1968 immediately after the events in Paris. Taking up a term used by Daniel Cohn-Bendit, Lefort uses the word "breach" (*la brèche*) to denote an "excess, that no photographic image can capture"[14]. At the same time, the word subtly calls to mind the storm on the Bastille as the integral act in implementing the modern revolution *par excellence*, the French revolution of 1789. In using the term, Lefort expresses the hope that something may have transpired from the student revolts in France in May '68, which was more than simply a transient or temporary state of emergency. The 'new disorder', according to Le-

---

12 See Laclau and Mouffe, *Hegemony*.
13 Lefort, "Le désordre nouveau", 45 (trans. J.B.).
14 Lefort, "Le désordre nouveau", 37 (trans. J.B.).

fort, denotes the readiness of the so-called *Enragés de Nanterre*, the 'zealots' of Nanterre, to persist in a state of illegality. The student revolt of May'68 was so ground-breaking, for the very reason that the students settled into this state of illegality fully in the public eye and in the form of acts that were able to impress and fascinate the collective imagination. The student revolt rendered "authority incapable of being wielded"[15], thereby, according to Lefort, rendering "the law itself open to question"[16].

A hallmark of the May '68 rebellion was the manner in which it constituted "a breach with conventional leaders of protests"[17]. It abandoned the course constantly taken by trade unions, political parties and other groups.[18] And in doing so, it took place *at* the university and was aimed *against* the university as a "[privileged] venue for the production and reproduction of dominant mental structures"[19]. In this way, it succeeded in creating a new arena or, more precisely, a 'non-venue' at the university, where the breach with society could take place and be extended over time.[20]

In his essay, Lefort further refers to the refusal of the *Enragés* of May '68 to accept responsibility for anything at all, neither for those who followed them, nor for what might happen the next day.[21] And he recalls a scene that epitomises this new freedom: On 10th May 1968, Daniel Cohn-Bendit, who was popularly stylised as one of the leaders of the movement, told journalists as he left the rector's office that he had been commissioned by no one and did not speak on behalf of a movement.[22] The May '68 movement was, according to Lefort, "from the very beginning without leaders, without hierarchy, without discipline"[23]. In precisely this aspect, according to the key hypothesis of Lefort's essay, the movement displayed a new austerity and a new realism – and specifically not, as is often alleged, in the form of utopianism and idealism. The students of May '68 did not attack the existing order with the aim of substituting a new order for it, born out of the vision of a better society. Rather, they endorsed a "disorder within society"[24] and sought by these means to expose what remains hidden in

---

15 Lefort, "Le désordre nouveau", 45 (trans. J.B.).
16 Lefort, "Le désordre nouveau", 45 (trans. J.B.).
17 Lefort, "Le désordre nouveau", 46 (trans. J.B.).
18 See Lefort, "Le désordre nouveau", 49 (trans. J.B.).
19 Lefort, "Le désordre nouveau", 54 (trans. J.B.).
20 See Lefort, "Le désordre nouveau", 49 (trans. J.B.).
21 See Lefort, "Le désordre nouveau", 47 (trans. J.B.).
22 See Lefort, "Le désordre nouveau", 47 (trans. J.B.).
23 Lefort, "Le désordre nouveau", 47 (trans. J.B.).
24 Lefort, "Relecture", 209 (trans. J.B.).

conventional social discourse. It was part of the essence of this revolt to overrule fundamental references of social life and reveal a new public sphere.

In his reflections, twenty years later ("*Vingt ans après*"),[25] Lefort came to identify an achievement of democracy in the fact that the breach of those years, the new disorder, was *not a veritable revolution*, and did not trigger the complete overthrowing of institutions. Lefort's reflections were now no longer obsessed with the phantasm of the unfulfilled revolution of 1789 that was widespread amongst French intellectuals. On the contrary, he allowed democracy as such, its symbolic regime, to fill the void and to take the place of the glorious revolution of 1789. Almost apologetically with regard to his own expectations twenty years earlier, Lefort writes that democracy is in fact a regime of disorder that can be neither threatened nor enduringly called into question by revolutionary events. It is within democracy that conflict, no matter how intensive, has its normal place. Indeed, he summarises, democracy may well even be more conducive to disorder than to order, for it constantly calls for and encourages change and radical transformation.

By implication, Lefort even maintains that it is an advantageous waywardness of democratic regimes that enables them, as it were, to 'resorb' disorder and illegality and all forms of revolt and occasional or intermittent states of emergency, without being destabilised in their governing mode or in their symbolic endowment of political reality on society. He further maintains that the student revolt of '68 was by no means concerned with the self-assertion of its own legitimacy, with securing its success or with the creation of new orders. Far rather, the '68 revolt was masterly in orchestrating its own social displacement, celebrating its rejection of order, hierarchy, leadership and discipline. In his later essay, Lefort extends these contentions to democracy as such, ascribing to it the attitude of a permanently revolutionary regime, of a fragile and at the same time, flexible political state of being.

Lefort's observations and assessment are furthermore sustained by a veneration for the revolutionary moment itself, such as is always characteristic of left-wing, post-Marxist thinking. In the process, this faith in the revolution is deeply inscribed in the deliberations on democracy and also in the critique of its existing form. The revolutionary aspect is, for Lefort, not authoritarian in the sense of prescribing a new social order, but it is authoritative and institutionary in the sense of serving as a manual for overruling form and legality. The revolutionary attitude is born out of historical contingency, but it does not owe its existence to

---

[25] See Lefort, "Relecture", 199–212 (trans. J.B.).

it. It breaks with faith in the existing order, yet without necessarily destroying that order totally.

The masterfulness of the revolution and/or of revolutionary phenomena consists for Lefort in two points: first, in its unprecedented form of action (the 'breach'); second, in its dispassionate realism that does not speculate on instituting order, but on instituting disorder, and through precisely that aspect remains open to the existing order without destroying it.

In retrospect too, May '68 thus continues to be a revolutionary phenomenon for Lefort, without, however, becoming a revolution in the sense of antagonism against the ruling system. By way of explanation, Lefort now states that democracy itself is for him a lasting revolution that therefore no longer has any need of revolutions, nor can it be antagonistically threatened by any such revolution. Democracy can, he writes, be destroyed by totalitarian movements, but never by staging social conflicts or by subversively making their illegalities public.[26] Gianni Vattimo has spoken in this sense of democracy as a life form of a 'guaranteed future' that, so to speak, generates 'the new' non-violently, and as an automatism of the system.[27]

It is now possible to emphasise precisely this feature as a merit of democracy, as Lefort does, or, by contrast, to accuse it of being, so to speak, its seductive illusion and its 'anaesthetic' against all genuine political action, as, for example, Slavoj Žižek has done. In his opinion, democracy no longer permits a genuine coup, a radical break, a real alternative to itself, for it is capable of presenting itself, as it were, not as the best of all possible political systems, but nevertheless as the most open and most flexible of all open and flexible political systems. Slavoj Žižek's project is inspired by the same revolutionary gesture and seeks to detect any loophole, no matter how small, for a truly revolutionary coup. With this end in view, Žižek in his texts has, for thirty years, obsessively analysed and commented on every political movement, every revolt, every demonstration and every awakening, no matter how small, that suits his purpose, hailing them in their potential to vastly disrupt the *status quo*. Just as a seismograph does, he registers and chronicles every vibration, small as it may be, and, by introducing suitable political categories, seeks to point the way to massive and radical change. The invocation of a master of the revolution, a political subject with his own order, who uniquely and alone paves the way to a wholly new world for the masses also belongs for Žižek to this awakening potency. Thus, in an article on the yellow vests movement in France published on 18th December 2018,

---

26 See Lefort, "Relecture", 211–212 (trans. J.B.).
27 See Vattimo, "The Bottle, the Net, the Revolution", xxix–xl.

Žižek proclaims that it is the much-acclaimed leaderless structure and the chaotic self-organisation of this political movement that ultimately inhibits their success. The yellow vests movement persists, like many other present-day political movements, in hysterical provocation of the ruling system of liberal democracy. By making impossible demands, which they cannot possibly meet, of the technocratic experts who hold sway in democracy, the movement fails to achieve its full and truly revolutionary potential. By contrast, what is required is a complete change of the existing system, and this can only be brought about by a 'genuine leader' whose authority unfolds out of loyalty to his own vision and not out of concessions he makes to the masses or out of impossible demands with which he provokes the technocrats. The true master is, accordingly, the person who "simply [follows; R.K.] his own wishes, so that it is up to the people to decide whether to follow him"[28]. The true master does not feed parasitically on attacking the existing system, but opens the door to a wholly new world.

The masterfulness of the master, of which Žižek speaks, thus bears totalitarian traits. For it is not a matter of keeping democratic unrest alive a little and bringing about 'disorder within the order', but about nothing less than a total transformation – radical not only in its disruption, but in its complete destruction and dissolution of the existing structures. It is not without reason that the excess of the revolutionary phenomenon alluded to by Lefort invariably assumes traumatically unsettling, rather than simply transgressive and shifting, features in Žižek's eyes. Nevertheless, Žižek's eagerness for a radical coup shares with Lefort's vision the political force of a revolutionary event, that moment of masterfulness, of a new form of action for which no precursors are known.

This gives rise to a quasi-paradoxical situation: Is the masterfulness of the revolution liberating, does it open onto something new, is it emancipatory in its effect? Or is the ideology of the revolution invariably totalitarian in its consequences and traumatically unsettling in its modality? Does it rest upon an effective illusion?

By way of comparison, let us now turn our attention to the current student movement bearing the label of political correctness, which seeks to create a breach with the ruling arcanum of the university. It is characterised by a species of illegality that is no less violent, no less self-flaunting than that of May '68, but also and additionally by a new invisibility and anonymity. Besides its numerous 'watchblogs' for professors on the internet, the public event and most visible trace of this movement – which, compared to the protagonists of May '68, has remained more unerring in its absence or lack of leadership – was almost cer-

---

28 Žižek, "Gelbwesten" (trans. J.B.).

tainly the occupation of the Social Sciences Institute at the Humboldt University Berlin in January 2017. It came to be known by the hashtag #holmbleibt. The slogan of the Berlin students "keep uncalm" comes very close, indeed, to the notion of the permanent revolution established by Lefort; the permanent renegotiation of the *status quo* as the essence of a radical understanding of democracy. The main concern of the initiators of the #holmbleibt hashtag is to maintain unrest, to 'keep uncalm', and to bring about disorder within order, so that society (i.e. the university) remains mobile and continues to be open(-minded). They are concerned with justice for everyone – whoever it may be who concretely seeks justice. The step towards total anonymity, which the digital revolution has made possible both technically and in terms of cultural praxis, can also be construed as a prolongation of the radical democratic moment of the permanent revolution. In his radical democratic ethics, for example, Oliver Marchart advocates the fundamental democratic right to anonymity and non-identity, and interprets this as the consistent implementation of democracy as an admittedly groundless and unfounded form of society.[29] Just as society itself is insubstantial and without foundation, so too, from a democratic viewpoint, is the revolution and the political subject who brings it about.

However, this raises the question: What can still be 'revolution' in a system of revolutionary change or flux in which, in principle, every kind of conflict is recognised, possible and non-dangerous? The exploratory movements already outlined also provide practical and theoretical evidence that the longing for a revolution, namely as redemption or deliverance into a *wholly other* world, has still not been satisfied, even in the age of a politics of immanence, in the age of post-metaphysical political philosophy and in the 'one' world with its globalised availability. Revolutionary politics – be that in the form of a conservative, a left-wing, or even a radical democratic revolution – currently enjoys immense popularity. It is the question of its political imagination, of its excessive illustration and dissemination, and of its sovereign implementation that would appear not yet to be settled. Thus, since the end of the Cold War, there is no longer any wall, no 'Iron Curtain' behind which one might project the vision of a countersystem, of a *wholly other* world, in which, as it were, all the longings of this world can be focussed and located. This means that there is also no longer any room or space for reflexion that might inspire and stimulate the political imagination. For the time being, political imagination is enclosed in a 'locked room' of immanence.

---

29 See Marchart, *Die politische Differenz*, 343.

3 Revolutionary politics

Beyond the 'locked room' of immanence,[30] Alain Badiou also addresses the problem of how revolution might be possible in a world 'without metaphysics', in a world without otherness, without transcendent truth, that is, in the 'one' globalised world. The notion of a revolutionary politics of truth stands at the centre of his analysis of contemporary political thinking and late-modern philosophy. It is not without reason that he works out his philosophical position in dialogue with the theological writings of the Apostle Paul and his 'discovery' of a new form of universalism.[31] Badiou's thinking assumes the form and shape of political theology.[32] He is of the opinion that during his lifetime, Paul sought to establish a universal singularity vis-à-vis the established institutions. Paul's attitude as a subject over against the authorities in the course of his 'conversion' was, according to Badiou, without precondition and incomprehensible.[33] In consequence of the truth event, Paul was radically dislocated and became a new subject, reflected in his staunch fidelity to this truth event, and which is also reflected in his Christian theology and in justification of Christian communities. He recognised that true universality can only be brought into the world without a centre and through an event of divine violence.

When he invokes Paul, Badiou does so in the context of his critique of the state of present-day philosophy, for which he sees the predicated end of metaphysics and philosophy's orientation towards Martin Heidegger, as being primarily responsible: "Philosophy lingers on in its incapacity to move forward in the element of metaphysics."[34] Philosophy administers the ruins of metaphysics while exercising its critique of metaphysics.[35] It teaches that that the contemporary world is a world shaped by the freedom principle and that there is no need to seek the advent of a better world.[36] This thwarts the very *raison d'être* of all revolt. But precisely this process of closing the debate on the basic and essential topics of philosophy, on universality and truth, and on the possibility of a 'wholly other' world has currently spawned malevolent symptoms: As long ago as 1996, Badiou wrote how the collapse of the grand collective subjects and their

---

30 This paragraph includes considerations of the author, which have already been published in: Klein, "Revolution im Zeitalter der Immanenz", 144–163.
31 See Badiou, *Saint Paul*.
32 See Finkelde, *Politische Eschatologie nach Paulus*.
33 See Badiou, *Saint Paul*, 15–16.
34 Badiou, "Gegenwärtige Welt", 16–17 (trans. J.B.).
35 See Badiou, "Gegenwärtige Welt", 34 (trans. J.B.).
36 See Badiou, "Gegenwärtige Welt", 9 (trans. J.B.).

rational presentation led to an eruption of collective, religious, racist and nationalist passions with their imagined "compensatory totalities" that "set their confidence in archaic subjects via processes of exclusion, marginalisation and polarisation", thereby evading the necessity of "having to express themselves or make decisions on their own behalf."[37]

According to Badiou, what is needed by way of contrast is a regenerated philosophy of the political subject that is capable "of deciding and thinking on its own behalf in the face of inhumanity"[38]. In his view, the emptying of the collective singulars and subjects – including truth, revolution, history, nation, etc. – that results from post-metaphysical thinking therefore calls for a combative answer. The proliferation of its symptoms in late modernity in the shape of new forms of authoritarianism and authoritarian movements can only be thwarted by a new conception of the revolution as 'politics of truth'. Such orientation towards revolutionary truth as brought about by a singular event then also allows for the differentiation amongst new political movements, between those which stand only for pseudo-emancipatory concerns and those which truly bring about an updated ethics in the implementation of freedom.

Badiou sets the political implementation of freedom at the centre of his vision of revolutionary politics. It is manifestly obvious in his argumentation that this is incapable of being practised or conceived of without a gesture that extends beyond the immanence of the political. It is political theologies – and not any renunciation of them – that therefore characterise the political situation and the political discourse of the present day. But since secular thought cannot of its own accord de-ideologise its revolutionary liberation and redemption fantasies – in terms of the advent of the radically new and wholly other – it must of necessity make of that advent a political absolute. Such an ideology of revolution, orbiting around the blind spot of treating its own emancipatory gestures and characters as absolutes, is to be observed, by way of example, in Badiou's invocation of a politics of truth, as it is too in Žižek.

But by no means does this apply only to the critics of (non-)political postmodernity, Badiou and Žižek. In the context of Frankfurt critical theory too, it is possible to observe such a canonisation of the revolutionary moment as, for example, in Christoph Menke's recent book *Autonomie und Befreiung*[39] (*Autonomy and Liberation*). Here Menke seeks to conceptualise liberation not only as a break with our nature, but also as surplus or excess beyond all social forms. It

---

[37] Badiou, "Gegenwärtige Welt", 31 (trans. J.B.).
[38] Badiou, "Gegenwärtige Welt", 30 (trans. J.B.).
[39] Menke, *Autonomie und Befreiung*.

calls for a polemical force, as Menke calls it, a force of negativity. This makes it possible to enter into a break with the contingent and the determined. More precisely, it enforces the ability to posit the self as undetermined and, put in theological terms, to thereby overcome the world.

Within these propositions of Menke's, however, there lies the idolisation of a certain negative power of disruption or at least withdrawal within the immanent that serves to overcome the myth of the revolution as a guaranteed future. With the help of an invocation of the power of negativity, the attempt is undertaken to bring the consummation of freedom to bear once more in the current discourse as a force that performatively brings about the reality of a *wholly other* world, at least as a possibility. It is further to be observed how various tendencies and varieties of existing political disruption and transformation mutually 'pass the buck' to and fro between each other with regard to whose concept of the revolution bears ideological and revitalising features for metaphysics, and thereby once again circumvents a truly emancipatory attitude.

It is not solely the negativity, nor its being born out of contingency, but the masterful, unsurpassable and singular that places revolutionary politics in the vicinity of a theological saviour figure. Where and how exactly this unsurpassable and non-illuminable, the 'arcane' of the political subject is to be located – in its absence, its anonymity, its traumatic separation or simply its indeterminacy expropriated from itself – is, as it were, only a marginal question. From Žižek to Menke, at any rate, it is one they all ask.

4 Carl Schmitt: Antagonism or the permeation of *occasio* and *causa*?

Finally, taking the ongoing debate on one of Carl Schmitt's early writings as an illustration, I would like to examine once more in greater detail the problem that is posed by the masterfulness of revolutionary politics. The strict opposition, indeed enmity, between *occasio* and *causa*, which Schmitt examined diagnostically in his *Political Romanticism* in 1919, proclaiming them polemically as the solution, shall serve as an example.

Schmitt himself described his paper on *Political Romanticism* as a course of action against the forces of the Reformation operative down to modernity. Schmitt described and opposed the romantic spirit as the consummation of Protestantism.⁴⁰ In his writing, he repeatedly makes clear that romanticism is not a natural ally of conservative ideas,⁴¹ but is rather similar in nature to rebellion and anarchy, insofar as it represents an intellectual structure that goes as far as the total annihilation of each and every form, the individualistic dissolution of every form of social order and even as far as escaping from concrete reality altogether.⁴²

The central figure in Schmitt's interpretation of romanticism is the opposition, exaggerated to a well-nigh binary degree, of two terms which he borrows from the founding of modern thinking, namely, from the reaction of Nicolas Malebranche to the philosophy of Descartes: *occasio* (chance or accident) and *causa* (ground or cause). *Occasio* here stands for a vital energy that is pitched against all attachments and norms, and *causa* for the obsessive attachment or binding of life to a ground or cause, to a principle or to what Schmitt at times simply calls concrete reality.⁴³ *Occasio* and *causa* appear ideally-typically as forces of releasing and binding which, in Schmitt's understanding, can be clearly separated from one another. They also covertly re-emerge, however, within the romantic conscience and its metaphysical view of life, namely in the "romantic conflict of possibility and reality"⁴⁴.

According to Schmitt, this romantic conflict is metaphysical in character because it gives expression to a particular view of the world with regard to a last or final instance and this is, in the case of romanticism, the possibility of life created by a subject and his/her aesthetic productivity that is unfailingly superior to and/or withdrawn from its reality.⁴⁵ The forces of romanticism are therefore those that promoted and expedited the "transformation of the reality of the world into a fantastical construct"⁴⁶. The resolution of the conflict between the modalities of being in romanticism can best be brought to bear by sharply rejecting all ties and causalities.

A further hallmark of the romantic conscience is, according to Schmitt, its de-dualisation strategy. Here again, the philosophy of Nicolas Malebranche figures as a model for his analyses. Thus, in the spirit of romanticism, all duality of being is invariably disarmed and professed to be illusory by the avoidance

---

40 See also Schmitt, *Political Romanticism*, 24: "The connection between Protestantism and romantism is obtrusive."
41 See Schmitt, *Political Romanticism*, 10.
42 See Schmitt, *Political Romanticism*, 19–21.
43 See Schmitt, *Political Romanticism*, 18–19.
44 Schmitt, *Political Romanticism*, 65.
45 See Schmitt, *Political Romanticism*, 18–19.
46 Schmitt, *Political Romanticism*, 74.

and mediation of a higher or all-encompassing third party (the idea, the state, or God).⁴⁷ The original opposition thus disappears into non-being. The force of romanticism therefore consists in escaping from one reality to the other, for neither of them can develop binding or ultimately authoritative normativity and, furthermore, they also cannot truly stand in sharp opposition to any other.

What Schmitt describes here is essentially a form of replication and relativism of realities, such that the label of post-modernism might also be attributed to it.⁴⁸ Post-modern theologies such as Patrick Cheng's queer political theology, for example, also justify an 'anything goes' view of the world with reference to an omnisexual kenosis, that is, a process that believes in the necessity of evoking God as gender-dissolving and polyamorous instance.⁴⁹ Accordingly, Schmitt also postulates: "The idiosyncrasy of romantic occasionalism lies therein, that it subjectifies the principal factor of the occasionalist system, God."⁵⁰ God operates as figure of the infinite encompassing third party only until – in the sense of Schmitt's secularisation theory – he can be replaced by worldly and temporal factors.⁵¹ The romanticist view of the world thus oscillates between two polar extremes: the dissolution of all reality in God and the acknowledgement of the positively real as such, whereby the latter can be neutralised in its potential for conflict and its contradictoriness precisely by that same radically subjectified God. Again, Schmitt names Malebranche as his referee, in whose system God's supremacy is enhanced to a fantastical magnitude. God acts here as the absolute instance of the system, and everything that happens in the world is a mere cause of his sole and exclusive efficacy.⁵² This 'God' is subsequently replaced by the state, the people, or the individual subject who suffuses the world with his aesthetic productivity.

In the final section of his paper, Schmitt then seeks to undergird the *causa*, (commitment to the norm) and with it, to normality as a counterpart to this quasi-boundless force of *occasio* and/or of an occasional cause or ground with its potential for totalitarianism. The latter, as the ultimate reference point of the world, renders a quasi-boundless instance absolute and, consequently, any number of diverse possibilities are made real. The normal, he maintains, is the

---

47 See Schmitt, *Political Romanticism*, 87–88.
48 The term post-modernism as developed by Wolfgang Welsch could operate as a basis here: Welsch, *Unsere postmoderne Moderne*.
49 See Cheng, *Radical Love*, 58.
50 Schmitt, *Political Romanticism*, 99.
51 See Schmitt, *Political Romanticism*, 17.
52 See Schmitt, *Political Romanticism*, 17.

epitome, the quintessence of un-romanticism.⁵³ At the same time, however, it is the fundamental bedrock of the political, the central question which asks what is right and what is wrong.⁵⁴ Without a notion of right and wrong, man cannot become politically active. To be sure, this opposition of right and wrong also would appear to occur in the spirit of romanticism, but there it is immediately neutralised. By endless mediation of the third party in romanticism, wrong is dissolved to become mere dissonance or a category that is accessible only to the romantic experience.⁵⁵

Schmitt, therefore, seeks to characterise romanticism as a fundamentally passive attitude to life. The romantic is (aesthetically) productive without being active. And this also replicates the essential inner conflict in the romantic conscience.⁵⁶ "Where political activity begins, political romanticism ceases,"⁵⁷ writes Schmitt and, assured of victory, he proclaims his political theology of the sovereign decision with which – thus the implicit subtext of his *causa* meditations – the romantic productivity of aesthetic practices will be successfully brought to a standstill in its underlying structure.

There have been intensive discussions in the research of the past two decades of whether Schmitt's diagnosis is adequately justified and of whether the strategic thrust of his (counter-)argumentation is useful and effective. Two interpretations are worth highlighting, the first being Friedrich Balke's early recognition of the importance of Schmitt's long underestimated paper on romanticism and its diagnostic value for the present.⁵⁸ According to Balke, Schmitt lays bare the true driving force behind his political theology in his paper: the culture and society of late modernity with its focus on diversification and permanent deferrals has been the real adversary of Schmitt's politics of sovereignty, geared as they are to dictatorship. In contrast to Schmitt, however, Balke allows not the force of *causa* – that is, authority, normality and sovereignty – to win the day, but instead *occasio* with its virtually limitless elusive force. He accuses Schmitt of simply wanting to allow his decisionist politics of sovereignty to be regenerated by the occasional system. This is doomed to failure, for – contrary to what Schmitt still believed – the occasional world completely eludes the metaphysical determination and the antagonism of *causa*.

---

53 See Schmitt, *Political Romanticism*, 161–162.
54 See Schmitt, *Political Romanticism*, 128–129.
55 See Schmitt, *Political Romanticism*, 161–162.
56 See Schmitt, *Political Romanticism*, 159–160.
57 Schmitt, *Political Romanticism*, 160.
58 See Balke, *Staat nach seinem Ende*.

Juliane Rebentisch has put forward an entirely different interpretation in her rehabilitation of the political value of aesthetic practices for a culture of freedom in democracy.[59] Rebentisch's thesis is that *occasio* and *causa* are dynamically interlinked, for aesthetic practices in themselves have political meaning. Namely, the 'distance to the social' that is inherent in the aesthetical allows the subject in his practical day-to-day living, to productively seek possible means of assimilating, but also of transforming and changing systems. And it is precisely this that is constitutive for a democratic culture of freedom – for a life form of democracy.

In the light of this, Rebentisch's interpretation differs from standard constructions of Schmitt's *Political Romanticism*, and she emphasises the dynamic connection of *occasio* and *causa* as opposed to their simple contraposition. According to her theory, "on account of his anti-aestheticisation premise" Schmitt is unable to "logically pursue the liberation theory motifs that are also inherent in his concept of sovereignty".[60] In Rebentisch's hands Schmitt becomes – as it were by sleight of hand – (partial) advocate rather than merely an opponent of the close connection of politics and aesthetics in the modern era.[61] According to Rebentisch, Schmitt's argumentation is at any rate characterised by a degree of ambivalence, which permits him to "borrow to an extent from the romantic insistence on the impenetrability of the subject"[62] and to allow this to also subsequently become incorporated into his thinking on sovereignty.

In view of some current developments, however, the question arises as to whether the structure of an antagonism between *causa* and *occasio*, of which Schmitt himself was the co-initiator can be said to have been dispatched by these means. It could only ever be disposed of by means of a mental or intellectual ban which, in practice, would be impossible to implement. An appropriate and meaningful course would be needed to undertake an intensive examination and discussion of the real option Schmitt points toward. By contrast, attempts to mitigate Schmitt's antagonism by undermining or circumventing the contraposition and incorporating elements of his theory in the liberal-democratic matrix of revolution by reformation cannot fully resorb the problem he has raised and the dialectic of *causa* and *occasio* introduced by it.

---

59 See Rebentisch, *Art of Freedom*.
60 Rebentisch, *Art of Freedom*, 178.
61 See Rebentisch, *Art of Freedom*, 145–180.
62 Rebentisch, *Art of Freedom*, 145.

5 Conclusion: Disorder or new order

In conclusion, a few observations can now be made on the question posed at the outset. I began by interpreting the motif of 'in need of a master' as a longing for the other – the small other and the large other, the small revolution of disorder within order and the large revolution of a totally new order, the possibility of changing the world or a wholly other world. Both possibilities, following Schmitt, can also be conceived as antagonisms in the context of an ultimately metaphysical attitude, an in a variety of ways theologically formed attitude to the world. However, post-metaphysical philosophies, as well as the critique of them, both obscure this point of their 'commonality', which is still present in Schmitt, namely that he analyses them both as ultimately being forms of political theology. This is most clearly demonstrated by Rebentisch's 'revolving door model'—the cheerful to-and-fro between disorder and new order in a democratic culture of the freedom of the subject. In her reading of Schmitt, she attempts to neutralise the antagonism between *causa* and *occasio* and to level out the difference between them. The re-emergence of this very antagonism in present-day politics and the polarisation, division and re-politicisation of post-democratic societies created by that antagonism is, however, real, and it presents a challenge to reflect anew not only on the mental confrontation of the two as substantially inaugurated by Schmitt and others, but also on their mutual interdependence and dialectic.

The article has been translated into English by James Brown.

Bibliography

Badiou, Alain. *Saint Paul: La fondation de l'universalisme.* Paris: Presses Universitaires de France, 1997.

Badiou, Alain. "Die gegenwärtige Welt und das Begehren der Philosophie," In *Politik der Wahrheit*, ed. by Alain Badiou and Jacques Rancière, trans. Rado Riha, 7–35. Wien: Turia & Kant, 2010.

Balke, Friedrich. *Der Staat nach seinem Ende: Die Versuchung Carl Schmitts.* Munich: Fink, 1996.

Cheng, Patrick S. *Radical Love. An Introduction to Queer Theology.* New York: Seabury Books, 2011.

Finkelde, Dominik. *Politische Eschatologie nach Paulus: Badiou, Agamben, Žižek, Santner.* Wien: Turia & Kant, 2007.

Heller, Ágnes. *Hegel oder das Ende der Philosophie.* Bochum Hegel Lecture, 25 June 2019, unpublished manuscript.

Klein, Rebekka A. "Revolution im Zeitalter der Immanenz: Die Macht des Vollzugs der Freiheit als Problem der Politischen Theologie," *Berliner Theologische Zeitschrift* 36 (2019): 144–163.

Laclau, Ernesto, and Mouffe, Chantal. *Hegemony and Socialist Strategy: Towards a Radical Democratic Politics.* London: Verso, 1985.

Lefort, Claude. "Le désordre nouveau," In *Mai 1968: La Brèche suivi de Vingt Ans Après*, ed. by Edgar Morin, Cornelius Castoriadis and Claude Lefort, 45–81. Brussels: Editions Complexe, 1988.

Lefort, Claude. "Relecture," In *Mai 1968: La Brèche suivi de Vingt Ans Après*, ed. by Edgar Morin, Cornelius Castoriadis and Claude Lefort, 199–212. Brussels: Editions Complexe, 1988.

Marchart, Oliver. *Die politische Differenz. Zum Denken des Politischen bei Nancy, Lefort, Badiou, Laclau und Agamben.* Berlin: Suhrkamp, 2010.

Menke, Christoph. *Autonomie und Befreiung: Studien zu Hegel.* Berlin: Suhrkamp, 2018.

Nancy, Jean-Luc. *Que faire?* Paris: Éditions Galilée, 2016.

Rebentisch, Juliane. *The Art of Freedom: On the Dialectics of Democratic Existence*, trans. Joseph Ganahl. Cambridge, UK: Polity Press, 2016.

Schmitt, Carl. *Political Romanticism*, trans. Guy Oaks. New Brunswick, NJ: Transaction Publishers, 2011.

Vattimo, Gianni. "The Bottle, the Net, the Revolution, and the Tasks of Philosophy: A Dialogue with Lotta Continua," In *Beyond the Subject: Nietzsche, Heidegger, and Hermeneutics*, Gianni Vattimo, ed. and trans. Peter Carravetta, xxix–xl. Albany, NY: State University of New York Press, 2019.

Welsch, Wolfgang. *Unsere postmoderne Moderne*, 5th ed. Berlin: De Gruyter, 2018.

Žižek, Slavoj. "Die Gelbwesten brauchen einen Führer," Die *WELT*, 18 Dec. 2018, https://www.welt.de/kultur/plus185687534/Philosoph-Slavoj-Žižek-Die-Gelbwesten-brauchen-einen-Fuehrer.html. (accessed 12 Oct. 2019).

Rasmus Nagel
Total Fidelity?
About the Exclusivity of the Excluded

Abstract: The article explores the recent modifications of Jan Assmann's critique of monotheism. Assmann's thesis about the 'Mosaic distinction' of true and false religion has not been mitigated but rather reinforced by focusing on its political structure: The Mosaic distinction distinguishes not so much between true and false religion but rather between exclusive fidelity and infidelity. The following text provides a theological response to Assmann's thesis and proposes a conceptualization a) of Christian existence as always simultaneously faithful and unfaithful – so that the faithful count themselves not against but rather among the unfaithful – and b) of faith as grounded in the exclusivity of the excluded, i.e. Christ – so that the exclusivity of Christian faith has to be understood in terms not of an absolutization of a certain religious worldview or order but rather as a fidelity to that which is excluded from it.[1]

Introduction

For more than twenty years, a debate has been taking place in the German-speaking world and beyond on the relationship between monotheism and violence. It was triggered by the thesis of the Egyptologist Jan Assmann that in the literary figure of Moses the distinction between true and false religion had been successfully made for the first time in history.[2] According to Assmann, the 'Mosaic distinction' bears the germ of intolerance and violence within itself and manifests in the later reception of Judaic, Christian and Islamic politics of religion. The religious exclusivism of such a 'total religion',[3] Assmann claims, is potentially violent, which is why one has to think about how religion could be de-totalized and thus civilized.

---

[1] The argument of this paper is carried out in more detail in the first chapter of my dissertation *Universale Singularität: Ein Vorschlag zur Denkform christlicher Theologie im Gespräch mit Ernesto Laclau, Alain Badiou und Slavoj Žižek* (forthcoming).
[2] See Assmann, *Moses the Egyptian*.
[3] See Assmann, *Totale Religion*. For an earlier version of the argument see Assmann, "Gotteszorn und Apokalypse".

Assmann himself modified his position several times in the course of the debate and finally reformulated it in a revised form.[4] I will refrain here from going into the details of the development of the debate and instead start my first section from Assmann's new version – especially since Assmann, in my view, has rather intensified his actual argument: namely in his accusation of 'total religion', which will then be the subject of my second section. In a third step I will then respond to Assmann's criticism from the perspective of Protestant theology.

1 The Mosaic distinction

In its first form the 'Mosaic distinction' aimed at the guiding difference of 'true' and 'false'. Only by introducing this difference into the realm of religion had monotheism made it possible "to distinguish between true religion and false religions, true God and false gods, and thus also to convert from false religions to true religions, or conversely to fall away from true to false religions."[5] The 'Mosaic distinction' therefore implies the introduction of the Parmenidean logic of either/or into the space of religion.

More recently Assmann has revised his thesis. The Exodus narratives are not primarily about the distinction between true and false religion but between fidelity [Treue] and infidelity [Untreue].[6] Now this distinction does not refer to the difference between Israel and the other peoples but rather differentiates *within* Israel between those who remain loyal to the covenant with God and those who fall away, "God's friends and his enemies"[7], and in doing so remains limited to the 'endosphere' of the people of Israel. God demands from Israel unconditional loyalty to the covenant but not from the other peoples. Assmann therefore speaks of a 'particular monotheism of fidelity' as the characteristic feature of the covenant theology in the Exodus narrative and of the corresponding Deuteronomistic elaborations.

---

[4] See Assmann, *Invention of Religion*, 79–90; earlier and in condensed form Assmann, "Mose und der Monotheismus der Treue", 16–33; as well as in Assmann, "Monotheismus der Treue", 249–267.
[5] Assmann, "Monotheismus der Treue", 16 (trans. R.N.).
[6] The English version of Assmann's *Exodus* translates 'Treue' as 'loyalty'. This translation focuses on the political dimension but misses the *theo*political point of Assmann's argument, which is why I choose 'fidelity' as translation of 'Treue'. 'Faithfulness' would also be a valid alternative.
[7] Assmann, *Invention of Religion*, 83, in reference to Dtn 5:9–10 and Ex 20:5–6.

Assmann identifies their extra-biblical model in Assyrian state loyalism.[8] The oath of fealty to the ruler gets "transferred"[9] with respect to the relationship to God, which thereby gets a political depth structure. This reception of the Assyrian oath of fealty in covenant theology brings about some important changes, as Assmann emphasizes: Firstly, the covenant relationship is specifically justified by the narrative of the liberation from Egypt. Because God is the liberator, the sole fidelity is reserved for him. In addition, the covenant relationship is characterized as a voluntary one that is not imposed on Israel, and finally, the biblical covenant theology repeatedly emphasizes God's patience and mercy with his covenant partner. However, despite these important changes with regard to the former model, Assmann notes: "That said, the friend-foe-distinction quite obviously derives from this source and with it, too, the problem of violence."[10]

Assmann now contrasts the particularistic fidelity monotheism with the biblical model of a 'universalistic monotheism of truth' or an 'ontological' monotheism.[11] Now here, indeed, the leading distinction between the true God and the false gods is decisive, but it is not a 'Mosaic' but rather a 'Deutero-Isaian' or 'Jeremian' distinction, whose essential characteristic is the ontological insight into the non-existence of the other gods. For Assmann the pagans in Deutero-Isaiah are not unfaithful apostates but fools who lack insight into the non-existence of their gods. On the one hand, this extends the theological judgment universally to other peoples and their gods. On the other hand, however, it is defused by not making the potentially violent, political distinction between friend and foe: religion-critical satire and mockery instead of persecution of the apostates.

Basically, Assmann thus takes up the classical distinction between monotheism and monolatry, while criticizing the monolatry concept for the danger of an evolutionist interpretation, as if the religion of ancient Israel had developed from a particularistic monolatry to a universalistic monotheism. Instead, Assmann stresses the continuity and simultaneity of both concepts in the biblical text. Instead of being replaced by its apolitical, universalistic variant, the covenantal monotheism of fidelity remains of central importance for the Jewish and also the Christian and Islamic tradition.

> "The one God in whom Jews, Christians and Muslims believe is considered both the only God, beside whom there are no other gods, and the one God who is to be loved and there-

---

8 Assmann refers here particularly to Otto, *Deuteronomium*.
9 Assmann, *Invention of Religion*, 205. See Assmann, *Herrschaft und Heil*, 50.
10 Assmann, *Invention of Religion*, 86. The German original text reads differently "das Problem von Intoleranz und Gewalt" ("the problem of intolerance and violence"): Assmann, *Exodus*, 114.
11 See Assmann, "Monotheismus der Treue", 252–255.

fore jealous, to whom unconditional fidelity is to be kept. The true religion is defined as the only religion that makes free – or in Christian reinterpretation 'blessed'. Freedom and truth coincide. This is something absolutely new in the history of religion."[12]

One could interpret Assmann in such a way that precisely this simultaneity becomes the actual problem. In themselves, both monotheisms would be relatively unproblematic: The particularistic fidelity monotheism is potentially violent by its political structure but at least limited particularistically – whereas the universalistic, ontological monotheism makes general truth claims but remains modest and rather intellectual than zealous. In the biblical combination, however, a universalistic concept of truth is now politically ammunitioned by the covenant-theological concept of fidelity and fools become apostates.

Above all "in the Christian concept of revelation with its paradoxical connection of exclusivity and universality"[13], Assmann sees this intertwining of fidelity and truth and thus a source of intolerance. The Christian concept of revelation with its Christological culmination joins, so to speak, the problems from both worlds, from particularist and universalist monotheism.

The new version of the 'Mosaic distinction' thus defuses Assmann's critique of monotheism by no means but focuses more on its political dimension. More recently, Assmann has also spoken of 'total religion',[14] which, as will be shown, duplicates Jewish or Christian universalism and its problems.

2 Total religion?

Analogous to Carl Schmitt's concept of the total state, Assmann puts forward the thesis that in the Abrahamic religions an idea of 'total religion' becomes visible. Assmann shows how the essential political ingredients for this can be found in the Old Testament: It is above all the wrath of God that Assmann interprets as a divine emergency, as a situation in which all other distinctions of social life are transcended, so that only fidelity (or infidelity) to the covenant with the God of Israel is the decisive issue. According to Assmann, Exodus 32 describes the quasi

---

12 Assmann, "Monotheismus der Treue", 27 f. (trans. R.N.).
13 Assmann, "Monotheismus der Treue", 33. It should be noted that this connection between fidelity and universality, as just shown, does not have to be specifically Christian, even if it is even more obvious in the case of the Christological culmination.
14 See Assmann, *Totale Religion*. In a similar sense, Peter Sloterdijk already spoke of 'total membership'. See Sloterdijk, *Mount Sinai*; for a shortened earlier version see Sloterdijk, "Im Schatten des Sinai", 124–149.

archetypal and pattern-forming emergency: God's wrath over the worship of the golden calf results in Moses' call to the ultimate decision. "Who is on the Lord's side? Come to me" (Ex 32:26). The bond established by the fidelity to God transcends all other ties, even the familial: "'Put your sword on your side each of you, and go to and fro from gate to gate throughout the camp, and each of you kill his brother and his companion and his neighbor'" (Ex 32:27b). Analogous to Schmitt's concept of the intensity of the political, the state of emergency not only creates another possibility of association among others, for instance the political – but in the state of emergency it is rather decided which of these associations is the *genuinely* political one: in this case the covenant of God. The fidelity relation to God makes a total claim by relativizing all other areas of human life. In the face of this ultimate, everything else appears as penultimate – and thus in the light of this ultimate. Since the covenant of God alone is at least potentially capable of suspending all other associations, it is political in Schmitt's sense. Therefore, according to Assmann, it is justified to speak of 'total religion' in this case. Just as Schmitt wanted – against the "functional differentiation of society in art, science, law and economics, politics and religion [–] the *whole* person, the *entire* people, the *total* state"[15], so too the monotheistic religions have the potential to become total religion in so far as they aim at the whole person.

In a similar way Peter Sloterdijk spoke of the phenomenon of 'total membership'. Also with regard to the Sinai episode of the Book of Exodus, Sloterdijk interprets the narrative of the Sinai scheme of the formation, break and restoration of the covenant as an "ethnogenetic"[16] oath, which for the first time "elevates a people to a programmatic total institution"[17]. The members of this people are committed to a form of "total membership"[18], whereby Sloterdijk explicitly emphasizes its participatory aspect. The forms of participation that encompass the whole person are combined with a strategy of self-singularization, i.e., of outward demarcation. Similar to Assmann, Sloterdijk asserts that total religion is fundamentally incompatible with modern, differentiated societies. Also, the changes during the Reformation are for Sloterdijk "merely alternative forms of total religious registration"[19]. Only with the development of 'religion' into an independent social subsystem did the actual reformation of religious life take place. For Sloterdijk, religious membership in modernity is principally optional

---

15 Assmann, *Totale Religion*, 117.
16 Sloterdijk, *Mount Sinai*, 50, 56.
17 Sloterdijk, *Mount Sinai*, 44.
18 Sloterdijk, *Mount Sinai*, 59. Assmann explicitly adopts this diction in *Totale Religion*, 158.
19 Sloterdijk, "Im Schatten des Sinai", 139 (trans. R.N.).

and plural;[20] the task today remains dealing with "the remnants of intolerance that survived the turn towards the subsystemization of religion"[21].

Following Assmann and Sloterdijk, it could therefore be argued that the combination of universal truth and total faithfulness leads to an unfortunate *duplication of universalism:* It concerns *everyone* and it concerns everyone *totally*. The universality of such a 'total religion' would therefore not only consist in its claim to be the only true religion but also in its refusal to be subsumed in principle as a social subsection and thus to be coordinated with others, and in its accompanying claim to orientate society and the lives of its members as a whole. In this way, the potential for conflict arises in relation not only to other religions but also to other 'secular' domains such as economy, art, media, etc. A theological reflection on Christian universalism will, therefore, have to consider not only the interreligious problematic but also the problem of its potential 'totalitarianism'.

3 Theological critique

With his new version of the thesis about the Mosaic distinction, Assmann politicized the question of truth and thus intensified it: (1) the close coupling of truth and politics by linking the distinction between true and false religion with that of fidelity and infidelity to God and the ensuing potential for violence within the logic of friendship and enmity; (2) the consequent universalization of this quasi-political call for fidelity to all people; (3) the claim of this fidelity to the whole life of all people and thus the refusal of total religion to allow itself to be subordinated as a social subsystem to an overarching whole.

Assmann's thesis of the Mosaic distinction has since its first version in *Moses the Egyptian* become the object of numerous criticisms but also of sympathetic continuations. I will pass over the various exegetical and historical concerns and proceed immediately to a systematic-theological evaluation.

---

20 See Joas, *Glaube als Option*, argues in a similar way. Joas, however, does not assess the increase of religious options in secular societies merely as relativization, but also in the sense of 'new opportunities for commitment'; see 139.
21 Sloterdijk, *Mount Sinai*, 62.

3.1 The theological (non-)sense of the distinction between friend and foe

The question remains: Does the Christian faith really distinguish between 'friends and foes of God' – and if so, how? The category of fidelity is *the* key description of the Christian God-human relationship already for the reason that *pistis* is best translated as faith or faithfulness. This translation has the advantage, apart from its proximity to the Hebrew *emunah*, of avoiding the cognitivist emphasis of 'belief' that is, for instance, present in the German *Glaube*. It also allows the theological point to be made that the New Testament can just as well speak of human as of divine *pistis*. 'Faith' describes the new covenant between God and man as mutual fidelity, with the emphasis that divine fidelity, personified in Jesus Christ, is asymmetrically the condition of the possibility of human fidelity – and is as such grace.

Similar to how God's faithfulness to humans is an undivided, *passionate* fidelity that fully involves God – so the fidelity that is required from humans encompasses *the entire human existence* with body, soul and mind. It is therefore indeed not possible to understand the relationship with God as a sub- and coordinated part of human life, which would possibly have to arrange itself with other areas against the background of a neutral third. Instead, the Christian concept of faith claims to permeate the entire human life in its multidimensionality and thus to orient it towards God. In fact, Assmann is not wrong with his provocative formulation of the 'totality' of faith.

At the same time – now I have to specify critically – the factual reality of 'unbelief' is to be noted both theologically and sociologically. In Christian terms this is interpreted as the expression and consequence of sin. Just as Assmann suspects, the concept of fidelity 'automatically' includes the concept of infidelity. But does this description not then make possible that fatal distinction between 'faithful friends of God' and 'unfaithful enemies of God', between believers and unbelievers? Sloterdijk was not wrong to point out the inner necessity of this opposition. Similar to the avantgarde counter-culture, monotheism always appears as counter-religion and speculates from the outset on its rejection: "There can be no universalism without set-theoretical paradoxes: one can only invite everyone if one can be sure that not everyone will come."[22] What Sloterdijk describes here in terms of cultural psychology, cannot be dismissed theologically either. At least in its factuality the phenomenon of unbelief demands its theological interpretation: no soteriology without hamartiology.

---

22 Sloterdijk, *God's Zeal*, 130.

A conceivable 'solution' lies in the theological paradox of Luther's formula *simul iustus et peccator*. The simultaneity of divinely bestowed justice and the lasting sinfulness of man is based on the reformatory radicalization of theological anthropology. Since humans with all their capacities are under the power of sin and are altogether unable to be faithful to God by their own efforts, they need the unconditional gift of divine grace again and again. What Assmann and Sloterdijk overlook in this perspective is the consequent and lasting universality of sin. According to the Reformation view, human infidelity to God is precisely *not* a suitable criterion for distinguishing between groups of people: For it is first the believer who knows of his lasting infidelity and need of salvation.

Since faith alone justifies, or since unbelief is accordingly the true sin of the human being, the translation of the Lutheran *simul*-formula into the form *simul fidelis et infidelis* is permissible. Interestingly, this transfer was first made verbally by the Catholic side. In the first volume of *Concilium* (1965) Johann Baptist Metz noted that

> "in the mirror of our concupiscent experience of faith and justification (Heil) we meet ourselves as just and unjust [heil und heillos], as spiritual and of the flesh (pneumatik [sic] und sarkisch), as believing and unbelieving. In this sense, the experience of the inner threat to us through sin can and must be called real sin; and Catholic theology recognizes the simul iustus et peccator. In this sense, the experience of the inner threat to our faith by unbelief (by what else?) can and must be called real unbelief; there is a Catholic understanding of simul fidelis et infidelis."[23]

Metz thereby opposed a widespread reaction of theology to secularization: to assume a hidden *fides implicita* even in the case of declared unbelief. For that would also be a possible theological option: to solve the problem of the fundamental difference between belief and unbelief by abolishing unbelief as a phenomenon to be taken seriously. It would be conceivable to assume a religious a priori, a primary relation to the divine, which appertains *nolens volens* to everyone, only that some are by appropriate socialization and education in a position to articulate this a priori adequately symbolically, whereas the others, whilst implicitly also possessing this religious primary relation, are only unable to make themselves conscious of it because they miss the religiously educated self-consciousness and the verbal means of expression. In this way the problem of a hard distinction between fidelity and infidelity, belief and unbelief, and thus also a distinction between friend and foe disappears. So, the option would be: universal solidarity in (implicit) belief: 'Somehow' everybody believes.

---

23 Metz, "Unbelief as a Theological Problem", 70 (Emphasis in original).

Metz disagrees. For Metz, the reality of unbelief is always a real threat to human existence and faith. He sees this inner antagonism formulated in the Lutheran *simul iustus et peccator* and applies it to the difference between belief and unbelief: *simul fidelis et infidelis*, at once faithful and unfaithful, believing and unbelieving. In this tension-filled simultaneity Metz sees not only the possibility to understand secularization as a real phenomenon of unbelief; the emphasis lies rather on a precise description of the Christian life of faith, which Metz with Luther sees as fundamentally contested.

Simon Peng-Keller has suggested that Luther's thesis should be understood as a confession of faith and as an expression of Mark 9:24 ("I believe, help my unbelief") and be limited to a *simul iustus et tentatus*, "without ontologizing the contingent fact of Christian unbelief."[24] What is undoubtedly true about this, is firstly that unbelief is not just a phenomenon of 'many' but of every faith, and secondly that the Lutheran *simul* only makes sense in the perspective of faith. Contestation [Anfechtung] is always parasitical, it presupposes the contested faith. But if Peng-Keller reduces unbelief to contestation or wants the former to be understood only in the light of the latter, he risks falling back behind Luther's paradox and watering down its imposition. For if faith were so powerful that unbelief could only appear as its accidental deficiency, then believing (i.e. not so genuine) unbelievers and (genuine) unbelievers could be distinguished from each other.

But this would be to play away the point of the Lutheran – and Pauline – doctrine of justification that especially in view of sin and unbelief "there is no distinction" (Rom 3:22) to be made here. This way, the universalistic potential would be lost, through which Paul develops his theology of grace against a soteriological separation of Jews and Gentiles.

The statement of the universality of sin does not necessarily mean its ontologization. It would be conceivable to distinguish a *de facto* being of humans under sin from their *de iure* being under grace; in Luther's lecture on Romans it reads "peccatores in re, iusti in spe"[25]. In other words: In the view of God, *coram Deo*, humans are righteous, but as far as they themselves are concerned, only their being a sinner is 'real' about them[26] – and in this respect Christians are no different from non-Christians. This becomes particularly clear inasmuch as

---

24 Peng-Keller, *Alte Passionen*, 528.
25 Luther, "Römervorlesung", 269,30.
26 "Christianus est dupliciter considerandus, in praedicamento relationis et qualitatis. Si consideratur in relatione, tam sanctus est, quam angelus, id est, imputatione per Christum ... Sed christianus consideratus in qualitate est plenus peccato". Luther, "Joachim Wörlin", 141,1–3.5 f.

Luther's simul must be read soteriologically as *totus iustus, totus peccator*.²⁷ In this sense, the simul, as Wilfried Joest writes, is not "the equilibrium of two mutually confining partial moments but rather the battlefield of two mutually exclusive wholes."²⁸ As a totality figure the simul describes a hard paradox: "rhyme there who can rhyme"²⁹, Luther polemicizes against Aristotelian logics. Applied to the distinction between belief and unbelief this would mean: *totaliter fidelis et infidelis*. In the soteriological full sense of the word the believer is to be qualified permanently as unbeliever. In this way, the hamartiological realism of reformatory theology makes at the same time also a hamartiological universalism possible: Instead of solidarity in implicit belief, solidarity in explicit unbelief would be the option here.

In this sense, the simul does not stand for a 'both-and' but for a paradoxical coincidence of 'either-or' – and that is why in the opposition of Assmann and Schmitt the latter is closer to 'truth' because he maintains the constitutive antagonism of fidelity and infidelity. Against Schmitt or beyond him, however, the universality of unbelief must be emphasized, which makes Christian particularism impossible. Friends and enemies of God are not two closed particular groups, but the Christian antagonism between righteousness and sin or between faith and unbelief is first of all a rupture that splits the Christian 'identity' from within and thus permanently undermines its full (or even: 'total') constitution. Christian identity finds the 'other', the unbeliever, which it would need in order to define itself in contrast to it, always and first of all within itself. Burkhard Liebsch noted in the context of cultural studies: "Contradiction [Widerstreit] and irresolvable conflict do not first occur to us in a Manichaean confrontation with others ... We encounter them within ourselves from the very beginning. We contradict ourselves."³⁰ This also goes for theology: the splinter in the eye of the other always

---

27 Wilfried Joest identified two different ways of using the simul formula in Luther's work and distinguished accordingly between a total aspect and a partial aspect. So, Luther, apart from speaking of the Christian as *totus iustus, totus peccator*, can also say: "pii partim iusti sunt, partim peccatores". Luther, "Antinomer", 542,5f. Joest interprets this partial simultaneity of justice and sin in reference to Luther's ethics and the question of a *tertius usus legis*. Also, for Luther, according to Joest, there is a possible "progressus" between the two poles. See Joest, *Gesetz und Freiheit*, 68. The given argument focuses on the soteriologically decisive total aspect of the simul formula.
28 Joest, *Gesetz und Freiheit* (see note 27), 58.
29 Luther, "Antinomer", 508,1.
30 Liebsch, "Kulturelle Lebensformen", 201 f. Liebsch's suggestion of a soteriological perspective is theologically to be shared, at least to a limited extent: "Seen in this light, it is only seemingly a paradox that the liberation *to* the recognized contradiction could liberate *from* it." (See 204; emphasis in original).

immediately reminds the believer of the plank in his own. This insight does not have primarily or necessarily a moralizing or self-critical meaning, but it clarifies the actual ('ontological', de facto real) universality of all people in their enmity to God. To put it another way: the multitude of unbelievers is not a subset of all human beings, or rather does not exhibit any specific difference to other groups of people – and is therefore *not particular but universal*. Every human being is addressable to his or her unbelief.

It is now the obvious question to ask in reverse: On the basis of which categories can those be described who would be counted to the set of believers? This leads to a strangely inconsistent asymmetry, although the simul actually would seem to suggest symmetry here: *On the one hand*, the group of believers can hardly be a particular subset in the sense described above. The antagonism of belief and unbelief cannot simply be translated into the juxtaposition of believers and unbelievers. Just as unbelief does not mark a specific difference, so too faith does not mark a particular group of people. As has just been established and put strictly: *no one* believes, so it is impossible to say that 'some' people believe and 'others' do not. *On the other hand*, there is faith, and so there are also 'believers' – and not only in the implicit, hidden sense, which in turn could quickly be extended to 'everyone', but in an explicit and concrete form. So, neither *everybody* believes, that is obvious – nor *some*, because precisely these know about their unbelief first. The binary paradigm of universality and particularity reaches here its inner limit, the point of its inner exception, which can also be described as singularity.

3.2 Singularity between exclusivity and exclusion

Eberhard Jüngel once specified the Christian claim to exclusivity – *solus Christus* – as 'exclusive inclusivity'.[31] This one is at the same time about everyone. But is this Christocentric form of inclusivism not an expression of the over-expansive tendencies according to which Assmann accuses universalized monotheism? It would be if this were a matter of universalizing something merely particular: a cultural or religious identity, for example. In contrast to this, my thesis would be that the group of believers is not defined by a particular, i.e. a *differentia specifica*, but is founded via relation to the singular. In this context I do not think of the singular as an individual instantiation of a universal but rather as the constitutive exception inherent in the universal. In this, I am following up

---

31 See Jüngel, *Justification*, 149–151.

on the ideas of Alain Badiou, Jacques Rancierè and Slavoj Žižek, according to which the singular marks that symptomatic site within a given order, the 'part of no part', which on the one hand must be excluded from this order to ensure its consistency, and on the other hand, where its organizing principle becomes visible. In contrast to the particular, which represents the ordered regular case within a whole, the singular is the immanent exception that eludes the order. Badiou speaks here of 'universal singularity'.

The universal solidarity in explicit unbelief therefore corresponds to the withdrawal dimension of the singularity of faith, whose claim to exclusivity does not refer to one's own religious system but to the singular excluded himself. Sloterdijk's fear that the believer's universal inclusion is ultimately based on the exclusion of the unbeliever can be answered from a Christian point of view in such a way that it is already the excluded, i.e. Christ, with whom faith begins. As a theology of the cross would have to explicate: The singularity of Jesus Christ is always the exclusivity of the excluded – and only as such universal in its claim.

There are two sides to this universality: On the one hand, the exception symptomatologically reveals the antagonistic exclusion on which every order is founded. It has a critical function in this respect. On the other hand, however, it can also function constructively by opening up the horizon of an open non-exceptionality, in which the exclusion that is constitutive for the community has already been anticipated [vorweggenommen] – and thereby overcome. In a theology of the cross such a universality would have its beginning in the 'end of all sacrifices'.[32] The decisive characteristic of this open community would then be that it does not define itself by an external but by an internal antagonism: exclusively faithful to that which it first excluded itself – and thus *simul fidelis et infidelis*.

Bibliography

Assmann, Jan. *Moses the Egyptian: The Memory of Egypt in Western Monotheism*. Cambridge, MA: Harvard University Press, 1998.
Assmann, Jan. *Herrschaft und Heil: Politische Theologie in Altägypten, Israel und Europa*. Munich: Hanser, 2000.
Assmann, Jan. "Gotteszorn und Apokalypse: Über den Ernstfall Totaler Religionen," *Zeitschrift für Ideengeschichte* 6 (2012): 67–82.

---

[32] See Stoellger, "Ende des Opfers", 62–78.

Assmann, Jan. "Monotheismus der Treue: Korrekturen am Konzept der Mosaischen Unterscheidung im Hinblick auf die Beiträge von Marcia Pally und Micha Brumlik," In *Die Gewalt des Einen Gottes: Die Monotheismusdebatte zwischen Jan Assmann, Micha Brumlik, Rolf Schieder, Peter Sloterdijk und Anderen*, ed. by Rolf Schieder, 2nd ed., 249–267. Berlin: Berlin University Press, 2014.

Assmann, Jan. *Exodus: Die Revolution der Alten Welt*. Munich: C.H. Beck, 2015.

Assmann, Jan. "Mose und der Monotheismus der Treue: Eine Neufassung der 'Mosaischen Unterscheidung'," In *Monotheismus unter Gewaltverdacht: Zum Gespräch mit Jan Assmann*, ed. by Jan H. Tück, 16–33. Freiburg i.Br.: Herder, 2015.

Assmann, Jan. *Totale Religion: Ursprünge und Formen puritanischer Verschärfung*. Vienna: Picus, 2016.

Assmann, Jan. *The Invention of Religion: Faith and Covenant in the Book of Exodus*, trans. Robert Savage. Princeton, NJ: Princeton University Press, 2018.

Joas, Hans. *Glaube als Option: Zukunftsmöglichkeiten des Christentums*. Freiburg i.Br.: Herder, 2012.

Joest, Wilfried. *Gesetz und Freiheit: Das Problem des Tertius Usus Legis bei Luther und die Neutestamentliche Parainese*, 2nd ed. Göttingen: Vandenhoeck & Ruprecht, 1956.

Jüngel, Eberhard. *Justification: The Heart of the Christian Faith: A Theological Study with an Ecumenical Purpose*, trans. Jeffrey Cayzer. London: Bloomsbury, 2014.

Liebsch, Burkhard. "Kulturelle Lebensformen – Zwischen Widerstreit und Gewalt," In *Handbuch der Kulturwissenschaften*, vol. 1, *Grundlagen und Schlüsselbegriffe*, ed. by Friedrich Jaeger and Burkhard Liebsch. Stuttgart: Metzler, 2004.

Luther, Martin. "Römervorlesung [1515/16]," In *Kritische Gesamtausgabe*, vol. 56, Martin Luther, ed. by Johannes Ficker. Graz: Akademische Druck- und Verlagsgesellschaft, 1970.

Luther, Martin. "Die dritte Disputation gegen die Antinomer [1538]," In *Kritische Gesamtausgabe*, vol. 39,1, Martin Luther, ed. by Heinrich Hermelink. Graz: Akademische Druck- und Verlagsgesellschaft, 1964.

Luther, Martin. "Promotionsdisputation von Joachim Wörlin [1540]," In *Kritische Gesamtausgabe*, vol. 39,2, Martin Luther, ed. by Heinrich Hermelink. Graz: Akademische Druck- und Verlagsgesellschaft, 1964.

Metz, Johann Baptist. "Unbelief as a Theological Problem," trans. Tarcisius Rattler, *Concilium* 1 (1965): 59–77.

Nagel, Rasmus. *Universale Singularität: Ein Vorschlag zur Denkform christlicher Theologie im Gespräch mit Ernesto Laclau, Alain Badiou und Slavoj Žižek* (forthcoming).

Otto, Eckart. *Das Deuteronomium: Politische Theologie und Rechtsform in Juda und Assyrien*. Berlin: de Gruyter, 1999.

Peng-Keller, Simon. *Alte Passionen im Neuen Leben: Postbaptismale Konkupiszenz als Ökumenisches Problem und theologische Aufgabe*. Freiburg i.Br.: Herder, 2011.

Sloterdijk, Peter. *God's Zeal: The Battle of the Three Monotheisms*, trans. Wieland Hoban. Cambridge, UK: Polity, 2009.

Sloterdijk, Peter. "Im Schatten des Sinai: Fußnote über Ursprünge und Wandlungen Totaler Mitgliedschaft," In *Die Gewalt des Einen Gottes: Die Monotheismusdebatte zwischen Jan Assmann, Micha Brumlik, Rolf Schieder, Peter Sloterdijk und Anderen*, ed. by Rolf Schieder, 124–149. Berlin: Berlin University Press, 2014.

Sloterdijk, Peter. *In the Shadow of Mount Sinai*, trans. Wieland Hoban. Cambridge, UK: Polity, 2015.

Stoellger, Philipp. "Ende des Opfers und Opfer ohne Ende: Neuere Systematisch-Theologische und Religionsphilosophische Perspektiven zum 'Opfer'," *Verkündigung und Forschung* 56 (2011): 62–78.

III Post-Political Theology

Philipp Stoellger
Das Relative als das Absolute?

Das Politische zwischen Kontingenz und Verkörperung

Abstract: The article shows that the figure of the master in the theological register is ambivalent. Within the biblical traditions it stands for claims of empowerment which delegitimize the interpretive power of other masters (disqualified as idols) and respectively legitimize the interpretive power of one's own claim to leadership (in the name of God as Lord and Master). The power of interpretation proves to be an antagonistic effort. In addition, the analysis focuses on the distinction between the need and the desire for the master. While need can be coped with, desire cannot. The latter refers to conflicting and unfulfillable passions such as those of sin and faith, as well as of evil and of the good. Finally, the article refers to the project, often associated with postmodernism, to abolish the Absolute and with it the reference to an all-powerful Master. It pleads for a theoretical space in-between relativism and the call for absoluteness where especially medium-theoretical questions prove to have an impact on the search for the master.

„Denn der HERR ist unser Richter,
der HERR ist unser Meister,
der HERR ist unser König; der hilft uns!"[1]
(Jes 33,22)

„Was hilft ein Bild?
Sein Meister hat's gebildet. (פֶּסֶל כִּי פְסָלוֹ יֹצְרוֹ)
Was hilft ein gegossenes Bild, ein falscher Lehrer?
Sein Meister verlässt sich auf sein Werk,
obgleich er stumme Götzen macht."
(Hab 2,18)

‚In Need of A Master' provoziert die Rückfragen: welcher Meister – und warum sollte man seiner bedürfen? ‚Der Meister' ist schon biblisch eine ambige Figur – eindeutig einerseits, andererseits verdoppelt eindeutig und damit hoch zweideutig. *Gott* als Meister aller Meister ist *jenseits* aller Zweideutigkeit. Und alle anderen Meister des Diesseits sind *mitten drin* in aller Zweideutigkeit dieser

---
1 Vulgata: legifer / Septuaginta: ἄρχων / Biblia Hebraica Stuttgartensia: מְחֹקְקֵנוּ.

Welt. Diesseits aller Zweideutigkeit ist zudem, dass der Meister als Bildner, Bildermacher eindeutig *negativ* besetzt ist: der Möchtegern-Demiurg, der nur stumme Götzen macht.

Die schlichte Folge der Meisterschaft Gottes scheint sein zu sollen: Alle anderen Meister einer theopolitischen Kritik zu unterziehen und zu zeigen, dass sie nur Fürsten dieser Welt sind, oder Götzenmacher, Sich-Selbst-zu-Götzen-Macher. Nur – diese Kritik träte auf im Namen des Herrn, der unser Meister sei. Entgeht *Gott* der Ambivalenz aller Meister (wenn denn nicht Liebe und Zorn oder *revelatus* und *absconditus* zum Problem würden)? Und falls Gott ihr hoffentlich entginge (spätestens in Christo), entgeht die theologisch möglichst meisterhafte Meisterkritik der Ambivalenz sicher nicht. Denn wer spricht, wenn Gott zum Meister erklärt wird? Wo fände da die Theologie ihren Ort, ihre Rolle und ihre Stimme? Vermutlich in aller Zweideutigkeit, die darum umso mehr Eindeutigkeit prätendiert und doch nicht erreicht, ohne von neuem in Zweideutigkeiten verstrickt zu werden.

Im Rekurs auf Gott finale und definitive Ambivalenzreduktion zu betreiben, ist leider seinerseits hochambivalent: ein Wille zur Macht, genauer zur Deutungsmacht, in der eine Meisterdeutung *Gott zum Meister macht* – wobei im Nebeneffekt eine Deutung die Meistertheologie von Gottes Gnaden zu sein beansprucht und sich damit in alle Ambivalenzen verstrickt, denen man entkommen wollte (oder etwa nicht?).

Wenn ‚alle Kreter lügen', kann man diesem Paradox theologisch nur schwer entkommen: Alle Theologie will von sich weg auf Gott allein als den Meister zeigen, aber darin wird sie praktisch zum Meistermacher, Meisterzeiger – zum Kreter, der kein Kreter sein will. Selbst die frömmste Geste eines Propheten, eines Johannes gar, von sich weg auf Christus zu zeigen, erliegt dem Paradox, dem wir so gerne entkämen.

Ist Religion Kommunikation mit Metaphern, Gleichnissen und Paradoxien, würde die Theologie meist gern endgültig entparadoxieren im Rekurs auf den Meister aller Meister, Gott selbst, oder im Rekurs auf die Vernunft, auf das absolute Subjekt oder besser gleich auf das Absolute, den absoluten Begriff. Wie auch immer die Figur des Meisters ‚aufgestellt' wird, die Theologie wäre gern Jesaja, aber läuft Gefahr, zu Habakuks Bildmeister zu werden. Theologie ‚von Gottes Gnaden' (wie Paulus es prätendiert) hat darin dasselbe Problem wie eine Theologie, die im Namen des Absoluten auftritt: Beide betreiben eine Selbstermächtigung zur Meisterdeutung des Deutungsmeisters. Auch wenn es einen Unterschied macht, ob einem diese Selbstermächtigung versehentlich unterläuft oder dezidert, also ob sie verleugnet wird oder gesucht. Wobei keineswegs klar ist, welche Version vorzuziehen wäre.

Um sich in diesem Dilemma etwas zu orientieren und vielleicht einen Ausweg aus dem Fliegenglas zu finden, sollen im Folgenden erörtert werden: 1) das *Bedürfnis und Begehren nach Meistern*, um den Fokus etwas zu präzisieren; 2) *das Relative als das neue Absolute*, Szenen der Fabrikation von Meistern; 3) ein Fazit: *No Need of A Master*; und als postscriptum der Ausblick auf die offene Aufgabe einer Entfaltung des *Medialen* jenseits des Musters von Meistern und Jüngern.

1 Bedürfnis und Begehren nach Meistern

Um welches Bedürfnis und welche Meister geht es? *In Need of a Master* fokussiert ein ‚need', kein ‚desire'. Also ginge es um ein Bedürfnis, nicht um ein Begehren. Damit ist bereits eine kritische Differenz markiert. Deskriptiv hieße das, es geht *nur* um ein Bedürfnis, das gestillt und entsprechend bewirtschaftet werden kann. Da aber *in vivo* faktisch mehr im Spiel ist – Übergänge ins Begehren, der Sehnsüchte und Fantasien –, ist vom ‚need' zu sprechen, womöglich kritisch und normativ. Überhöhungen politischer Bedürfnisse als Begehren seien zu reduzieren auf das praktisch Machbare, Stillbare. Solch einer Ernüchterungsgeste kann man gerne folgen. Oder ist mehr im Spiel? Ein theologisch-kritischer Ton etwa dergestalt, immanente Probleme politischer Verhältnisse seien *als* Bedürfnisse zu behandeln, nicht als transzendenzorientierte Formen des Begehrens? Wer politisch zu begehren beginnt, übertreibt das Endliche ins Unendliche, was theologisch wie politisch eine unselige Übertreibung wäre: Sei es die Übertreibung des Begehrten, wenn aus Endlichem Unendliches fingiert wird; oder die Übertreibung des Begehrenden, des intrinsisch infiniten Subjekts, oder die Übertreibung des Begehrens selber als Infinitisierungsdynamik.

Nicht dass ‚Übertreibung' als solche ‚illegitim' wäre, wie Alexander Düttmann geklärt hat.[2] Gerade in religiösen Kontexten gibt es Übertreibungen in, mit und von denen wir leben, etwa in Liebe und Hoffnung. Bernhard Waldenfels untersuchte das unter dem religionshermeneutischen Topos der ‚Hyperphänomene'.[3] Aber in politischen wie kirchlichen Konstellationen sind Übertreibungen weder nötig noch wünschenswert, wenn sie in der Suche nach Meistern zur Sucht werden – und entsprechende Entzugserscheinungen und Katerstimmungen nach sich ziehen.

Zum Hintergrund sei angemerkt: Glaube wie Sünde sind Formen des Begehrens – und darum einander so nah wie fern. Mag man Gott begehren oder

---

[2] Vgl. Düttmann, *Übertreibung.*
[3] Vgl. Waldenfels, *Hyperphänomene.*

besser noch *wie* Gott begehren, trifft die aktuale Infinität des Begehrens ein passendes Gegenüber. Aber – in politischen wie ökonomischen Konstellationen scheint das ‚Objekt' des Begehrens überlastet zu werden von dessen Infinität und Transzendenzlust.

1.1 Meister?

Zum hier thematischen Begriff des ‚*master*', deutsch als ‚Meister' verstanden, ist vorab wenigstens ungefähr zu sagen, was damit gemeint sein mag. Denn ‚Meister' ist *scilicet* kein etablierter *Begriff*, sondern ein polysemer Ausdruck, meist eine Metapher, was auch sonst. Daher muss man ihn etwas näher bestimmen, um nicht über völlig Disparates zu handeln.

‚Meister' wird hier verstanden als *Figur der Macht*, ähnlich dem metonymischen ‚Herr-Knecht'-Verhältnis. Meister ist ein Relationsausdruck gegenüber ‚Jünger', ‚Schüler', ‚Adept' oder denen, die dem Meister folgen, sich ihm unterwerfen. Insofern ist das Modell ‚stratifikatorisch' und operiert mit einer Machtrelation von ‚oben und unten'. Als *Machtfigur* ist ein Meister nicht gleich ‚Herrscher'. Es geht in Meister-Verhältnissen nicht notwendig um Herrschafts-, sondern um Machtverhältnisse: nicht nur um *potestas*, sondern auch um *charisma* bzw. *potentia*.

Dabei ist Meister – nicht nur in seiner Anwendung auf politische Verhältnisse – ein suggestiver Ausdruck. Denn er insinuiert ein *Legitimitätsversprechen:* Der Meister sei Meister aufgrund seiner Meisterschaft, einer besonderen Kompetenz, die ihn zum Meister mache und als solchen legitimiere. Damit wird für einen politischen Herrscher durch diese Metapher schnell zu viel insinuiert: zwar keine Legitimität *qua* Geburt oder Gottes Gnaden, aber doch eine *qua* Kompetenz.

Darin steht der Meister dem Charismatiker nahe, dem eine besondere Geistpräsenz zugeschrieben wird, die ihn legitimiere. Während ein Charismatiker im religiösen Sinn typischerweise seine Auszeichnung als Gabe und Widerfahrung ausgibt (möglichst ‚wider Willen', vgl. Mose und die Propheten), wird der Meister auf seine Werke, seine Erfahrung, *phronesis* und daher wohlverdiente Meisterschaft *in etwas* verwiesen.

Wird im Deutungsmuster des ‚Meisters' *Kompetenz* mitgesetzt, impliziert das: der Meister habe *wirklich* etwas zu sagen (und nicht nur qua Amt ‚das Sagen'). Eine Urszene dessen wäre Aristoteles als Meister gegenüber dem Herrscher namens Alexander; oder Platons *Politeia* mit der begehrlichen Fantasie eines Philosophenkönigs, oder die Sehnsucht nach einem ‚Bundesphilosophen', der den Politikern sagt, wo es lang gehen sollte. Sollte man das Begehren der ‚*public theology*' analog als eines nach einem Bundestheologen oder -ethiker verstehen?

Im politischen Kontext sind Meister meist im Hintergrund zu suchen, nicht im Vordergrund auf der politischen Bühne der Herrscherfiguren, sondern daneben oder dahinter: die Berater, grauen Eminenzen, vermeintlichen Kompetenzfiguren, die nicht herrschen, sondern den Herrscher beim Regieren beraten (so er denn mit diesem mühsamen Geschäft des Regierens zu tun hat). Theologische, vor allem ethische Politikberatung spielt in diesem Register.

Wenn der Herrscher so weise wäre, sich hoffentlich klug beraten zu lassen, *ermöglicht* er zumindest, seine Entscheidungen kompetenzgestützt zu treffen. Ist doch eines leicht zu lernen, wenn man an parlamentarischer Arbeit partizipiert (z. B. in Synoden): politische Entscheidungsprozesse sind alles Mögliche, aber keineswegs notwendig *kompetenz*gestützt.

Spricht man von ‚Meistern' sind sicher ‚dark master' und ‚light master' zu unterscheiden, dunkle und helle. Widriges, Störendes, Fremdes zu personifizieren und *als Feind* zu identifizieren, letztlich womöglich, um *den* Feind auszumachen, ist die andere, dunkle Seite der ‚Meistermacherei', im Grenzwert ‚den Teufel an die Wand zu malen', im Glauben, damit das Böse bannen zu können. Mit genug Teufelsglauben glaubt man vielleicht wirklich, der Teufel sei der Grund allen Übels und mit einem Sieg über den so produzierten Teufel könne man letztlich alles Übel beseitigen.

Auf der dunklen Seite der Macht mit ihrem Teufels- oder Feindesglauben lässt sich etwas an der ‚Meisterei' klären: Sie operiert mit der Kulturtechnik der *Delegation* an den einen Anderen, Fremden, Bösen; der *Verkörperung* zur Verehrung oder Verteufelung; der Vereinfachung bzw. Prägnanz; und der Stellvertreterrituale, als könnte man mit dem Sieg über *den* Bösen *das* Böse meistern. Und als würde man mit dem Sieg über den Bösen selbst zum Meister aller Meister.

1.2 Orientierungs- und Ordnungsbedarf

Basal und unverdächtig ist wohl phänomenologisch wie hermeneutisch davon auszugehen, dass es *Orientierungsbedürfnisse* gibt, wo gehandelt und gelitten wird. Immer wieder ist etwas zu entscheiden, geht man links oder rechts lang, und dafür bedarf es der Orientierung.[4] Fährt man im Rhein-Neckar-Raum oder im Ruhrgebiet auf der Autobahn, wäre man ohne Wegweiser schnell so hilflos wie orientierungslos. Je komplexer das Entscheidungsproblem, desto schwieriger wird es – und desto hilfreicher sind Orientierungsmarken, die vorgegeben sind oder werden.

---

4 Vgl. Stegmaier, *Orientierung*.

Man muss *nolens volens selbst* entscheiden, wo es lang geht. Nur, um zu entscheiden, bedarf es, je komplexer das Problem, desto dringlicher der Anhaltspunkte und Markierungen, die man nicht selbst gesetzt hat, sondern hoffentlich vorfindet. Dem *Orientierungsbedürfnis* korrespondiert ein *Ordnungsbedarf*. Daher bedarf es der Vorgaben wie einer Beschilderung, und entsprechend der vorgängigen und antizipativen Delegation von Entscheidungen (Stadtplanung etc.), die grundsätzlich heteronom operieren: Es geht lang, wo die Wege gebahnt wurden und sich schon ‚Geländer des Daseins' finden. In der üblichen ‚anthropologischen Situation' von ‚Evidenzmangel und Handlungszwang' (Blumenberg) sind solche Heteronomien durchaus hilfreich, wenn nicht sogar überlebensnotwendig. Um es ‚anwendungsorientiert' zu sagen: Wenn jeder Chirurg erst einmal drauflos schneiden würde in fröhlicher Autonomie, hätten die Patienten unabsehbare Risiken und Nebenwirkungen zu ertragen, wenn sie es denn überleben würden. Die hoch heteronom strukturierte Medizinerausbildung ‚sagt, wo es lang geht', etwa beim Schneiden.

Geht man dagegen *dogmatisch* vom autonomen, handlungsmächtigen Subjekt mit Wachbewusstsein und in voller Gesundheit aus, sind solche Vorgaben und Heteronomien störend oder unzulässig. Ganz anders hingegen klingt ‚In Need of A Master', wenn man schwer krank ist und eine lebensrettende OP braucht.[5] Dann braucht man einen ‚Meister', in dessen Hände man sich begibt: nicht einen ‚Schamanen' oder Gesundbeter, auch nicht einen allzu autonom veranlagten Chirurgen, sondern Professionalität, Methode und System – alles andere als autonome oder herrschaftsfreie Vorgaben. In physischen und psychischen Notlagen ist man jedenfalls auf hilfreiche, gar heilsame Andere angewiesen: auf lebensrettende Heteronomie. Wer hingegen ‚Heteronomie' nur als Verletzung der Autonomie begreifen kann, läuft Gefahr, nicht begreifen zu können, dass Autonomie eingebettet ist in Angewiesenheit auf Andere und Anderes.

Dabei ist eine entscheidende Frage, ob ‚*Vertrauen*' hier eine Rolle spielt. Denn Meister insinuieren Vertrauensverhältnisse. Bedarf es dessen? Zumal es so überaus riskant ist zu vertrauen? Oder ist die Umbesetzung durch Verlässlichkeit von Strukturen und Institutionen nicht viel empfehlenswerter, um das Vertrauensrisiko zu minimieren? Die Ambiguität wird manifest in medizinischen Kontexten: In Grenzlagen müssen wir uns auf Andere verlassen, würden denen womöglich auch gerne vertrauen, aber Struktur und System bieten bestenfalls verlässliche Verhältnisse. Die Professionalisierung von Systemen entlastet vom Vertrauensrisiko, bietet dafür aber lediglich verlässliche und im Fehlerfall verklagbare Substitute. Der Meister hingegen fordert Vertrauen (blindes?) und bedient das Begehren nach

---

[5] Oder anders und ähnlich, wenn man in Seenot ist und dringend Rettung braucht.

mehr als bloßer Verlässlichkeit. Das Risiko im Gegenzug ist erheblich, der affektive Gewinn allerdings auch.

1.3 Bedürfnis und Begehren nach Meistern

Es gibt Bedürfnisse – wie Orientierungsbedürfnisse und Ordnungsbedarf –, die zu einem Begehren eskalieren können, zum Begehren nach einem ‚Master':
- einem Meisterdenker,
- einer Meistertheorie,
- einer Meisterdeutung,
- einem Meister in Lebenshilfe und der Religionspraxis,
- einem absoluten oder wenigstens souveränen Herrscher,
- oder einem ‚immer noch absoluteren' Gott.

Die Geschichte des Gott-Denkens erscheint im Rückblick der Regel zu folgen, ihn möglichst hoch zu treiben, immer noch höher, auf dass Größeres nicht gedacht werden könne, mehr noch: auf dass er größer werde, als dass er noch gedacht werden könnte.[6] Diese Eskalationen des Begehrens nach dem Absoluten sind nicht nur theologisch und philosophisch immer noch lebendig (mancherorts zumindest), sie können auch kirchlich dazu führen, sich nach der Größe der politischen Meister zu sehnen, um sich in deren Schatten zu sonnen. Solche Formen des Begehrens fabrizieren *Figuren* der Meister – wenn das Begehren figurativ operiert: sich seine begehrten Figuren fabriziert.

Das ist irgendwie verständlich, ohne darum Verständnis dafür haben zu müssen oder gar Einverständnis.[7] Solche Formationen und Figurationen zu beschreiben, um zu verstehen, ist das eine; wie man darauf antwortet das andere. Und wie dieses Begehren bewirtschaftet wird das dritte. Denn es wird je nach Kontext oder Format sehr unterschiedlich bewirtschaftet.

Das Begehren nach ‚neuen Meistern' ist immens und anscheinend allgegenwärtig, in ganz verschiedenen kulturellen Kontexten. In *Politik* und *Ökonomie*, im *Recht* (BVerfG, EuGH) und in der *Kunst*, wenn nach den ‚alten Meistern' neue gesucht und ernannt werden, üblicherweise vor allem kraft des ‚Kunstmarkts'. In der *Religion*, wenn das Amt des Höchsten plötzlich von einem Charismatiker besetzt scheint; oder wenn ein Amtsträger *fällt* – und anders als ein gefallener Bundespräsident dann zum Charismatiker avanciert. In der *Technik* in Gestalt des

---

6 Vgl. zu Gottes Eskalationen: Blumenberg, *Matthäuspassion*, 83 ff.
7 Vgl. Stoellger, „Verständigung mit Fremdem", 164–193.

neuzeitlichen Erfinders und Entdeckers, der nach dem Geniekult des 19. Jahrhunderts abgelöst wird von Programmierern und Algorithmen. In der *Philosophie* mit der Vernunft als *dem* Meister und den Meisterphilosophen, nach denen es umso mehr Bedarf zu geben scheint, je weniger religiöse Autoritäten das Sagen haben (d. h. zugeschrieben bekommen). Gegen die Meistervernunft und Vernunftmeister notierte übrigens schon Luther in seiner *Disputatio de homine:*[8] „[N]icht einmal über seinen Entschluß oder seine Gedanken hat er [der ach so vernünftige Mensch] volle und zuverlässige Gewalt, sondern ist darin dem Zufall und der Nichtigkeit unterworfen."[9] Die vermeintlich absolute Vernunft ist kontingent oder, schlichter gesagt, Menschenwerk und damit weder etwas Göttliches im Menschen noch einfach neutral oder sündlos.

Die ‚akademische' Bewirtschaftung des Meisterbegehrens ist gleichwohl ungebrochen, seien es Meisterinstitutionen wie Exzellenzuniversitäten oder phänomenal das Begehren mancher Wissenschaftler nach Anerkennung, öffentlicher Geltung und Medienpräsenz. Die ‚akademische' Sehnsucht bleibt merklich: ‚Wenn die Welt auf uns hören würde, wäre sie eine bessere Welt; die Kirche eine bessere, der Mensch ein besserer …'. Dem entspricht das Meisterbegehren mancher Studierender: den großen Meister als Lehrer. Ob bei Studierenden oder Lehrenden und Forschenden: die Wissenschaftsvorstellung des 19. Jahrhunderts lebt noch immer – mit ihrem Begehren nach Heroisierung, als könnte ein großer Held die Rätsel der Welt lösen und sie retten. Es ist anscheinend eine tiefsitzende Erwartungsgewohnheit: Luhmann werden oder Habermas oder Ricœur, als wäre ein genialer Meisterdenker der Messias, der uns von allem Übel erlösen könnte.

Das Verfahren ist ebenso bekannt wie seine Vergeblichkeit: Komplexitätsreduktion durch Personalisierung, Heroisierung und Stilisierung. Man könnte das auf ein Prägnanzbegehren zurückführen, nur geht das offensichtlich an den inter- und transdisziplinären Problemen und Herausforderungen komplett vorbei. Daher ist die wissenschaftlich belastbare Alternative dazu: *Methode* statt Meister. Aber kaum ist die Methode als entpersonalisiertes Verfahren aufgerufen, geht der Streit von neuem los: um die Meistermethoden, seien sie empirisch und historisch, quantitativ und rein objektiv. So operiert auch die Politik, die Ökonomie oder das Recht; aber vor allem Kunst und Religion scheinen besonders disponiert für die ewige Wiederkehr des Meisterbegehrens.

---

[8] Luther, „Die Disputation de homine", 175–177.
[9] These 18 in: Luther, „Die Disputation de homine", 176 (Übers.; Ph.S.).

Jedenfalls erscheint Luhmanns Pathos, in der Wissenschaft gehe es um Wahrheit, so wunderbar wie sympathisch alteuropäisch.[10] Das Begehren sucht nicht Wahrheit, sondern den wahren Meister (als personalisierte Verkörperung der Wahrheit?). Das tiefste Begehren ausgerechnet der nüchternen Naturwissenschaften ist bekanntlich der Nobelpreis. Einem solchen Meister scheint dann alles erlaubt zu sein. Wer hoch genug dekoriert ist und seine Exzellenz bestätigt bekam, hat das Sagen – und entsprechende Aufmerksamkeit – plötzlich in allerlei Hinsicht. Der Ökonom und Nobelpreisträger Friedrich von Hayek (1899–1992, Nobelpreis 1974), Sohn einer Biologenfamilie, vertrat dezidiert die ‚Aussiebung' durch den Markt. Er hielt eine hohe Arbeitslosenquote für wünschenswert, die die natürliche Selektion durch den Markt ermögliche,[11] weil die individuelle Freiheit an die (freiwillige) Unterwerfung unter die ‚unpersönlichen Kräfte des Marktes' (Hayek) gebunden sei. Oder im Originalton: „Wenn wir garantieren, daß jeder am Leben erhalten wird, der erst einmal geboren ist, werden wir bald nicht mehr in der Lage sein, dieses Versprechen [die ausreichende Ernährung aller Menschen] zu erfüllen. Gegen die Überbevölkerung gibt es nur die eine Bremse, nämlich daß sich nur die Völker erhalten und vermehren, die sich auch selbst ernähren können"[12].

Während einem die ‚Doktorwürde' auch wieder aberkannt werden kann, wenn man sich ihrer im Laufe seines Lebens als unwürdig erweist, fungiert der Meistertitel des Nobelpreisträgers offenbar wie ein römischer ‚*character indelebilis*': unverlierbar und unantastbar. So werden Meister fabriziert, die dann lebenslang als Orakel für alles Mögliche durch die Weltgeschichte laufen dürfen – und erstaunliche Anerkennung finden.

Auch ein ‚Zen-Meister' kann sagen, was er will (auch den größten Unsinn), verlangen, was er will, tun und lassen, was er will: Er ist ein kleiner Willkürgott also – wie ein Orakel, das einer Begründung weder fähig noch bedürftig ist. Er ‚ist', oder besser gesagt, er wird vom Meisterbegehren dazu gemacht – und muss einigen Unsinn erfinden, um sich dem zu widersetzen.

Meister sind ein Muster absolutistischer Machtverhältnisse. Der gern geglaubte Absolutismus einer Unterwerfungslust, ist erstaunlich persistent, wenn der Meister einmal ‚erwählt' und ernannt wurde. Ist das dann im Grenzwert auch ein *Gewalt*verhältnis? Arendt meinte: „[S]o sollten wir wissen, daß der Hang zur Unterwerfung, der Trieb zum Gehorsam und der Schrei nach dem starken Mann in

---

10 Wissenschaftspolitisch ist die begründete Geltung längst von Geld als Geltungsgrund überholt worden: Wer genug Drittmittel hat, hat das Sagen und kann das Wort erteilen. Anerkennung operiert über Umsätze und Quoten der Zitation etc.
11 Vgl. Schönborn, *Ziel oder Zufall?*, 179.
12 von Hayek, „Ungleichheit", 3; vgl. dazu Schui, „Rechtsextremismus", 52f.

der menschlichen Psychologie eine mindestens ebenso große Rolle spielt wie der Wille zur Macht, und daß diese Unterwerfungsinstinkte politisch vermutlich erheblich relevanter sind."[13] Dann ist das Meisterverhältnis zumindest potentiell, latent gewaltsam. „Der Extremfall der Macht ist gegeben in der Konstellation: Alle gegen Einen, der Extremfall der Gewalt in der Konstellation: Einer gegen Alle."[14] Das wird akut, wenn einmal fabrizierte Meister als imaginäre Figuren eine Eigendynamik gegenüber den Ernennenden entfalten und so von aktuellen Anerkennungsprozessen abgekoppelt werden. Religiöser, politischer, auch akademischer Absolutismus (wie bei den Nobelpreisträgern) kann anscheinend eben dazu führen.

‚Quia voluit' war die Grundformel des Allmachts-Absolutismus seit Augustin, und in Form der Allmachtdefinition: Er kann, was er will, und was er will, kann er auch. Was einem Allmachtsgott recht ist, ist dem Meister billig. Mag diese (soteriologisch leere, christologisch unhaltbare) Allmacht bei Gott zum Wesensbegriff gehören, zumindest wenn man einem Ontotheismus anhängt, ist das in *religiösen* Beziehungen zwischen Menschen *scilicet* eine Delegation: des ‚Eigenwillens' an den Willen des Meisters mit entsprechender Unterwerfungslust (von *beiden* Seiten).

Dabei lässt sich eine leicht zu übersehende Komplikation entdecken. War ‚Delegation' spätestens seit Blumenberg (*Arbeit am Mythos*) bekannt, hatte er anscheinend etwas übersehen: das Phänomen der ‚Re-Delegation'. Der delegierte Wille kehrt im Modus der Antizipation des Meister-Willens zurück. Das banale Beispiel dafür wäre: Man putzt, bevor die ‚Putzfrau' kommt (oder der ‚Raumpfleger'). Auf die Meisterfrage übertragen: Man gehorcht vorauseilend, bevor der Meister etwas sagt. Als wäre der Meister nur dazu ernannt, sich zuvorkommend selbst zu disziplinieren. Der ‚vorauseilende Gehorsam' ist nicht nur die Internalisierung des Meisters, sondern genauer besehen ein Re-Delegations-Phänomen. Der Umweg über die Delegation an den Meister könnte – kraft der List des Begehrens – gerade dazu dienen, im Modus der Antizipation ‚selber zu wollen, bevor der Meister will'.

---

[13] Arendt, *Macht und Gewalt*, 40 f.
[14] Arendt, *Macht und Gewalt*, 43.

1.4 Mächte und Meister

Was für Meister *in welcher Hinsicht* ist differenzierungsbedürftig:

a) *potestas*

Im politischen Kontext ist der Meister eine Figur der *potestas:* ein Herrscher. Ungeachtet der Differenz von Herrschen und Regieren geht es in der *potestas* um die Macht, bindende Entscheidungen zu produzieren – mehr nicht: Gesetze machen, durchsetzen, sanktionieren etc. Da *potestas* fabriziert wird, also Herrscher (bzw. Herrschaftsstrukturen) *gemacht* werden, ernannt, gewählt, ‚geboren‘, kann politische Herrschaft nur relativ sein, nicht absolut. Das ist im Machtbegriff von Hannah Arendt oder Hans Jonas ja wiederholt erörtert und geklärt worden. Macht (im politischen Sinn der *potestas*) wäre keine Macht, wenn sie nicht relativ wäre, ein Beziehungsphänomen: Macht ist stets Macht über andere, die daher von denselben abhängig ist und bleibt (Anerkennung, Verfahren etc.). Absolute Macht wäre eine *contradictio in adjecto:* als absolute bzw. Allmacht wäre sie beziehungslos und damit machtlos.

Wie auch immer die Herrschaft legitimiert und legalisiert sein mag, ist sie abhängig von Anerkennung und Zuschreibung, von Verfahren und Strukturen, die sie einbetten, einbinden – und damit *binden* an ein Woher (und Wozu) von Herrschaft. Alle *potestas* ist relativ zu Anerkennungsverhältnissen. Daher ist das Begehren nach Unabhängigkeit von Anerkennung ebenso verständlich – wie konstitutiv selbstwidersprüchlich. Wieweit dieser Selbstwiderspruch ‚absoluter Macht‘ als kalkulierte Absurdität brauchbar wäre, wäre eigens zu verhandeln. Analog der Absurdität einer *creatio ex nihilo* könnte das *negativistisch* andeuten, Herrschaft wie Herstellung nicht auf Gott übertragen zu können, ohne eine Absurdität zu produzieren.

b) *potentia*

Im theologischen Kontext ist der Meister nicht primär eine Figur der *potestas*, sondern vor allem eine der *potentia:* kein politischer Herrscher, sondern Schöpfer, Erhalter, Versöhner und Vollender. So wird die Macht Gottes nicht unter dem Begriff einer *omnipotestas*, sondern der *omnipotentia* erörtert – anders als in den Machtkonflikten zwischen Kaiser und Papst, in denen es um *potestas* ging, nicht um *potentia*.

Augustins kurz gefasster Allmachtbegriff war bekanntlich: Gott kann, was immer er will – also bereits die Kurzformel eines Absolutismus: ‚Nichts ist unmöglich ...'. *Omnipotentia* ist erst mit Hieronymus in die Bibelübersetzung eingewandert (als vermeintliche Übersetzung von Pantokrator und *El Shaddai*).[15] Nur zur Erinnerung sei notiert, dass im Alten und Neuen Testament nirgends von Allmacht die Rede ist, auch bei Hiob nicht. Daher sind auch Bibelübersetzungen nur als dogmatischer Anachronismus verständlich, sofern sie im Alten Testamten vom ‚Allmächtigen' sprechen – sprechen *lassen*, machen und so eine Machtfantasie in die Texte eintragen. Selbst die Lutherrevision von 2017 bedient noch solch ein Allmachtsbegehren. Diese Machtfantasie hat sich seit der Vulgata erstaunlich schnell und bis heute frömmigkeitsprägend durchgesetzt, als wäre sie die passende Figur für das religiöse Begehren. Dass damit eher Machtbegehren und Machtfiguren verehrt werden, als Gott im christologisch verantwortbaren Sinne, ist merklich.

Mit *potentia* geht es um Möglichkeit in mehrfacher Hinsicht: um Ermöglichung (von ansonsten Unmöglichem), um Verwirklichung (von Möglichem) und um Vernichtung (von Wirklichem) – *da capo al fine*. Dabei sind stets Selektionen als Kehrseite präsent: Ermöglichung exkludiert ebenso wie Verwirklichung und Vernichtung. In Bezug auf Gott gilt dieser modale Zirkel der *potentia* vor allem als *kreativ* und *rekreativ:* Er ermöglicht und verwirklicht – und vernichtet, wenn, dann hoffentlich nur das Übel.

Daher ist die logische oder ontologische Omnipotenz theologisch weder unnötig noch sinnvoll. Es geht um Macht als *potentia*, und sei es höchste Macht (oder wie die Bibel in gerechter Sprache formuliert für *El Shaddai:* der Macht über die Macht hat) und zwar strikt als Schöpfung, Erhaltung, Versöhnung und Vollendung der Welt, also als deren *Ermöglichung und Verwirklichung* (und *Vernichtung* des *malum*). ‚Allmacht' ist die hyperbolische und paradoxe Wendung für eine schöpfungstheologische, soteriologische und eschatologische Eigenschaft Gottes. Daher bedarf es keiner metaphysischen Eskalation eines abstrakten Allmachtsbegriffs.

Die Kritik der Eskalation der *potentia* zur *omnipotentia* ist das eine, das andere ist, dass mit der *potentia als Ermöglichung* etc. ein *anderer* Machtbegriff im Spiel ist. Der hilft gegen die Reduktion von Machtfragen auf *potestas* und personale Trägermedien, auch gegen ‚vermögenspsychologische' Reduktion der *potentia* auf Handlungsvermögen, ‚Vermögen' eines ‚Subjekts' bis hin zum Geldvermögen. *Potentia* ist eben nicht nur personal, sondern nicht zuletzt strukturell und medial konzipiert.

---

15 Vgl. Bauke-Ruegg, *Allmacht Gottes*.

Als kritische Norm ließe sich aus dem *potentia*-Konzept folgern: Derjenige ‚Meister' wäre eine theologisch sinnvolle Figur, der Neues *ermöglicht*, also eröffnet und erschließt. Nur ist das noch zu formal und *in vivo* zu unbestimmt. Wäre derjenige Meister zu begrüßen, der das ‚Overton-Fenster' weit öffnet und bisher Unsägliches salonfähig werden lässt? Ermöglichung *des Übels* ist, spätestens seit dem Griff zum Apfel, keineswegs per se zu begrüßen. Auch wenn der deutsche Idealismus meinte, der Sündenfall sei die Erweckung zur Freiheit (und darin der Sabbatianischen Mystik folgte). Daher ist die *potentia* als Ermöglichung und Verwirklichung im Zeichen kreativer Fremderhaltung sinnvoll zu nennen; was allerdings auch noch der Näherbestimmung bedarf. Denn nur solche Fremderhaltung wäre normativ vorzüglich, die eine selbstkritische Differenz von ‚alt versus neu' geltend macht (oder Analoges).

c) *auctoritas (charisma, exousia)*

Im religiösen (wie auch politischen) Kontext *kann* der Meister auch eine Figur der *auctoritas* sein, des Charisma bzw. der ἐξουσία, was die Verhältnisse weiter differenziert. Denn der Charismatiker herrscht nicht, noch regiert er, aber er ist auch nicht Schöpfer, Versöhner oder Vollender. Ist er doch nicht an *potestas* oder *potentia* orientiert, sondern an Darstellung und Deutung. Daher ist er vor allem eine Figur der *Deutungsmacht*. Er hat – so die Vorstellung – etwas zu sagen, ohne politisch oder qua Amt das Sagen zu haben. Seine ‚Vollmacht' ist hybrid: anscheinend primär die der Person, die vollmächtig erscheint; dabei aber (wie beim Propheten) abkünftig von dem, der ihn legitimiert (Gott); genauer aber abhängig von dem, was er denn *wirklich* zu sagen hat (Wort); und nicht zuletzt abhängig von denen, die ihm folgen, ihn anerkennen und zum Charismatiker machen (Hörer).

Wer ‚hat' *das Sagen* oder wer hat *wirklich* etwas zu sagen? So zu fragen, heißt zu unterscheiden zwischen dem Anspruch, ‚das Sagen' zu haben (etwa qua Amt, Institution oder Struktur), und einem Sagen, dessen Anspruch offen auf Ratifikation angewiesen bleibt. Machtwort und Wortmacht sind deutlich zu unterscheiden, wie ‚das Sagen haben' oder *wirklich* etwas zu sagen zu haben.[16] Jemand hat das Sagen, der in einer Position ist, Entscheidungen zu treffen, zu sagen ‚wo es langgeht'. Wer in solcher Position oder ohne sie *wirklich* etwas zu sagen wagt, setzt sich aus und ist den Anderen ausgesetzt ‚*à fond perdu*'. Ob er etwas zu sagen hat und ob das Gehör und Anerkennung findet, ist höchst fraglich – wie das Schicksal der Propheten demonstriert.

---

[16] Vgl. Stoellger und Kumlehn, *Wortmacht/Machtwort*.

2 Absolute Meister: das Absolute als politische Figur

Die Frage nach einem ‚Meister' hat, wie gezeigt, sehr verschiedene Register. Eins ist nach dem Bisherigen aber evident: Meister werden gemacht, mal gewählt, mal ernannt oder auch schlicht gelost, an der Uni wie in der Politik und der Religion, nicht ohne Gründe meistens, aber sie sind Resultate von Praktiken, Verfahren, Prozessen, Konstellationen und Kontingenzen: Figuren als Folge von Figurationen. Insofern gehören ‚Meister' ins Register der Medienanthropologie, einer Figurenlehre, die aus Praktiken der Figuration entstehen.[17]

Der geliebte Glaube, die Gründe für die Ernennung eines Meisters seien zwingende oder letzte Gründe, im Grunde also sei der Meister ‚alternativlos', ist so beruhigend wie selbsttäuschungsanfällig. Denn Meister werden erst Meister, wenn sich Schüler finden, die ihnen folgen. Analoges gilt bekanntlich auch für Charismatiker, wie Max Weber zu Recht meinte. Kann man ‚von außen' von Meistern im Plural sprechen, scheint von innen in politischer wie religiöser Hinsicht zu gelten: ‚Es kann nur einen geben ...'. Ein Meister liegt nicht im Konflikt mit anderen, alternativen Meistern, sondern er ist – einmal ernannt, gewählt, geliebt – *selbstverständlich* in seiner Autorität. So ist der Meister in seiner Selbstverständlichkeit, Unantastbarkeit, Erhabenheit etc. eine eminente Figur von Deutungsmacht: Er hat das Sagen – und nur wenn es *gut* geht, hat er auch *etwas* zu sagen (‚wirklich' etwas zu sagen) und nicht nur *das* Sagen.

Das Deutungsmuster des ‚Meisters' ist politisch wie religiös in der Regel allerdings *einschläfernd* (wie andererseits auch die Überführung der Politik in postpolitische Bürokratie). Im Grunde gebe es nichts zu verhandeln, nichts zu streiten, nichts zu entscheiden. Denn der Meister hat das Sagen und sagt, wo es lang geht. So wirkt die Genealogie des Meisters wie eine Metonymie auf die Struktur der *Konstitution des Absoluten*.

Die Konstitution des Absoluten als Entlastung und Delegation *ist* eine *politische* Figur, mit der Machtverhältnisse organisiert werden: abkünftig von Figurationspraktiken, verkörpert in Figuren, verdichtet in Szenen. Es sind *Figuren* – des Fühlens und Begehrens, Denken, Sprechens – und der Ordnung wie Organisation und Orientierung. Dabei geht es stets um Deutungsmacht, also wer ‚das Sagen' und ‚wirklich etwas zu sagen' habe, sei es König wie Papst, Kaiser wie allmächtiger Theismusgott.

---

17 Vgl. Stoellger, *Figurationen*.

Das ließe sich in vier Schritten behandeln, von denen hier nur der erste und der letzte näher erörtert werden kann: Die Konstitution des Absoluten qua Figuration; die kompetitive Eskalation in politisch-religiösen Konfigurationen; die antiabsolutistische Wende der Neuzeit und die ewige Wiederkehr des Absoluten im Relativen. Die letzte Wendung führt in die Frage, ob denn derzeit vor allem *das Relative als das Absolute* gilt.

2.1 Konstitution des Absoluten durch Figuration

Mit dieser These geht es *hier* nicht um die ‚Selbstkonstitution' der immanenten Trinität, etwa nach Manier Hegelscher Logik. *Diese* Theorie des Absoluten wäre vor allem die Selbstkonstitution der absoluten Theorie, von der noch manche Dogmatiken ihren Nektar saugen.

Es geht vielmehr um Szenen der Figuration von möglichst absoluten Meistern, der dann eine Formation entspricht. In Formen werden Figuren ‚gegossen'; und Figuren formen ihrerseits das sie Umgebende. Wie eine Gussform die Figur formt; so die Figur den Gips, wenn ein Abguss genommen wird.

a) Eine pointierte Urszene solcher Figuration ist die Genese des Königtums in Israel. Seitens der königskritischen Theologien wird der *Sünder als König* und der *König als Sünder* dargestellt. Schlicht gesagt, das Königtum ist ein Witz, und zwar ein unfrommer, schlechter Witz. Denn wo Jahwe allein herrscht, ist die Figur des Königs als Herrscher weder nötig noch erwünscht. Stattdessen operieren Jahwes ‚Regierungsmittel': Tempel und Tora, Prophetie und Weisheit. Dass damit eine Differenzregel angewandt wird, ist klar: Mag den anderen Völkern der König an Gottes statt auftreten, gar *als* Gott, gilt in Israel diese Repräsentationsregel gerade nicht. Dass diese Königskritik nur für manche Theologien des AT gilt, ist klar, vor allem im Zeichen von Tora und Deuteronomismus, der Zionstheologie mit Tempel und Priestern und der Prophetie in Moses Tradition; aber weniger für Weisheit und königstreue Traditionen.

b) Wurde alttestamentlich der Sünder zum König gemacht und der König ein Sünder, ist umso erstaunlicher, dass im Investiturstreit des Mittelalters eine Schubumkehr der Deutung programmatisch wurde – und bis heute für manche Kulturwissenschaftler geblieben ist: Kantorowicz' immer gern wiederholte Lehre der ‚Zwei Körper des Königs' ist bekanntlich einem königstreuen Text des Mittelalters entnommen: dem sogenannten ‚Anonymus von York'. Christus als König zu deuten, ermöglicht, den König wie Christus in zwei Naturen zu deuten (womit allerdings die Pointe einer unauflösbaren personalen Einheit verkannt wird: Die *unitio* und *unio personalis* wie die *communicatio idiomatum* wird politisch *nicht* rekonstruiert).

‚Rex non potest peccare' oder ‚The King can do no wrong' ist das entsprechende Rechtsprinzip, nachdem der Souverän ‚immun' ist oder ‚infallibel' (der Papst unter Umständen *ex cathedra*). Da alles Recht vom Souverän ausgeht, *ist* Recht, *was immer* von ihm ausgeht. Die Legitimität des Souveräns gilt als (von Gottes Gnaden) gesetzt, so dass die Legalität seines Handelns ausnahmslos entschieden ist. Dass eine Differenz von Legitimität und Legalität auftreten könnte oder auch die Legitimität selbst in Zweifel stehen könnte, gilt dann als ausgeschlossen. „*Quod principi placuit legis habet vigorem*"[18], lehrten die Digesten Justinians. Dem entspricht der andere Grundsatz, „*Princeps legibus solutus est*"[19]. Daher galt der Kaiser als Inhaber der absoluten Deutungsmacht über das Recht: „*conditor quam interpretes legum*"[20].

c) Dabei ergab sich beim Anonymus von York im Nebeneffekt eine deutlich interessantere Papsttheorie: Die *Figur* des Papstes hat *drei Körper* (was Kantorowicz ebenso übersah wie die meisten seiner Leser). Analog zur alttestamentlichen Königskritik versteht der königstreue Anonymus den *Papst als Sünder:*

> „Eine solche Person ist nicht einfach, sondern vielfältig, sie vereinigt in sich mehrere Personen. Der Papst vereinigt in sich die Person des obersten *Bischofs*, die des *Menschen* und die eines *Mörders* oder irgendeines anderen Sünders [...]. *Als oberster Bischof* sündigt er nicht, sondern vergibt er die Sünden; als solcher wird er von allen verehrt, geehrt und von niemandem gerichtet. *Als Mensch* dagegen kann er keine Sünden vergeben, auch wenn er selbst nicht sündigt; man muss ihn zwar ehren, aber er kann auch wie jeder andere Mensch gerichtet werden. *Als Sünder* schließlich darf er weder verehrt noch geehrt werden, und *er muss gerichtet werden wie jemand, der unter dem Menschen steht*. Denn es ist nicht gerecht, daß wir gleichzeitig einem Apostel und einem Mörder oder Ehebrecher, dem allerheiligsten Bischofsamt und dem Verbrechen eines Mörders oder Ehebrechers Ehre und Verehrung erweisen"[21].

---

18 Dig. 1,4,1 (Behrends u.a., *Corpus Iuris Civilis II*). Vgl. Inst. 1,2,6 (Behrends u.a., *Corpus Iuris Civilis: Institutionen*).
19 Dig. 1,3,31 (Behrends u.a., *Corpus Iuris Civilis II*). Vgl. dazu auch Inst. 2,17,8: „secundum haec divi quoque Severus et Antoninus saepissime rescripserunt: 'licet enim' inquiunt 'legibus soluti sumus, attamen legibus vivimus'" (Behrends u.a., *Corpus Iuris Civilis: Institutionen*) und Dig. 32, 23: „decet enim tantae maiestati eas servire leges, quibus ipse solutus esse videtur." (Behrends u.a., *Corpus Iuris Civilis V*). Zur Betrachtung dieses Prinzips im mittelalterlichen Byzanz vgl. Simon, „Princeps legibus solutus", 449–492.
20 Cod. I,14,12 (Krueger, *Corpus Iuris Civilis II*); vgl. dazu Gaudemet, „L'empereur interprète du droit", 169–203. Die Konstitutionsprobleme eines ‚absoluten Souveräns' lassen sich an Barbarossa (im Ronkalischen Landfrieden) zeigen. Vgl. das Scholarenprivileg in: Appelt, *Die Urkunden Friedrichs I.*, 36–40, Nr. 243; vgl. zum Landfrieden in: Weiland, *Constitutiones*, 245, Nr. 176.
21 Übersetzung nach Bagliani und Wildermann, *Der Leib des Papstes*, 76 f; im Original: Pellens, *Anonymus*, 6.

Das erscheint so undenkbar, dass es unsichtbar bleibt, ungelesen, unbedacht und anscheinend ‚tabu': Der Papst ist *in persona* auch ‚Mörder oder irgendein Sünder'.[22] Als solcher steht er *unter* dem Menschen und müsse so gerichtet werden. Was Luther später vom Christenmenschen sagen wird, er sei *simul iustus et peccator* findet hier eine verwandte Bestimmung. Auch der Papst bleibt nicht von der *anthropologischen* wie *hamartiologischen* Differenz verschont: als Mensch sowohl Kreatur als auch *gefallene* Kreatur zu sein. Auch der Papst ist ‚unter der Macht der Sünde' – was allerdings eine ungeheure Spannung, einen Machtkonflikt in dieser dreifachen Person impliziert.

d) Den politischen Klimawandel der Neuzeit im Zeichen der Autonomie artikuliert *Kant* – meint man und findet eine überraschende Königstreue. Denn Kant zufolge gilt, wer ein Widerstandsrecht in Anspruch nehme, maße sich die Position des Souveräns an, womit ein *logischer* Widerspruch zum faktischen Souverän entstehe.

> „Wider das gesetzgebende Oberhaupt des Staats giebt es also keinen rechtmäßigen Widerstand des Volks; denn nur durch Unterwerfung unter seinen allgemein-gesetzgebenden Willen ist ein rechtlicher Zustand möglich; also kein Recht des Aufstandes (seditio), noch weniger des Aufruhrs (rebellio), am allerwenigsten gegen ihn als einzelne Person (Monarch) unter dem Vorwande des Mißbrauchs seiner Gewalt (tyrannis) Vergreifung an seiner Person, ja an seinem Leben (monarchomachismus sub specie tyrannicidii). Der geringste Versuch hiezu ist Hochverrath (proditio eminens), und der Verräther dieser Art kann als einer, der sein Vaterland umzubringen versucht (parricida), nicht minder als mit dem Tode bestraft werden. – Der Grund der Pflicht des Volks einen, selbst den für unerträglich ausgegebenen Mißbrauch der obersten Gewalt dennoch zu ertragen liegt darin: dass sein Widerstand wider die höchste Gesetzgebung selbst niemals anders als gesetzwidrig, ja als die ganze gesetzliche Verfassung zernichtend gedacht werden muss. Denn um zu demselben befugt zu sein, müßte ein öffentliches Gesetz vorhanden sein, welches diesen Widerstand des Volks erlaubte, d.i. die oberste Gesetzgebung enthielte eine Bestimmung in sich, nicht die oberste zu sein und das Volk als Unterthan in einem und demselben Urtheile zum Souverän über den zu machen, dem es unterthänig ist; welches sich widerspricht und wovon der Widerspruch durch die Frage alsbald in die Augen fällt: wer denn in diesem Streit zwischen Volk und Souverän Richter sein sollte (denn es sind rechtlich betrachtet doch immer zwei verschiedene moralische Personen); wo sich dann zeigt, daß das erstere es in seiner eigenen Sache sein will."[23]

---

[22] Dass das auch für den König gelten müsste, ist so klar wie es auffällt, dass der Anonymus darauf nicht zu sprechen kommt. Könnte es sein, dass der König nicht ‚Mörder und Sünder' sein kann, da er nicht mordet, sondern legitimerweise tötet (was die Kirche bekanntlich nicht durfte)? Selbst wenn dem so sein sollte, würde der dritte Körper des Königs hier unthematisch gehalten, nicht ohne Grund vermutlich.

[23] Kant, *Metaphysik*, 320. Vgl. Unruh, *Herrschaft der Vernunft*.

e) Die vermeintliche Selbstwidersprüchlichkeit eines Widerstands gegen den Souverän und die rationale Notwendigkeit des Gehorsams gegenüber dem Staatsoberhaupt war Kants These. *Bonhoeffer* korrespondiert auf gut lutherische Weise mit seiner Affirmation staatlicher Ordnung: „Gerade in der Wahrung der strengen Gerechtigkeit, des Schwertamtes, der *Gnadenlosigkeit staatlicher Ordnung*, d. h. der echten Weltlichkeit, wird die Christusherrschaft, d. h. die Herrschaft der Gnade, ganz ernst genommen"[24]. Die Affirmation dieser Gnadenlosigkeit wird nicht allein christologisch begründet (was schon seltsam genug ist), sondern im engeren Sinne auch *theologisch* mit dem Zorn Gottes: „Die Menschwerdung Gottes, d. h. die Menschwerdung der Liebe wäre mißverstanden, wenn man nicht auch die weltlichen Ordnungen der strengen Gerechtigkeit, der Strafe und des Zornes Gottes als Erfüllung dieser menschgewordenen Liebe verstehen wollte"[25]. Das heißt nicht weniger, als dass *um Christi willen* die ‚strenge Gerechtigkeit' in ‚Zorn' und ‚Gnadenlosigkeit' anzuerkennen sei. Die Gründe dieser lutherisch-preußischen Auffassung finden sich in Bonhoeffers Transformation der alten Schöpfungsordnung in seiner ‚Mandatenlehre': der „Lehre von den 4 göttlichen Mandaten: Ehe und Familie, Arbeit, Obrigkeit, Kirche"[26]. Diese Ordnungen seien darin göttlich, „daß sie einen konkreten in der Offenbarung begründeten und bezeugten göttlichen Auftrag und eine göttliche Verheißung haben"[27].

Man wird biblisch-theologisch allerdings fragen können und auch müssen, ob diese ‚Offenbarungsbegründung' von kulturellen Formen wirklich ‚biblisch' ist. Man wird kulturhermeneutisch fragen müssen, ob sie tragfähig ist und warum sie wünschenswert sein sollte. Und systematisch-theologisch ist die Frage, woher Bonhoeffer das weiß, was er als so zwingend behauptet. ‚Weltliche Obrigkeit' jedenfalls war, wie oben erwähnt, in der Geschichte Israels hochumstritten. Und Jesu Anerkennung der religiösen wie politischen Obrigkeiten war überaus zurückhaltend – und hatte im Zweifelsfall klar die Form der Kritik, nicht des radikalen Gehorsams.

Bonhoeffer schreibt in seinem „Theologischen Gutachten: Staat und Kirche" hingegen, dass der Obrigkeit gegenüber Gehorsam gelte, „unabhängig von ihrem Zustandegekommensein"[28]. Deswegen kann Kirche nicht zum Widerstand gegen

---

[24] Bonhoeffer, „Theologisches Gutachten", 559 f. (Herv.; Ph.S.).
[25] Bonhoeffer, „Theologisches Gutachten", 560; Bonhoeffer fährt fort: „[W]enn man nicht das Gebot der Bergpredigt auch im echten staatlichen Handeln gewahrt sähe. Nicht Verchristlichung oder Verkirchlichung der weltlichen Ordnung, sondern ihre Befreiung zur echten Weltlichkeit ist Sinn und Ziel der Christusherrschaft" (ebd.).
[26] Bonhoeffer, „Theologisches Gutachten", 561.
[27] Bonhoeffer, „Theologisches Gutachten", 561.
[28] Bonhoeffer, „Theologisches Gutachten", 517.

die Obrigkeit aufrufen, weil diese einen „göttlichen Charakter"[29] habe. Damit wird eine Differenz gemacht, die später entscheidend werden wird: die von ‚Staat' versus ‚Obrigkeit'. ‚Staat' sei eine eigenmächtige menschliche Begründung der ordnenden Macht des Gemeinwesens ‚von unten'. ‚Obrigkeit' hingegen entzieht sich aller menschlichen Begründung, und eben das mache ihren ‚göttlichen Charakter' aus. „Obrigkeit ist von Gott geordnete Vollmacht, weltliche Herrschaft in göttlicher Autorität auszuüben. Obrigkeit ist Stellvertretung Gottes auf Erden. Sie ist nur von oben her zu verstehen",[30] genauer: die „echte Begründung der Obrigkeit ist also Jesus Christus selbst"[31]. „Obrigkeit geht nicht aus dem Gemeinwesen hervor, sondern sie ordnet das Gemeinwesen von oben her"[32]. Bonhoeffer geht so weit, Obrigkeit als „Engelmacht" zu deuten, um „ihre Stellung zwischen Gott und der Welt" zu bezeichnen.[33] „Die obrigkeitlichen Personen sind Gottes ‚Liturgen', Diener, Stellvertreter (Röm. 13,4)"[34]. So kann er mit Nietzsche formulieren, die Obrigkeit sei in „gewissem Sinne jenseits von Gut und Böse" und verliere auch „durch ein ethisches Versagen noch nicht eo ipso ihre göttliche Würde"[35].

1941 entfaltete Bonhoeffer in seiner Ethik eine eigenartige ‚Katechontik'[36]:

> „Vor dem letzten Sturz in den Abgrund kann nur zweierlei bewahren: das Wunder einer neuen Glaubenserweckung und die Macht, die die Bibel als ‚den Aufhaltenden', κατέχων (2Thess 2,7) bezeichnet, das heißt, die mit starker physischer Kraft ausgerüstete Ordnungsmacht, die sich den in den Abgrund Stürzenden erfolgreich in den Weg stellt [...]. Das ‚Aufhaltende' ist die innerhalb der Geschichte durch Gottes Weltregiment wirksam werdende Gewalt, die dem Bösen seine Grenze setzt. Der ‚Aufhaltende' selbst ist nicht Gott, ist nicht ohne Schuld, aber Gott bedient sich seiner, um die Welt vor dem Zerfall zu bewahren. Der Ort, an dem das Wunder Gottes verkündigt wird, ist die Kirche. Das ‚Aufhaltende' ist staatliche Ordnungsmacht"[37].

Darin tritt geschichtstheologisch verdichtet sein Staatsdenken zutage: der Staat als Ordnungsmacht in Gottes Auftrag. Andererseits spricht er von jenem „Rest an

---

29 Bonhoeffer, „Theologisches Gutachten", 532.
30 Bonhoeffer, „Theologisches Gutachten", 507.
31 Bonhoeffer, „Theologisches Gutachten", 514.
32 Bonhoeffer, „Theologisches Gutachten", 507f.
33 Bonhoeffer, „Theologisches Gutachten", 508.
34 Bonhoeffer, „Theologisches Gutachten", 517.
35 Bonhoeffer, „Theologisches Gutachten", 518.
36 Vgl. Berger, „Die Katechon-Vorstellung", 33–56; auszugsweise in: Rauchensteiner und Seitter, Katechonten, 92–102.
37 Bonhoeffer, Ethik, 122f.

Ordnungsmacht, der sich noch wirksam dem Verfall widersetzt"[38]. Das meint *nicht* die Kirche – auch nicht den einzelnen Widerständigen –, sondern dass die ‚staatliche Ordnungsmacht' auseinandertritt, so dass hier die pervertierte Ordnungsmacht ihrem *Rest* gegenübersteht, vermutlich der militärische Widerstand dagegen. Dieser *Rest* als ‚das Aufhaltende' wird dann im Namen von Gottes Mandat als Gottes Medium begriffen: „Gott bedient sich seiner[,] um die Welt vor dem Zerfall zu bewahren"[39].

f) Ein ‚Meister' ist nichts anderes als ein Relatives, das zum Absoluten ernannt wurde – etwa ein Mensch zum König, oder ein anderer zum Papst, der später womöglich noch zum Heiligen promoviert wird. Insofern manifestiert sich in der Figur des ‚Meisters' das Relative als das Absolute. Während die alttestamentliche Königskritik diese Überhöhung eines Endlichen theozentrisch kritisierte, kann eine ‚Philosophie der Autonomie' wie diejenige Kants noch den politischen Souverän als Figur des immanenten Absoluten überhöhen. Und eine Theologie in lutherischer Tradition wie diejenige Bonhoeffers kann sogar die Obrigkeit als Figur von Gottes Gnaden übertreiben. Das ist deswegen so doppelt bemerkenswert, als sowohl die Autonomiethese Kants wie auch die Christologie Bonhoeffers (von seiner politischen Widerständigkeit abgesehen) gerade gegenläufige Obrigkeits*kritik* erwarten ließen. Figuren der ‚Meister' und die politische Version obrigkeitlicher Souveränität sind – einmal etabliert und Tradition geworden – offenbar hartnäckiger als die philosophischen oder theologischen Widerstandspotentiale.

Das Relative als das Absolute zu übertreiben, ist allerdings hoch ambig. Auf Augustinisch hieße das: Endliches als Unendliches zu übertreiben oder präziser: zu pervertieren. Wenn es gut geht, wehrt sich der so gemachte Meister mit allen Mitteln gegen diese Übertreibung – wie Mose und die Propheten. Aber wer kann schon solch einer Ernennung widerstehen? So gewinnt meist das Meisterbegehren, noch im Entzug des Meisters.

Auf diesem Hintergrund ist die kaisertreue Papstkritik des Anonymus von York theologisch wie politisch brisant, allemal brisanter als das übliche Deutungsmuster der ‚zwei Körper'. Und es ist nicht weniger brisant, wenn die papstkritische Kaisertreue des Anonymus zum kulturwissenschaftlichen Paradigma avanciert. Theologisch gesagt: Der Meister ist nicht nur Relatives, das zum Absoluten ernannt wurde, er bleibt auch ‚Mörder und Sünder'. Alle Meister also sind im Grunde ‚Mörder und Sünder' – alle, bis auf einen?

---

[38] Bonhoeffer, *Ethik*, 123.
[39] Bonhoeffer, *Ethik*, 123; vgl. Stoellger, „‚Ich aber sage euch'", 123–151.

g) Die Überhöhung des Relativen ins Absolute ‚von unten' gilt theologisch als ‚Insubordination' oder ‚Perversion'. Aber – der Übergang ‚des Absoluten ins Relative', also ‚von oben', gilt als legitim (Offenbarung), mehr noch als *grundlegend* für das Judentum in den Figuren der Tora und des Tempels, wie für das Christentum in der Inkarnation. Wenn also der Absolute zum Relativen wird – ist das erwünscht und begrüßt. Das wäre die Urszene der theologisch einzig legitimen Koinzidenz von Absolutem und Relativem. Es hat nur das Risiko wie die Nebenwirkung: der Relative wird zum Absoluten gemacht: Jesus zum Sohn Gottes *ernannt*.

Was so religionskritisch klingt, ist allerdings solenne Theologie, wie sie von Eberhard Jüngel vertreten wird. Ist doch seine christologische Grundformel die der „Identifikation Gottes mit dem Menschen Jesus [...], die sich darin ausspricht, daß dieser Mensch *Sohn Gottes* genannt zu werden verdient. Denn in dieser Identifikation vollzieht sich das Sein Gottes als Liebe."[40] Dass diese Formulierung kein Einzelfall ist, belegt beispielsweise die folgende Variante: Das „Ereignis der Auferweckung" werde in der ältesten Überlieferung – die Jüngel hier affirmativ anführt – „als Offenbarung der Gottessohnschaft Jesu, ja sogar als das Ereignis, in dem Jesus zum Sohn Gottes zum Kyrios und Christus ‚gemacht' bzw. ‚definiert' wird, verstanden (Röm 1,4; 10,9; Apg 2,36)"[41]. Und er verweist nicht zufällig auf die einschlägige Formulierung aus Apg 2,36: „So wisse nun das ganze Haus Israel gewiss, dass Gott diesen Jesus, den ihr gekreuzigt habt, zum Herrn und Christus gemacht hat" (καὶ κύριον αὐτὸν καὶ χριστὸν ἐποίησεν ὁ θεός, τοῦτον τὸν Ἰησοῦν ὃν ὑμεῖς ἐσταυρώσατε).

Die retrospektive Deutung des Gekreuzigten als Inkarnierter, also die retrospektive Verlängerung der Passionsgeschichte in die ‚ewige Sohnschaft' bis hinein in die immanente Trinität führt zu einer Eskalation der Deutung, die sich metaphysisch verselbständigen kann. Der Relative schlechthin, *der* ‚schlechthin Abhängige', der Gekreuzigte, wird zur Figur des Absoluten gemacht.

Das Ambige daran ist die Überhöhung bis zur Übertreibung – was im Grenzwert dazu führen kann, die Auferstehung als Revokation der Passion misszuverstehen oder schon Passion als Inthronisation (Johannes). Ist doch die Pointe der Passion vielmehr die Deeskalation Gottes, in der Relativierung des Absoluten, seiner abgründigen Erniedrigung im Kreuz. Die ganze Ambivalenz tritt in dieser Differenz zutage: Ist die Christologie von einer Theorie des Absoluten prästabilisiert und dann lediglich eine ‚Repräsentation' Gottes? Damit würde das Absolute in aller Niedrigkeit doch wieder so perfektioniert, dass es auch noch

---

40 Jüngel, *Gott als Geheimnis der Welt*, 447.
41 Jüngel, „Zur dogmatischen Bedeutung", 238.

capax finiti (und *mortis*) sei. Alle Ohnmacht des Gekreuzigten wäre nur noch die inklusive Steigerung der vorgängigen Allmacht. Oder ist die Christologie in ihrer Zuspitzung als Kreuzestheologie gerade der Abbau solcher Eskalationen des Gottdenkens? Wer hier ein Sowohl-Als auch verträte, würde doch wieder einer Aufhebung der Differenz im Zeichen einer weiteren Eskalation das Wort reden. Wer diese Differenz schärft, dem bleibt vermutlich nur der Abschied von *der* Figur religiösen und theoretischen Begehrens: einer perfektiblen Meisterfigur.

h) Diese Meisterfigur ist die Urszene der immer noch größeren Omnipotenz: bei noch so großer Ohnmacht eine immer noch größere Macht und bei noch so großer Niedrigkeit eine immer noch größere Hoheit zu begehren und zu behaupten. Anselms Denkregel des *quo nihil maius cogitari possit* (bis zum *maius quam cogitari possit*) folgt der Logik von Gottes Eskalationen, wie sie Blumenberg beschrieb und diskret dekonstruierte.

Gott als einzig legitimer absoluter Souverän, als Meister aller Meister – führt zu einer Passionslosigkeit, oder aber zu Vorstellung, als wäre Gottes einzige Passion die seiner Eskalation ins Absolute. ‚Christus als das eine Wort Gottes', dem allein man zu vertrauen und zu gehorchen habe, wie Barmen I formuliert, richtet sich gerade gegen solche Souveränitätsfantasien, wie sie theopolitisch betrieben wurden. Nur wiederholt sich in der Gegenbesetzung das Problem, das gelöst werden sollte: Gegen einen falschen Absoluten hilft nur der wahre Absolute? Dann würde im Gottesbegriff wiederholt und verdichtet, was als politisches Problem gelöst werden sollte. Das ist nur eine Problemverschiebung und Verfestigung. Die *Funktion* oder (mit Blumenberg) *Position* des Absoluten provoziert ewige *Wiedergänger*.

Gegen die allzu menschlichen, nur zu theologischen Souveränitäts*sehnsüchte* hilft ein theologischer *Entzug:* die Passion als *Entlastung vom Absoluten*.[42] Angesichts von ‚Gottes Eskalationen' bedarf es gegen das Begehren nach Meistern offenbar immer wieder der Deeskalation. Nur, wie man diese Deeskalationen beschreiben und betreiben könnte, ohne doch wieder De-Eskalationen zu wiederholen, bleibt ein Problem. Was wären probate Therapeutika gegen das eskalierte Begehren nach dem Meister?

Vakanz scheint schwer erträglich und provoziert Neubesetzungen dieser Position. Umbesetzungen, Schubumkehr, Autonomie, Selbstsorge oder Selbst-Meisterschaft, das absolute Subjekt oder die Ästhetik der Existenz, Delegation, infinite Delegation als Aufschub ad infinitum, Pluralisierung bis zur infiniten (und seriellen) Individualität? Figuren des Absoluten zerfallen in der Pluralisierung. Aber – wäre dann das Kontingente, das Plurale oder das Relative doch

---

42 Vgl. Stoellger, „Die Passion als ‚Entlastung vom Absoluten'", 225–257.

wieder ein Absolutes: Absolut sei, dass alles relativ sei? Und daher das Relative absolut?

3 Das Relative als das Absolute?

Die Hintergrundmusik des Bisherigen war die vermeintliche Alternative zweier Deutungsmuster bzw. einer eingefleischten Denkgewohnheit: Vom Absoluten aus zu denken; oder im Grunde alles für relativ zu halten.

‚Es gibt das Absolute', sei es das Subjekt oder ‚der große Andere' oder wer oder was auch immer. Und wenn es das *noch* nicht gäbe, muss man es erfinden, wie das unmittelbare Selbstbewusstsein oder den Begriff des Absoluten. Und wer glaubt, das gäbe es nicht, hat es nur noch nicht erkannt oder wahrgenommen. Der Wille zum Absoluten greift zur Not auch zur Gewalt. Dann wird das Denken gezwungen, die Notwendigkeit des Begriffs des Absoluten zu erkennen, oder andernorts das unfehlbare unmittelbare Selbstbewusstsein und sein Abhängigkeitsgefühl zu erkennen. Und wer das nicht erkennt – gehört nicht zur Gemeinschaft der Denkenden.

Im Unterschied dazu ist manche Theologie und Phänomenologie deutlich kontingenztoleranter: Es wird die Kontingenz des Gegebenen, Sichzeigenden zugestanden und nicht eine absolute Gabe oder Gabe des Absoluten behauptet und argumentativ erzwungen. Dass sich an dieser Kontingenztoleranz die Geister scheiden in Theologie wie Philosophie, ist klar. Eine Apologetik oder natürliche Theologie kann von der Notwendigkeit nicht lassen, dem *ens necessarium* des absoluten Meisters.

Die vermeintliche Alternative lautet: Alles ist relativ, was denn sonst.[43] Die Liquidierung des Absoluten, seine Verflüssigung im Zeichen der Quecksilbrigkeit allen Seins, die Dekonstruktion und Dissemination, der *cultural turn*, alles sei kulturrelativ, findet als Echo in religiösen Belangen, alles sei doch individuell. Für die meisten versteht sich dann von selbst, dass ‚alles relativ' ist: Religion kulturrelativ, historisch, perspektivisch, milieuspezifisch, diskursrelativ etc.

Die gängige Schubumkehr universaler Relativierung ist kulturell, sozial, historisch oder vermeintlich auch ontologisch (weil physikalisch) die dominante Selbstverständlichkeit. Nur hat die Omnirelativität einen paradoxen Nebeneffekt: das Relative als das neue Absolute zu verstehen. Alles ist relativ – nur dieser Grundsatz nicht? Die hegemoniale Voraussetzung der Omni-Relativität ist bemerkenswert: der Grundsatz gilt so fraglos, ist also derart deutungsmächtig, dass

---

43 Vgl. Fuhrmann-Koch und Mohr „Die Sterne tanzen", 6–15.

er glauben lässt und macht, es sei tatsächlich alles so relativ – und uns verkennen lässt, dass dieser Grundsatz selbst dann als ‚absolut' gültig anerkannt wird.

‚Wahrheit ist Interpretation', *auch nur* Interpretation, lautet die bekannte Paradoxierung Nietzsches. Das gilt dann in der Regel als performativ inkonsistent und daher als unwahr. Denn der Satz über die Interpretativität von Wahrheit gebe sich selbst als generelle Behauptung aus, nicht als verhandelbare Interpretation. Der Satz widerlege in seiner Form, was er als Inhalt behauptet. Übertragen auf die ‚Omni-Relativität' gälte dann dasselbe: Die gängige Prämisse, alles sei relativ und es gebe kein Absolutes, ist ‚autodestruktiv' in ihrer Inkonsistenz.

Allerdings – kann man zweifeln, ob Nietzsche so ‚dumm' war, wie in der gängigen Widerlegung angenommen wird. Eine These, die so offensichtlich performativ inkonsistent ist, könnte kalkuliert sein: *Noch in der generellen Behauptung der Omnirelativität von Wahrheit wird die Unhaltbarkeit dieser generellen Behauptung destruiert.* Damit würde nicht nur etwas gesagt, sondern gezeigt (epideiktisch, deiktisch): es wird *ad occulos* demonstriert, dass solch eine ‚generelle Wahrheit' unsagbar ist. Im performativen Selbstwiderspruch bestätigte sich dann das Gesagte im Modus des Zeigens.[44]

Die Konsequenz ist unbehaglich: Der Ort der absoluten Wahrheit bleibt leer, unbesetzt, noch nicht einmal durch eine generelle Negation besetzbar – die sich in ihrer selbstwidersprüchlichen Generalisierung selbst untergräbt. Wer hier zu schnell an die ‚leere Bundeslade' denkt, oder den leeren Thron oder die Kipporet, hätte mit einem nur ‚wiedererkennenden Verstehen' die Befremdung zu schnell inkludiert und überwältigt.

Viele könnten meinen, für die Theologie sei solch eine Vakanz nicht nur unbehaglich, sondern unerträglich. Allerdings gälte das nur dann, wenn man einen theistischen Gottesbegriff voraussetzte (sei es platonisierend, sei es aristotelistisch); oder wenn man eine metaphysische oder subjektmetaphysische Form der Theorie des Absoluten voraussetzte. Für solche Denkformen ist die Vakanz des Absoluten vielleicht unerträglich; für andere mitnichten. Sowenig Macht ‚absolut' begriffen werden kann, sowenig also ‚Allmacht' ein religiös oder theologisch notwendiges Konzept ist, sowenig muss man Wahrheit als ‚absolut' begreifen. Sie kann allemal besser als perspektivisch begriffen werden.[45]

Nur ist mit einer Azentrizität (Derrida) oder leeren Mitte (Lefort) wenig gewonnen. Die Reflexionsfiguren des negativen Absoluten oder der Negation des Absoluten bis zur radikalen Negativität (Mersch) sind von Blumenberg in ihrer Aporetik durchreflektiert worden: Die unbesetzte Funktionsstelle behält ihre

---

44 Vgl. zur Sache Stoellger, „Interpretation zwischen Wirklichkeit und Konstruktion", 93–128.
45 Vgl. Dalferth und Stoellger, *Wahrheit in Perspektiven*.

Gravitationskraft für neue Besetzungen. Oder anders: Sie zieht neue Besetzungen auf sich, provoziert das Begehren umso mehr. Religionstheoretisch ist das ebenso bekannt wie politisch oder ästhetisch: Die neuen Meister kommen, um die tradierten Orte zu bespielen.

4 No Need of A Master

Das Begehren nach ‚Meistern' ist nicht neu oder innovativ, sondern so alt, dass man meinen könnte, ‚es riecht schon'. Ohne von ‚anthropologischen Konstanten' sprechen zu wollen, scheint es sich um eine ebenso vielgestaltige wie verbreitete Grundfigur sozialer Beziehungen zu handeln. Daher sind die Ökonomien, also Bewirtschaftungsformen des Meisterbegehrens auch so allgegenwärtig wie Gott selbst.

Der Meister aller Meister, Moses selber, wenn auch wider Willen, das Königtum, die religiöse Meisterlust im Umgang mit Jesus, oder die Genese von Amt und Hierarchie in den ‚Kirchen der alten Christenheit'. Mit ‚expliziter' politischer Theorie geladen wird dieses Begehren in Dionysios Areopagitas ‚Himmlischen Hierarchien', der Leittheorie für einen militärisch strukturierten Himmel wie seiner Entsprechung in den kirchlichen Hierarchien. Theologisch ‚tiefergelegt' wird das in der bei manchen bis heute beliebten Erfindung der ‚Schöpfungsordnung' als Legitimierung von Herrschaftsverhältnissen, Diskriminierungen und Exklusionen. Selbst ein preußischer Offizier wie Bonhoeffer hing an seiner Meisterdeutung der Mandatenlehre und deren antidemokratischen Implikationen.

Das Meisterbegehren sucht Entlastung durch Delegation. Es verschärft sich angesichts von Überkomplexität, Ausdifferenzierung, Unübersichtlichkeit bis zur Undurchsichtigkeit. Wenn sich die Entlastung *vom* Absoluten als keineswegs so entlastend herausstellt, wenn das Relative als das neue Absolute als Überforderung wirkt, alles allzu relativ, dann ist nur zu verständlich, dass neue Figuren des Absoluten ernannt werden, ohne dass ein Verstehen dieser Dynamik Einverständnis voraussetzen oder anstreben müsste.

Auch eine sich selbst durchsichtige Subjektivität bleibt ein nostalgisches Therapeutikum gegenüber ‚externalisierten' Meistern. Im theologischen Kontext ist exemplarisch Bultmanns Pathos der ständig immer wieder neuen ‚Entscheidung' zur Eigentlichkeit eine leer laufende Subjektivität. Als wäre das Subjekt ‚Herr im eigenen Haus'. Die Subjektivitätsmetaphysik wirkt theologisch wie politisch allzu transparent: eine Subjektivität der Selbstkontrolle und der Selbstüberwachung. Ob der Andere zum Meister ernannt wird oder im Gegenzug man selbst in emphatischer Autonomie – diese Gegenbesetzung ähnelt einander auffällig.

Das Begehren nach Meistern bleibt regressiv. Sollte doch der ‚Meister' als Leiter oder Geländer allenfalls vorübergehend genutzt und möglichst bald als unnütz zurückgelassen werden. Würde man am Meister hängen, würde man hängen bleiben am Vorübergänglichen. Wer sich auf Dauer an Übergangsobjekte klammert, hat offenbar ein Problem.

So erscheint weder deskriptiv noch normativ naheliegend, das neue Meisterbegehren als ‚*political awakening*' zu deuten. ‚Ich würde lieber nicht' – den mittlerweile schon wieder müde werdenden Neu-Populismus als Erwachen des Politischen begreifen, als politische Erweckungsbewegung. So zu deuten, ist nicht nur in Gefahr einer politisch-theologischen Überhöhung einer politischen wie religiösen Ökonomie, und es ist nicht nur theologisch in Gefahr einer pneumatologischen Überqualifizierung des Willens zur Macht, sondern es folgt einer Verunendlichung des Endlichen, der Übertreibung eines Orientierungsbedarfs als Meisterbegehren, als ginge es darin um das Transzendenzbegehren. Der ‚Schritt zurück' in populistische Pathospolitik ist allenfalls unterkomplex. Im religiösen Kontext ist diese Unterkomplexität allerdings auch beliebt: so lange und hartnäckig zu vereinfachen, bis eine schwarz/weiß-Differenz und moralische Eindeutigkeit entsteht.

Ich würde es normativ gesehen vorziehen, auf neue Meister zu verzichten. Denn Meisterverhältnisse sind Abhängigkeits- und Unterwerfungsverhältnisse. Auch manche Theologie hat die lustvollen Unterwerfungen seit langem bewirtschaftet und damit Theologiegeschichte gemacht. Und nicht zuletzt protestantische Theologien scheinen anfällig für ‚Meister-Verhältnisse' zu sein. Exemplarisch etwa Manfred Josuttis, der je später desto vehementer versucht hat, dieses Meisterbegehren zu bespielen mit dem Motto ‚Ego eimi'. Selbst bei denen, die die Autonomie so liberal feiern, steht es nicht viel anders in dieser Personalisierung und Verkörperungslust.

Im katholischen Kontext ist immer schon und ohnehin klar, wer das Sagen hat, und über das Sagen wie Gesagte entscheidet im Zweifel das Heilige Officium. Also sind Herrschafts- und Deutungsmachtverhältnisse geklärt, fraglos – auf ewig. Protestanten hingegen haben diese Klarheit und Eindeutigkeit nicht, weder kirchlich noch theologisch. Umso verständlicher, dass die poly- oder azentrischen Organisationsverhältnisse des Protestantismus ‚blass' aussehen im öffentlichen Wettkampf um die markantesten Meister.

Darauf allerdings zu reagieren mit dem Motto ‚*Let's go public, theology!*', ist für die einen so attraktiv, wie für die anderen etwas durchsichtig. In laizistischen Kontexten oder in solchen der Religionsunterdrückung ist der Wille zur Öffentlichkeit sinnvoll. Aber in Deutschland, in der Berliner Republik zumal? Da klingt das eher nach neuem Deutungsmachtbegehren der Religion. Als suchten Religionsvertreter die Nähe der Mächtigen, um sich in deren Schatten zu sonnen. Die politische Sportart der Produktion von Meistern und die religiöse der ‚Figuration heiligen Personals'[46] passen gut zueinander.

Postskriptum: Das Absolute und das *Mediale*

Wie wäre der christliche Glaube *ohne Absolutes* zu verstehen? Ohne Meisterbegehren? Und kirchliche Praxis ohne die Figuration heiligen Personals? Eine Christologie jenseits der Unterwerfungsverhältnisse und damit auch jenseits einer divinen Souveränität gegen die der Welt oder gar die diabolische? Eine Kirchenpolitik ohne Charismaprätention der Kirchenführer? Ein Glaube ohne infallible und absolute Gewissheit?

Mit dem Absoluten wird eine Differenz gemacht: alles Relative und das Absolute (in schlechter Unendlichkeit), und um das erfolgreich zu steuern, wird das Absolute inklusiv expandiert (Universalismus als Inklusivismus, der den infernalen Rest produziert). Das Absolute evoziert allerdings einen ‚Zwischenraum' mit dem Problem der Differenz und Distanz – was *Medien* des Absoluten evoziert: den himmlischen Hofstaat, die Engel, alle möglichen Medien, die dazwischentreten: Boten, Repräsentanten etc. Indirektheit, Mittelbarkeit. Und je mehr Medien dazwischentreten, desto mehr Unmittelbarkeitsbegehren.[47] Das Begehren nach Unmittelbarkeit und Eigentlichkeit verkennt Mittelbarkeit, Medialität, Indirektheit.

Zwischen Absolutem und Relativem operiert das *weder* Absolute *noch* nur Relative, genauer gesagt: das Nichtbeliebige und Nicht-Alternativlose, eine bestimmte Form der Kontingenz, Figuren des Dritten etwa. Statt dem Deutungsmuster von ‚Meister und Jüngern' zu folgen, empfiehlt sich womöglich ein Sinn für nicht-beliebige Kontingenzen, für mediale Operationen in den lateralen Zwischenlagen der Sozialität: also eine Aufmerksamkeit für feine Differenzen der Medialität.

Nur fragt sich dann: *welche* Medienpraktiken und *in welchem Geist?* Organisations- und Ordnungsverfahren, die ‚durchrechnen', was geht und was nicht? Nur was sich kirchenpolitisch rechnet, hat Bestand und Daseinsrecht? Jenseits

---

46 Vgl. Stoellger, „Figuration und Funktion", 212; Stoellger, „Migration des Heiligen und heilige Migranten", 263; Stoellger, „Anthropologie der Figuration", 251–299.
47 Zur ‚nahen Gnade' in der Mystik wie auch bei Luther (De libertate): Gottunmittelbarkeit als Grundfigur religiösen Begehrens vgl. Hamm, „Die ‚nahe Gnade'". Vgl. dazu auch schon in den Psalmen: Hartenstein, *Das Angesicht JHWHs*.

von Wort oder Bild also die Herrschaft der ‚Zahl', im Grunde eine algorithmische Eschatologie (oder Apokalyptik)? Oder auf der medialen Oberfläche dann kirchlicher Populismus mit der Suche nach einem charismatischen Retter?

Am Ende von Blumenbergs Arbeit am Höhlenmythos findet sich eine *theopolitische Parabel*. „So muß auch im finalen Höhlengleichnis eine Rückkehr in eine Höhle stattfinden"[48], notiert er gegen Ende seiner phänomenologischen Kulturtheorie, den ‚Höhlenausgängen'. Im Schlusskapitel ‚Vorgaben für einen letzten Höhlenentwurf' endet er mit einer indirekten Mitteilung. Er zitiert schlicht unter dem Titel ‚Ein anderer Mythos' eine rabbinische Parabel auf die Grenzen der Mystik – von einer glühenden, feurigen Mystik über eine göttlich auferlegte Kontemplation als Wende in die *vita activa*:

> „Ein anderer Mythos
> Einst saßen R. Jehuda, R. Jose und R. Simon beisammen, und der Proselytenabkömmling Jehuda war unter ihnen. Da begann R. Jehuda und sprach: Wie schön sind doch die Werke dieser Nation [sc. der Römer]! Sie haben Straßen angelegt, Brücken gebaut und Bäder errichtet. R. Jose schwieg. Darauf nahm R. Simon b. Johaj das Wort und sprach: Alles, was sie errichtet haben, geschah nur in ihrem eigenen Interesse. Sie haben Straßen angelegt, um da Huren zu setzen, Bäder errichtet zu ihrem Behagen, Brücken gebaut, um Zoll zu erheben. Der Proselytenabkömmling Jehuda erzählte ihr Gespräch weiter, und es wurde der Regierung bekannt. Diese beschloß dann: Jehuda, der gelobt hat, soll erhoben werden, Jose, der geschwiegen hat, soll nach Sepphoris verbannt werden, und Simon, der geschmäht hat, soll hingerichtet werden. Da ging er hin und verbarg sich mit seinem Sohne im Lehrhause; dahin brachte ihnen seine Frau täglich Brot und einen Krug Wasser, und sie speisten. Als aber [die Verfolgung] verschärft wurde, sprach er zu seinem Sohne: Frauen sind leichtsinnig; wenn man sie quält, könnte sie uns verraten. Hierauf gingen sie und versteckten sich in einer Höhle. Da geschah ihnen ein Wunder und es wurde für sie ein Johannisbrotbaum und eine Quelle erschaffen. Sie zogen die Kleider aus, setzten sich bis zum Halse in den Sand, und studierten den ganzen Tag; zur Zeit des Gebetes kleideten sie sich an, bedeckten sich und verrichteten das Gebet, nachher aber zogen sie die Kleider wieder aus, damit sie nicht verschleißen. Nachdem sie zwölf Jahre in dieser Höhle gesessen hatten, kam Elijahu, stellte sich an den Eingang der Höhle und sprach: Wer verkündet dem Sohne Johajs, dass der Kaiser gestorben und sein Befehl aufgehoben ist? Darauf kamen sie heraus und sahen Leute pflügen und säen. Da sprach er: *Sie lassen das ewige Leben und befassen sich mit dem zeitlichen Leben.* Jeder Ort, auf den sie ihre Augen richteten, ging sofort in Flammen auf. Da ertönte eine Hallstimme und sprach zu ihnen: Seid ihr herausgekommen, um meine Welt zu zerstören? Kehret in euere Höhle zurück. Darauf kehrten sie zurück und saßen da ein Jahr von zwölf Monaten. Sodann sprachen sie: Das Strafgericht der Frevler in der Hölle dauert ja nur zwölf Monate. Da ertönte eine Hallstimme und sprach: Verlasset euere Höhle! Da kamen

---

48 Blumenberg, *Höhlenausgänge*, 812.

sie heraus. Überall, wo R. Elehzar schlug, heilte R. Simon. Er sprach zu ihm: Mein Sohn, *die Welt hat an mir und dir genug.*"[49]

Als offenes Ende einer Kulturphilosophie ist diese Fabel symptomatisch und emblematisch: Wenn Kultur sich in Höhlen entwickelt und die Höhle zur Grundmetapher der Kultur wird, ist die Höhlenzeit der feurigen Mystiker Einübung in die Endlichkeit: eine Kultivierung des überhitzten Begehrens, über die Kultur hinaus zu kommen. Denn sonst würde die Welt unter dem Blick des Begehrens verbrennen. „*Philosophie* wäre dann auch die ‚Disziplin', von dem zu reden, was man sich nicht mehr leisten kann", und „von dem zu reden, was man sich zumuten muß an Konzession und Kontraktion"[50]. Der Theologie könnte diese Disziplin nur zum Besten dienen, zumal gegenüber neuen Meisterbegehren.

Bibliographie

Appelt, Heinrich, Hg. *Die Urkunden Friedrichs I.: 1158–1167*. Hannover: Hahnsche Buchhandlung, 1979.

Arendt, Hannah. *Macht und Gewalt*, übers. v. Gisela Uellenberg, 17. Aufl. München: Piper, 2006.

Bagliani, Agostino Paravicini, und Wildermann, Ansgar. *Der Leib des Papstes: Eine Theologie der Hinfälligkeit*. München: C.H. Beck, 1997.

Bauke-Ruegg, Jan. *Die Allmacht Gottes: Systematisch-theologische Erwägungen zwischen Metaphysik, Postmoderne und Poesie*. Berlin: De Gruyter, 1998.

Behrends, Okko; Knütel, Rolf; Kupisch, Berthold, und Seiler, Hans Hermann, Hg., *Corpus Iuris Civilis II. Digesten 1–10: Text und Übersetzung*. Heidelberg: C.F. Müller, 1995.

Behrends, Okko; Knütel, Rolf; Kupisch, Berthold, und Seiler, Hans Hermann. Hg., *Corpus Iuris Civilis. Die Institutionen: Text und Übersetzung*, 3. Aufl. Heidelberg: C.F. Müller, 2007.

Behrends, Okko; Knütel, Rolf; Kupisch, Berthold, und Seiler, Hans Hermann, Hg., *Corpus Iuris Civilis V. Digesten 28–34: Text und Übersetzung*. Heidelberg: C.F. Müller, 2012.

Berger, Martin. „Die Katechon-Vorstellung 2Thess 2,6f: Dietrich Bonhoeffers Interpretation im Kontext der Rezeptionsgeschichte", *Protokolle zur Bibel* 5, Nr. 1 (1996): 33–56.

Blumenberg, Hans. *Matthäuspassion*, 9. Aufl. Frankfurt a. M.: Suhrkamp, 1988.

Blumenberg, Hans. *Höhlenausgänge*, 3. Aufl. Frankfurt a. M.: Suhrkamp, 2007.

Bonhoeffer, Dietrich. *Ethik*, hg. v. Ilse Tödt, Heinz Eduard Tödt, Ernst Feil und Clifford Green. München: Chr. Kaiser, 1992.

Bonhoeffer, Dietrich. „Theologisches Gutachten. Staat und Kirche", In *Konspiration und Haft*, hg. v. Jørgen Glenthøj, Ulrich Kabitz und Wolf Krötke, 505–593. München: Chr. Kaiser, 1996.

---

49 Blumenberg, *Höhlenausgänge*, 819 f.; Blumenberg nennt als Quelle Goldschmidt, *Der babylonische Talmud*, Traktat Shabbat II,6 (Herv.; Ph.S).

50 Blumenberg, *Höhlenausgänge*, 810.

Dalferth, Ingolf U. und Stoellger, Philipp, Hg. *Wahrheit in Perspektiven: Probleme einer offenen Konstellation*. Tübingen: Mohr Siebeck, 2004.
Düttmann, Alexander G. *Philosophie der Übertreibung*, 2. Aufl. Frankfurt a. M.: Suhrkamp, 2004.
Fuhrmann-Koch, Marietta und Mohr, Mirjam. „Die Sterne tanzen: Kontrollierte Pluralität: Im Gespräch mit Jana Zaumseil und Philipp Stoellger. Interview geführt v. Marietta Fuhrmann-Koch und Mirjam Mohr", *Ruperto Carola* 14 (2019): 6 – 15
Gaudemet, Jean. „L'empereur interprète du droit", in *Festschrift für Ernst Rabel*, Bd. 2, *Geschichte der antiken Rechte und allgemeine Rechtslehre*, hg. v. Wolfgang Kunkel und Hans J. Wolff, 169 – 203. Tübingen: Mohr Siebeck, 1954.
Goldschmidt, Lazarus. *Der babylonische Talmud: Berakoth, Mishna Zeraim, Shabbat*. Königstein i.Ts.: Jüdischer Verlag, 1980.
Hamm, Berndt. „Die ‚nahe Gnade' – innovative Züge der spätmittelalterlichen Theologie und Frömmigkeit", In *„Herbst des Mittelalters"? Fragen zur Bewertung des 14. und 15. Jahrhunderts*, hg. v. Jan A. Aertsen und Martin Pickavé, 541 – 557. Berlin/New York: de Gruyter, 2004.
Hartenstein, Friedhelm. *Das Angesicht JHWHs. Studien zu seinem höfischen und kultischen Bedeutungshintergrund in den Psalmen und in Exodus 32 – 34*. Tübingen: Mohr Siebeck, 2008.
von Hayek, Friedrich A. „Ungleichheit ist nötig: Interview mit Stefan Baron", *Wirtschaftswoche* 11 (6. März 1981): 3.
Jüngel, Eberhard. „Zur dogmatischen Bedeutung der Frage nach dem historischen Jesus", In *Wertlose Wahrheit: Zur Identität und Relevanz des christlichen Glaubens: Theologische Erörterungen*, Bd. 3, Eberhard Jüngel. München: Chr. Kaiser, 1990.
Jüngel, Eberhard. *Gott als Geheimnis der Welt: Zur Begründung der Theologie des Gekreuzigten im Streit zwischen Theismus und Atheismus*, 8. Aufl. Tübingen: Mohr Siebeck, 2010.
Kant, Immanuel. *Die Metaphysik der Sitten*. Berlin: Reimer, 1906.
Krueger, Paul, Hg. *Corpus Iuris Civilis II: Codex Iustinianus*. Berlin: Weidmann, 1888.
Luther, Martin. „Die Disputation de homine: 1536", In *Kritische Gesamtausgabe*, Bd. 39,1, Martin Luther, hg. v. Heinrich Hermelink. Weimar: Hermann Böhlau Nachfolger, 1926.
Pellens, Karl, Hg. *Die Texte des Normannischen Anonymus*. Wiesbaden: Steiner, 1966.
Rauchensteiner, Meinhard, und Seitter, Walter, Hg., *Katechonten: Den Untergang aufhalten*. Berlin: Syndikat, 2001.
Schönborn, Christoph. *Ziel oder Zufall? Schöpfung und Evolution aus der Sicht eines vernünftigen Glaubens*. Freiburg i.Br.: Herder, 2007.
Schui, Herbert. „Rechtsextremismus und totaler Markt: Auf der Suche nach gesellschaftlicher Klebmasse für den entfesselten Kapitalismus", In *Neoliberalismus und Rechtsextremismus in Europa: Zusammenhänge – Widersprüche – Gegenstrategien*, hg. v. Peter Bathke und Susanne Spindler, 48 – 59. Berlin: Karl Dietz Verlag, 2006.
Simon, Dieter. „Princeps legibus solutus: Die Stellung des byzantinischen Kaisers zum Gesetz", In *Gedächtnisschrift für Wolfgang Kunkel*, hg. v. Dieter Nörr und Dieter Simon, 449 – 492. Frankfurt a. M.: Vittorio Klostermann, 1984.
Stegmaier, Werner. *Philosophie der Orientierung*. Berlin: De Gruyter, 2008.
Stoellger, Philipp. „Interpretation zwischen Wirklichkeit und Konstruktion: Konstruktionistische Interpretationstheorie als Antwort auf konstruktivistische Übertreibungen", In

Die Wirklichkeit als Interpretationskonstrukt? Herausforderungen konstruktivistischer Ansätze für die Theologie, hg. v. Andreas Klein und Ulrich H.J. Körtner, 93–128. Neukirchen-Vluyn: Neukirchener Verlag, 2011.

Stoellger, Philipp. „Die Passion als ‚Entlastung vom Absoluten': Negative Christologie im Zeichen der Tränen Gottes", In *Permanentes Provisorium: Hans Blumenbergs Umwege*, hg. v. Michael Heidgen, Matthias Koch und Christian Köhler, 225–257. München: Fink, 2015.

Stoellger, Philipp. „Figuration und Funktion ‚un/heiligen Personals': Zur Figurenlehre medialer Anthropologie", In *Mediale Anthropologie*, hg. v. Christiane Voss und Lorenz Engell, 201–250. München: Fink, 2015.

Stoellger, Philipp. „Migration des Heiligen und heilige Migranten, oder: Machen Medien Menschen – heilig?", In *Medien des Heiligen*, hg. v. Friedrich Balke, Bernhard Siegert und Joseph Vogl, 176–188. Paderborn: Fink, 2015.

Stoellger, Philipp. „‚Ich aber sage euch, dass ihr nicht widerstehen sollt dem Übel …'? Gründe und Ungründe des Widerstandsrechts im Anschluss an Bonhoeffer", In *Bonhoeffers Friedensgedanke und Frieden in Ostasien: The 2nd Heidelberg University – Seoul Theological University International Academic Conference*, hg. v. Suk-Sung Yu, Jürgen Moltmann, Michael Welker, Johannes Eurich und Phillip Stoellger, 123–151. Seoul: Seoul Theological University, 2016.

Stoellger, Philipp. „Verständigung mit Fremdem: Zur Hermeneutik der Differenz ohne Konsens", In *Verstehen und Verständigung: Intermediale, multimodale und interkulturelle Aspekte von Kommunikation und Ästhetik*, hg. v. Klaus Sachs-Hombach, 164–193. Köln: Herbert von Halem Verlag, 2016.

Stoellger, Philipp, und Kumlehn, Martina, Hg. *Wortmacht/Machtwort: Deutungsmachtkonflikte in und um Religion*. Würzburg: Königshausen & Neumann, 2017.

Stoellger, Philipp. „Anthropologie der Figuration: Konfigurationen von Mensch und Medium zwischen De- und Transfiguration", In *Figurationen des Menschen: Studien zur Medienanthropologie*, hg. v. Philipp Stoellger, 251–299. Würzburg: Königshausen & Neumann, 2019.

Stoellger, Philipp, Hg., *Figurationen des Menschen: Studien zur Medienanthropologie*. Würzburg: Königshausen & Neumann, 2019.

Unruh, Peter. *Die Herrschaft der Vernunft: Zur Staatsphilosophie Immanuel Kants*, 2. Aufl. Baden-Baden: Nomos, 2016.

Waldenfels, Bernhard. *Hyperphänomene: Modi hyperbolischer Erfahrung*. Berlin: Suhrkamp, 2012.

Weiland, Ludwig, Hg. *Constitutiones et Acta Publica Imperatorum et Regum: 911–1197*. Hannover: Hahnsche Buchhandlung, 1893.

John Milbank
Theopolitics Today

The Crisis of the Symbolic Order

Abstract: The contemporary global political crisis can be understood as a crisis of the symbolic order. Human beings are ultimately bound together by objects of their love which are at once concrete and significant. But capitalism prises the symbol apart into empty matter and meaningless sign or number. The extremity of this process has resulted in a division between an elite of the signs and numbers on the one hand and a mass of people reduced to marginalised dependence on leached material resources. The former group tends ideologically to favour liberal univeralism; the latter a particularist nationalism. In order to mediate the particular and the universal we must recover the symbolic. This is rooted in a religious mediation of transcendence. We value to a degree the specific just because our grasp of the universal is as yet incomplete, as with analogy and negative theology. Thus, there can only be religious solutions to our current dilemma and Christianity most of all is the religion of the paradoxical coincidence of the most general and the most concrete.

1

Our widest categories of political analysis are doubly stuck and belated. First, they remain too confined to the polarity of right versus left, which has to some extent been supplanted by a new polarity of liberal versus postliberal. But secondly, even this simple polarity seems woefully inadequate to understand what is now going on. For both the liberal and the postliberal camps are themselves bifurcated and sometimes act in complex collusion. For a long time now, capitalism has become so unquestionably dominant that supposed 'conservatism' takes mainly the form of foregrounding economic liberalism. Conversely, left liberalism increasingly confines itself to cultural liberalism, focussing on issues of rights, identity and licensed transgression.

Much dishonesty is involved in this supposed cleavage, since what Thomas Piketty calls the 'Merchant' branch of the middle classes may adopt what he calls 'Brahmin' stances in its leisure time, while regarding an artificially preserved past or a questioning avant-garde as equally vital sources for investment and profit.[1] Meanwhile, the Brahmins tends to adopt economic critiques only to the extent of suggesting designer-chic modifications of capitalist practice.

In deeper reality, the entire middle class is increasingly subordinate to the growing dominance of an international moneyed elite. One can construe this dominance, as Piketty does, in terms of the natural long-term tendency of capitalism towards the increased concentration of financial wealth and its intensified securing in landed, inheritable property.[2] In the shorter term, one can understand it in terms of the ever-greater recourse of Western capital to financial speculation and debt-funding, in the face of a sustained crisis of the rate of profitability (linked to the overcapacity of production), and its associated threat to Western hegemony, ever since the Nineteen-seventies.[3]

The financial super-elite is also super-mobile and extra-terrestrial. It congregates in certain islands, both literal and metaphorical: large cities and small nations. It associates itself with the most mobile and instant forms of digital technology and their expanded capacities for mass surveillance and continuous spectacle, which controls through fascination. As Christophe Guilluy has argued, one large but far less prosperous, though comfortable section of the highly educated middle-class links itself to this destiny.[4] Typically, it enjoys the various services of mobile immigrant labour, more exploitable than the indigenous working classes which it often displaces.

The latter become marginalised, either geographically or culturally (or both), but then, as Guilluy points out, so also does a very substantial section of the middle class, whose education, locations and inherited instincts renders it less cosmopolitan and less up to date. One is tempted to say that, in this combination within the UK, one has the make-up of the narrow Brexit majority, even if that would be somewhat of an exaggeration. But certainly something like this combination forms in very many countries the backbone of 'national populist' opposition to the prevailing liberal order.

This newly marginalised majority is nonetheless dialectically related to the tinctured gin-sipping world of finance and information of which it is so suspicious. The most basic tendency of capitalism, one can argue, is to accumulate through simultaneous aggregation and abstraction. It sunders all naturally and immediately felt reality, which is at once, for our general human experience, both physical and significant. Land is enclosed and agglomerated, the life of the

---

[1] See Piketty, *Capital and Ideology*
[2] See Piketty, *Capital in the Twenty-First Century*.
[3] For a historical summary see Anderson, "Situationism à L'Envers?", 47–93.
[4] See Guilluy, *No Society*.

labourer is torn apart from his own meaningful labour, the desires of the consumer cease to be really her own. Symbolic value, which lies so close to the domain of the religious, is now engrossed and hoarded as sheerly numerical, while land and people are left denuded and bereft, artificially 'naturalised'.[5] The inherent logic here is the pursuit of short-term interested wealth at the cost of the literal destruction of natural ecology, our real shared abundance, as is now all-too evident. Thus all tends to a world of statistics recorded within a wasteland.

The elite and their assistants inhabit the statistic-hoarding citadels. The remainder inhabit the surrounding wasteland. Thanks to further economic, and to a lesser degree technological developments, the comparatively warm and human realm of the industrial complex has increasingly diminished, now globally and not just in the West. Given the increased slowing of profits and lowering of output in relation to productivity ever since the Nineteen-seventies (the real cause of under-employment today and not the increase of automation)[6] more and more capital has been diverted from industrial production into less-productive services and still more into speculative finance, which more and more segregates and insulates an ever-richer minority. Meanwhile, under 'disorganised capitalism', the majority are thrown back upon their own meagre resources: their own bodies, skills, families, houses, ornaments, pets, streets and neighbourhoods. What is now shared is not so much an economic destiny of common oppression, as with an older proletariat, but rather, and paradoxically, isolation. This tends to characterise populism and to yield, as with the *gilets-jaunes* in France, spontaneous mass furies that periodically peter out for lack of organisation.

For similar reasons, a suspicion of all forms of expert mediation tends to arise: either the marginalised people are confined to themselves, or any mass articulacy tends to be agglomerated and centralised. And this can be regarded as ironic, if populists sometimes and understandably long for lost community and thick local and shared identity.

In consequence, one can see that there is not simply an oppositional 'standoff' between the liberal-tending castles of virtual information and the postliberal real hinterlands – symbolised by the polluted tracts of nature that now surround and intersperse our towns and cities. Instead, their contradictory linkage was already dramatically illustrated by the sub-prime mortgage crisis in the USA, where the most elevated and irresponsible speculations directly linked their fates to the most desperate plights of ordinary people seeking basic shelter.

---

5 See Milbank and Pabst, *The Politics of Virtue*, 93–127.
6 See Benanev, "Automation and the Future of Work", 5–38.

One can also witness it in the way already a capitalist chancer like Silvio Berlusconi was able nonetheless to articulate populist grievances as a basis for his power through his exploitation of media spectacle. It is today manifest again in the predilections of many populists, both in Italy and in Britain, to use social media to override all editorial and sifting mediations, including representational ones in the political arena.

Thus today this dialectical intertwining of nostalgia and futurism has become more intense and more complex, as we have seen with Farage in Britain, Trump in America, Salviani in Italy and Bolsonaro in Brazil.

Fully to understand the simultaneous stand-off and yet complicity between abstracted sign and leached place however, one needs to see that the crucial third, mediating factor is in fact the political state itself. The latter can benefit from and even base itself upon capitalist money, but it cannot be reduced to that, because ultimately power is more about force than lucre: it is force alone that renders power ultimately enforceable, and force is inextricably linked to terrain and to the people who command a specific terrain. It is not ultimately the case that the state depends on finance but the very reverse: speculation is undergirded by the relative reliability of government bonds, backed ultimately by naked power and the authority to print money, besides the knowledge that the state will always bail-out the banks whose credit they require. Of course the more this happens, the more a further license to speculation is granted, as we have seen since 2008.

This is why Fernand Braudel rightly concluded that one only has fully-fledged capitalism when the state is run by and for the bourgeoisie, when the interests of State and of Capital have become one. Likewise Giovanni Arrighi was basically right to argue that one cannot entirely understand the neoliberal revolution unless one sees it in the geopolitical context of the attempt of the West to try to stave off the rising power of both the East and the South. Naturally declining rates of profit, and periodically successive crises of over-production and demand, were also crises of diminishing Western and especially American influence, with inherently-linked economic, demographic, and political dimensions. Thus, for example, increased military spending was at once a matter of security and of Keynesian economic stimulation. Equally, the ever-greater recourse to debt was both an effort to sustain the wealth of American citizens and to lock rising China into economic dependence upon the nation that still held the overwhelming military advantage.[7]

---

7 See Arrighi, *Adam Smith in Beijing*.

Of course, the American fear has for long been that its massive indebtedness must eventually backfire. And this is what characterised the moment of Trump, along with the perception that American military capacity could be dangerously wasted upon ideological foreign adventures yielding little benefit, and recently just the reverse. An economic rebalancing was sought, in keeping with the truth that the USA (unlike the UK) has always been divided between a financial and commercial economy fully locked into the world system and a vast Continental economy that is relatively independent and relatively traditional. Some attempts were accordingly made to further protect American manufacturing and agriculture and to re-balance the finance/goods ratio of trading with China.

But this was not fundamentally a retreat from neoliberalism, even if more attention was now paid to infrastructure and there are more gestural offers of public help to certain large clientage groups. Instead, internal deregulation was perpetuated, along with lowered rates of taxation for the rich. In all likelihood any current boom in public spending, tending to increased debt, would have been used to justify further tax-cuts for the few and some further retrenching austerity for the many in the future.

Through the combination of external protection and internal liberty it was hoped to attract investment back into the US, but these are not the only inducements to such a combination. Rather it is the case that the more Capitalism dominates in its most characteristic form of financial speculation and enforced debt (which in one way or another is always the basis of its excessive and unjust profits) then the more also it becomes entangled in politics.

In the short term this may not seem to be so: as private finance proves more flexible than the state mode and money escapes to increasingly obscure tropical bases. But in the long run it is the case: those bases themselves still have governments, and it is precisely the absoluteness of various national sovereignties which assists the escaping of the frameworks of international regulations based on formal liberal principles of fair contracting and dealing. And then those rival absolute positions can be played off against each other by the monetary cosmonauts.[8]

In the long run, credit secures itself with the securest guarantor, which is the large state. Thus, as with the sub-prime crisis, but on a far vaster scale, just because financial speculation is so airily daring, uncertain and unpredictable, it requires an ultimate guarantee of payment, measurement and investment-realisation in ever more literal, exploited, aggregated and defensible territory. At this point indeed Capital *is* the State, has mutated into the State. The latter has

---

8 See Hendrikse and Fernandez, "Offshore Finance".

evolved from being the bourgeois market-state to being instead a more militaristic state-market.

To this consideration one can add the dialectics of both technology and globalisation. In the first case automation may at first favour dispersed global production, but can increasingly allow instead domestic concentration, reducing transport costs. In the second case, global corporations may at first out-compete local firms, but in the long run these are able to marry a catch-up expertise with greater local knowledge. Thus we see a 'slowbalising' retreat of corporations to their homelands, to some degree and to some extent.

Given this context, the seemingly contradictory combination of favouring the free-flow of money but restrictions on that of goods and especially of people may make sense. A more culturally and ethnically uniform labour-force, rooted in a single place, can be seen as offering more reliability and pliability. For this reason, neoliberal extremists may seek to make a strategic and cynical alliance with populist resistance to high levels of immigration.

How does this Trump-moment relate to the Boris Johnson one? One can suggest that it does so in ways that puncture two delusions.

The first would be that of so many British Remainers that the Tory Right which is now in power under Boris Johnson is itself deluded. It is merely consoling to think so. For this political Right is not pursuing a dream of a past buccaneering empire. Instead, in keeping with the observed economic contrast of the USA and the UK already made, it has been shown that from the outset in the Nineteen-fifties the City of London was at the heart of an ever wilder and extra-terrestrial capitalism. This was indeed an hyper-exploitative successor project to that of empire. Not a fantasy, or rather a fantasy ever since all-too much entertained, but with all-too concrete consequences. Of course, how far the UK is really in control or could remain in control of this new mode of empire is quite another question. But it can certainly mean much increased power for a substantial section of the British elite.

And here one can point out another seemingly contradictory linkage between the fluid and the settled: the tendency of Brexit-voting beneficiaries of speculatively-based pensions to favour the wilder shores of Capital *just because* they now dwell in landed security, but at the same time at a cultural level may resent the ethnos and mores of London-based youngsters and incomers.[9]

Thus the Hard Brexit which is now imminent after Boris Johnson's victory may be all too frighteningly practicable, if not at all to the real benefit of most British citizens.

---

9 See Davies, "England's rentier alliance".

The second delusion about Boris Johnson is to imagine that he is in any way genuinely a High Tory, Communitarian and Postliberal, or that his accession must eventually betoken such a direction of travel. That is no more plausibly the case in Britain than in the United States. Johnson is all too manifestly a typical modern liberal: a perfect fusion of both its economic and cultural senses. His citizenship of everywhere is genuine, his rootedness in his own country fake.

What is surely most symbolic about him is his famed writing, after the announcement that the referendum would take place, of two opposite Daily Telegraph articles, one on the Remain side, the other for Leave, before plumping for the latter. On a personal level this just illustrates a cynical calculation that has now brilliantly paid off. But on a more cultural level it can be seen as a fable of a wider division and hesitation. Capitalism has never been united within itself: there has always been a constitutive tension between a steady capitalism cycling along with fairy-wheel stabilisers which travels securely but slowly, and the Boris-bike capitalism without stabilisers giving a wobbly but much faster and more flexible ride.

Today, with ever-greater financialisation, this contrast is much accentuated. What seems to go under-discussed is just why there should be a division within neoliberalism over Brexit.

To be sure, most businesspeople and most (though a significantly smaller proportion of) bankers favour Remain. Naturally, they support a system of predictable rules that has already secured the dominance of an ultra-capitalism. To a large degree this has been upheld by a Merkel-led Germany looking to create a law and norm-guided rather than democratically-based Europe that would be mainly shaped by Germany, just as once the former lands of the Holy Roman Empire were reshaped by Prussia.[10] Left-wing supporters of Brexit might seem to be right in supposing that the EU is now a neoliberal conspiracy against popular rule which surely gives capitalists everything that might dream of. Has not the power of the German-backed Euro already unseated or re-directed governments in Italy and Greece?[11]

So can Brexit be understood as a basically postliberal and communitarian resistance to these neoliberal depredations? Surely not, for this would be to ignore the fact that in Britain it is rather anarchic neoliberal ultras that have always been in command of the drive towards dismantling the European Union. For them, even the German mode of neoliberalism remains too residually ordo-liberal and regulative in character.

---

10 See Hawes, *The Shortest History of Germany.*
11 See Lapavistas, *The Left Case Against the EU.*

And one can argue that such more extreme capitalists are always bound to be the more authentic ones. For capitalism of its very nature, and especially when aligned with the State, is a process of going ever-further, of wanting always more, for that is its only *raison-d'être*. Eventually, the capitalist process comes up against limits as to the increase or expansion of the range of profits if it is not to destroy itself. Only so much more can be extracted from the existing pools of enclosed land, organised apparatus and controlled labour. Thus the remaining way, as both Marx and Joseph Schumpeter delineated, that it can sustain its native and non-negotiable inner drive, is by embracing destruction itself – both by making windfall profits from the resulting destitution (appropriating underpriced assets and so forth) and by clearing the way for the setting up of more advanced and inhumanly uncompromising technologies and procedures.

Unquestionably this is the sort of right-wing accelerationist programme favoured by Johnson's key advisor Dominic Cummings, who openly admires China and perhaps wishes to replace personal political participation with rule by experts backed by continuously updated streams of digital information and algorithmic calculations.[12] It follows that all the Remainer prophecies of impending doom are quite beside the point for assessing this band of cunning conspirators operating at the margins of legality.

A sophisticated political analysis needs therefore now to be quadrilateral. Clearly there is a spilt within the liberal camp between the more tender-hearted and the more logical liberals, happy to embrace the nihilism at the heart of 'liberalism' (in the restricted sense of individualism and utilitarianism) itself. But what of the postliberal camp? Here too one sees division. For reasons already advanced, the excluded majority may readily fall prey to unmediated democratic aggregation and to control by a seemingly benign centre and the rule of a strong man. This is already happening in several places. What is more, it is not even clear that all populists are communitarians at all: to the contrary, the evidence from Brazil and elsewhere is that they are sometimes, in despair at failed state-enterprise, happy to embrace a 'Protestant' (or indeed Protestant) promise of success to the individually hard-working, alongside a disdain for the indigent and and marginalised, now blamed for their own fates. On the other hand, there is also much evidence that many within the excluded majority (and even considerable numbers of the under-troops of the elites in the citadels) are looking for a combination that is not as yet on offer from any significant political party anywhere: greater economic equality combined with moderate social conservatism

---

12 See Meek, "The Dreaming of Dominic Cummings".

that is pro-family, life and childhood, combined with a respect for tradition, identity and place in both cultural and ecological senses.

It is clear that to a considerable degree this combination accounts for the success of the current regimes in Poland and Hungary, which should not be too readily placed in a 'far right' category. There are indeed reasons to be suspicious of their authoritarian tendencies which worsen by the day, often cravenly supported by some Catholics all too happy to trade support for nationalism for a sustaining or increase of ecclesiastical power. Yet at the same time western commentators underestimate the sheer difficulty of changing from totalitarianism to democracy. On both countries judicial, bureaucratic and media cadres retained corrupt habits of mind all too happy to block democratic decisions in their own interests, now sometimes disguised by a liberal discourse of rights. Removing such people and attitudes was probably unavoidable, even if it incurs a terrible risk of a new state control of the judiciary and the organs of information.

And another factor here is that we tend too readily to assume that the American model of the absolute separation of the executive from the judiciary is the only legitimate one – even though, for example, this has not been, prior to Tony Blair's changes, the traditional British way of doing things. A counter argument here would be that any absolute separation of legislation from legal application tends to found the former only in aggregated will, and the latter only in positive precedent. By contrast, their ultimate linkage (as pertained in the UK up till Blair's creation of a Supreme Court) tends to require that they can only be constrained by a shared reference to a natural law foundation in the objectively Good – a foundation that sustains the natural continuity of enactment with interpretation and ensures a hermeneutic resistance to the rigidity of either.[13]

Similarly, one should try harder to understand Eastern European unease about the effects of an excessively liberal toleration of freedom of opinion and the supplying of supposed information. There is an understandable fear in the East that powerful opinion-informing agencies can actually undermine a democratically-shared desire to sustain an inherited local or national culture. Not without reason did Burke and Carlyle realise that the press had come to constitute a 'Fourth estate' answerable to no one but itself and its interested financial backers. In the UK the tabloids have virtually hounded to death one princess and now persecute another. An Australian-based media empire has helped to undermine much of British culture (including the game of cricket and its unique values) and now British political power and unity with respect to the Brexit campaign. The latter also feeds off the further deregulation supplied by social media.

---

13 See Bastit, *Naissance de La Loi Moderne*.

Conversely, it is the case that populist news outlets exploit the justified sense of many that a dominant liberal media speaks only in the name of the interests and attitudes of more successful urban populations. Naturally, as with the case of the judiciary, one can fear that the restricting of liberal news licence will only result in its displacement by populist dishonesty and propaganda in Eastern Europe.

Thus today we can see on either side more acutely how real freedom depends paradoxically on an initially well-informed and responsible editorial sifting of news and opinion, rooted in a more fairly distributed ownership and control of news-outlets. In reality, responsible freedom is only possible within some sort of shared sense of the bounds of decency and commonly-shared goals of human relating. Responsible government should indeed be concerned about enabling this, even if such concern is all too likely to spill over into manipulative oppression.

Parallel considerations mean that one cannot just dismiss out of hand Eastern European and Italian concerns with the cultural coherence of European communities. This is not at all to say that newcomers, including Muslims, cannot be successfully integrated, but to pretend that the arrival in unprecedentedly large numbers of people with different (but by no means necessarily simply 'false') cultural values presents no serious problems of integration is something of a bourgeois delusion on the part of those who do not have to bear the brunt of these difficulties. Some obvious upshots of Merkel's excessive and sudden opening of the floodgates to refugees who were often not genuine refugees at all, have illustrated this very clearly. And from the example of Scandinavia especially, we should now be all too aware of the degree to which tolerant, egalitarian and welfare-based cultures readily accepting social reciprocity and a requisite degree of self-sacrifice depend upon a shared sense of deep understanding and co-belonging that can alone foster a high degree of mutual trust.[14]

Therefore, today in politics, we face not a binary but a triple choice: neoliberalism as we know it, genuine communitarian postliberalism or destructive capitalist accelerationism combined with Caesarian populism, prepared, as already shown by Johnson's contemptuous treatment of the UK Parliament, to break with representative democracy. Triple not quadruple, because the most extreme neoliberalism and the more atavistic mode of populism tend to combine, even though the tensions between the two will also remain and cannot ever be perfectly resolved.

---

14 See Murray, *The Strange Death of Europe*.

2

In what sense might all this possess a theological dimension? Perhaps the most crucial point here is the question of the symbolic, as already invoked. I have suggested that capitalism can be read as the sundering of the symbol, as its dissolution into mere things on the one hand and mere abstractions or numbers on the other. I have also suggested that this sundering relies upon and is paralleled by a political dimension that backs up and reinforces abstraction with naked power. Just as money is empty, but its manipulators prove all too palpably brutal, so also the modern state offers a site of power that is entirely neutral, yet which just for that reason can only be rendered operative in terms of arbitrary forces and interests, however much these may represent current majority opinion. Democracy requires that a government be deemed legitimate when it is supported by the combined voice of ironically disaggregated individuals, taken one by one, and abstracted from their concrete communities, regions, loyalties, religions and families. And yet these people are pre-selected by national boundaries which presuppose an identity which democracy at once contradictorily assumes and yet is supposed constitutionally to forget.

Legitimacy in these modern circumstances is inherently fragile. It depends upon habit and channels of procedure, but when these break down, as currently in the United Kingdom, it becomes rapidly unclear just in whose voice government is supposed to be speaking. Lost to view from modernity are older claims of government to be operating in the name of an 'other', of national tradition and purpose, ultimately mediating transcendent, divine norms. Politics, as Carl Schmitt rightly surmised, was always inherently theological, because deciding on what we should do in common is an existential question, inseparable from the metaphysical one of how things ultimately are, of 'what Being is' and therefore of how it should authentically be mediated.

So if one tries to get rid of the theological dimension of politics, then what can this mean? There would seem to be three possibilities.[15] First, the Hegelian or perhaps Heideggerean one of trying to translate religion into philosophy and image into concept, such that politics becomes the supposedly rational mediation of Being as the other to human existences. Yet such rationalism either implies an implausibly measurable progress guaranteed by logic, or else ironically a rational support for the fatality of a racial, class or national destiny – a manifestation of will through existential and competitive struggle (Hegel and Heidegger respectively). Nor is the idea that concept can emphatically rise above the

---

15 See Lefort, "The Permanence of the Theologico-Political?", 148–187.

range of image and metaphor, and so philosophy indisputably trump religion, itself plausible, given that we are embodied creatures of feeling, never able to escape from metaphorical, materially-based expressions.

The second possibility is the Marxist one. Long before Schmitt's meditations, Marx had concluded that the very notion of a political state involves an 'alienation' of the human essence in a religious manner, a fantasised imagination of an identity and power over-against us (even though we have ourselves projected this power). Today various writers, such as Giorgio Agamben and Jean-Luc Nancy, play variations on this anarchic theme, often in the hopelessly ironic postmodern mode of a ceaseless striving to escape the imaginary and symbolic framework which can never be finally escaped at all. The flight from politics to the purely animal or angelic is the last remaining but despairing gesture of an anti-political political hope. But such anarchy is itself in strange continuity with capitalism after all, in terms of its fantasy of a non-symbolic humanity, of an impossible human society not assembled together in the name of a mode of mythic self-representation taken to mediate the 'other' that is Being as such.

The third possibility seeks either for a mode of purely civil religion, ever since Rousseau, or else for a politics entirely freed from the theological. After our experiences of totalitarianism we have every reason to renew an originally Christian suspicion of civil religion as involving a dangerous sanctification of the state. The quest for a non-theological politics would then alone remain legitimately standing.[16]

But is this quest simply a phantom? Does the sudden and largely unexpected global political crisis through which we are now living demonstrate exactly *that* truth? For human beings are symbolically oriented creatures. They gather and assemble around shared rituals and meanings. They cannot not do so. Denying this, in the case of capitalism, proves to be a process of literal destruction, now extending to nature herself, which may after all be constituted by more unconscious processes of symbol-formation at sub-human levels.[17]

Denying this primacy of the symbolic in the case of secular democracy may be equally destructive, because it leaves a representational vacuum at the heart of our communities. Just what is it that our governments stand for if they claim to represent regions and nations and empires (including the mode of empire that is the EU) and not simply a body of individuals arbitrarily bounded and assembled? In what name are these various beings coming together other than their

---

16 See, for example, Nancy, "Church, State, Resistance", 102–112.
17 See Whitehead, *Modes of Thought*.

various individual ones? If it is only an aggregate of the latter, then why not dissolve the state? Why should Marx not be right? But we have seen that he is not right, because the fantasy of the post-philosophical (we should seek to change, not to understand the world) and even of the post-religious, is merely the fantasy of a post-symbolic humanity. This is impossible, because language as such is already metaphysical, already a wager as to the ultimate nature of the real and of its mediations, in the name of which alone we can come more than instinctually and so spiritually together (in a more than animal mode, or in our own spiritual mode of animality).

What can therefore be suggested in that today once more, as in the Nineteen-thirties, secular liberalism is in trouble, because, relatively decent as it may be, and superior to so many alternatives, it is still insufficient and even, in the end, incoherent. By suppressing the theological dimension of the political, it renders the political as such problematic. For if politics ceases to be answerable to an other beyond the human and to its representatives, to some sort of 'church', then sooner or later it will cease to appear legitimate – either to large minorities, or to many individuals as individuals, or, as today, to majorities themselves. For it will have ceased to claim to symbolise a people in terms of their ultimate cherished horizons. A vacuum will be inchoately discerned, and an inchoate rebellion will follow, as we now see almost everywhere.

In the Nineteen-thirties this rebellion was linked to race and to pseudo-science, and to an unholy hybrid of nostalgia with futurism. Some of those combinations pertain again today, but perhaps because of an increased suspicion of the modern trajectory as such, the difference today is the return of religiously-based or religiously-linked political movements everywhere from the USA to India, to Italy, to Russia, Eastern Europe and of course Islamic countries. Everywhere, also, there is the danger that an appeal to transcendence inverts into an instrumentalised use of the mediations of transcendence, tending to a new mode of what can only be described as a kind of religious fascism.

Thus now as in the Thirties, what we see is a rebellion against the economically and politically abstract; a revolt against the impossible attempt to undo symbolic identity, undertaken in the name of exaggerated particulars, thereby too often fostering prejudice and intolerance. Of course, this exaggeration of the particular *equally* betrays the symbolic and the metaphorical, which inherently seek to invoke the universal and the spiritual by way of particular sacramental and theurgic presences.

Therefore, as the Argentinian political theorist Ernesto Laclau noted, our political dilemmas today are curiously like the theological dilemmas that we face in seeking to speak of God.[18] Every name of God must be negated because none are adequate to him. This also means, as Laclau underscored, that every name of God, is in respect to him *equivalent* as a name – goodness becomes being becomes beauty becomes truth becomes even worm and leaf and stone. But does this mean, as he rightly asked, that therefore God can be more literally recognised as sheer identity and equivalence which would be virtually identical with nothing, as for Hegel? Such a theological move is not accidentally, in view of this invocation, akin to the celebration of the modern state as sheerly neutral, empty and indifferent, the mere mediator of agreed-upon rights, contracts, precedents and procedures – however much these might be upheld by 'corporate' loyalties as inducing a certain quasi-solidarity (to invoke Hegel's political thought).

In order instead to speak of God as a plenitude and a lure, to link God to certain ethical preferences as to how we should travel through this world (a question we cannot really avoid) we need also to name God affirmatively in terms of his own positive utterances in what is taken to be his Creation and his self-disclosure through various human traditions of oracular revelation. Our necessary negation of these natural and revealed names is now seen to be also a path of deepening insight into their eminent possession by God. To know, for example, that God exceeds any 'goodness' we might predicate of him, becomes nonetheless a mystical journey of discovery of his ever-greater generosity and our ever-greater possibility of sharing in that generosity.

In other words, the religious quest for God is in part about how we combine the universal and the particular, how we prevent our devotion to the universal being ethically empty, merely formal and nihilistic on the one hand, and how we prevent the sacramental and iconic from being idolatrous on the other. How to cleave to the particular as a pilgrim path that opens up and links to other particulars and beyond all of them, rather than proving to be a blank wall of prejudice and division before which we are self-stopped.

This is of course the theological question of the possibility of analogy, of a seemingly impossible paradoxical linkage of identity with difference, of the universal with the concrete. Without this possibility it seems that we cannot really speak of God at all. But also that without it we cannot truly have the political because we cannot have the theological. For we can then no longer discover a just way of binding particular people and peoples together under more general symbolic attachments. For Christians this space is the Church, for Jews it is mystical Israel, for Muslims it is the Ummah, for Buddhists the Sangha and so forth.

---

18 See Laclau, "On the Names of God", 137–147.

But unless this secular political space in some sense defers to and is measured itself by this sacred and prophetic space, how shall it be even political at all? How shall it be more than merely empty, lacking in a symbolic sufficiency such as really to bring different individuals and diverse groups together? And it is not enough, as Laclau advocated, in an Hegelian gesture (rather akin to that of Gillian Rose) that is scarcely distinguishable after all from postmodern despair, to recommend a ceaseless and unresolved dialectical shuttle between the abstractly universal and the populist particular as the very agonistic heart of politics. In reality this would be an anti-politics, a merely endless oscillation between a tyrannically removed rationalism and an equally tyrannical imposed set of prejudices.

Viewed in this light, our emerging global political crisis seems to be indeed a theological one. Beyond liberalism and national populism we need to find a third, postliberal direction. Insofar as this involves an analogical linking of the universal and the particular in order to achieve political connection, this proves to be inseparable from the theological quest to find an adequate symbolic language to speak of the normative other that is Being itself to which our human existences must seek somewhat blindly to correspond. In contrast to the later historical reflections of Henri Bergson I would suggest that there needs to be a way to develop from local to more universal sympathies; that the two are not generically different impulses.[19] Our local attachments are more than the necessary disciplines of defensive armies because they are rooted in a more fundamental instinct for individuals to cooperate and exchange. Yet Bergson was right to say that ethics sinks into such mere military preparedness if it cannot open out into something wider, embracing not just all humans but also all creatures, the entire cosmos.

And with the earlier Bergson but beyond him and in terms suggested by his disciple Charles Péguy, I would suggest that the key to this opening lies in the operation of grace.[20] The sacred is not fundamentally the pre-given: it is rather secular technocracy that thinks only in terms of manipulating what is already there (the *tout fait*), of further amalgamating and dividing it, of speeding it up, maximising and minimising it, further communicating and imaging it. But always the same old thing, however new one's iPhone. It is rather the human spirit itself, in its mysterious subjective depth, that experiences time as the ever-constantly new and realises that we cannot calculate the future, just be-

---

19 See Marrati, "Mysticism and the Foundation of the Open Society", 591–601. And in contrast to the political Bergson, see Milbank, "Divine Logos and Human Communication", 3–24.
20 See Milbank, "Foreword", xi–xxxv.

cause possibility is not stored up in an embalmed past. Instead, new possibility constantly arrives as the virtuality of the actual, as Gilles Deleuze rightly (in this instance) reads Bergson. Or in Péguy's Christian terms it arrives as grace, as a teleological horizon unexpectedly descending to us from above, but synergically, through our own creative actions, ever weaving a new poetic and symbolic thread for human guidance and inhabitation.

Within this perspective, the universally uniting is not something general and abstract, but more the result of converging openings within the various particulars, a further expansion of their unique disclosures that can generate a shared culture, besides shared principle, just as villages come together in an identifiable region and regions in identifiable countries and continents.

As the religion of the analogy of being and as the religion of grace, Christianity should be particularly concerned with the problematic of mediating the universal with the particular and of sustaining our human inherited traditions as genuinely alive only insofar as they are open to a non-identical repetition in the future. This is both the theoretical question of naming God and the practical question of how to live politically and socially together. Uniting the two is the project of the Church, which also transcends and orients any merely legal and coercive co-existence. As the Body of Christ, the *totus Christus*, the Church recalls and sustains the Incarnation of God as Man. This continuing event is most of all the analogical combining of the most negatively general and divine with the most entirely and humanly positive and particular, since it goes to both extremes at once. In social terms this suggests that what finally unifies humanity symbolically is simply one past contingent human figure who might in that sense be 'anyone', and yet as *thereby* concretely and historically situated begins to join us all paradoxically under the auspices of one specific and yet uniquely open and grace-bearing lineage.

Humans cannot be united by following either the particular or the universal commands of a 'Father', of a transcendent authority over-against us, whether that be of embalmed tradition or of scientific abstraction. But as Christians we have faith that they *can* after all be united under the ultimate heavenly Father who only constitutes his authority through its exemplary symbolic manifestation by the Son, in terms of his both eternally and historically presented 'metaphorical' transfer of negative mystery into positive flesh. Here the political or rather post-political law is paradoxically enacted through its perfect observance in one unique instance. Its sheer unrepeatable particularity renders it further observable by all human beings only in the continuous mode of an interpretation of its spirit, the collective project of realising different individual interpretations of Christ as also harmoniously compossible and compatible with those of others.

In a very stuttering and imperfect way, this 'Church' project has all the same shown historically its reality in a myriad projects and benefits that have produced those historically unique and convivial 'free associations' (from monastery to sports club and trade union) around shared positive enterprises and attachments that both transcend and fulfil the merely political. The resumption and extension of this Christological task of seeking to shape a 'community of communities', whose overall concrete form cannot be known in advance, but is always received again by grace, has to be our main theological and practical Christian response to the new crisis of the symbolic order and our seeming inability to mediate the particular and the universal.

Bibliography

Anderson, Perry. "Situationism à L'Envers?," *New Left Review* 119 (2019): 47–93.
Arrighi, Giovanni. *Adam Smith in Beijing: Lineages of the 21st Century.* London: Verso, 2009.
Bastit, Michel. *Naissance de La Loi Moderne.* Paris: Presses Universitaires de France, 1990.
Benanev, Aaron. "Automation and the Future of Work – 1," *New Left Review* 119 (2019): 5–38.
Davies, Will. "England's rentier alliance is driving support for a no-deal Brexit," *New Statesman*, 1 Aug. 2019, https://www.newstatesman.com/politics/brexit/2019/08/england-s-rentier-alliance-driving-support-no-deal-brexit. (accessed 03 Jan. 2020)
Guilluy, Christophe. *No Society: La fin de la classe moyenne occidentale.* Paris: Flammarion, 2018.
Hawes, James. *The Shortest History of Germany.* London: Old Street, 2018.
Hendrikse, Reijer, and Fernandez, Rodrigo. "Offshore Finance: How Capital Rules the World," *Transnational Institute Longreads,* https://longreads.tni.org/state-of-power-2019/offshore-finance/. (accessed 03 Jan. 2020)
Laclau, Ernesto. "On the Names of God," In *Political Theologies: Public Religions in a Post-Secular World,* ed. by Hent de Vries and Lawrence E. Sullivan, 137–147. New York: Fordham University Press, 2006.
Lapavistas, Costas. *The Left Case Against the EU* (Cambridge, UK: Polity, 2019)
Lefort, Claude. "The Permanence of the Theologico-Political?," In *Political Theologies: Public Religions in a Post-Secular World,* ed. by Hent de Vries and Lawrence E. Sullivan, 148–187. New York: Fordham University Press, 2006.
Marrati, Paula. "Mysticism and the Foundation of the Open Society: Bergsonian Politics?," In *Political Theologies: Public Religions in a Post-Secular World,* ed. by Hent de Vries and Lawrence E. Sullivan, 591–601. New York: Fordham University Press, 2006.
Meek, James. "The Dreaming of Dominic Cummings," *London Review of Books* 41, no. 20 (2019), 24 Oct. 2019, https://www.lrb.co.uk/the-paper/v41/n20/james-meek/the-dreamings-of-dominic-cummings. (accessed 03 Jan. 2020)
Milbank, John. "Divine Logos and Human Communication: A Recuperation of Coleridge" In *The Future of Love: Essays in Political Theology,* John Milbank, 3–24. London: SCM, 2009.

Milbank, John, and Pabst, Adrian. *The Politics of Virtue: Postliberalism and the Human Future*. London: Rowman and Littlefeld, 2016.

Milbank, John. "Foreword: Charles Péguy and the Betrayal of Time," In *Notes on Bergson and Descartes: Philosophy, Christianity, and Modernity in Contestation*, ed. by Charles Péguy, trans. Bruce K. Ward, xi–xxxv. Eugene, Or.: Cascade Books, 2019.

Murray, Douglas. *The Strange Death of Europe: Immigration, Identity, Islam*. London: Bloomsbury, 2018.

Nancy, Jean-Luc. "Church, State, Resistance," In *Political Theologies: Public Religions in a Post-Secular World*, ed. by Hent de Vries and Lawrence E. Sullivan, 102–112. New York: Fordham University Press, 2006.

Piketty, Thomas. *Capital in the Twenty-First Century*, trans. Arthur Goldhammer. Cambridge, MA: Harvard University Press, 2014.

Piketty, Thomas. *Capital and Ideology*, trans. Arthur Goldhammer. Cambridge, MA: Harvard University Press, 2020.

Whitehead, Alfred North. *Modes of Thought*. New York: The Free Press, 1966.

Daniel Weidner
Smashing Words

Prophetic Words and Alternative Political Theologies

Abstract: The paper conceives a Prophetic Political Theology by reading prophetic texts from the Hebrew bible and from James Baldwin as an alternative to contemporary Political Theology. It argues that the contemporary discussion of Political Theology is too narrow and too focused on a specific Idea of Political Theology, namely, on Carl Schmitt's theory of sovereignty. Instead of focusing on the political ruler, an alternative Political Theology would also take into account other political notions such as hope, solidarity, justice, or comfort. Instead of focusing on theological-political concepts, it would also refer to other speech acts, such as admonitions, appeals, and even to poetic images. Thus, both the early and late prophets of the Bible show how complex the relation between divine and human power is figured in the biblical corpus and that these figurations essentially depend on the literary form of the biblical text. James Baldwin's criticism of liberal democracy's disavowal of racial suppression shows how modes of prophetic speech are still used fruitfully in modern political discourse.

One of the most remarkable aspects of the recent religious turn in theory is the renaissance of Political Theology. What has been a rather esoteric discourse for specialists of medieval and early modern political thought has become one of the vibrant fields of political theory. Political Theology seems to be able to conceptualize both the growing religious fundamentalism in the East and the West and the more general crisis of political representation that haunts even the most secular liberal democracies today. However, this criticism does not come without ambivalence, since political theology's insistence of the fundamental nature of sovereignty and its radical criticism of the liberal illusions of democracy runs the risk of throwing the baby out with the bathwater. Even if we are skeptical against the liberal promises, human rights, the rule of law, the current global trends towards authoritarianism does not really suggest that the stress on sovereignty is the answer to that skepticism. Perhaps we should be careful to not so easily discard these promises, perhaps we should look for new modes of appealing to them, rather than pursuing yet another, more radical criticism. For radicalism is not necessarily an indicator of political prudence nor does the depth of conceptual foundation characterize a deep understanding of what is happening today.

Remarkably Political Theology today mostly speaks in an oracular tone and has a predilection for an odd, esoteric terminology: the *catechont*, the *oiconomia* – these words suggest an exclusivity and aim both towards the arcana of political power and to an academic community of the happy few. This is all the more remarkable since being a political discourse by its own claim, Political Theology would be expected to take place in the public sphere. Historically before the twentieth century, it was a rather popular and populistic discourse that used the then familiar language of religion to address political issues, think, for example of Georg Büchner, who coined the heavily biblical slogan "Peace to the hovels! Death to the palaces!" to incite a social revolution among the conservative peasants. Such a slogan, however, is neither addressed to the sovereign, nor is it a 'concept' in any meaningful sense. Rather, it is a speech-act that is addressed to a general public and a speech act which neither simply integrates theological thought in a political theory, nor dignifies a political vision with the aura of theological dogmatic but moves on the verge of biblical language and political action.

This example reveals that our understanding of Political Theology is a very narrow one and in fact more often than not bound to the thinker that is often thought to have coined the term: to Carl Schmitt and his political theology of sovereignty. True, Schmitt's formulations and statements are suggestive enough to be reinterpreted. But can we also envision other, more fractured, open, and weaker form of political theology? Can we think of concepts of Political Theology that do not merely concern power, but other concepts such as hope, solidarity, maybe even comfort? And maybe not only concepts, but also things that are not concepts at all, but speech acts, slogans, poems, or stories?[1] For, insofar as Schmitt is concerned, not only is his focus on power an irritating one, but similarly, his political theology is strikingly one-sided in its affinity to dogmatics and concepts. In religion as well as elements in politics, however, there are forms of speech and forms of action that are much less dogmatic than those to which Schmitt refers. Forms that, therefore, cannot simply be dogmatized into concepts that are then ready to hand, but which must, nonetheless, be read carefully.

How productive such readings can be are shown by the approaches to Paul brought forward by Agamben, Žižek, and Badiou.[2] However, even here there is a clear – philosophical, or political-theological? – tendency to move from reading to dogmatization that goes hand in hand with the tendency to overestimate the

---

[1] See Lebovic and Weidner: "Prophetic Politics."
[2] See Finkelde, *Politische Eschatologie nach Paulus*; Blanton and Vries, *Paul and the Philosophers*.

originality of Paul at the cost of the greater context, that is, to read Paul as a theoretician, as the one and single apostle instead of viewing him as part of the larger biblical tradition. When, for example, Giorgio Agamben reads Paul, he distinguishes him from the prophets, who speak *about* something, whereas the apostolic proclamation is indistinguishable from what it proclaims: "Each time the prophets announce the coming of the Messiah, the message is always about a time to come, a time not yet present. This is what marks the difference between the prophet and the apostle. The apostle speaks forth from the arrival of the Messiah. At this point, prophecy must keep silent, for now prophecy is truly fulfilled."³ However, as we will see shortly, this is not only a Christian (mis)reading of prophecy which does not speak about a coming messiah but about the very present state of crisis, it also completely underestimates the complex literary structure of prophetic texts, including the Pauline ones. In fact, these texts, as well as the entire prophetic tradition is decidedly ignored by the Schmittian perspective, despite, in the biblical corpus, it is prophecy that negotiates the relation between divine and mundane sovereignty. It is precisely this negotiation that the Schmittian identification of these sovereignties tries to suppress. However, the task of Political theology should probably be less the sacralization of power but the observation of this borderland and the negotiations that take place in it.

This is not merely a biblical phenomenon. Throughout the history of Christianity, and in particular the early modern period, the prophetic tradition is invoked again and again in movements of protest, and of social and cultural criticism.⁴ The Enlightenment and Romantic periods figured the prophets as moral critics of politics, or as artists that point to a different, more communal, less alienated form of government.⁵ In the late nineteenth and twentieth century, the prophets are figured as Charismatics or – as in Max Weber – as political pamphletists and radical intellectuals.⁶ And this legacy carries on in the twentieth century, both in the American Jeremiad that bemoans the loss of values and the crisis of the social bond, or in the civil rights movement that heavily referred and still refers to prophetic modes and tropes of justice, hope and renewal.⁷

Could we think of these discourses as part of a different political theology? Different, but not other, for my interest is not so much to construct another political theology, a Jewish against a Christian one, or a left against a right. Rather,

---

3 Agamben, *The Time that Remains*, 61.
4 See Walzer, *Exodus and Revolution*.
5 See Balfour, *The Rhetoric of Romantic Prophecy*.
6 See among others Schneidau, *Sacred Discontent*.
7 See Bercovitch, *The American Jeremiad*; Darsey, *The Prophetic Tradition*.

prophecy is a site to rethink political theology, to broaden its meaning, to reflect its paradoxes and to develop a new methodology, less dogmatic than philological in the sense of reading the prophetic. This is all the more necessary since prophetic politics is essentially a politics of speech, a politics that consists in words rather than action, a politics that is related rather to the public sphere than to the arcana of power. For the prophet has no means of power but his words in order to castigate and smash the existing order – a procedure that is always risky since smashing words tend to turn against oneself. In what follows I will sketch three different readings of these traditions: the earlier prophets and their relation to power, the later prophets and their relation to speech and, in a sketchier way, James Baldwin as a modern prophet who stirs up the liberal public sphere.

1

The earlier prophets designate the historical books Joshua to Kings in the Jewish Bible, whereas the later prophets comprise the scriptural Prophets, Isaiah, Jeremiah, Ezekiel and the smaller prophets. This fact in itself is central, for it shows that prophecy and history are related in that the prophets are part of a larger narrative and that the corpus consists of both stories about the prophets and words of the prophets. We can read the earlier prophets essentially as a piece of narrative political theory: a reflection on the nature and emergence of political power and of sovereignty.[8] Since this emergence is taking place within a larger story that goes on between the human and the divine, we can also read it as a piece of narrative Political Theology. It is Political Theology proper since it speaks about two scenes of politics, the earthly and the divine, and it is a complex one, since the relation between these two scenes is given in narrative form, that is: in a form that can suggest more than it actually states explicitly.

The most prominent, but also quite complex event is the establishment of the Kingdom in Israel in 1 Samuel 8–12. The people, weary of its weak rulers – the temporary charismatic leaders from the book of Judges – address the prophet Samuel:

> "Behold, you are old and your sons do not walk in your ways. Now appoint for us a king to judge us like all the nations." But the thing displeased Samuel when they said, "Give us a king to judge us." And Samuel prayed to the Lord. And the Lord said to Samuel, "Obey the

---

8 See Halbertal and Holmes, *Beginning of Politics*.

voice of the people in all that they say to you, for they have not rejected you, but they have rejected me from being king over them." (1 Sam 8:5–7, English Standard Version)

Already this small scene is slightly confusing, for on the one hand the final verdict seems to clearly state that the desire for a king is wrong and sinful, on the other the Lord asks Samuel to obey. Two concepts of political theory seem to crash into each other: the radical theocentric "The Lord is King" limits all sovereignty to the divine and models the divine according to the near eastern King with his imperial powers. It has its own tradition in the Hebrew Bible, for already Gideon answered the desire of the people to be ruled by him with: "I will not rule over you, and my son will not rule over you; the Lord will rule over you." (Judges 8:23) God is the only legitimate source and site of power – one could posit here a doctrine of theocratic anarchism as developed by Martin Buber.[9] On the other hand, there is the people's desire for a king 'like the other nations', implying that every nation deserves a king to become a political unity, here: to persist in the struggle with other nations – a doctrine of Realpolitik. It is this theory that the Lord also seems to accept when he repeats "'Now then, obey their voice; only you shall solemnly warn them and show them the ways of the king who shall reign over them.' So Samuel told all the words of the Lord to the people who were asking for a king from him." (1 Sam 8:21–22)

The two positions seem to be irreconcilable. However, there is a third one which enables a dialogue, a movement of meaning, a plot that makes the relation between divine and monarchical sovereignty even more complex and ambiguous. For the action takes place on different stages connected only by the prophet, who brings the plea from the people to the Lord and vice versa. The prophet is essentially less a foreteller as the Greek *prophetes* would suggest, but a messenger, as the Hebrew *nabi* suggests.[10] A representative, if you will, someone speaking in the name of someone else. It is through these representatives that the Lord actually ruled Israel, namely through judges which were also prophets, like Samuel. But this third position is never neutral and the mediation is never pure, which thus makes this text truly blurry. For being a messenger would actually imply repeating the message truly and faithfully. The text, however, suggests something different. Whereas the people ask Samuel to "appoint" a king, he is displeased that they want him to "give" them a king. And as the narrative goes on, we realize that Samuel does not, indeed, seem to tell "all

---

9 See Buber, *Kingship of God*.
10 For the intermediate position of the Prophet see Sternberg, *Poetics of Biblical Narrative*, esp. chapter 3., Polzin, *Samuel and the Deuteronomist*, esp. chapter 3.

the Words of the Lord" to the people. From verse 11–16 he develops a detailed list of all the things that the King will do, a list that can count as a warning on behalf of the Lord to be given to the people. What Samuel, however, does not say, or what the narrator does not tell us that he says, is the rigorous position that the wish for a king is a rejection of the Lord.

Moreover, as the Lord's repeated stress that Samuel shall obey the voice of the people indicates, there is a certain reluctance on Samuel's part, who will end up waiting a couple of chapters with a lot of digressions before making Saul king. And even after the anointment of the king, the prophet will not disappear but will stay on the scene to comment on the behavior of the king – a constellation that will lead to endless conflicts throughout the biblical books. Nor does the anointment represent the last stage in the story of Saul and Samuel. The bitter irony of this story is that Saul, just after being installed by Samuel and the Lord, is being rejected after he failed to perform God's command to kill the captured enemy king. "Then the word of the Lord came to Samuel: 'I regret that I have made Saul king, for he has turned back from following me and has not performed my commandments.'" (1 Sam 15:10–11) Now Samuel has to act the other way round: first he tries to object to the Lord, then he tells Saul that the Lord turned away from him, and then when the King asks what he can do to repent for his sins, Samuel answers that this will be of no use: "And also the Glory of Israel will not lie or have regret, for he is not a man, that he should have regret." (1 Sam 15:29)

What is in question here is obviously the puzzling nature of divine sovereignty, since we just heard that God declare his regret that Samuel is not willing or able to communicate to the king. As if this is not enough, the narrator closes the chapter "And Samuel did not see Saul again until the day of his death, but Samuel grieved over Saul. And the Lord regretted that he had made Saul king over Israel." (1 Sam 15:35) The Lord *does* regret and the sovereign does change his mind, which leaves his representative, the prophet, in an even more problematic position – the story of Jonah will be the ultimate articulation of this problem. Moreover, as in the rendering of Samuel's reluctance to appoint the king, we hear a further voice beyond that of the Lord, the King, the Prophet, and the people – namely the voice of the narrator who subtly or maybe not so subtly undercuts the authority of the prophet. Therefore, sovereignty is not only divided among these different instances but their relations are also fundamentally blurred.

What we encounter here is a discourse in which sovereignty is constantly discussed on two levels: both on the divine and the human, and it is this very interaction, at times ambivalence, that is at the core of the narration. Being much more than a mere statement about the limited sovereignty of rulers and kings, it also implies that divine sovereignty is anything but a simple notion, since it also depends on a certain form or narration and an implied epistemology of divine, prophetic, and narrative knowledge that is not so easy to disentangle. What is at stake, finally, is also a question implicit with respect to the discourse of Political Theology, namely, what kind of theology it implies, or, if theology is possible at all.

2

I will now turn to the later prophets, i.e. what is considered as the prophetic corpus in the Christian bible. Here, we have a mixture of prophetic words and prophetic legends as in the earlier prophets, but the focus now lies on the prophetic words, that is, on the performative dimension of discourse. How, then, is it possible to speak prophetically and to proclaim sovereignty, be it the sovereignty of the king or of the Lord? In fact, sovereigns usually have a rather uneasy relation to those who annoint them: on the one hand, they need someone to proclaim and even explain his or her sovereignty, and on the other hand, they are haunted by the fear that this theorizing might limit sovereign power. Moreover, the very notion of proclamation implies a performative dimension and uncannily borders theatrical simulation. which only seems to do what it actually contradicts.

To understand this performative moment in prophecy we have to read a little more closely. Take for example the first five verses of the book of Isaiah which open the corpus of the later prophets,

> "The vision of Isaiah the son of Amoz, which he saw concerning Judah and Jerusalem in the days of Uzziah, Jotham, Ahaz, and Hezekiah, kings of Judah:
> Hear, O heavens, and give ear, O earth; / for the Lord has spoken: "Children have I reared and brought up, / but they have rebelled against me. / The ox knows its owner, / and the donkey its master's crib, / but Israel does not know, / my people do not understand." / Ah, sinful nation, / a people laden with iniquity, / offspring of evildoers, / children who deal corruptly! / They have forsaken the Lord, / they have despised the Holy One of Israel, / they are utterly estranged. / Why will you still be struck down? / Why will you continue to rebel? / The whole head is sick, / and the whole heart faint." (Isa 1:1–5)

Three general observations can be made: first, as the historicizing superscription of verse 1 highlights, prophetic books are situated in a history of Israel in which we would find the kings mentioned in 2 Kings. At the same time, they are heavily anchored in the biblical canon, since verse 2 is not only an allusion to Genesis 1 (the creation of heaven and earth) but even more explicitly to the end of the mosaic books, where after the completion of the Torah (the book of laws and precepts) Moses taught the Israelites a song or a poem that begins "Give ear, O heavens, and I will speak, and let the earth hear the words of my mouth." (Deut 32:1) In content, form, and function, Moses' song is very similar to Isaiah 1, given that it addresses a future when the people will have left the Lord and forgot the Torah. Thus, from the very beginning, written revelation is accompanied by an oral supplement, and prophecy is no more related to the future than to the past which it repeats but also transforms.[11]

Secondly, it is important to note that verses 2–4 are poetry, characterized by parallelism, metaphoricity, wordplay, and a shift of address. There is parallelism on different levels, between that of heaven and earth, of nourishing and rebellion, or even phonetically in the *schm'u schamaim*, "Hear, o heavens". Parallelism, often seen as a mere device of memory, is a basic structural quality of poeticity if defined, following Jakobson, as the projection of the principle of equivalence from the axis of selection to the axis of combination.[12] As far as the imagery is concerned, the text regularly gives first an image and then the meaning: the rebellious children, ox and ass, followed by Israel who does not consider or understand. The verb used here for consider *bi'jn* also resonates with the *ben*, the children of verse 2, suggesting that not understanding means not being a good child, similar punning will structure the following lines. The text is thus poetic in the structural sense of reflecting upon its own making and its own language, here, upon the topical imagery of a land of milk and honey.

Thirdly, this passage exhibits a feature that is very common in Hebrew poetry and structurally important for the prophetic discourse: a complex and actually shifting situation of speech. Apart from the anonymous scribe of verse 1, we seem to read the poetical voice of Isaiah who quotes the Lord. And indeed, Prophecy is in large part reported speech, the word of the Lord by the word of man. However, as we have already seen, this reporting is not always transparent. The formula "the Lord has spoken" has the function of a quotation mark and is usually interpreted as a messenger formula, a seal intended to authenticate a transmitted message.[13] Be this as it may, in written language this formula has an ambivalent function, since the Hebrew construction, *ki adonai dibber* can mean both present and past: does the Lord actually speak, or has he spoken? Nor is the address clear: if the Lord (or the prophet) begins addressing "my people" as an object in the third person ("they have forsaken me") he turns to "you" in verse 5. The discourse is thus essentially hybrid, and we might argue that this

---

11 See Fisch, *Poetry with a Purpose*, esp. chap. 5.
12 See Jakobson, *Selected Writings*, 121–144.
13 See Westermann, *Basic forms of Prophetic Speech*.

as an important function to simulate divine discourse in human discourse. Oscillating between different speech acts, prophetic discourse has "an implied element of 'as if'", as Robert Alter states: "If we could actually hear God talking, making His will manifest in words of the Hebrew language, what would He sound like?"[14] This again, has theological consequences that might also have implications for Political Theology. A Sovereign, or at least divine one, cannot be expressed directly but only by a mixed discourse, by a discourse in movement.

The instability of discursive levels also affects the very meaning of prophetic speech, for the movement just mentioned is hard to stop. This becomes obvious shortly thereafter in the poem. After threatening the unfaithful people that they might be deserted as Sodom, the prophet repeats his initial address, however, this time not to Heaven and Earth: "Hear the word of the Lord, you rulers of Sodom! Give ear to the teaching of our God, you people of Gomorrah!" (Isa 1:10) The text moves from comparison to identification, from 'you might become like Sodom and Gomorra' to 'you are actually Sodom and Gomorra' – and you know what happened to them, the turn seems to imply. However, being put in the second person, this admonition leads to paradox: you do not only know what happened to those who did not listen, but you are actually Sodom and Gomorra and thus do not and will not listen. It is actually hard to imagine a harsher bashing of the audience. No wonder that the prophetic books narrate again and again how the actual audience of the prophets, the people of Israel, either became aggressive towards the prophet, or, more cynically, simply turned away. Already here, after 10 verses, the prophetic proclamation seems to have reached a dead end.[15]

Moreover, not only do the Israelites no longer hear the word, God won't hear them either. The poem goes on to state that there will be no offerings (verse 11) nor prayers, as verse 15 stresses: "When you spread out your hands, I will hide my eyes from you; even though you make many prayers, I will not listen; your hands are full of blood." As is repeatedly stated in the prophetic corpus, God will henceforth not hear the crying of the people (Jeremiah 11:11, Ezekiel 8:18), nor will He listen to its representative, the prophet: "As for you, do not pray for this people, or lift up a cry or prayer for them, and do not intercede with me, for I will not hear you." (Jeremiah 7:16) This renders the prophet in a paradoxical position: if prophecy traditionally has been part of a symmetrical and reciprocal relation, part of the institution of the covenant, a necessary means to mediate between its parties, then it now no longer is. Prophecy thus becomes

---

14 Alter, *The Art of Biblical Poetry*, 141.
15 See Fisch, *Poetry with a Purpose*, esp. chapter 4.

the paradox of the communication of non-communication, the announcement that there will be no more announcements. The prophetic proclamations again and again question the covenant which Israel had broken, by doing so, however, they also place themselves into question as part of this very institution: if neither God nor prophet hears the message, then what remains to be done for the prophet?

To be sure, this paradox is far from being complete. Communication does not end even if it is distorted and twisted, the condemnation is never complete, or, in other words, prophecy constantly rotates around the question about what remains to be done in a desolate situation. The harsh admonishments and whips against the stubborn audience can as abruptly turn to hope and consolation as it turned against the audience. Even if Israel has forgotten the Lord and will be destroyed completely, there might be a small remainder from which a new Israel will grow, as Isaiah 6 suggests. Despite a whoring Zion who betrayed her husband as in Hosea 1, she might still come back to her lover. What Harold Fisch called a "poetics of violence" works both ways, by terror and seduction, but in either case it will be extreme.[16] It has an affective dimension that might be constitutive for any theological discourse as well as for any political theology, since it also works with terror and seduction, i.e. it depicts apocalyptic demise in the near future but also suggests that we might be those who already understand the future and can begin to act upon it.

3

Since, in prophecy, the place of power and the place of truth do not coincide, it remains an attractive option not only for the politics of the powerlessness but also for democratic politics which is built around an empty space. Thus, the nineteenth and twentieth century faced a long line of prophetic or charismatic politics.[17] Often, it is a politics of crisis and of revolution, a politics that tends to criticize not only the ruling sovereign but also the institutions that surround him as bonds and contracts. However, it can also affirm these contracts and remember an idealized past to which the present must return. In any case, it suffers from the paradoxes of its performative setting, which we have already seen in the biblical material. As Kathleen Kaveny has argued, prophetic rhetoric has to walk a fine line, since it refers to fundamental ethical concerns and delivers fun-

---

16 See Fisch, *Poetry with a Purpose*, 135.
17 See Gutterman, *Prophetic Politics*; McKanan, *Prophetic Encounters*.

damental critique of the present, while at the same time it has to be careful not to fall into contempt for its listeners.[18] It also has ambiguous effects. It can enliven the public sphere, breaking up distinctions and routines, surprising and invigorating political discourse, but also runs the danger of polarization and moralization, of ripping the public sphere completely apart. It is a form of antipolitics that transgresses the limits of a given situation, but also runs the risk of destroying any political situation whatsoever. Could it renew an engagement with what we consider as fundamental moral questions, or does it rather reify these questions into rhetorical formulas? Would this allow, as I argued in the beginning, a shift of Political Theology's attention from questions of sovereignty to broader questions of modern society and subjectivity?

In conclusion, let me develop my third example, James Baldwin, whose essay *The fire next time* has gained an uncanny actuality in the context of reemerging racial tensions. Quoting a traditional spiritual "God send the rainbow as a warning sign. No more water, the fire next time" – we are, thus, not too far from the discourse of signs and warnings of biblical prophecy, and obviously this title and the whole essay and Baldwin as such stands in the tradition of black political theology, think only of Martin Luther King, Jr. To be sure, Baldwin does not transfer a religious proclamation, but he does speak in the name of the American tradition and in the name of a reality that is disavowed by his audience in a way that is not completely different from Isaiah who has to convince his hearers that they are not as elected as they assume.[19]

The situation in which Baldwin speaks and the audience which he addresses makes his address equally instable and precarious, but also similarly powerful as the Hebrew prophets we read. For imagine a society that is inherently divided into masters and slaves, into those who are free and sovereign individuals, and others whose freedom is denied – but this denial is never outspoken and always rationalized by other reasons, as the other being immature, uncivilized, or dangerous. Or, in Baldwin's words:

> "The white man's unadmitted – and apparently, to him, unspeakable – private fears and longings are projected onto the Negro. The only way he can be released from the Negro's tyrannical power over him is to consent, in effect, to become black himself, to become a part of that suffering and dancing country that he now watches wistfully from the heights of his lonely power, and armed with spiritual traveler's checks, visits surreptitiously after dark."[20]

---

18 See Kaveny, *Prophecy without Contempt*.
19 See Shulman, *American Prophecy*, esp. chapter 4.
20 Baldwin, "The Fire Next Time", 341.

The Negro is the product of the projection of those who consider themselves white, for becoming white always meant to disavow all that does not fit into the image of the sovereign self. It is a democratic paradox, for in democracy selfhood is not created through subjecting oneself under the sovereign but by subjecting others to oneself, Baldwin suggests. Even more important is to deny this very subjection, to consider oneself as innocent, that is, unknowledgeable and not willing to accept what has happened. Therefore, and this already touches the paradox of the address, Baldwin mostly speaks to the innocent, i.e. the good willing white liberals:

> "They are, in effect still strapped in a history which they do not understand, and until they understand it, they cannot be released from it. The have had to believe for many years, and for innumerable reasons, that black men are inferior to white man. Many of them, indeed, know better, but, as you will discover, people find it very difficult to act on what they know. To act is to be committed. And to be committed is to be in danger. In this case, the danger in the mind of most white Americans, is the loss of their identity."[21]

In a society of free individuals, individuality is still founded on dominion, only that it is not political dominion, but social a one that first of all rests on the premise that it can be ignored. Raising one's voice, claiming these ideals also for oneself is thus disturbing in itself, but might not be enough, for as mentioned, it is improbable that it would be heard, and even if heard it is improbable that it will create commitment. It does not suffice to convince the audience which is locked into this play of projection, but it has to be moved – moved affectively and moved out of the deadlock. One means of doing so is the purposefully ambiguous use of the address, of the 'we' in Baldwin. Quite often, he speaks in the name of the black community and even tends to claim exclusive authority to do so: whites are not able to understand what blacks experience. But in order to be able to do so, he must refer to a broader 'we': "In short, we, the black and the white, deeply need each other here if we are really to become a nation – if we are really, that is, to achieve our identity, our maturity, as men and women."[22] There is also a more fundamental covenant, both a memory and a premise which might allow for slave and master to acknowledge what was and what is. As every promise, this covenant to build a new nation also implies a threat:

> "It is a terrible thing for an entire people to surrender to the notion that one-ninth of its population is beneath them. Until the moment comes when we, the Americans, are able to accept the fact that my ancestors are both black and white, that on that continent we

---

21 Baldwin, "The Fire Next Time", 294.
22 Baldwin, "The Fire Next Time", 342.

are trying to forge a new identity, that we need each other ... – until this moment comes there is scarcely any hope for the American dream. If the people are denied participation in it, by their very presence they will wreck it."[23]

However, also when he uses a much narrower 'we', the black 'we', or even the private 'we', as in the letter to his nephew that makes up the first part of *The fire next time,* he can ask for much more than just for the abstract and general principles of mutual recognition, for he can reverse the demand of recognition: "And if the word integration means anything, this is what it means: that we, with love, shall force our brothers to see themselves as they are, to cease fleeing from reality and to begin to change it."[24] Even here in the demand of love, the dialectic of master and slave does not disappear and is not denied – but it is played in a fundamentally different way as to place the sovereign agency in the slaves hand and in the same move to transform this force from a force of suppression or revenge into the force of love. "I know that what I am asking for is impossible. But in our time, as in every time, the impossible is the least that one can demand."[25] Here, then, is another political theology, for if politics is the art of the possible, still the impossible is needed to break up the denials and disavowals that might be the main problems of democratic politics.

Bibliopgraphy

Agamben, Giorgio. *The Time that Remains: A Commentary on the Letter to the Romans*, ed. by Werner Hamacher, trans. Patricia Dailey. Stanford: Stanford University Press, 2005.
Alter, Robert. *The Art of Biblical Poetry*. New York: Basic Books, 1985.
Balfour, Ian. *The Rhetoric of Romantic Prophecy: Cultural Memory in the Present*. Stanford: Stanford University Press, 2002.
Baldwin, James. "American Dream and American Negro," In *Collected essays*, James Baldwin ed. by Toni Morrison. New York: Penguin Books, 1998.
Baldwin, James. "The Fire Next Time," In *Collected essays*, James Baldwin ed. by Toni Morrison. New York: Penguin Books, 1998.
Bercovitch, Sacvan. *The American Jeremiad*. Madison, Wis.: University of Wisconsin Press, 1978.
Blanton, Ward, and Vries, Hent De, eds., *Paul and the Philosophers*. New York: Fordham University Press, 2013.
Buber, Martin. *Kingship of God*, trans. Richard Scheimann. New York: Harper & Row, 1967.

---

23 Baldwin, "American Dream", 718–719.
24 Baldwin, "The fire next time", 294.
25 Baldwin, "The fire next time", 346.

Darsey, James. *The Prophetic Tradition and Radical Rhetoric in America*. New York: New York University Press, 1979.
Finkelde, Dominik. *Politische Eschatologie nach Paulus: Badiou – Agamben – Žižek – Santner.* Wien: Turia & Kant, 2007.
Fisch, Harold. *Poetry with a Purpose: Biblical Poetics and Interpretation*, Indiana University Press, 1988.
Gutterman, David. *Prophetic Politics: Christian Social movements and American Democracy.* Ithaca: Cornell University Press, 2005.
Halbertal, Moshe, and Holmes, Stephen. *The Beginning of Politics: Power in the Biblical Book of Samuel.* Princeton: Princeton University Press, 2017.
Jakobson, Roman. *Selected Writings*, vol. III, *Poetry of Grammar and Grammar of Poetry.* Cambridge, MA: Harvard University Press, 1987.
Kaveny, Cathleen. *Prophecy without Contempt: Religious Discourse in the Public Sphere.* Cambridge, MA: Harvard University Press, 2016.
Lebovi, Nitzan, and Weidner, Daniel, eds. "Propehtic Politics." Special Issue, *Political Theology* Nr. 21/1–2 (2020), https://www.tandfonline.com/toc/ypot20/21/1-2.
McKanan, Dan. *Prophetic Encounters: Religion and the American Radical tradition.* Boston: Beacon Press, 2011.
Polzin, Robert. *Samuel and the Deuteronomist: A Literary Study of the Deuteronomic History*, vol. 2: *1 Samuel*, New York: Harper & Row, 1989.
Schneidau, Herbert N. *Sacred Discontent: The Bible and Western Tradition.* Berkeley: University of California Press, 1976.
Shulman, George. *American Prophecy: Race and Redemption in American Political Culture*, Minneapolis, MN: University of Minnesota Press, 2008.
Sternberg, Meir. *The Poetics of Biblical Narrative: Ideological Literature and the Drama of Reading*, Bloomington: Indiana University Press, 1985.
Walzer, Michael. *Exodus and Revolution.* New York: Basic Books, 1985.
Westermann, Claus. *Basic forms of Prophetic Speech*, trans. Hugh Clayton White. Philadelphia: Westminster Press, 1967.

Florian Grosser
On the Abuses and Uses of Political Theology
Schmitt, Arendt, and the 'Trump Moment'

Abstract: This paper offers a critical analysis of the role of political theology in contemporary political praxis and theory. In particular, it examines the idea that a retrieval of politico-theological thinking can counter what some theorists describe as the disorienting effects of 'postmodern relativism'. With a focus on the United States, the paper first shows that the political landscape there attests to an excessive political theology that is 'messianic' in structure and that carries markedly Schmittian traits on the level of its content as it detaches decision-making from prudential and ethical concerns. Subsequently, it argues that the fact that 'new political theology' in its currently dominant (messianic, decisionist, and conflictual) form is incompatible with cornerstones of what Hannah Arendt defines as 'real democracy' does not preclude a different return to conceptual resources provided by the politico-theological tradition: This productive alternative is elaborated with the help of Arendt's reinterpretation of two notions central to Schmitt's discourse, sovereignty and the miracle.

In his 2012 *Manifesto of New Realism*, Italian philosopher Maurizio Ferraris argues that the 'irrealism' of postmodern thought is a key explanatory factor for the rise of populism and the resulting crisis of democracy: on his account, postmodernism with its strategies of 'ironization' and 'deobjectification', its rejection of 'grand narratives' and, above all, its claim as to the "primacy of interpretations over facts",[1] has not only undermined whatever emancipatory aspirations might have fueled it originally. What is more, it has paved the way for an ideological appropriation of its tenets by neo-Machiavellian types who exploit the diffuse, latently relativistic sense of disorientation that, disseminated by various forms of postmodern-inspired cultural production and reiterated by mass media outlets, has increasingly caught hold of Western societies since the 1980s. From close by, Ferraris witnessed how such a type – the entertainer, businessman, and media mogul Silvio Berlusconi – stepped out of the TV screen to seize the 'empty place of power' and became the longest-serving prime minister in post-war Italy. Against the predominance of a 'realitism' that blurs fiction and reality he advo-

---
[1] Ferraris, *Manifesto of New Realism*, 2.

cates for a 'realist transformation' of philosophy: a transformation that finds expression in an insistence on experience and perception, in "a new openness toward the external world".[2]

Although they suggest remedies other than 'ontology, criticism, enlightenment', analyses strikingly similar to Ferraris's have gained renewed momentum in political theory in the aftermath of the 2016 US presidential election. While some see Donald Trump as a figure that capitalizes on what Ferraris describes as an 'implosion' of the postmodernist worldview by spinning 'alternative facts', others regard him as an indicator that deconstructive movements and their agenda of revealing the unfounded character of nation-state and religion, of individual and collective identity have exhausted themselves – while a third group perceives his ideology and policies as a bulwark against contingency. Whether such analyses are critical of the 'The Donald Trump Moment'[3] in contemporary politics, whether they read this moment as symptomatic of a shift in democratic tectonics, or whether they affirm it, they converge in relating its emergence to diversifying and destabilizing tendencies promoted by representatives of postmodern thought such as Jean-François Lyotard, Jacques Derrida, or Judith Butler. One suggestion as to how firm(er) ground can be regained—how political order and community can be reconceived in post-post-metaphysical, non-contingent categories—envisages a turn not to a 'new realist' ontology but to a 'new political theology'.[4] In addition to overcoming the disorientation induced by postmodernism, the creative return to a discourse significantly initiated and shaped by Carl Schmitt is thought to open up transformative possibilities that transcend the status quo and point beyond the immanence characteristic of our late-modern present – beyond, to borrow a term form Eric Santner, our deep 'stuckness' within an economic and social (neo-)liberalism of global reach that plays out on the levels of political language and imagination, procedures and institutions.

It is the cogency and validity of this interpretative framework, composed of an analytical part (the idea of *postmodern disorientation*) and a remedial or aspirational part (the idea of *politico-theological reorientation*), that the following remarks seek to examine. To this end, the first section assembles observations on contemporary US politics: consulting empirical data on voter behavior while con-

---

[2] Ferraris, *Manifesto of New Realism*, 18.
[3] This is the title of a 2016 conversation between *New York Times* columnists Gail Collins and Arthur Brooks.
[4] For pertinent interventions that discuss the revolutionary potential of the notion of 'divine violence' and the paradigmatically revolutionary figure of St. Paul see Žižek, *Violence* and Badiou, *Saint Paul* respectively.

ceptually drawing on Michael Walzer's distinction between 'mosaic' and 'messianic' politics, today's political landscape, it is argued, attests to an *excess* rather than a *deficit* of political theology (I). Following the discussion of its 'messianic' structure, the substance of this excessive political theology is probed. Here, it is held, that this substance is best understood in terms of Carl Schmitt's thought – in particular, his considerations on politics in relation to the religious sphere. Juxtaposing Schmitt's 1922 *Political Theology* with discourses that provide ideological support to the US administration, it is shown that the manner in which its decision-making is detached from both prudential and ethical concerns carries markedly Schmittian traits (II). Against the background of this cross-section of American politics, the subsequent section takes up the suggestion at the heart of the interpretative approach described above: it reassesses the role of postmodern thought in the resurgence of a problematically theologized messianic, decisionist, and conflictual politics (III). The final section takes up the aspirational element of this approach, i.e. the idea of politico-theological reorientation. While 'new political theology' in its presently dominant Schmittian form is incompatible with cornerstones of what Hannah Arendt defines as 'real democracy'[5], this does not preclude the possibility of a different return to conceptual resources provided by the politico-theological tradition. This possibility will be elaborated with the help of Arendt's reinterpretation of two notions central to Schmitt's discourse, the notions of *sovereignty* and, especially, of the *miracle* (IV).

1 The temptation of messianism

Although it has received little attention by political commentators, the phenomenon of so-called 'Obama-Trump voters' is one of the more striking features of contemporary US politics. As studies show, nine percent of those who had voted for Barack Obama in the 2012 presidential election voted for Donald Trump four years later; and thirteen percent of those who voted for Trump had voted for Obama before – a total number of at least six million people.[6] In face of the apparent differences between the successive presidents as to

---

[5] See Arendt, "Nation-State", 255–261. This point will be taken up in the concluding section.
[6] Such studies have been conducted by the bipartisan *Democracy Fund* and *American National Election Studies*, a voter survey run by the University of Michigan and Stanford University. See https://www.voterstudygroup.org/search-results?s=obama+trump+voters (accessed 04. Dec. 2019) and http://politicaledu.org/2017/07/26/obama-trump-voters/#_ftn1 (accessed 04. Dec. 2019).

their worldviews, agendas, and policies, their backgrounds and personalities, this voter behavior seems odd. Yet, certain parallels become discernible if one takes into account discursive underpinnings of the approaches to politics presented to the public in both their candidacies; and if one considers their self-descriptions in relation to what both disparagingly referred to as 'the system': what partially explains the significant number of 'Obama-Trump voters' is the recognition that their anti-status quo rhetoric, their air of change and disruption, their narratives of awakening and return, tapped into a deep ideological reservoir overabundant with notions of salvation and deliverance. That the majority of these voters are evangelical Christians suggests that such affective energies were indeed mobilized in their presidential campaigns – all the more so since sixty percent of evangelicals, the largest religious group in the US, consider a 'second coming' of Christ 'likely' to happen by 2050. In this climate of anticipation, both candidates could cast themselves as rescuer and redeemer, could strategically deploy and politicize theological notions.[7]

Evidently, there are considerable divergences regarding these politico-theological mobilizations by Obama and by Trump respectively;[8] and there are even more fundamental differences in the extent to which these mobilizations have been brought to bear in actual policy-making.[9] Yet, what their applied political theologies have in common is the promise of a *solid ground* and of a *way out* – to the comfort of a substantial part of the electorate they are offered as cure-alls for the ills of ideological looseness and institutional stuckness. Whether we broadly understand 'political theology' as a dispute concerning the *general relation* between religious concepts and attitudes on the one hand and political life on the other or whether we understand it in terms of a *specific relation* in which such ideas and comportments actually shape the political sphere, these brief observations indicate why the present American situation can hardly be described as lacking in political theology.

---

[7] These observations might also allow one to better comprehend how the current holder of the office could redirect these enormous expectant energies to his advantage by depicting his predecessor as 'false messiah' when addressing evangelicals who had voted for Obama; and as 'demon' when addressing the vast majority within this key voting bloc who had always been hostile toward the Obama presidency.
[8] Particularly during his first campaign, Obama's approach was heavily imbued with *eschatological* motives. In contrast, Trump has presented himself as a bulwark against decline and, not least, as a leader who holds back the forces that undermine or attack America as a Christian nation, thereby insinuating something more akin to the logic of the *katechon*.
[9] The contrast between Obama's (messianic) campaigning and his (mosaic) governing style may have contributed to former supporters feeling 'let down' after having been 'uplifted'.

Beyond pointing to its prevalent guises, it is necessary to grasp the structures of belief and desire that are expressed as well as driven forward by such brands of political theology. For a first approximation, Michael Walzer's distinction between an 'exodus politics' and 'political messianism' can provide some insight:[10] whereas the former '*mosaic*' approach accepts that politics unfolds within history, that its success depends on individual and collective effort, and that such effort is notoriously threatened by 'backsliding', the latter '*messianic*' approach largely places its bets on divine intervention;[11] and whereas mosaic politics, cautious in formulating expectations, strives for gradual improvement, 'utopianist' messianic politics hopes for radical transformation. The wide resonance of the slogans of change and disruption suggests that for many ('Obama-Trump' and other) voters mosaic considerations are overridden by messianic desires for transcendence and overcoming – or, in Walzer's terms, for reaching Eden rather than Canaan. What is at stake in committing to one of the two modes with their irreconcilable takes on temporality and agency, on difference and conflict, is one's relation to democracy. Walzer leaves no doubt that messianism, simultaneously generative of 'quietude' and zealous, aggressive displacement activities amounts to an 'anti-politics' corrosive of democratic coexistence as defined by 'argument', 'compromise', and 'interpretation'. "Messianism", he concludes, "is the great temptation of Western politics."[12]

2 In a Schmittian key

In light of the degree to which American politics seems to succumb to this temptation, it is required to further examine the content transported by today's messianic political theology. In broad terms, its gaining currency is attributable to the fact that it addresses the desire for the abovementioned combination of looseness and stuckness, the sense of uncertainty on the one hand, of paralysis on the other, to be overcome: in its promise to resolutely act disruptively (i.e., independent of the 'tinkering' of established democratic agents, procedures, and institutions) and restoratively (i.e., allowing for the retrieval of lost integrity), it lays claim to stable foundations and non-contingent ways forward. This *foundational-directional* thrust finds condensed expression in the slogan of 'Mak-

---

[10] For a concise discussion see Walzer, *Exodus*, 133–149.
[11] For Walzer, the only form of politically relevant human agency recognized in this messianism consists in 'forcing the end', i.e. in contributing to an apocalyptic moment that precedes 'messianic times'.
[12] Walzer, *Exodus*, 135.

ing America Great Again' and the corresponding narrative according to which a re-solidified and unstuck future is achieved by means of re-appropriating a past order that has been systematically hollowed out and contaminated, disregarded and disrespected by 'un-American' ideological and social forces.

The substance and inner logic of this narrative with its messianic underpinnings can be better grasped by paying attention to affinities it reveals to the politico-theological theory of Carl Schmitt. For the examination undertaken here, this is not a matter of documenting any direct influence – even though Schmittian thought undoubtedly enjoys a vivid afterlife in the 'alt right'.[13] Instead, what is of interest is how certain mechanisms at work in the present administration's policy-making and in its understanding of the underlying justificatory basis relate to notions at the center of Schmitt's writings. Rather than aiming at a comprehensive account, a few elements of Schmitt's messianic political theology are selected that can illuminate the applied messianism of the 'Trump moment'.[14] A first cluster of affinities emerges around a *personalist understanding of political authority*. The idea of absolute sovereignty concentrated in *un seul architecte* as the ultimate, in fact the only political subject is not only at the root of Schmitt's early, approving interest in Rousseau's *législateur* and Hobbes's *Leviathan*;[15] it also crystallizes in the opposition he posits between a pseudo-politics marked

---

[13] Remarkable direct connecting lines and processes of reception have been documented by scholars like Mark Koyama and journalists like Peter Maas. Their works show that Schmitt is a major ideological influence on agenda setters in 'alt right' media outlets as well as on high-ranking members of the administration. One prominent example is Michael Anton who, prior to serving as a senior national security official in the Trump government, advocated for a Trump presidency in his 2016 article "The Flight 93 Election". The article casts the then-candidate as katechontic restrainer and America's last rescue.

[14] Although some commentators read Schmitt as a 'counter-messianic' theorist who ultimately dissolves religious matters including Christian messianism into mere political history (e.g., Bernard Bourdin), the messianic dimension of Schmitt's reflections on 'sovereignty', conceived in terms of 'divine creation' *ex nihilo* and of the 'miracle', is cogently analyzed by others (e.g., Antoni Abat i Ninet): In his remarks on Donoso Cortes that tie sovereign leadership directly to the notion of 'divine miracle', Schmitt suggests that 'miracles' of sovereignty are required to prevent the victory of the forces of evil. While in the context of the mid-nineteenth century Cortes is concerned with 'the decisive battle between Catholicism and atheist socialism', Schmitt brings to bear Cortes upon his own time and his own critique of what he labels as 'bourgeois liberalism'. For him, versions of such a 'battle' take effect the moment political activity is transposed from talk and negotiation to sovereign decision and open confrontation. See Schmitt, *Politische Theologie*, 50–55.

[15] Carl Schmitt will seek to further immunize Hobbes's theory of the 'strong state' in his 1938 *Leviathan*. He concludes this work, written under the impression and in defense of the National Socialists' rise to power, with the exclamation '*Non iam frustra doces, Thomas Hobbes!*'.

by 'discourse' and 'debate' and a politics proper defined by the 'independent significance of the subject of decision-making' or, in short, by 'dictatorship'.[16] As Schmitt holds (and affirms), such sovereign authority is modeled on the idea of an almighty God which all modern endeavors in secular politics have denied but failed to do away with. Such authority remains silent insofar as it rejects all modes of exchanging and thinking through ideas in expert consultations, in parliamentary debates, or in engaging with the governed. In denying that other persons' perspectives and concerns can play a political role, decision-making turns into a quiet monologue, a matter of gut feeling on the part of the sovereign. That notions like 'the interest of the people' are occasionally invoked thinly veils the fact that the only standard is the personal experience and intuition of the one 'strong' enough to make decisions.

With this cancelling out of exchange, a further affinity becomes apparent between what is laid out by Schmitt and carried out by the current US leadership: political life is detached from the *aspiration of approximating truth*. In a peculiar double-attack on the relevance of truth (aspirations) for politics one finds, firstly, an appeal to the notion of privileged access to truth by those in power – to truth in capital letters, so to say, which is removed entirely from common discourse. Schmitt introduces a *foundationalist* element into his reflections when he refers to 'metaphysical truth', gesturing to its content in the registers of Heraclitean thought (a universe shaped by *polemos*) and, primarily, of Catholic teaching (a universe governed by an almighty God). On the other hand, conceptions of truth, whether as correspondence or as coherence, are discredited when Schmitt holds that genuine decision is 'born out of nothing'. By thus introducing an openly *anti-foundationalist* element, truth is not only marked as inaccessible for the many but as categorically unattainable. In combination with his personalist understanding of authority, this leads to an embrace of what can be described as active nihilism.[17] This anti-foundationalism not only deeply informs Schmitt's central idea that the extra-legal constitutes the ground floor dimension of legality but it also essentially shapes his own brand of 'post-truth politics' indebted to Hobbes's formula: *auctoritas, non veritas facit legem*.[18]

---

16 See Schmitt, *Politische Theologie*, 33.
17 Throughout his writings, Schmitt sets such active nihilism apart from what he describes as the passive, impotent nihilism of liberalism which, he holds, discursively and procedurally dissolves all authentic opposition.
18 The formula is mentioned when Schmitt remarks on the fundamental difference between 'discussion' and 'dictatorship'. This foundationalist/anti-foundationalist hybrid further culminates in the characterization, indebted to Joseph de Maistre, of sovereign decision as 'infallible' and 'unappealable'. See Schmitt, *Politische Theologie*, 46, 50.

Rather than a (hostile) takeover of postmodern strategies of 'deconstructing' and of 'making meaning slide' by the Right, the Hobbesian formula and its idiosyncratic recurrence in Schmitt seem to be a plausibly traceable source of present-day American politics with its proliferation of 'alternative facts'. The hybrid of foundationalism and anti-foundationalism might also help to explain the alliance between a president who, invoking 'executive privilege' and ruling by decree and executive order,[19] holds in contempt any exterior, inter-subjective, codified, or transcendent frame of reference; and a vice-president who describes himself as an 'Evangelical Catholic'. It might also partially account for the appeal of these strange bedfellows to an electorate in which a radically individualist, voluntarist attitude of 'free choice' coexists with notions of divine providence and 'God's own country'.

It is thus a trait of the contemporary excess of messianic political theology that many of its themes and motives play out in a Schmittian key. Deployed against much-bemoaned *Immanenzvorstellungen*,[20] two distinct, yet interrelated moments – *originalist-metaphysical* and *decisionist-active nihilist* – coincide in this version of messianism that insinuates to transport a collective disenchanted and disillusioned by ordinary politics to an extra-ordinary sphere thanks to 'miraculous' sovereign conduct unbound by explanation, justification, or accountability. As to its content, this late-modern iteration of what Michael Walzer refers to as the 'anthropomorphic theology' at the heart of early-modern absolutism,[21] can be spelled out along Schmittian lines in yet another way: for the epitome of authority, the sovereign *fiat* to be effective as a cure for immanentism, its proponents consider it vital to unleash unmediated conflict against enemies who are identified (or invented) through essentializing operations – a point to return to in the following section.

3 What disorientation? Which postmodernism?

In considering configurations of enmity that energize protagonists and partisans of today's messianic political theology, it seems advisable to return to the initial concern with the role postmodern theory has played for its formation and in the resurgence of related phenomena of authoritarianism and nationalism. Is there

---

[19] The strategy of undercutting state agencies and bureaucracy (or, in the terminology of Trump allies, 'the deep state') by leaving thousands of high- and mid-level government positions unfilled fits into this picture, too.
[20] See Schmitt, *Politische Theologie*, 44.
[21] See Walzer, *Regicide and Revolution*, 8–34.

any evidence that postmodern projects of 'diversifying identity' have contributed to bringing about the desire – at least partially satisfied by Schmittian originalist-decisionist, conservative-revolutionary political theology – to regain safe ground while pushing forward into the exhilaratingly new? Or that such projects have provoked a longing for a rock solid, hyper-integrated collective identity by having advocated for plural, fluid, hyper-atomized individual identities?

All indications suggest that, in the American case, the significance of postmodernism is *marginal* – all the more so when it is compared to other developments that have induced stuckness in uncertainty. The limited influence it exerts in the context of politico-cultural controversies is further based on selective, mostly *distortive* references to Derridean, Rortyan, or Butlerian ideas.[22] Let me support these assertions regarding marginality and distortion in turn. To reduce the risk of philosophical speculations on the 'Trump moment' going awry, it is worth taking into consideration factors identified as impactful in producing disorientation by empirical social research. To name only a few, such factors include the drawn-out crisis of democratic representation that has resulted in oligarchic, plutocratic structures gaining ground (and, as a reaction, to a growing number of disillusioned and, therefore, unaffiliated 'independents', today the largest segment in the electorate); the corresponding neglect of the 'social question' across the political spectrum that has occurred at a moment when the economic and professional world have undergone dramatic changes, due to new technologies and new economies with their demand of individual 'responsibilization', of keeping up and fitting in; and an aggravating environmental crisis made manifest in wild fires, mud slides, floods, hurricanes, and declining air and water quality, which no amount of denial and misinformation can cover up. In light of these phenomena and their tangible effects on social justice, economic inclusion, and political participation, the perception that the world is out of joint and in need of anchoring, cohesion, and direction, and that the available tools of democratic politics are insufficient to escape a downward spiral is hardly surprising; neither is the broad resonance of political endeavors that promise resolute leadership and secure homely belonging, in particular among the groups most directly affected by these developments. In all this, there is little

---

[22] It must be noted that these ideas typically do not even break through the walls of comparative literature and rhetoric departments to enter political philosophy syllabi or political science curricula – let alone leave behind the academic world to have an impact on public consciousness and discourse.

to suggest that 'postmodern relativism' – a rather broad and inconclusive category of analysis[23] – might be on par with such momentous disorienting factors.

Although set in the specific context of Germany during the 1960s, Theodor Adorno's recently published reflections on 'new right-wing extremism' prove instructive for our discussion.[24] There, Adorno retraces how the (well-substantiated) perceptions regarding the 'tendency towards concentration of capital' (*Konzentrationstendenz des Kapitals*) and the 'spectre of technological unemployment' (*Gespenst der technologischen Arbeitslosigkeit*), together with the (largely ungrounded) 'feeling of a foreign threat' (*Gefühl der außenpolitischen Bedrohung*), bring about the societal conditions for such extremism.[25] From the vantage point of social psychology, his analyses address the seemingly paradoxical way nationalist ideology unfolds its 'demonic' destructive force at the moment in which the nation-state is losing its status as the main political unit in processes of supra-national integration. On Adorno's account, however, it is precisely because even the supporters of nationalism recognize this development as objective that their commitment is so uncompromising. This attitude of defiance also explains their fascination with visions of apocalyptic doom – rather than facing the disappearance of what they take to be the essential basis of their collective identity, they embrace 'the end'.[26] With an eye to political strategies that exploit and actively fabricate such attitudes, Adorno mentions propaganda (which, he argues, becomes 'the substance of the matter'); the 'permanent repetition' of unfounded assertions that verge on lies; a 'concretism' composed of pseudo-objective data and hyper-subjective anecdotes and, thus, immunized against questions of proof; and an appeal to 'punitiveness', *Straffreudigkeit*, directed against antagonists from within and without. A further characteristic of such ideological 'revenants' consists in their muttered allusions to 'support behind them' – an unspecific 'support' beyond ordinary politics which is supposed to function as a 'guarantor' for sweeping success.[27] Undoubtedly, current messianic political theology, with its promises of deliverance by miraculous, sover-

---

23 With a specific focus on 'poststructuralism' – in itself "an array of theoretical and methodological approaches", yet only one strand of 'postmodernism' – Gerald Posselt and Sergej Seitz critically examine the charges of 'constructivism' and 'relativism' that have been levelled against it by, for instance, Jürgen Habermas, Axel Honneth, or Paul Boghossian. See Posselt and Seitz, "Relativism and Poststructuralism", 133–143.
24 See Adorno, *Aspects*.
25 See Adorno, *Aspects*, 2–4.
26 Adorno points to the figure of Wotan in Richard Wagner's *The Ring* as an archetype for thus 'wanting the end'.
27 See Adorno, *Aspects*, 12.

eign forms of unchecked, unrestricted truth and power, provides suggestions for how the empty container of such an enigmatic 'support' can be filled with content. For Adorno, this ideological 'praxis without concepts', its 'techniques' and 'tricks' cannot be countered by means of moralizing. The satisfaction provided by displays of grandiose gestures of authority and the stirring up of a rhetorical-affective union can only be unmasked as vain if the 'disastrous' consequences inherent to nationalism with a messianic 'support behind it' are demonstrated to its supporters. While Adorno mentions the unfree disciplining effects on the private sphere and lifestyle of the youth, his argument concerning 'drastic interests' might well be extended to economic inequality, social outclassing, and political disenfranchisement when applied to the contemporary American situation.[28]

If identity diversification is nonetheless invoked as destabilizing by partisans of the 'alt right' in the 'cultural war' fought in blogs, online forums, and on Twitter, one must keep in mind that their contact is not with postmodern thought but with mediatized derivations thereof that typically amount to caricatures.[29] What makes these derivations attractive, easy targets and flammable fuel for 'anti-liberal' resentment, is the fact that they operate by the principle that 'what does not fit is made to fit'. For one thing, the *epistemological frameworks* in which postmodern theorizing unfolds are misunderstood, neglected, or simply ignored – both by its culture-industrial epigones on the left and its fervent critics on the right. For instance, the emphasis on 'interpretation' and 'perspective' is by no means equivalent to promoting relativism. As is the case in Nietzsche or in important strands of phenomenological and existentialist thought, the idea of seeing aspects from plural angles does not constitute an attack on objectivity and truth but is understood as an essential precondition for both.[30] More importantly, popularized postmodernism turns a blind eye on *normative commitments* in dominant strands of postmodern moral, political, and social thought: its sustained commitment to global equality, anti-racism, and anti-sexism, to 'solidarity', 'hospitality', 'recognizability', or an 'ethics of cohabitation' – not to mention its profound indebtedness to Kantian and Hegelian moral philosophy or to the political theologies of thinkers like Franz Rosenzweig, Walter Benjamin, and Em-

---

28 Here, the current administration's completed tax reform, its measures against *The Patient Protection and Affordable Care Act* or against voter registration come to mind.
29 This is proliferated by segments of the 'liberal' media and culture industry, by TV shows like *Transparent*, or in self-help literature like *The Transgender Child*.
30 The political implications of such multi-perspectivism have been spelt out by Hannah Arendt: For her, it is what prevents the collapse of a 'common world' and, with it, of politics proper – a point to come back to in the concluding section.

manuel Levinas.³¹ No, it is not Nietzsche who had Trump elected.³² And neither is it in reaction to *Grammatology* or *Gender Trouble* – or the alleged effects of such theoretical works like same sex marriage, transgender bathrooms, or LGBTQ+ pride events³³ – that people in the deindustrializing Rust Belt or in rural Alabama have been receptive to his messianic nationalism. While their resentment is at times transposed to such (removed) phenomena and their (perceived) sources in 'liberal intellectualism', it springs from the disorienting uncertainty they have to live through under the conditions of a late-capitalist economic, political, and social order.

What further supports the claim that 'postmodern relativism' is of limited significance in contemporary constellations is the identification of 'enemies' by both the political leadership and those who are most intensely carried away by the 'Trump moment'. Rather than turning to proponents of a new, fluid identity politics (of diversity), those with whom (to briefly return to Schmitt) 'dialogue' and 'synthesis' is impossible, are marked based on criteria of an old static identity politics (of essential otherness).³⁴ The 'battle' to safeguard American identity is *not* to

---

31 As Gerald Posselt and Sergej Seitz elaborate, even the postmodern category of 'contingency' – often described as postmodernism's key relativistic pitfall by its critics – is not without certain normative implications. They write:

"[O]ne of the crucial insights of poststructuralism consists in emphasizing the necessity of a critical attitude and argumentative practice that cannot retreat to a safe shelter of ultimate foundations without denying the necessity (and urgency) of contingent foundations and of articulating universal claims. In stark contrast to the 'relativist' claim that all grounds are 'contingent' and therefore 'equally valid,' poststructuralism sees 'contingency' itself as a normative criterion to evaluate conflicting truth claims, social structures, moral norms, and political institutions. It is precisely in this sense that 'the only democratic society is one which permanently shows the contingency of its own foundations' (Laclau 2000, 86), which is also the criterion to critically evaluate existing democracies, societies, moral systems, etc." (Posselt and Seitz, "Relativism and Poststructuralism", 140).

32 See Alloa, "Nuit de la philo".

33 It is far from obvious whether and how a tangible causal relation can be established between postmodern theory on the one hand and what is labeled as its practical outcomes on the other. Among other things, one runs the risk of unduly aggrandizing the social and political influence of the intellectual sphere in suggesting such a relation.

34 The heat and noise with which issues labelled as show pieces of a new, diverse, fluid identity politics are discussed online or in radio talk shows cannot conceal their negligible impact on policy-making: in three years, the Trump administration has embraced a rhetoric of 'traditional' gender roles but has done little to actually roll back legislation. However lukewarm the sentiment, however strategic the calculation – during his acceptance speech at the Republican National Convention, Trump, to the applause of the delegates, promised that he would do 'everything to protect our LGBTQ citizens' from, and this is quite telling as to how 'enemies' are set up, 'the violence and oppression of a hateful foreign ideology'.

be waged against queer or trans subjects and groups – as far as gender and sexual politics is concerned, the achievements of feminist and civil rights movements are under attack in attempts to change policy and legislation in favor of 'pro-life'. Moreover, otherness as enmity is primarily imagined and desired to play out along three lines: first, along *religious lines* – the blatant Islamophobia and resurgent Anti-Semitism provide ample evidence here; second, along *ideological lines* that date back to the 'cold war' – as can be seen in the fighting terms 'Marxist', 'socialist', and 'communist', which are notoriously used to discredit political rivals like Bernie Sanders, Elizabeth Warren, or Alexandria Ocasio-Cortez; and finally, along *racial lines* for, to be sure, today's reactionary movements in America are an essentially white attempt at coping with stuckness and looseness – an attempt that causes as much consternation as it does fear among all other ethnic groups. One should not forget that for many on the right, Barack Obama has been the epitome of all these existential threats since he first ran for office and that Trump effectively blazed his trail into the political arena with his 'birther' (conspiracy) theory, a discourse fully compatible with apocalyptic depictions of the first president of color as 'Anti-Christ' and 'Satan'.[35] It is *this* landscape of old identity politics in which neo-Schmittian messianic political theology can thrive and exist in dangerous excess.

The policy area to which notions of enmity are applied the most by the current administration is *immigration*. It is in relation to migrants (or, rather, to what Thomas Nail's recent work describes as fabricated 'figures of the migrant'), it is at the border that the allegedly decisive confrontation between 'authority and anarchy' – celebrated by Schmitt in his dictatorial suspension of legitimacy and embraced in current American politics – is concretely weaponized: the walls, fences, travel bans, deportations, and family separations, the sustained attack on so-called 'chain migration', and the demand of 'assimilation' (a term that has recently been substituted for 'integration' in official documents concerning immigration) reveal that deliverance from those who are foreign, those who are not native, is at the core of the promised miracle of sovereign decision that overcomes paralysis and disorientation. What is at stake is the recuperation of a closed stable community of those who share identical values, traditions, beliefs, and interests. For Michael Anton, the committed Schmittian and former high-ranking member in the Trump administration mentioned above, this constitutes the 'final test' for 'the American nation'. Tellingly, his intervention, which

---

35 For Walzer, the identification of 'Satanic enemies' is a distinguishing feature of messianic politics. See Walzer, *Exodus*, 141–143.

declares that Trump represents this nation's last best hope, concludes with the polemical question: 'a million more Syrians, anyone?'.

4 Political theology, give or take: Arendt on the 'miracle' of give-and-take

Drawing on Hannah Arendt, it is precisely with regard to migration that the final section examines the possibility of an alternative political theology and its capacities to overcome immanence. For the fact that katechontic, decisionist, inimical messianism is currently predominant does not preclude different, more 'mosaic' ways of politicizing certain conceptual resources of theology. Granted, despite her academic socialization amidst this "largely Germanic"[36] debate unfolding in the 1920s, the connections of Arendt's thought to political theology are rather inconspicuous; and her scattered remarks on the subject are ambiguous, wary, or outright critical.[37] Yet, her deep concern with Walter Benjamin's reflections on 'weak messianism' or the manifold reverberations of her early work on Augustine's concept of love in her later work indicate that she is neither unaffected by nor categorically opposed to the idea that theology can live on in modern politics – its self-understanding as secular notwithstanding. In fact, the question of the secular constitutes the center of her reflections on "the problem of the relationship between religion and politics".[38] It is primarily in this context that Arendt engages with Schmitt's politico-theological doctrine.

After a 'hidden dialogue' had been speculated about for some time,[39] recently published marginalia in her copies of *The Concept of the Political*, *The Nomos of the Earth*, *Theory of the Partisan* and *Political Theology* have confirmed the role of Schmitt as a point of reference and, ultimately, repulsion: while she repeatedly "travel[s] a great distance in Schmitt's company, [she] reach[es] an alternative destination."[40] Differing in their elaborateness and main focus, Arendt's annotations, for instance, give insight into how she sets her understanding of law (as

---

[36] Moyn, "Hannah Arendt on the Secular", 71.
[37] Her interpretation of the notion of 'necessity' in Marx as an anti-political 'absolute' equivalent to conceptions of an almighty God or her critical remarks on Rousseau's concept of the 'General Will' and his sigh *il faudrait des dieux* are cases in point. This has led commentators to conclude that Arendt's theory remains at a distance to the political-theological debate. See Gordon, "The Concept of the Apolitical", 855–878.
[38] Arendt, "Religion and Politics", 368.
[39] See Kalyvas, *Democracy*; Sluga, "The Pluralism of the Political", 91–109.
[40] Moyn, "Arendt on the Secular", 82.

lex rather than *nomos*) apart from Schmitt's 'pseudo-ontological' analysis that traces the law back to the conquest of land and soil;[41] they are less illuminating when it comes to politico-theological questions. Still, one marginal note in her copy of the 1933 second edition of *Political Theology* reflects what her distance to Schmitt is owed to: "*Entscheidung = Unheil = Willkür!*", Arendt scribbles on top of page 41.[42]

The note captures Arendt's 'alternative destination' in a nutshell: although she shares the concern of an 'end of politics' with Schmitt, she insists on the antidotes of mutuality, promise-making, contract, and concerted, discursive action. Her considerations are situated in the same problem horizon of stuckness and transformation as Schmitt's but in her understanding of both, she parts company: change, for Arendt, can only be achieved in plural 'worldbuilding' that takes seriously starting conditions of difference ('a chaos of difference' that breaks open with inter-subjectivity, i.e. long before and independent of concrete phenomena of 'immigration' or 'multi-cultural' societies) and that seeks to cope with rather than eliminate these conditions; and immanence, on her account, does not only manifest itself in political systems, procedures, and practices but also in political thinking that fails to discard inherited patterns. From her vantage point, Schmitt's political theology appears as such a failure since it reproduces and presents as inescapable the dependence of the political realm on the religious sphere. Against Schmitt's central claim that key political concepts are based on covered-up religious categories, she stresses the historicity and contingency of politico-theological constellations and, in particular, conceptions of sovereignty when she writes that "the long alliance between religion and authority does not mean that the concept of authority is itself of a religious nature."[43] The relation of dependency Schmitt posits between sovereignty and divine omnipotence or the state of exception and the miracle is *only one* attempt in the Western political tradition "to enforce absolute standards on a realm whose very essence seems to be relativity".[44] Thus, it is entirely conceivable

---

[41] For a detailed account of her critical reading see Jurkevics, "Hannah Arendt reads Carl Schmitt's The Nomos of the Earth", 345–366.
[42] Scanned versions of Arendt's Schmitt marginalia can be found at https://blogs.bard.edu/arendtcollection/marginalia/ (accessed 17 Oct. 2019).
[43] Arendt, "Religion and Politics", 372.
[44] Arendt, "Religion and Politics", 383. Departing from Schmitt's account once again, she argues that, rather than paradigmatic notions of absolute authority, 'Plato's myth of a Hereafter' and its medieval reformulations as 'the doctrine of Hell' are to be seen as the most, in fact the only effective 'political element in traditional religion'.

for her that, despite recurring 'trends that see religion everywhere',[45] the politically motivated search of an absolute can develop without recourse to theology and, for instance, embrace technological standards instead;[46] or that recourse to the religious domain can take forms that no longer look for any absolute foundation or external 'sanction' but are satisfied with partial, disjointed impulses and orientations.

It is this latter possibility that Arendt's own politico-theological interventions explore. As if taking up the warning against 'theocracy' in Benjamin's *Theologico-Political Fragment* – his reminder that politics can neither directly realize nor build on the religious – she rejects Schmitt's dependency claim and inverts his theologically grounded notion of miraculous sovereign decision. On the foil of her general conviction, expressed in *The Human Condition*, that 'the miracle of action' enables new, at times even revolutionary beginnings, her writings on migration seem to spell out her understanding of *the miracle of another sovereignty* in particular clarity: such miraculous sovereignty occurs bottom-up; it is made possible by plural forms of political subjectivity and agency; and it crystallizes in the encounter between 'strangers' – i.e., the very moment pervasive motifs of top-down decision-making are suspended and the 'bad spectator-like relation to reality'[47] and to the political sphere is overcome by individuals or groups.

Though Arendt puts emphasis on migrant 'newcomers' not 'shirking', 'defending themselves', and 'fighting for', on their part-taking and rights-taking (and such parti-cipation in the literal sense might well transgress codified law),[48] she does not suggest that their agency is self-sufficient or privileged. This becomes clear in the reflections on the *'right to have rights'* and *'real democracy'* at the core of her thinking on migration.[49] Without discussing problems of

---

[45] See Arendt, "Religion and the Intellectuals", 228–231, where she refers to such trends as "puffs of Zeitgeist" that "have followed their zigzag line ever since the Enlightenment, which was followed so closely by romanticism" and that have occurred in every generation. She concludes: "[I]t would be much more surprising if the rapid decline in religious belief which has taken place in Western culture during the last three hundred years were not interrupted by these intellectual memories".

[46] For a reconstruction of Arendt's critical reflections on 'political technology' see Van Camp, "Hannah Arendt and Political Theology", 19–35.

[47] See Adorno, *Aspekte*, 55.

[48] For more detailed discussions of Arendt's reflections on democratic part-taking by migrants see Honig, *Democracy*; Grosser, "Von Wolkenkratzern, Schmetterlingen und 'wirklicher Demokratie'", 99–129.

[49] Her reflections on the subject are systematically developed in the essays *We Refugees* (1943) and *Es gibt nur ein einziges Menschenrecht* (1949) as well as in the analysis of imperialism in *The Origins of Totalitarianism* (1951).

predominant, one-sidedly legalistic interpretations of this idiosyncratic 'right' here, systematically central passages in Arendt's writings reveal that it is not understood in terms of a codified protection of the politico-legal status of migrants in national, intra-, or supranational frameworks. She insists instead that the dangers of rendering particularly vulnerable persons and groups 'superfluous' through denaturalization, deportation, and detention[50] can only be reduced by means of a lived *praxis* and through a 'system of relations' where one is judged based on one's actions and convictions.[51] Any tangible realization of the 'right to have rights' is therefore not only contingent on acts of *taking* on the part of 'newcomers'; it equally depends on acts of *giving* on the part of those who are established 'members' of 'receiving' states and societies. For Arendt, it is citizens rather than institutions and procedures that give and guarantee the rights of others – especially, after the experiences of the twentieth century have shown that codified civil and human rights have failed in preventing expulsion, persecution, and the production of 'outlaws' such as 'displaced' and 'stateless persons'.[52] In this vein, Werner Hamacher encapsulates Arendt's position when he writes that "the sole human 'right' exists only if there are those who care for it and take care of it, who transfer it over to others and thereby maintain it in the movement of giving."[53] What thus emerges is the idea of a double-movement of *mutual give-and-take* in which inter-subjective relations and, thereby, a 'common world' are 'built' across lines of difference. What takes shape in this double-movement that transforms democratic community is referred to as a 'performative we' in the political phenomenologies of Judith Butler or Bernhard Waldenfels.[54] It is in opening up new forms of communal coexistence that the 'miracle of action' as the miracle of another sovereignty manifests itself: Such sovereignty is 'mosaic' in character as it springs from an effort in or of plural 'togetherness', as it is

---

50 Arendt's analyses of the extreme danger of being turned into 'nothing but human beings' and reduced to 'the abstract nakedness of being human' faced by stateless persons and refugees are taken up in Agamben's reflections on *homines sacri*. See Agamben, "We Refugees", 114–119.
51 Such a 'system', for her, characterizes a genuinely 'political community'. The formulations are taken from the *Menschenrecht*-essay. The key term *Beziehungssystem* used by Arendt, (mis-)translated into English as *framework*, confirms the irreducibility of her considerations to juridical matters.
52 Similar ideas of a relationally, inter-personally grounded politics, ethics, and law have recently been elaborated in the works of Song, "The Significance of Territorial Presence", 225–248; Wallace, *The Moral Nexus*; and Shachar, *Birthright Lottery*.
53 Hamacher, "The One Right No One Ever Has", 962.
54 See Butler, *Notes toward a Performative Theory of Assembly*; and Waldenfels, *Sozialität und Alterität*. For an interpretation of Arendt's political thought that takes her self-description as 'a sort of phenomenologist' as its point of departure see Loidolt, *Phenomenology of Plurality*.

aware that ever-new decisions will be required to allow for improvement (or to prevent 'backsliding'), and as it is open-ended with regard to the (more or less institutionalized) form it will take in processes of 'worldbuilding'. It is a miraculous sovereignty defined by 'encounter rather than command', by giving 'orientation' rather than demanding 'obedience'.[55]

Understood in this Arendtian key, miracles thus imply the need to reconceive of traditional citizenship and, first and foremost, sovereignty. A critical reconsideration of state and popular sovereignty is undertaken in Arendt's 1963 public lecture *Nation-state and Democracy*.[56] First, she points out that the notion of the sovereign nation-state and people, have their historical origins in absolutism. What is more, sovereignty must be seen as inherently tied to 'racial thinking' and, therefore, one of the root causes of the violent forms of nationalism during the twentieth century. These forms, Arendt stresses, are anything but limited to totalitarian regimes and anything but eliminated after the defeat of Hitler's Germany and Mussolini's Italy. Instead, the idea of national sovereignty resurfaces in an increasingly interconnected world. While anachronistic, it is tantamount to 'a dangerous megalomania' that goes hand in hand with 'xenophobia', an aggressive variation on 'folklore and *Heimat* kitsch'. Her conclusion is clear: as long as nationalism "with its egocentric narrow-mindedness"[57], appealing to sovereignty, continues to shape politics, the prospects for reforming the meaning of political community along the lines of common 'worldbuilding' are poor; and as long as established patterns of organization, determined by the 'trinity of people, territory, and state', are in place and political legitimacy depends on "nothing more than the consistent protection of citizens' basic rights",[58] the criteria for what Arendt calls 'real democracy' (*wirkliche Demokratie*) are not met. This is only the case if the *demos* is reconceived in terms of an uncommon community that neither relies on foundationalist notions of preexisting commonalities (e.g., by invoking shared traditions and values as constitutive of a 'natural' communal

---

[55] For a detailed discussion of these notions that draw on Arendt and, especially, Franz Rosenzweig to reject the Schmittian understanding of miracle see Honig, "The Miracle of Metaphor", 78–102.
[56] In this lecture, the term *Einwohner*, resident or (co-)habitant, is positioned as an alternative category to that of the *Bürger*, citizen; it thus indicates Arendt's reconceptualization of political community and membership. The idea of a *Mitverantwortlichkeit* with respect to one's *Mitmenschen*, invoked in her *Menschenrecht*-essay, underlines that such community and membership exceed the group of those who happen to be born into the same political order. The critique of the 'people's sovereignty', a crucial factor in the problematic 'identification of the rights of man with the rights of peoples', is anticipated in Arendt, *Origins of Totalitarianism*.
[57] Arendt, "Nation-State", 261.
[58] Arendt, "Nation-State", 260.

bond) nor on anti-foundationalist notions of deciding between friend and enemy (e. g., by invoking violent conflict as constitutive of such a bond). If we take "the right for all people [aller, i.e. all residents or co-habitants; FG] to participate in public affairs and to appear in the public realm and make themselves heard" as the principal criterion, it becomes evident that "democracy in the nation-state has never been in particularly good shape."[59]

Despite the bad shape American democracy is in in this 'Trump moment', are there any signs, however faint, that miracles as envisaged by Arendt are taking place? Some recent phenomena seem to suggest that this is indeed the case – the support of citizens for the *Día sin inmigrantes*, a day of boycott on which neither 'legal' nor 'illegal' migrants went to work, opened their businesses, spent money, or sent their children to school; their readiness to protest at airports across the country against *Executive Order 13769*, the 'Muslim ban'; or their approval for 'sanctuary' policies and jurisdictions that protect 'illegal' immigrants from deportation. However, these phenomena primarily occur in coastal and other metropolitan areas and, consequently, might be dismissed by sweeping objections from the Right as the work of 'naïve', 'unrealistic do-gooders' who fail to see that they contribute to a foreign invasion. Or they might be discredited as manifestations of 'secret privilege', sources of 'surplus enjoyment' on the part of 'liberal multi-culturalists' by a fashionable hermeneutics of suspicion formulated by self-declared 'radical leftists' like Slavoj Žižek (a 'paradox' gratefully adopted and exploited by reactionary agenda setters like Steve Bannon or Ann Coulter). Then what about Morristown, Tennessee – a small town in a state in which 61 percent, a county in which 76.6 percent of the votes had gone to Trump – where *Immigration and Customs Enforcement* and other state agencies arrested over one-hundred 'undocumented' immigrants employed at the local meatpacking plant on April 7, 2018? There, the sense that fellow residents and neighbors had been targeted unjustly spread throughout the conservative constituency. In order to prevent deportations, it led local government, business, and religious institutions to spontaneously collaborate with organizations in support of migrants as well as with affected families. And it led citizens to write character references for those arrested in droves, to connect them to lawyers, to raise funds for the legal costs to be covered, and to offer their families sanctuary sites in homes and churches.[60] The direct experience of 'urgent prox-

---

59 Arendt, "Nation-State", 260.
60 Local as well as national (for, NPR and *The New Yorker*) media have covered the events in Morristown.

imity',[61] the recognition of lived communal relations, and the resulting political *praxis* contributed to the prompt release of more than half of the arrested. Not to mention the profound re-orientation in questions of who belongs, who counts as a moral and political subject, who gets to decide matters of belonging and counting, and what justifies such decisions: "Miracles happen when we find ourselves able to suspend a pattern ... whereby one 'culpabilizes' the Other or ... cultivates *ressentiment*, with respect to a fundamental dysfunction or crisis within social reality."[62]

Hannah Arendt refers to miraculous moments in which sovereignty is reformed and community is founded anew not only in terms of mutual promises and guarantees of a 'right to have rights'. In an even more openly politico-theological tonality she also describes such moments as inter-subjective instantiations of the 'grace of love'. With direct reference to democratic coexistence under conditions of large-scale migration she holds that the dangers of violent exclusion "can be adequately dealt with only by the unpredictable hazards of friendship and sympathy, or by the great and incalculable grace of love."[63] Arendt's political considerations thus draw on two key theological notions ominously absent in Schmitt – and forgotten or brushed off by contemporary discourses in politics dramatically overdetermined by technological and economic categories. She thus demonstrates that what it takes to unstuck and reorient ourselves are neither new masters who model their dangerous (and equally laughable) grandstanding and strongarming on religious notions of unlimited might; nor new master narratives that, yearning for the altogether extraordinary and murmuring about the inevitability of conflict in reaching it, lend them support by invoking salvific history. What is needed instead are masterful re-connections, to critical re-appropriations of entries in the lexicon of theology to enrich our political language and imagination and, with that, to move the boundaries and break open the limits of our political world.

Bibliography

Adorno, Theodor. *Aspects of the New Right-Wing Extremism*, trans. Wieland Hoban, Cambridge/Medford, MA: Polity Press, 2020.

---

[61] Drawing on Rosenzweig and Benjamin, Eric Santner describes such experiences as "truly inhabiting the midst of life [by] being answerable to our neighbor and the demands of the day, *die Forderung des Tages*". Santner, "Miracles Happen", 133.
[62] Santner, "Miracles Happen", 89–90.
[63] Arendt, *Origins of Totalitarianism*, 301.

Agamben, Giorgio. "We Refugees," *Symposium* 49 (1995): 114–119.
Alloa, Emmanuel. "Nuit de la philo. Pourquoi ce n'est pas Nietzsche qui a fait élire Trump," *Libération*, 14 Nov. 2018, https://www.liberation.fr/debats/2018/11/14/nuit-de-la-philo-pourquoi-ce-n-est-pas-nietzsche-qui-a-fait-elire-trump_1692038 (accessed 04 Dec. 2019)
Arendt, Hannah. *The Origins of Totalitarianism*. New York: Houghton Mifflin Harcourt, [1951] 1973.
Arendt, Hannah. "Religion and the Intellectuals [1950]," In *Essays in Understanding: Formation, Exile, and Totalitarianism, 1930–1954*, Hannah Arendt, ed. by Jerome Kohn, 228–231. New York: Penguin Random House, 1994.
Arendt, Hannah. "Religion and Politics [1953]," In *Essays in Understanding: Formation, Exile, and Totalitarianism, 1930–1954*, Hannah Arendt, ed. by Jerome Kohn. New York: Penguin Random House, 1994.
Arendt, Hannah. "Nation-State and Democracy," In *Thinking Without a Banister: Essays in Understanding 1953–1975*, Hannah Arendt, ed. by Jerome Kohn. New York: Penguin Random House, 2018.
Badiou, Alain. *Saint Paul: The Foundation of Universalism*, trans. Ray Brassier. Stanford: Stanford University Press, 2003.
Butler, Judith. *Notes toward a Performative Theory of Assembly*. Cambridge, MA: Harvard University Press, 2015.
Ferraris, Maurizio. *Manifesto of New Realism*, trans. Sarah De Sanctis. Albany: SUNY, 2014.
Gordon, Peter E. "The Concept of the Apolitical: German Jewish Thought and Weimar Political Theology," *Social Research* 74 (2007): 855–878.
Grosser, Florian. "Von Wolkenkratzern, Schmetterlingen und 'wirklicher Demokratie'. Hannah Arendt und Günther Anders als Phänomenologen der Migration," In *Quertreiber des Denkens: Dieter Thomä – Werk und Wirken*, ed. by Emmanuel Alloa, Michael G. Festl, Federica Gregoratto and Thomas Telios, 99–129. Bielefeld: transcript, 2019.
Hamacher, Werner. "The One Right No One Ever Has," *Philosophy Today* 61 (2017): 947–962
Honig, Bonnie. *Democracy and the Foreigner*. Princeton, NJ: Princeton University Press, 2001.
Honig, Bonnie. "The Miracle of Metaphor: Rethinking the State of Exception with Rosenzweig and Schmitt," *diacritics* 37 (2007): 78–102.
Jurkevics, Anna. "Hannah Arendt reads Carl Schmitt's The Nomos of the Earth: A Dialogue on Law and Geopolitics from the Margins," *European Journal of Political Theory* 16 (2017): 345–366.
Kalyvas, Andreas. *Democracy and the Politics of the Extraordinary*. New York: Cambridge University Press, 2008.
Loidolt, Sophie. *Phenomenology of Plurality: Hannah Arendt on Political Intersubjectivity*. New York: Routledge, 2018.
Moyn, Samuel. "Hannah Arendt on the Secular," *New German Critique* 35 (2008): 71–96.
Posselt, Gerald, and Seitz, Sergej. "Relativism and Poststructuralism," In *The Routledge Handbook of Philosophy of Relativism*, ed. by Martin Kusch, 133–143. London: Routledge, 2019.
Santner, Eric. "Miracles Happen: Benjamin, Rosenzweig, Freud, and the Matter of the Neighbor," In *The Neighbor: Three Inquiries in Political Theology*, ed. by Slavoj Žižek, Eric L. Santner and Kenneth Reinhard, 76–133. Chicago: University of Chicago Press, 2005.

Schmitt, Carl. *Politische Theologie: Vier Kapitel zur Lehre von der Souveränität.* Munich: Duncker & Humblot, 1922.
Schmitt, Carl. *Der Leviathan in der Staatslehre des Thomas Hobbes: Sinn und Fehlschlag eines politischen Symbols*, ed. by Günter Maschke, 2nd ed. Stuttgart: Klett-Cotta, 1995.
Shachar, Ayelet. *The Birthright Lottery: Citizenship and Global Inequality.* Cambridge, MA: Harvard University Pres, 2009.
Sluga, Hans. "The Pluralism of the Political: From Carl Schmitt to Hannah Arendt," *Telos* 142 (2008): 91–109.
Song, Sarah. "The Significance of Territorial Presence and the Rights of Immigrants," In *Migration in Political Theory: The Ethics of Movement and Membership,* ed. by Sarah Fine and Lea Ypi, 225–248. Oxford: Oxford University Press, 2016.
Van Camp, Nathan. "Hannah Arendt and Political Theology: A Displaced Encounter," *Revista Pléyade* 8 (2011): 19–35.
Waldenfels, Bernhard. *Sozialität und Alterität: Modi sozialer Erfahrung.* Berlin: Suhrkamp, 2015.
Wallace, R. Jay. *The Moral Nexus*, Carl G. Hempel Lectures. Princeton, NJ: Princeton University Press, 2019.
Walzer, Michael. *Regicide and Revolution: Speeches at the Trial of Louis XVI*, trans. Marian Rothstein. London: Cambridge University Press, 1974.
Walzer, Michael. *Exodus and Revolution.* New York: Basic Books, 1985.
Žižek, Slavoj. *Violence: Six Sideway Reflections.* New York: Picador, 2008.

List of contributors

Ino Augsberg is Professor of Legal Philosophy and Public Law and Co-Director of the Hermann Kantorowicz Institute for Fundamental Research in Law at Christian-Albrechts-University Kiel. He has published on the correlation of law and religion, on human dignity and on Martin Heidegger. Recent publications include: *Kassiber: Die Aufgabe der juristischen Hermeneutik* (Tübingen: Mohr Siebeck, 2016); "Im Namen des Volkes," in *Volk als Konzept in Recht und Politik*, eds. Jochen Bung and Milan Kuhli. (De Gruyter, forthcoming 2019).

Luca Di Blasi is Associate Professor for Philosophy at the Institute for Systematic Theology at the University of Bern. His areas of research are philosophy of religion, cultural and political philosophy as well as poststructuralism. Recent publications include: *Dezentrierungen: Beiträge zur Religion der Philosophie im 20. Jahrhundert* (Turia & Kant, 2018); *Der weiße Mann: Ein Anti-Manifest* (Bielefeld: Transcript, 2013).

Dominik Finkelde SJ is Professor for Epistemology and Contemporary Philosophy at the Munich School of Philosophy. He has published on contemporary philosophy and German Idealism, especially on Hegel, Kant, Frege, Wittgenstein, and Badiou. Recent publications include: *Excessive Subjectivity: Kant, Hegel, Lacan, and the Foundation of Ethics* (New York: Columbia University Press, 2017); "Lack and Excess / Zero and One: On Concrete Universality in Dialectical Materialism," *Philosophy Today* 63, no. 3 (forthcoming 2019); "Logics of Scission: The Subject as 'Limit of the World' in Badiou and Wittgenstein," *Philosophy Today* 61, no. 3 (2017), 595–618.

Florian Grosser teaches philosophy at California College of the Arts and is Visiting Associate Professor, at the University of California at Berkeley. His current work primarily focuses on the politics and ethics of forced migration. Recent publications include: *Revolution denken: Heidegger und das Politische 1919 bis 1969* (München: C.H. Beck, 2011); *Theorien der Revolution zur Einführung*, 2nd revised edition (Hamburg: Junius, 2018 [2013]).

Rebekka A. Klein is Professor for Systematic Theology at the Faculty of Protestant Theology and Director of the Ecumenical Institute at Ruhr-Universität Bochum. Her main areas of research include political theology and radical democratic theory. Recent publications include: "Revolution im Zeitalter der Immanenz: Die Macht des Vollzugs der Freiheit als Problem der Politischen Theologie," in *Berliner Theologische Zeitschrift* 36 (2019), 144–163; *Depotenzierung der Souveränität: Religion und politische Ideologie bei Claude Lefort, Slavoj Žižek und Karl Barth* (Tübingen: Mohr Siebeck, 2016); *Sociality as the Human Condition: Anthropology in Economic, Philosophical and Theological Perspective* (Leiden: Brill, 2011).

Burkhard Liebsch is Adjunct Professor for Philosophy at Ruhr-University Bochum. He has published on social and political philosophy. Recent publications include: *Europäische Ungastlichkeit und "identitäre" Vorstellungen: Fremdheit, Flucht und Heimatlosigkeit als Herausforderungen des Politischen* (Hamburg: Meiner, 2019); *Einander ausgesetzt – Der Andere und das Soziale*, 2 Vol. (Freiburg: Karl Alber, 2018); co-edited with Michael Staudigl and Philipp

Stoellger, *Perspektiven europäischer Gastlichkeit: Geschichte – Kulturelle Praktiken – Kritik* (Weilerswist: Velbrück, 2016).

John Millbank is Professor Emeritus and Director of the Centre of Theology and Philosophy at the University of Nottingham. He is also Principal of the Methexis Institute in Charlottesville, Virginia. He has published on theology and social theory, on politics, ethics, and aesthetics. Recent publications include: Edited with Adrian Pabst, *The Politics of Virtue: Post-Liberalism and the Human Future*, (London: Rowman & Littlefield, 2016); *Beyond Secular Order: The Representation of Being and the Representation of the People* (Oxford: Blackwell, 2013); *The Future of Love: Essays in Political Theology* (Eugene, OR: Wipf & Stock, 2009).

Rasmus Nagel is research fellow at the chair of Systematic Theology in Heidelberg. He has published on the interrelation of Christianity and poststructuralist thought as well as on the philosophy of Slavoj Žižek. Recent publications: *Universale Singularität: Ein Vorschlag zur Denkform christlicher Theologie im Gespräch mit Ernesto Laclau, Alain Badiou und Slavoj Žižek* (Tübingen: Mohr Siebeck, forthcoming 2019); "'Das Fiasko Gottes ist immer noch das Fiasko Gottes': Slavoj Žižek als kreuzestheologischer Barthianer", in *Gottes schwache Macht: Alternativen zur Rede von Gottes Allmacht und Ohnmacht*, eds. Rebekka A. Klein and Friederike Rass (Leipzig: Evangelische Verlagsanstalt, 2017), 83–96.

Clemens Pornschlegel holds the chair of German Studies at Ludwig-Maximilian-University München. He publishes on the presence of religious motifs in modern German literature. Recent publications include: *Allegorien des Unendlichen: Hyperchristen II – Zum religiösen Engagement in der literarischen Moderne: Kleist, Schlegel, Eichendorff, Hugo Ball* (Turia & Kant, 2017); "Deutung als dogmatische Funktion: Überlegungen zur institutionellen Struktur exegetischer Rede", in *Was heißt Deutung? Verhandlungen zwischen Recht, Literaturwissenschaft und Psychoanalyse*, eds. Susanne Lüdemann and Thomas Vesting (Paderbon: Wilhelm Fink, 2017), 39–55.

Philipp Stoellger holds the chair of Systematic Theology and Philosophy of Religion at the University of Heidelberg. He has published on media theory, visual anthropology and philosophy of religion. Recent publications include: edited volume, *Figurationen des Menschen: Studien zur Medienanthropologie* (Königshausen & Neumann, 2019); edited with Martina Kumlehn, *Bildmacht – Machtbild. Deutungsmacht des Bildes: Wie Bilder glauben machen* (Königshausen & Neumann, 2018).

Günther Thomas holds the chair of Systematic Theology, Ethics and Fundamental Theology at Ruhr-Universität Bochum. He is also a Research Associate at the Faculty of Theology, Stellenbosch University. He has published on Public Theology, Media Theory and Ethics. Recent Publications include: *Im Weltabenteuer Gottes Leben* (Leipzig: Evangelische Verlagsanstalt 2000); *Gottes Lebendigkeit: Beiträge zur Systematischen Theologie* (Leipzig: Evangelische Verlagsanstalt, 2019); edited with Markus Höfner, *Ewiges Leben: Ende oder Umbau einer Erlösungsreligion?* (Tübingen: Mohr Siebeck, 2018); edited with Heike Springhart, *Exploring Vulnerability* (Göttingen: Vandenhoeck & Ruprecht, 2017).

Dimitris Vardoulakis is the deputy chair of the Philosophy Research Initiative at Western Sidney University. His research interests range from the relation between literature and philosophy to theories of power and sovereignty. Recent publications include: *Stasis Before the State: Nine Theses on Agonistic Democracy* (New York: Fordham, 2017); *Freedom From the Free Will: On Kafka's Laughter* (New York: SUNY, 2016); *Sovereignty and Its Other: Toward the Dejustification of Violence* (New York: Fordham, 2013).

Joseph Vogl holds the chair of Literature and Cultural Studies at Humboldt University Berlin and is Permanent Visiting Professor at the Department of German at Princeton University. His fields of research are the history and theory of knowledge, media theory and history of literature. Recent publications include: edited volume with Veronika Thanner and Dorothea Walzer, *Die Wirklichkeit des Realismus* (Paderbon: Wihelm Fink, 2018); *The Ascendancy of Finance* (Cambridge: Polity, 2017); *The Specter of Capital* (Stanford: Stanford University Press, 2014); *On Tarrying* (Chicago: Chicago University Press, 2011).

Daniel Weidner is Professor for the Study of Culture and Religion at the Institute for Cultural History and Theory and Associate Director of the 'Leibniz-Zentrum für Literatur- udn Kulturforschung' (ZfL) at Humboldt University Berlin. His research interests include religion and literature, history of literary theory and German-Jewish literature. Recent publications include: *Handbuch Literatur und Religion* (Stuttgart: J.B. Metzler, 2016); "The History of Dogma and the Story of Modernity: The Modern Age as the Second Overcoming of Gnosticism," in *Journal for the History of Ideas* 30 no. 1 (2019), 75–90.

Index

Abensour, Miguel   1, 12, 169, 171, 182
Adorno, Theodor W.   15, 294f., 300
Agamben, Giorgio   2, 5, 10, 36, 122, 264, 272f., 301
– bare life   5
Agonism   170, 172–175, 177
– Agonistic   1, 169–171, 177, 267
Alexander the Great   80
Allmacht, Omnipotence   9, 59, 187, 189, 230–232, 242, 244, 299
Althusser, Louis   1, 78f., 154
Anarchism   170, 275
Ancien Régime   21, 29, 31
Antagonism   11, 13, 43, 45, 170, 173–175, 177, 193, 198, 201–203, 213–216
– Antagonistic, Antagonistisch   11, 14, 99, 112, 130f., 167, 169, 216, 221
Arendt, Hannah   15, 71, 112, 123, 125, 127f., 229–231, 285, 287, 295, 298–304
Aristocracy   74f., 86
Aristotle, Aristoteles   5, 74, 77
– Aristotelian   214
Assmann, Jan   13, 121, 205–212, 214f.
Augustine, Saint   98, 298
Ausnahme   49f., 54, 60, 66
– Authoritarian, Autorität   2f., 8, 10–15, 76, 88f., 112, 120–122, 125, 130, 136f., 156, 165–167, 174, 177, 179, 190, 192, 197, 261
– Authoritarianism, Autoritarismus   2, 7, 9, 11, 12, 15, 77–79, 84, 89f., 111f., 116, 120, 137, 139, 165–167, 170, 197, 271, 292

Badiou, Alain   2, 5f., 61, 187, 196f., 205, 216, 272, 286
Baldwin, James   15, 271, 274, 281–283
Balibar, Étienne   169, 173
Barth, Karl   96, 99f.
Beauvoir, Simone de   147, 154
Belief   1, 80, 88, 171–173, 211–215, 289, 297, 300

Benjamin, Walter   33, 295, 298, 300, 304
Bergson, Henri   267f.
Bewunderung   23, 57, 112, 127
Biopolitics   73, 79, 81f.
Bodin, Jean   36f., 39
Bondage, Knechtschaft   13, 28, 29, 112, 113, 137, 81
Bonhoeffer, Dietrich   96f., 99f., 238–240, 245
Braudel, Fernand   43, 256
Büchner, Georg   272
Bürger, Citizen   4, 81–84, 88, 125, 175, 256, 258, 296, 301–303
Butler, Judith   147, 158, 173, 286, 301

Capitalism, Kapitalismus   1f., 8, 14, 29, 33, 43, 116, 159, 188, 253–260, 263f.
Catholic, Katholisch   212, 261, 291f.
– Catholicism   100, 290
Chomsky, Noam   115f.
Christ, Christus   74, 99, 108f., 150f., 205, 211, 216, 268, 288, 297
Christian   2, 7, 11–14, 71, 93, 95, 100f., 107, 150f., 183, 196, 205, 207f., 210f., 213–216, 264, 266, 268f., 273, 277, 288, 290
– Christianity, Christentum   10, 12, 14, 94–97, 100, 121, 150, 241, 253, 268, 273
Cisgender   12, 145f., 148f., 152, 154
Citizen, Bürger   4, 81–84, 88, 125, 175, 256, 258, 296, 301–303
– Citizenry   85, 131
– Citizenship   175, 259, 302
Civil Religion   4, 98, 264
Climate Change, Klimawandel   149, 237
Community, Gemeinschaft   2, 6, 8f., 15, 85, 94, 150, 173–181, 188, 216, 255, 269, 272, 282, 286, 297, 301f., 304
– Communitarian, Kommunitaristen   117, 174, 179, 259f., 262

Contingency, Kontingenz 2, 5 f., 103, 107, 170–172, 174 f., 177, 180, 187, 192, 198, 286, 296, 299
Conversion 46, 97 f., 149, 165 f., 177 f., 184, 196

Dasein 126, 187, 226
Deleuze, Gilles 28, 45, 120, 268
Democracy, Demokratie 1–3, 5, 12 f., 15, 74 f., 86, 106, 131, 165–167, 169, 173 f., 177, 180, 182, 184, 188, 190, 192–195, 202, 261–264, 271, 282, 285, 287, 289, 298, 300, 302 f.
Derrida, Jacques 2, 9, 62, 75, 134, 244, 286
Descartes, René 199
Desire, Verlangen 10, 80, 83, 138, 171 f., 176, 178, 183 f., 189, 221, 223, 255, 261, 275, 289, 293
Devil, Teufel 104, 107, 225
– Satan 297

Ecclesiology 97
Embodiment, Verkörperung 46, 108, 188 f.
Enlightenment 4, 148, 150, 273, 300
Eschatologie 196, 248, 272
Essence 153, 171, 175, 192, 195, 264, 299
Essentialism 4, 153, 177
Eurocentrism 183
– Eurocentric 183
Evangelical 97, 288, 292
Exclusivity 13, 205, 208, 215 f., 272
Existential 166, 263, 297
– *Ex Nihilo* 54, 231, 290

Faith, Glaube 8, 13 f., 46, 98 f., 101, 108 f., 154, 192 f., 205, 211–216, 221, 268
– Fidelity 13, 196, 205–212, 214
– *Pistis* 13, 211
Fanon, Frantz 154
Fantasy 179, 258, 264 f.
Fascism, Faschismus 8, 121, 183, 265
– Fascist 6, 180
Faust 9, 21–27, 30–32
Ferraris, Maurizio 285 f.
Fetish 187–190
– Fetishization 12 f.

Feuerbach, Ludwig 96
Flesh 4, 55, 108, 212, 268
Foucault, Michel 10, 21, 24, 35 f., 45, 79, 82 f., 122 f., 125, 154
Foundationalism 291 f.
– Foundationalist 15, 291, 302 f.
Frankfurt School, Frankfurter Schule 155 f., 158
French Revolution 71, 190
Freud, Sigmund 29, 61, 66, 111, 121, 124, 155, 165 f., 172, 179
– Freudian 166
Fukuyama, Francis 6, 32, 162
Futurism 256, 265

Gebet, Prayer 23, 96, 248, 279
Gemeinschaft, Community 2, 6, 8 f., 15, 85, 94, 150, 173–181, 188, 216, 255, 269, 272, 282, 286, 297, 301 f., 304
Gender, Geschlecht 6, 12, 138, 146–152, 154 f., 157, 160, 166–169, 172, 180, 200, 296 f.
Glaube, Faith 8, 13 f., 46, 98 f., 101, 108 f., 154, 192 f., 205, 211–216, 221, 268
Globalisation, Globalisierung 258
Goethe, Johann Wolfgang von 9, 21–25, 27–31
Grace, Gnade 211–213, 222, 224, 236, 238, 240, 247, 267–269, 304
Greek, Griechisch 50, 60, 73–75, 97, 275
Grotius 75
Guattari, Félix 28

Habermas, Jürgen 2, 4, 7, 100, 228, 294
Hamartiology 211
– Hamartiological 214
Hegel 22, 121 f., 183, 187, 263, 266
– Hegelian 153, 263, 267, 295
Hegemony, Hegemonie 1, 5, 12, 128, 167, 170 f., 190, 254
– Hegemonic 5, 12, 167–169, 171–173, 177 f., 181 f.
Heidegger, Martin 9, 21, 125, 127, 153, 180, 196, 263
Hermeneutics, Hermeneutik 56, 64, 74, 76, 151, 303
Heteronomy, Heteronomie 12, 167, 226

Hobbes, Thomas   10, 59, 75, 179, 290f.
- Hobbesian   292
Honneth, Axel   156, 158, 162, 294
Human Rights, Menschenrechte   98, 100f., 105f., 271, 301
Husserl, Edmund   153
Hysteria   8, 147

Identity Politics   12, 145–147, 149, 152–163, 296f.
Ideology, Ideologie   4f., 9, 78f., 149f., 171, 181, 183, 194, 197, 254, 286, 294, 296
- Ideology Critique   190
Imago Dei   98, 100
- Vater-Imago   120
Immanence, Immanenz   1, 3f., 8, 10f., 21, 36, 47, 108, 188, 195–197, 286, 298f.
Immigration   166, 177f., 258, 297, 299, 303
Inclusion   103, 216, 293
- Inclusivism, Inklusivismus   215, 247
Invisible, Unsichtbar   9, 64, 103, 149, 237
- Invisibility   5, 194
Irrealism   285
- Islamic   205, 207, 265
Israel   13, 86f., 206–208, 235, 238, 241, 266, 274–280
- Zion   280

Jesus   96, 108, 211, 216, 239, 241, 245
Jewish   2, 15, 73f., 88, 96, 153f., 207f., 273f.
- Jew   72–74, 86, 88, 120, 150, 152–154, 156, 159, 161, 207, 213, 266
Joas, Hans   210
Jonas, Hans   96, 231
Josephus, Flavius   72–76, 89
- Josephism   74, 84
Judaism, Judentum   10, 12, 14, 73, 121, 150f., 241
- Rabbinic   150
Jüngel, Eberhard   215, 241

Kant, Immanuel   4, 111, 114, 189, 237f., 240
- Kantian   295
- Kantianism   95
Kantorowicz, Ernst   4, 39, 43, 236

Kapitalismus, Capitalism   1f., 8, 14, 29, 33, 43, 116, 159, 188, 253–260, 263f.
Katechon   239, 288
- Katechontic, Katechontik   239, 290, 298
Katholisch, Catholic   212, 261, 291f.
Keller, Catherine   31, 96
Kelsen, Hans   174
King, Jr., Martin Luther   4, 42f., 76, 80, 85, 87–89, 161, 236, 274–277, 281
Klimawandel, Climate Change   149, 237
Knechtschaft, Bondage   13, 28, 29, 112, 113, 137, 81
Kojève, Alexandre   71, 153
Kontingenz, Contingency   2, 5f., 103, 107, 170–172, 174f., 177, 180, 187, 192, 198, 286, 296, 299

Lacan, Jacques   7, 120, 136, 154
Laclau, Ernesto   1, 5, 12, 136, 169–174, 176, 183, 190, 205, 265–267, 296
Lefort, Claude   1–3, 5, 13, 169f., 190–195, 244, 263
Levinas, Emmanuel   134f., 296
Levites   11, 77, 86–89
Liberalism   8, 253, 260, 265, 267, 286, 290f.
Locke, John   10, 26, 58f., 75
Love   11, 14, 78, 93f., 98–109, 200, 253, 280, 283, 298, 304
Löwith, Karl   113, 116, 118, 125
Luther, Martin   212–214, 228, 237, 247, 281
- Lutheran   96, 99, 212f.
Lyotard, Jean-François   286

Machiavelli   72, 78, 81, 84
Marchart, Oliver   1, 175, 195
Marx, Karl   27f., 32, 44, 46, 153, 155, 260, 264f., 298
- Marxism   100, 155, 169
Master, Meister   9–14, 19, 21, 49, 56, 71f., 77, 82f., 94, 102, 111–113, 115, 124, 127, 137, 139, 153f., 157, 162, 165, 172f., 178, 184, 193f., 203, 221, 223–227, 245, 281–283, 304
Mediation   14, 200f., 253, 255f., 263, 265, 275

Index

Menke, Christoph   181 f., 197 f.
Menschenrechte, Human Rights   98, 100 f., 105 f., 271, 301
Merleau-Ponty, Maurice   125
Messiah, Messias   106, 228, 273, 288
– Messianic   14 f., 97, 285, 287–290, 292, 294–297
– Messianism   287, 289 f., 292, 298
Metaphysics, Metaphysik   3, 108, 196, 198, 237
Metz, Johann Baptist   212 f.
Michael, Walzer   96, 99, 156, 159 f., 287, 289 f., 292, 297
Miracle   285, 287, 290, 297–304
Mission   57, 97 f., 101
Modernity   1–5, 7–9, 45, 55, 71, 74, 87, 102, 187, 190, 197 f., 201, 209, 263
Moltmann, Jürgen   96 f., 99
Monolatry   207
Monotheism   205–208, 211, 215
– Monotheistic   209
Moses   10 f., 27, 59, 71 f., 74, 77, 85–89, 205, 209 f., 235, 245, 277 f.
– Mosaic   205–208, 210, 277, 287–289, 298, 301
Mouffe, Chantal   1, 5, 12, 112, 169–175, 182 f., 190
Mythology   71
– Mythic   97, 99, 264
– Mythos   230, 248

Nancy, Jean-Luc   9, 13, 187–189, 264
Negativity, Negativität   133, 135, 198, 244
Neoliberalism   79, 162, 257, 259, 262
Nietzsche, Friedrich   22, 94, 125, 239, 244, 295 f.
Nihilism   260, 291
Nomos   10, 49–57, 60–66, 298 f.
– Nomos der Erde   50–53, 55, 66
Nostalgia   108, 256, 265

Object, Objekt   10, 14, 36–39, 93, 106, 148, 153, 156, 160, 177, 188, 210, 253, 276, 278
– Objectification   155 f.
– Objectivity   295

Öffentlichkeit, Public Sphere   15, 64, 129, 173, 192, 272, 274, 281
Omnipotence, Allmacht   9, 59, 187, 189, 230–232, 242, 244, 299
Ontology   3, 5, 170, 286
– Ontological, Ontologisch   2, 6 f., 12, 153, 155, 165, 167, 175, 207 f., 215, 232, 243, 299
Orthodox   100

Papst   231, 234, 236 f., 240
Paradox   1, 8, 57, 71, 112, 114, 211–214, 222, 232, 243, 274, 279 f., 282, 303
Passion   197, 213, 221, 241 f.
Pathos   116, 182, 229, 245
Patriarchal, Patriarchalisch   52, 178 f.
Patronomie   50 f., 66 f.
Paul, the Apostle, Paulus   129, 196, 213, 272 f., 286, 294
– Saint Paul   6, 150, 196, 286
Péguy, Charles   267 f.
Peng-Keller, Simon   213
Phantasmagoric   8, 175
– Phantasmagorias   175
Phenomenology, Phänomenologie   128, 183, 243, 301
– Phenomenological, Phänomenologisch   115, 121, 153, 155, 225, 248, 295
Piketty, Thomas   253 f.
Plato   3, 74, 299
– Politeia   224
– Republic, The   3, 43, 71, 74–77
Pluralism   12, 169, 173 f., 182, 298
– Plurality, Pluralität   132, 171, 173, 182, 301
Poem   272, 277, 279
– Poetic, Poetisch   22, 23, 268, 271, 275, 278, 280
– Poetry, Poesie   23, 278–280
Political Theology, Politische Theologie   3 f., 8 f., 13–15, 36, 55, 82, 94 f., 99 f., 187, 189 f., 196, 200 f., 203, 219, 271–274, 277, 279–281, 283, 285–290, 292–294, 297–300
Polybius   74 f.

Populism, Populismus   111, 112, 115, 117, 131, 145f., 149, 154, 158, 162, 246, 248, 255, 262, 267, 285
- Populist   6, 9, 117f., 147, 160–162, 180, 254–256, 258, 260, 262, 267
Post-metaphysical   2–7, 108, 180, 195, 197, 203, 286
Postmodernism   1, 15, 221, 285f., 292–296
- Postmodernity, Postmoderne   4, 133, 200
- Post-secularism   95
Poststructuralism   294, 296
- Poststructuralist   154
Prayer, Gebet   23, 96, 248, 279
Prophets   14f., 72, 271, 273–275, 277, 279, 281
- Prophetic   14, 267, 271–274, 277–280
Protestantism, Protestantismus   93–95, 98, 199, 246
Psychoanalysis   154f.
Public Sphere, Öffentlichkeit   15, 64, 129, 173, 192, 272, 274, 281

Queer   147, 154, 200, 297

Radical Democracy Theory, Radikale Demokratietheorie   1, 167, 170–173, 175–177, 180, 182–184
Radicalization   11, 93, 212
Rancierè, Jacques   216
Realpolitik   136, 168, 173, 275
Recognition   155–158, 160–163, 169, 180, 201, 283, 288, 304
Relativism   1, 6–8, 14, 200, 221, 285, 294–296
Relativität   243f.
Renaissance   41, 45f., 120, 271
Republican   76, 173f., 177, 296
Revolution   1, 13, 31, 55, 75, 77, 187, 190, 192–198, 202f., 256, 272f., 280, 292
Ricœur, Paul   11, 71, 111, 121f., 124, 133, 137, 228
Romantic, Romantik   120, 198–202, 273
- Romanticism   198–202, 300
Rorty, Richard   155
Rose, Gillian   267
Rosenzweig, Franz   295, 302, 304

Rousseau, Jean-Jacques   4, 125, 264, 290, 298
Santner, Eric   1, 4, 55, 286, 304
Sartre, Jean-Paul   111, 114f., 125, 137, 152–157, 159
Schmitt, Carl   3, 8f., 13, 15, 49–56, 60–67, 83, 120, 124, 174–176, 179–181, 183, 187, 198–203, 208f., 214, 263f., 272, 285–287, 290–292, 296–300, 304
Schöpfer   25, 27, 231, 233
Sex   147–151, 154, 296
- Cissexual   148, 150, 152
- Heterosexual   2, 145f., 150, 152, 156f., 160–162, 167–169, 172
- Sexuality   172
- Transsexual   148, 152
- Sinner, Sünder   213, 235–237, 240
Sloterdijk, Peter   125, 208–212, 216
Socialism, Sozialismus   55, 100, 166, 290
- Socialist   170, 290, 297
Social Media   256, 261
Sociology   95
Soteriology   211
Sovereignty, Souveränität   4f., 7, 10, 13, 15, 35–41, 45, 47, 73, 75, 82f., 89, 94, 101, 118, 122f., 187f., 201f., 240, 247, 271–277, 281, 285, 287, 290, 299–302, 304
Spinoza, Baruch   9–11, 71–74, 76–90
Spirit, Geist   26, 29, 61, 97, 99, 108f., 114, 121, 128, 129, 136, 183, 198f., 201, 224, 247, 267f.
- Spiritual, Spirituell   12, 120, 212, 265, 281
Spivak, Gayatri   177
- Stoicism   183
Subject, Subjekt   1, 5–7, 10, 35, 38, 77–80, 84, 102, 148, 153–155, 157, 165, 171, 176, 178, 182, 188, 193, 195–200, 202f., 206, 290f., 297f., 300, 304
- Subjectivity, Subjektivität   2, 245, 281, 299f.
Symbol   14, 150, 253, 263f.
- Symbolic   2, 4, 8, 14, 160, 178, 192, 253, 255, 259, 263–269
- Symbolic Form   8

Symptom 3, 8, 115, 117, 122, 136, 155, 165f., 173, 184, 196f.

Taylor, Charles 11, 98, 108, 111, 120, 138
Teufel, Devil 104, 107, 225
Theism 95f.
– Open Theism 97
Theocracy 11, 72f., 75–77, 81–83, 86, 88–90, 300
– Hebrew Theocracy 9f., 71, 76, 82f., 85–89
Theology 2, 4, 11–13, 15, 94–97, 99, 196, 206f., 212–214, 216, 224, 246, 253, 277, 292, 298, 300, 304
– Protestant 11, 74, 93–97, 100, 104, 206, 246, 260
Theopolitical, Theopolitisch 94, 206, 222, 242
– Theo-political 93f., 99–101, 104, 107
Tillich, Paul 99
Totalitarian 151, 182, 193f., 302
– Totalitarianism 200, 210, 261, 264, 300, 302, 304
Total Religion 13, 205f., 208–210

Transcendence, Transzendenz 1–5, 8, 10, 14, 21, 28, 36, 47, 65, 98, 108, 146, 153, 189, 253, 265, 289
Tyranny 77, 79, 83–85, 89f.
– Tyrannical 267, 281
– Tyrant 77, 84, 89f.

Universal 14, 29, 83, 98, 105f., 168f., 171, 175, 179, 182f., 196, 205, 210, 212, 215f., 243, 253, 265–269, 296
– Universalism, Universalismus 14, 168, 171, 180, 196, 208, 210f., 214, 247

Victim 80, 158, 161f., 168f., 172, 176, 181f.
– Victimhood 166–169, 172, 176, 180, 182
Verlangen, Desire 10, 80, 83, 138, 171f., 176, 178, 183f., 189, 221, 223, 255, 261, 275, 289, 293
Verkörperung, Embodiment 46, 108, 188f.

Waldenfels, Bernhard 223, 301
Weber, Max 9, 21f., 29, 72, 234, 273
Whitehead, Alfred North 96, 264

Žižek, Slavoj 1f., 6f., 13, 136, 166f., 178f., 193f., 197f., 205, 216, 272, 286, 303

www.ingramcontent.com/pod-product-compliance
Lightning Source LLC
Chambersburg PA
CBHW020830160426
43192CB00007B/588